Pierre M. Irving and Washington Irving:
A Collaboration in Life and Letters

Pierre M. Irving, *circa* 1870

The photograph of Pierre M. Irving opposite the title page is reproduced from the original, by N. S. Bowdish of Richfield Springs, New York, in the Collection of American Literature, Beinecke Rare Book and Manuscript Library, Yale University.

Washington Irving, *circa* 1859

The portrait of Washington Irving opposite the title page is reproduced from an oil painting by Henry F. Darby (c. 1831-?) in the collections of Sleepy Hollow Restorations, Inc.

Pierre M. Irving and Washington Irving: A Collaboration in Life and Letters.

Wayne R. Kime

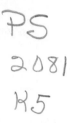

11/1979
Am. Lit.

Canadian Cataloguing in Publication Data

Kime, Wayne R., 1941-
    Pierre M. Irving and Washington Irving

Includes index.
ISBN 0-88920-056-4 bd.   ISBN 0-88920-055-6 pa.

1. Irving, Washington, 1783-1859 – Biography.
2. Irving, Pierre Munro, 1802-1876. 3. Authors,
American – 19th century – Biography. I. Title.

PS2081.K55   813'.2   C77-001528-X

Cover design by Michael Baldwin MSIAD

For Alicia

Preface

This is a study of the collaborations between Pierre M. Irving and Washington Irving which began shortly after the two men first met as adults, in 1826, continued until the death of the author in 1859, and in a sense extended even beyond that date. In compliance with the wishes of his uncle, Pierre took up during Irving's lifetime the roles, among others, of research assistant, proofreader, real estate agent, attorney, financial adviser, comptroller, co-researcher, literary critic, editor, confidant, and nurse. No one worked so closely with Irving during the second half of his career as Pierre, and no one came to know him so well as he. After 1859, Pierre continued his services to his late uncle chiefly by compiling a delegated biography, *The Life and Letters of Washington Irving*, 4 vols. (New York, 1862-1863), which remained for three generations the standard biographical portrait of the author. Yet, although he was by all odds the closest associate of the later Irving and exerted a great influence in shaping his posthumous fame, Pierre is still virtually unknown to us. Amidst the assiduous research undertaken in this century into the details of his uncle's eventful life history, many features of Pierre's life—for example, such basic ones as his birthdate and the correct spelling of his name—have remained uncertain or unknown. Accordingly, using the limited materials available for the purpose, I have attempted in this work to provide as complete a biography of him as possible. He was a talented individual in his own right and was on familiar terms with many of the dignitaries of his day besides Irving, but I believe that his place in history is as an associate of his uncle. A biographical sketch of him is thus a natural accompaniment of an account of his relationship with Irving, particularly since during the years of their association their interests, their opinions, their activities, and their circles of friends gradually came to be almost indistinguishable.

In my portrayal of Irving I have made no attempt to present an exhaustive biographical compilation but have relied largely upon published material, including the *Life and Letters* and the monumental biography by Stanley T. Williams, *The Life of Washington Irving*, 2 vols. (New York and London, 1935). No one who engages in research in Irvingiana can fail to be conscious of his deep indebtedness to the latter work, nor to recognize the high standard of scholarship enjoined upon him by the example of Stanley T. Williams' meticulousness and thoroughness. The most ambitious researcher must continually reckon with the thought that his own completed labours will perhaps amount to no more than an addendum to the *Life*, but at the same time he must also feel a grateful sense of obligation to Williams for having brought together in that work a wide range of information for use in further interpretation of Irving's life and writings. Naturally, in its authoritative bulk the *Life* has exerted an influence over Irving scholarship and criticism in the forty years since it was published. In order to define the aims of the present work as a contribution to Irving studies, it will thus be helpful briefly to summarize Williams' general approach in his biography and to survey his views of Irving's later career.

Williams portrayed Irving primarily as a "public figure," a "clarifying mirror of some aspects of culture in America"; more specifically, he presented the author as a representative figure in "an era which consistently intermingled the aims of art, morality, politics, and business" (I, xiv). In Williams' view, Irving achieved his greatest successes as a literary artist during his youth in New York and his seventeen-year sojourn in Europe. Upon his return to the United States in 1832, he was confronted with an American society which had grown superficial, sentimental, self-gratulatory, materialistic, and indifferent or even hostile to the pursuit of art for its own sake. He lacked sufficient personal force to resist the influence of this society, and gradually "America . . . drew him to herself, developing further the substantial, worldly, matter-of-fact qualities in his nature" (II, 50). "Imperceptibly" the "ideals" of American civilization became his own, until by 1846, when he returned again to his country after four years' service as its Minister to Spain, his early alertness and dedication to the craft of writing had diminished into "intellectual sterility" and "apathy toward literature" (II, 52, 211). Even though he had continued to write since 1832, he had done so without inspiration —and often simply to earn money. For example, his *Astoria* (1836) was "a stupendous piece of hack work" (II, 75), and his final publication, *The Life of George Washington* (1855-1859) was to be "a biography almost wholly divorced from literature" (II, 209). As Williams presented it, Irving's later career typified "the fate of scores of gifted Americans, from Freneau to Bryant, living in Philistia. . . . [H]aving proved that he could write, he turned to issues that, he thought, really mattered; the pen became an embellishment for the statesman or man of affairs" (II, 209).

Modern students of Irving's life and writings have not called into question Williams' formulation of the author's relation to American life after 1832, and they seem to have accepted his harsh judgments of the works written after that date insofar as they have tended to ignore them in favour of the earlier productions. The major critical volume which has appeared since the *Life*, William L. Hedges' *Washington Irving: An American Study, 1802-1832* (Baltimore, 1965), exemplifies this continuing climate of opinion. In the preface to his work, Hedges writes: "The justification for not treating the last twenty-seven years of Irving's life is that with his celebrated return to the United States in 1832 his career was in one sense completed. The works on which his reputation as the nation's first successful author primarily rests were behind him. . . . He kept on writing but not developing as a writer" (p. viii). Hedges' suggestive book is the evidence of his belief that it is possible, in his words, "to define [Irving's] major contributions as a writer and to work out in detail his relation to his intellectual environment" (p. viii) without taking into account his life and writings after 1832.

Although I do not propose to contend with the view that Irving's post-1832 career was intrinsically less significant and successful than what preceded it, I do believe that this thesis remains undemonstrated. Within a few years we can expect to have available a complete edition of the author's published works, journals, notebooks, and letters which will afford us the tools necessary for a thorough reexamination of his entire career, and perhaps at some future time we will be able to see it as a unitary whole rather than as falling into two easily separable and unequally important parts. For the present, the aim of this work is merely to shed some new light on Irving's later life by approaching it from a fresh point of view. Whereas Williams presented the author primarily as a public figure and Hedges approached him through "literary analysis and comparison" of his earlier published works (p. viii), I attempt to portray him chiefly as a private person. I do consider his status as a public personality in relation to his character as a private individual, and I do discuss those of his works which were affected in various ways by his collaborations with his nephew. Nevertheless, I believe that the greatest potential of a study of Irving's relations with Pierre and other members of his family is for the insight it can afford us into his private life.

Since in my account of Irving's relations with Pierre I often address myself to topics which Williams treated in terms of Irving alone,

I present these with an emphasis different from his. At some points, too, the facts of the collaboration between the two men call into question the interpretations of Williams. However, as a study of Irving this work is intended as a whole to be supplementary rather than corrective. As regards Pierre, it should serve to correct a few erroneous remarks or innuendoes published in this century about his personality and his performance as a biographer, but it is essentially an autonomous work. As a study of the relationship between Pierre and his uncle, I hope that it will have interest in itself as the record of an unusual and fruitful collaboration in life and letters between two engaging personalities.

In preparing this book I have received assistance from a great many individuals, to whom I am happy to express my sincere thanks. However, to a few persons my indebtedness is so deep as to require a more particular acknowledgment here. The late Professor Ernest J. Moyne maintained a lively interest in the project from its inception, and successive drafts of the manuscript benefited from his thoughtful study and wise counsel. The late Professor Herbert L. Kleinfield offered suggestions which facilitated my original search for unpublished material relating to Pierre M. Irving and Washington Irving, and the late Professor Henry A. Pochmann gave sound advice as to the form the results of my research might eventually take. Patricia E. Smith, formerly the librarian at Sleepy Hollow Restorations, Inc., shared with me again and again her extensive knowledge of Irvingiana. I am grateful to Miss Smith, to Professor Ralph M. Aderman, and to Professor Lewis Leary for their readings of the manuscript. My mother, Mrs. Betty Wendt, provided much clerical and other assistance, and my wife, Mrs. Alicia Kime, promoted the undertaking in numberless ways.

I wish to thank the following libraries for their permission to quote from unpublished material in their collections: Boston Public Library; Phillips Exeter Academy; Historical Society of Pennsylvania; Houghton Library, Harvard University; Henry E. Huntington Library; University of Illinois Library; Library of Congress; Massachusetts Historical Society; New-York Historical Society; Henry W. and Albert A. Berg Collection, New York Public Library; Manuscript Division, New York Public Library; New York Society Library; George Peabody Department, Enoch Pratt Free Library; University of Rochester Library; Sleepy Hollow Restorations, Inc.; Watkinson Library, Trinity College; Washington Irving Collection, Clifton Waller Barrett Library, University of Virginia; Collection of American Literature, Beinecke Rare Book and Manuscript Library, Yale University. A few citations of quoted material include a reference both to the repository in which the original manuscript survives and also a page-reference to the *Life and Letters,* in which the quoted passage was first published and from which it is reproduced. Unless otherwise indicated (e.g., Chapter Seven, footnote 136), the texts from the two sources are identical in substance. Because Pierre M. Irving ordinarily reproduced his source material with a high degree of accuracy—and because treating letters published in the *Life and Letters* as "quoted quotations" is a cumbersome procedure—documents from the biography are ordinarily given here as if they were the originals. That is, when presented as parts of the text they are enclosed within only a single set of quotation marks ("..."), and when set off from the text they are enclosed within no quotation marks.

A part of the research for this book was made possible by a Travel Grant from the Canada Council in 1969. The book has been published with the help of a grant from the Humanities Research Council of Canada, using funds provided by the Canada Council. To both these institutions, and to the Wilfrid Laurier University Press, I wish to express my grateful appreciation.

Port Credit, Ontario, 1977   *W. R. K.*

Table of Contents

Part III: The Continuing Collaboration

List of Abbreviations

Unless otherwise specified, citations of the works of Washington Irving refer to volumes of the Connoisseur Edition (13 vols., Philadelphia: University Library Association, [*ca.* 1900]), which was printed using plates derived from the Author's Revised Edition published between 1848 and 1850 by George Putnam.

The following abbreviations are employed in the footnotes:

Libraries	*Abbreviation*
Houghton Library, Harvard University	Harvard
Henry E. Huntington Library	Huntington
University of Illinois Library	Illinois
New-York Historical Society Library	N-YHS
Henry W. and Albert A. Berg Collection, New York Public Library	NYPL, Berg
Manuscript Division, New York Public Library	NYPL, MS
George Peabody Department, Enoch Pratt Free Library	Peabody
University of Rochester Library	Rochester
Sleepy Hollow Restorations, Inc.	SHR

Clifton Waller Barrett Library, University of Virginia   Virginia

Beinecke Rare Book and Manuscript Library, Yale University   Yale

Persons and Places

Washington Irving	WI
Pierre M. Irving	PMI
Sunnyside	SS

Published Works

Irving, Pierre M. *The Life and Letters of Washington Irving.* 4 vols. New York: G. P. Putnam, 1862-1863.   LLWI

Williams, Stanley T. *The Life of Washington Irving.* 2 vols. New York and London: Oxford University Press, 1935.   Life

Unpublished Works by Pierre M. Irving

Account Book, 1859-1866, recording his transactions as Executor of the Estate of Washington Irving. (Manuscript Division, New York Public Library)   Account Book

"The Genealogy of the Irving Family. Compiled for the Information of the Descendants of William Irving the first settler of that surname in the city of New York . . . ," with documents by other hands. (Sleepy Hollow Restorations, Inc.)   Irving Genealogy

Holograph notebook containing a record of Washington Irving's activities and physical condition, February 28-November 28, 1859, with other notes. (Berg Collection, New York Public Library)   1859 Journal

Holograph notebook containing an outline of the *Life and Letters of Washington Irving.* (Berg Collection, New York Public Library)   MS Outline

Holograph notebook containing notes on Pierre M. Irving's accounts as a lawyer [this is the same notebook as the one containing the outline of the *Life and Letters*; the legal register is at the other end]   Legal Register

Holograph notebook containing notes for
    study of the Irving family genealogy,
    information concerning Irving's
    ownership of land, excerpts from letters
    written by him, notes on his
    publications, and other material.
    (Manuscript Division, New York Public
    Library)

Misc. Notebook

Part I

Pierre M. Irving and
Washington Irving, 1826-1848

Chapter One

An Independent Nephew, 1826-1834

To the surprise of Washington Irving, who for his convenience had recently been accredited as an American attaché at Madrid, the diplomatic mail pouch delivered to the United States Legation there on May 5, 1826, contained a letter addressed not to himself but to Pierre M. Irving,[1] a twenty-four-year-old nephew[2] of whose presence in Europe he had received no previous indication. This mute testimony of Pierre's possible proximity to Madrid left Irving "extremely tantalized," and also rather nettled to think that the family in New York had apparently not seen fit to inform him beforehand that his relative was journeying to Spain from his home there.[3] He was sensi-

---

[1] *The Journals of WI*, eds. William P. Trent and George S. Hellman, 3 vols. (Boston, 1919), III, 24—cited hereafter as *Journals; WI and the Storrows: Letters from England and the Continent, 1821-1828,* ed. Stanley T. Williams (Cambridge, Mass., 1933), p. 82.

[2] PMI was born to William Irving and Julia Paulding on April 3, 1802. The family origin of his given names, if any, is unknown. A distant relation on his mother's side bore the name Pierre: this was Pierre Bauduin, who settled at Boston in 1687 and was the first of several generations of prominent Bowdoins in America (PMI, Misc. Notebook). The name Munro was apparently without precedent in PMI's family history.

[3] *WI and the Storrows,* p. 82.

tive about slights from the transatlantic Irvings such as this seemed to be, for having lived in Europe for the past eleven years, he recognized uneasily that his early intimacy with them was diminishing. When he had sailed from New York on a supposedly "temporary" mission to Liverpool in 1815, Pierre Munro, the fourth child of his eldest brother, William,[4] had been only a boy; and during his long absence fully seven of the twelve children in his elder brother Ebenezer's family had been born.[5] Despite the faithful efforts of Ebenezer, his sister Catharine,[6] and such loyal friends as Henry Brevoort[7] to keep him abreast of affairs at home, inevitably he was becoming a stranger to the new generation of Irvings. A desire to allay the trend was no doubt at the root of his excitement over the possibility of renewing acquaintance with Pierre.

Immediately upon receipt of the mysterious letter he made inquiries after his nephew, and within a few days he was informed by the United States Consul at Gibraltar that the person in question had touched there the previous fall, bound for Italy, but for some reason had decided to spend the winter in southern Spain.[8] The Consul's reply only teased Irving the more; for if accurate, it meant that Pierre had been living within a few days' journey of Madrid, where he and his brother Peter had resided since February.[9] He made further inquiries, but in vain; and on June 12, after a month's wait, he wrote to his friend Thomas W. Storrow that he was still uncertain of his nephew's whereabouts. "Should he come to Paris," Irving added, "and you hear of him pay him attentions for my sake[.] He has grown

---

[4] William Irving (1766-1821) was married to Julia Paulding (1768-1823) in 1793; a genealogical chart of the children born to the couple is in *Life*, II, opposite 255. The fullest sketch of William Irving is by Stanley T. Williams in the *Dictionary of American Biography*, eds. Allen Johnson and Dumas Malone (New York, 1928-1937), V, 511-12—cited hereafter as *DAB*. Information on his career as a businessman is in Walter Barrett [pseud. Joseph A. Scoville], *The Old Merchants of New York*, 5 vols. (New York, 1889), II, 79-81 *et passim*.

[5] Ebenezer Irving (1776-1868) was married to Elizabeth Kip (1784-1827) in 1805; a genealogical chart of the children born to the couple is in *Life*, II, opposite 255.

[6] Catharine Rodgers Irving Paris (1774-1849), WI's eldest living sister, who adopted a half-motherly manner toward him.

[7] The correspondence between WI and Henry Brevoort, Jr. (1782-1848), his close friend in youth, has been edited by George S. Hellman as *The Letters of WI to Henry Brevoort*, 2 vols. (New York, 1915), and *The Letters of Henry Brevoort to WI, together with other unpublished Brevoort Papers*, 2 vols. (New York, 1918). Two-volume-in-one editions of both works, to which subsequent citations refer, were published in 1918.

[8] *WI and the Storrows*, p. 82.

[9] WI and Peter arrived in Madrid on February 15. Acting on a suggestion by Alexander Everett, the United States Minister to Spain, WI had planned while in Spain to translate into English a long-awaited work on Columbus compiled by Don Martin de Navarrete, the distinguished Spanish scholar. However, a preliminary study of the work quickly convinced him that it would not appeal to a wide audience, being "rather a mass of materials for a history, than a history itself." Further thought along these lines led him to the conclusion that "a history faithfully digested from these various materials, was a desideratum in literature" ("Preface," *Life and Voyages of Christopher Columbus*, I, 18). In May 1826, WI was at work on the latter project.

up since I left New York; he was a very promising boy and I am told is very clever and very amiable. There can be very little chance of his being still in Spain & I have to give up hope of meeting with him. It grieves me excessively for the idea of meeting with a relative and one of the young stock in which I feel such great interest, had quite occupied my thoughts."[10] Abandoning the search, Irving returned to work on the literary project occupying him that spring—a biography of Christopher Columbus—and to a pleasant routine of social life among the diplomatic community and the hospitable native families in the Spanish capital.

Early in June, 1826, Pierre Munro Irving set out northward from Cadiz through Spain, bent on seeing the sights thoroughly but frugally. Traveling by coach, he passed along the Guadalquivir River to Seville and thence westerly toward the ancient city of Cordova, at the edge of the Sierra Morena.[11] From Cordova his itinerary took him farther west into Andalusia and again northward into La Mancha, a region renowned both as the home of Don Quixote and as the resort of the most feared bandit tribes of all Spain. Owing perhaps to his modest equipage, he had the unusual good fortune to avoid being waylaid;[12] and at last, not long after crossing the Tagus River, his coach came within sight of Madrid, its steeples and cupolas gleaming in the clear sky. Arriving there on Monday, June 19,[13] he managed to locate a suitable inn and prepared for a leisurely exploration of the place. Madrid was seldom visited by foreigners at this period, but it offered an imposing array of buildings and monuments of interest to an intelligent tourist. Pierre idled about contentedly for a few days, but on June 24 he was thunderstruck to be informed that his Uncle Washington was in the city, living at the home of Obadiah Rich, a wealthy American merchant and bibliophile of international reputation. Hurrying there, he came upon his relative seated in Rich's extensive library of Spanish history and literature, hard at work on *The Life and Voyages of Christopher Columbus*.[14]

The reunion was animated on both sides. So far as it interfered with Irving's progress on his ambitious biographical undertaking, the

---

[10] *WI and the Storrows,* p. 82.

[11] Except as otherwise indicated, details concerning the cities and regions which PMI visited and traversed in Spain are drawn from Alexander Slidell (who later changed his name to Alexander Slidell MacKenzie), *A Year in Spain,* 2 vols. (London, 1831). Slidell (1803-1848) entered Spain in October 1826, and while at Madrid he made the acquaintance of WI. *A Year in Spain* won WI's hearty approval. He reviewed the work in the *Quarterly Review,* 44 (February 1831), 319-42, praising it for its wealth of detail, "given with the . . . persevering and conscientious fidelity of a Flemish picture" (320).

[12] Alexander Slidell did not, and in *A Year in Spain* he gave a chilling account of his party's being attacked by robbers while traversing this region (II, 65-76). PMI's itinerary from Cadiz to Madrid was the exact reverse of Slidell's.

[13] PMI, MS Outline, Chapter 46 (1826).

[14] *LLWI,* II, 253. WI wrote in his journal on June 24: "Pierre M. Irving arrived – passed greater part of the day talking with him – strolling the Prado, etc –" (*Journals,* III, 29).

arrival of Pierre had come at an inopportune moment; yet the author was clearly more pleased than distracted by the unhoped-for visit, and as Pierre later recalled, he was "in excellent spirits."[15] For Pierre, the fortuitous meeting was perhaps an even more notable occasion than for his uncle. Irving's reputation as a successful literary man had formed part of the milieu in which his nephew had grown to adulthood. For example, at the same commencement ceremony in which Pierre was granted his A.B. degree from Columbia College, Irving had received an honorary A.M. degree *in absentia,* the first the institution had ever bestowed.[16] If Pierre was far too self-possessed an individual to feel any strong impulse toward hero-worship, he respected his uncle's literary achievements and justly regarded him as something of a celebrity. Probably his greatest pleasure in the reunion at Madrid, however, was simply at having so unexpected an opportunity to see Irving again. He had failed to contact him during the eight months of his stay in Spain thus far, and but for this coincidence he might have missed a visit entirely. He and Irving spent the remainder of the day in conversation together. The latter was full of talk about his present literary undertaking, but he was also curious to learn from Pierre the circumstances of his residence in Europe.

Although Irving had conveyed to Thomas W. Storrow the impression that he knew enough of Pierre's career in New York to warrant characterizing him as "very clever and very amiable," he was in fact almost ignorant of his nephew's activities in the past few years. He had demonstrated this unawareness rather egregiously only a few months before, when upon learning from a niece[17] that Pierre was considering a journey to Europe, he had immediately damned the notion as "idle." Holding up his own protracted wanderings as a bad example, through an intermediary he had lectured his nephew on the pernicious effects of youthful travel. "The knowledge to be gained by a mere ramble through Europe is of all things the most useless and superficial," he wrote. "It may give fashionable interest to a fine gentleman of England, who is a man of fortune & leisure and merely seeks to accomplish himself for society, but with a young American, who has to earn his mere bread by his talents and his industry this superficial polish is worse than useless." Adding that his advice proceeded solely from "a high opinion of Pierre" which inspired "anxiety for his welfare," Irving expressed a wish that he would "fix himself steadfastly to something useful; and go on to inform & strengthen his mind." After all, Pierre would gain "more in one year by studying soundly at home than in three by wandering abroad."[18]

Irving dated his cautionary letter from Paris on August 29, 1825. Pierre failed to enjoy the benefit of its counsel, however, for by the

[15] *LLWI,* II, 253.

[16] Milton H. Thomas, *Columbia University Officers and Alumni 1754-1857* (New York, 1936), pp. 135, 285.

[17] Julia Irving (1803-1872), the eldest of PMI's three sisters.

[18] WI to Pierre Paris Irving, Paris, August 29, 1825 (SHR).

time it reached New York he was already a passenger aboard the brig *Columbia* bound for Europe.[19] Yet even had he read his uncle's advice, he probably would not have been influenced by it in the least. Well intended as Irving's maxims doubtless were, his notion that "Pierre stands in need rather of something to fix than to unsettle him" was in most respects simply unfounded. Certainly there is no evidence that he thought it necessary to reprimand his young relative for his presence in Europe once the latter had made his appearance in Madrid. On the contrary, he was pleased to discover in Pierre not only a personable companion but an individual well acquainted with the "useful" matters which he professed to regard as so important.

Had Pierre read Irving's pronouncement that one year of study in New York outweighed three of travel in Europe, he might have retorted that his four years of study recently completed in the city seemed an ample price to pay for a *Wanderjahr* abroad. Upon graduating from Columbia College in 1821, he had shown no want of steadiness in preparing himself for a profession. Several years of looking on while his brave father slowly killed himself with overwork and anxiety in an attempt to make ends meet for a large family[20] had taught him a lesson he would never forget; and well before the death of William Irving in December 1821, Pierre had resolved to pursue a reliably remunerative line of work. Perhaps under the guidance of his Uncle John Treat Irving, at that time recently installed as Judge of the New York Court of Common Pleas,[21] he became a student in a New York law office. Pierre's mother, Julia Paulding Irving, was so affected by the loss of her husband that she declined steadily afterward; and in the few months prior to her own death in January 1823, when she was unable to care for the household or even herself,[22] Pierre was often needed at home.

Yet even in these bleak times he kept at his studies and also managed to enjoy a limited social life. He was a member of the Calliopean Society, a semi-secret organization which met on Tuesday evenings to hear original compositions and to discuss topics of literary and scientific interest.[23] He attended "literary seances," read the works of "The Croakers"—Fitz-Greene Halleck and Joseph Rodman

[19] New York *Evening Post*, September 15, 1825, p. 2, col. 5; Ebenezer Irving to Genl. Richard Dodge, New York, September 29, 1825 (N-YHS).

[20] William Irving was financially ruined by losses his importing agency sustained following the War of 1812. In the years afterward he attempted to repay his debts and provide for his family while at the same time fulfilling his obligations as a United States Congressman from New York. In 1819 he was forced by failing health to vacate his seat in Congress, and in the ensuing months his persistent efforts to repay his debts further undermined his condition.

[21] John Treat Irving (1778-1838) was the first person to hold this post, which he assumed in 1818. He served with distinction until his death in 1838.

[22] See *Life*, II, 261.

[23] Eleanor B. Scott, "Early Literary Clubs in New York City," *American Literature*, 5 (March 1933), 13, 16.

Drake—then being circulated in manuscript,[24] and became friends with David Berdan, another law student who also had lost his father recently.[25] Berdan, a sometime student of medicine at Columbia College and a graduate of Union College in Schenectady, New York,[26] was a more ebullient personality than Pierre, but the two shared many ideas and tastes in common. While Pierre may not have felt so vehemently as his acquaintance an "aversion to the business of life [which] arose from his devotion to books, and to nature," he fully shared Berdan's ambition to be, as the latter delicately put it, "in possession of a competency."[27] Eventually they took rooms together, and in the evenings they regularly coached each other in Cicero[28] before turning to more congenial topics. Levelheaded as Pierre ordinarily was, undoubtedly he did second to some degree David's weary impatience with legal studies.[29] He was never to regard the practice of law as anything more than a convenient recourse, a necessary means to a more agreeable mode of occupation, or at best, a tolerable way to make ends meet.[30] However, unlike his Uncle Washington, who as a young man had fought an inconclusive bout with the study of law, Pierre persevered and mastered the trade. He was unwilling to expend his entire energy on legal, commercial, and financial affairs, but he showed his family's respect for ability in these spheres of activity. Thus, while he must have taken the attitudes of the perfervid Berdan with a few grains of salt—perhaps, indeed, noticing the similarity

[24] PMI to Fitz-Greene Halleck, New York, February 29, 1864 (Boston Public Library).

[25] David Berdan (b. ca. 1803) was the son of James Berdan, Sr., a New York grocer. The elder Berdan had died in 1820, in part from the effects of exposure suffered in 1819 while on a tour of the Ohio Valley as an agent of the New York Emigration Society (Longworth's [New York] City Directory for 1804, 1820, 1821; Newton Bateman, et al., Historical Encyclopedia of Illinois . . . [Chicago, 1929], I, 45).

[26] Berdan was enrolled in the Columbia College of Physicians and Surgeons for the session of 1814-1815 (Thomas, Columbia, p. 231). In 1817 he entered Union College, where he immediately showed literary talent and became a leader of the Adelphic Society. He graduated in 1821. Most of the information available about David Berdan is in a memoir of him by William H. Seward, "David Berdan," Knickerbocker Magazine, 14 (December 1839), 471-82; reprinted in The Works of William H. Seward, ed. George E. Baker (Boston, 1887), III, 117-27. Subsequent citations of Seward's memoir refer to the reprinted text.

[27] David Berdan to an unidentified correspondent, n.p., August 1822; Seward, pp. 119, 121.

[28] It was not customary during this period for a law student in New York to read Cicero as part of his studies. The task was probably set Berdan by his employer, John Anthon (1784-1863), a leading lawyer in the city whose brother, Charles Anthon (1794-1867), was Professor of Ancient Languages at Columbia College. The identity of PMI's employer is unknown. Details of a law student's life in New York from 1820 to 1822 are given by William H. Seward in his Autobiography from 1801 to 1834 (New York, 1877), pp. 47-48.

[29] Seward, pp. 119, 121.

[30] In this he was in agreement with Berdan, who according to Seward had "determined to secure an acquaintance with the practical duties of an attorney, as a contingent resource, and at the same time to prepare himself for literary pursuits" (Seward, p. 121).

between his written effusions and the sentimental prose of Laurence Sterne or even "Geoffrey Crayon,"[31] Pierre shared his literary tastes, his boredom with legal training, and something of his restlessness.

Late in 1822, Pierre and Berdan began to discuss the possibility of journeying to Europe for an extensive tour to be made "in the plainest dress" and rendered economical by eating only "the plainest food." David was at first the more ardent in advocating this splendid idea, but at some time after the death of Pierre's mother his own enthusiasm increased. His responsibilities at home had now eased, leaving him with a new degree of freedom to regulate his activities as he wished. Gradually his desultory conversations with Berdan about a great escape to Europe in the indefinite future became more serious and specific. Their mutual labours on midweek evenings also changed emphasis: they continued to trudge grimly through *De Legibus*, but they now began to garnish the task with elementary readings in Italian and French. Berdan hired a tutor in French who supplemented his instructions with descriptions of travel in the countries they proposed to visit, and they both patronized the local circulating libraries for published accounts by recent travelers in Europe.[32] Thus they pursued their legal studies in a responsible fashion, looking forward to a revolt from considerations of practical necessity once they should be admitted to the bar. Only one consideration posed a threat to their anticipations: David's delicate health. Early in 1824 he confided to a friend his alarm that "from the symptoms I have observed . . . I am in the first stage of consumption." Nonetheless, he professed to regard Europe with such "poetic feeling" that he would journey there if he had even "strength enough to climb the vessel's side."[33] Meanwhile, he and Pierre lived frugally and quietly, often visiting with each other's family. Pierre enjoyed the evenings at the home of Mrs. Berdan

[31] For example, compare the tone of the following statement by Berdan, probably written in 1821 or 1822, to that of "Westminster Abbey" or "Rural Funerals" in Irving's *The Sketch-Book* (1819-1820): "You speak eloquently of military burial, and your train of thought is elevated. It is different from my own. I had a prejudice in favor of a military life, but my habits and feelings have been so opposite, that they have effected a revolution of opinion. Through all the pomp and circumstance of ceremony, I see the march of corruption, the emptiness of renown. When, as a simple citizen, I stand and view the burial of a soldier, I involuntarily smile at the pageantry with which he is committed to the earth. I turn to the quiet procession, the unadorned pall, to the light yet thrilling sound of the earth that is thrown upon the coffin, with a finer feeling. I leave the grave of the soldier with sensations that do not accord with the ordinary tone of my mind, because I feel that I can not suppose my burial may be like his; but I quit the spot where an obscure and unknown individual has been consigned to his native dust, with a hallowed feeling, that is exalted by the internal conviction of its correspondence with what is to be my own fate" (Seward, p. 120).

[32] David Berdan to an unidentified correspondent, n.p., October 1822; Seward, p. 122. The Calliopean Society maintained a lending library which they may also have drawn upon (Scott, "Early Literary Clubs," p. 16). Publications dealing with the recent conflict between France and Spain were numerous, and familiarity with them may have helped sway PMI and Berdan toward their somewhat unusual decision to visit the latter country.

[33] David Berdan to an unidentified correspondent, n.p., [1824]; Seward, p. 122.

in Broome Street, a short walk from their rooms.[34] There he regularly saw David's two brothers, John, a young businessman, and James, a good-natured undergraduate at Yale College, and also his sister, Margaret, a girl of sixteen.

In May 1825 Pierre and David both passed their examinations and were licensed to practice as attorneys in the state of New York. True to plan, they wasted no time tarrying in the city; but rather, on the sound theory that it was "absurd to seek knowledge of foreign countries, without first having made acquaintance with... [their] native land,"[35] they set out on a tour of the United States. They sailed northward on the Hudson River toward Lake George, near the border with Upper Canada, where they rendezvoused with William H. Seward,[36] a mutual friend. Seward accompanied them back to Albany and thence along the Erie Canal toward Niagara Falls, bidding them goodbye as they turned southward on a long semicircular route through Pennsylvania, Ohio, and Virginia to the Atlantic coast, and finally northward back to New York. According to Seward, on this "romantic excursion" through the semi-wilderness the travelers occupied themselves in "renewing... love of country upon battlefields, and paying the homage of grateful and enthusiastic devotion to nature."[37] Sailing down the Ohio River, they decided to search for "Harmon Blennerhassett's Island," where they hoped to locate the ruined home of that notorious associate of the accused traitor Aaron Burr. By good fortune they were able to discover the remains of the Blennerhassett mansion; and having meditated for a few moments in the shadow of this American ruin, they commemorated the visit by carving their names on a slab of plaster and passed on, taking with them a fragment of the structure "as a relic."[38]

After an exhausting tour of over twelve hundred miles, they returned to New York in mid-summer with their eagerness for the European journey unabated. Even though the western trek had taxed David's health, their planned itinerary for the next excursion was ambitious: they would travel on foot through "part of France, Switzerland, Italy, England, perhaps Scotland, and withal... touch at

---

[34] In 1822 Mrs. Berdan moved from the home she had occupied during her husband's lifetime, at 3 Park Place, to 419 Broome Street. She is not listed in *Longworth's Directory* after 1829.

[35] Seward, p. 123. The thought is attributed to Berdan.

[36] Seward (1801-1872), later a distinguished statesman, met David Berdan at Union College, where he matriculated in 1816 and graduated in 1820. His friendship with Berdan grew closer in the fall of 1820, when he began a legal apprenticeship under John Anthon, David's employer. Within a few months Seward moved to the office of two other prominent New York lawyers, John Duer and Ogden Hoffman. Presumably he met PMI at about this time.

[37] Seward, p. 123.

[38] David Berdan to an unidentified correspondent, n.p., summer 1825; Seward, p. 124. "Blennerhassett's Island" was thirteen miles south of the then village of Marietta, Ohio.

Gibraltar."[39] Probably they expected to visit various members and friends of the Irving family along their way, but it is noteworthy that Pierre had never given Irving any direct indication of his plans, nor, indeed, even written him during his two years' methodical preparations for the journey. He knew that Irving was familiar with most of the countries he and Berdan proposed to traverse, yet he made no effort to solicit his advice. The motives underlying this uncommunicativeness are impossible to specify with certainty, but Pierre may simply have assumed that nothing useful could come from making contact with his uncle on so sensitive a topic as this. He knew that Irving tended to be sternly unsympathetic toward young relatives who showed an inclination to follow in what he seemed to consider his own errant footsteps. Recently, for example, he had directed a blunt warning to Pierre's cousin and namesake Pierre Paris Irving against pursuing a professional literary career. In reply to a confiding letter from this nephew,[40] who was clearly seeking encouragement, Irving had dismissed his ambition as "pernicious," counselling him to become instead a "practical man of business."[41] Surprised and utterly deflated, Pierre Paris had thereupon quietly retreated to a clerkship in his father's prosperous New York importing agency.[42] Pierre Munro may well have inferred from this minor catastrophe that his best policy was to remain silent. Another possible explanation for his failure to write Irving is suggested by a prominent feature of his own character: a deep-seated determination to make his own decisions and commit his own errors, which made him unwilling to seek favours from anyone. Certainly as his father's son he had a legitimate

[39] David Berdan to an unidentified correspondent, n.p., October 1822; Seward, p. 122. The geographical sequence of places in this early listing is chaotic. By 1825 the two must have formed a more coherent plan of their progress, but their itinerary as finally laid out is unknown, except that they intended to begin in southern Italy and hike northward into France.

[40] Pierre Paris Irving (1806-1878), the eldest son of Ebenezer Irving, graduated from Columbia College in 1824. According to PMI, at about this time Pierre Paris "ventured into print in some contributions to a little periodical, called The Fly, which ran through five numbers and expired" (*LLWI*, II, 218). He enclosed some of these articles in his letter to WI as samples of his work.

[41] WI to Pierre Paris Irving, Paris, December 7, 1824; *LLWI*, II, 218-22. This letter was an expression of WI's concern for the entire brood of his distant nephews and nieces whose welfare, he wrote, was "a constant source of solicitude" to him. Disappointed at the unflattering reception given his most recent publication, *Tales of a Traveller* (1824), he was uncertain of his future as a professional author and disposed to regard himself too harshly as an utter failure. He was pained to think that his young relations, being absent from him, might regard his career as glamorous and worthy emulating; hence he responded to any indications of his nephews' following in his footsteps by urging them to seek "useful" careers—unlike himself, who "never could find a calling." WI to Pierre P. Irving, Paris, August 29, 1825 (SHR).

[42] *LLWI*, II, 233-34. After the dissolution of P. & E. Irving & Co., in 1820, Ebenezer Irving kept a store at the same address as before, 122 Pearl Street (*Longworth's Directory* for 1821, 1822); in 1826 he moved his business to 127 Water Street, where he remained until he was burnt out in 1835 (Scoville, *Old Merchants*, II, 79). He then set up a new store at 12 Platt Street, where he remained in business until his retirement in 1841.

claim on Irving's good will and assistance; but the events of his later life reveal that except in times of real need he was never prepared to exact it simply as his due. Whatever his motives, whether discretion, independence, or perhaps diffidence of approaching his uncle, Pierre kept silence.

The preparations for their departure being complete, on September 15 Pierre and David said goodbye to James Berdan at the docks of New York, boarded the *Columbia,* and presently felt themselves possessed by "the wild delight of children at the arrival of a long-expected holiday." According to David, during the first few days of the voyage even the "graceful undulations of the waves" satisfied their famished appetites for diversion. They sneered at their former "abode in the city, as captives talk of their captivity after liberation"[43]—temporarily ignoring their awareness that to preserve David's strength they must pursue their explorations with prudence. As the first installment of their travels in Europe they intended to walk the entire length of Italy from south to north; and hence for the greater part of the voyage they counselled each other on the importance of mastering Italian. However, well before the *Columbia* dropped anchor at Gibraltar they had resigned themselves, owing to David's condition, to postponing the tour of Italy and spending the winter months more quietly in Spain. Thus they disembarked at this bustling jumping-off place, paid their respects to G. G. Barrell, the overworked American Consul,[44] wandered about for a day or two, and made their way via steamboat from Gibraltar to the coastal city of Cadiz.

The ensuing months passed pleasantly for these two young Knickerbockers. With its elegant domestic architecture and its countless memorials of the Spanish, Roman, Greek, and Phoenician past, Cadiz was rich with scenic interest. It was also a distinctly cosmopolitan place, being crowded with English, French, Italian, Dutch, Moorish, and Spanish travelers passing along the main post road to and from Madrid in the north; and at this period it was further enlivened by the presence of ten thousand French troops, an occupation force stationed there in the aftermath of the Franco-Spanish conflict of 1823-1824. The native residents of Cadiz were themselves a worthwhile study as one promenaded the Alameda in the cool evenings—particularly the young women, whose eyes shone behind their coyly expressive fans. Alexander Slidell, an American who visited the city a few months after Pierre and Berdan, proclaimed the ladies of Cadiz "of all creatures in creation . . . the most enchanting," and affirmed that they exerted a fascination so powerful as to batter down "the barrier of the most stubborn morality."[45] Like their countryman, these temporary residents were sensible of all the exotic scenery in the place. Once they

---

[43] David Berdan to an unidentified correspondent, at sea, September 1825; Seward, p. 124.

[44] This was the official who was to answer WI's query in June 1826 as to the whereabouts of PMI. See *Life,* I, 331, and 483, note 38.

[45] *A Year in Spain,* II, 214, 215.

Rue de Boulogne, while among other topics for conversation the four wrangled over points of theology. With "all the complacency of ignorance," as Pierre ruefully put it a few years later, he and Storer undertook to enlighten Longfellow "on the subject of Christianity"—a creed in which the young poet claimed to discern "evidences of a higher origin than earth."[63]

In December Pierre had written a note to Irving, mentioning his return to Paris and his plans to proceed toward London within a few weeks. Since he did not expect to see his uncle again while in Europe, this message seems to have been essentially a gesture of courtesy. Certainly when he wrote it he had no inkling of the importance which Irving would attach to it nor of the great pleasure with which it would be received. In the past few months Irving had kept up communications with him so sporadically that he was almost ignorant of his uncle's activities since they had parted in July. Very naturally, he assumed that the author was at work on the *Life of Columbus*. In fact, however, Irving had been indulging himself during almost the entire period in an extended literary whim. In the course of his research for the *Columbus* he had grown so interested in the history of the conquest of Granada, the Moorish capital of mediaeval Spain, that he had temporarily suspended his efforts on the biography to begin writing a second Spanish narrative. While Pierre was traversing Italy, Irving was exploring this seductive new topic, and by the close of 1826 he had almost completed a draft of the narrative that would eventually be published as *A Chronicle of the Conquest of Granada*. Meanwhile, the weightier *Columbus* lay untouched and still far from finished.

Despite the still embryonic status of the latter work, on December 24 Irving wrote to John Murray, his publisher in London, claiming that it was "nearly ready for the press."[64] This untruth was prompted by an anxious wish to keep Murray interested in the book, on which the publisher had never really committed himself since it had first been proposed to him eleven months before. On January 16 he received a reply from Murray which was to begin months of suffering as a consequence of his mendacity: without going so far as to offer a price for the completed book, the wily publisher expressed strong interest in it and urged him to send the manuscript along immediately![65] Irving was mortified at having manoeuvred himself into so potentially embarrassing a corner; obviously he must turn his attention back to the long-forsaken topic without delay. Even as he did so, however, he was bedeviled by a complex problem associated with putting the completed work through the press. Until he had received Murray's bittersweet communication, he had assumed that he would be able to prepare and market the *Columbus* by whatever schedule and in what-

[63] PMI to Henry W. Longfellow, Northampton [Massachusetts], July 3, 1830 (Harvard).

[64] Ben H. McClary, ed., *WI and the House of Murray . . . 1817-1856* (Knoxville, 1969), p. 85.

[65] Only a fragment of Murray's reply survives. See McClary, p. 88.

ever manner he chose. Thus, in order to secure profits from sales of the book both in England and in the United States as well, he had planned to avert transatlantic piracy by adopting his usual procedure of arranging for roughly simultaneous publication in both places. To realize this aim he had intended, upon completing the manuscript, first to have it copied out at Madrid, and then to dispatch one copy to Murray and the other to Ebenezer, his agent in New York, so that the printers in both places could begin setting the work in type at approximately the same time. Murray's letter altered the whole complexion of affairs, however, and Irving was distressed to think that the time and expense of copying the manuscript must be added to the indeterminate period still to elapse before he could even finish writing his book. Would he be able to placate Murray long enough to keep the man's mercurial interest from waning?

On January 18, two days after receiving the letter from Murray, he was seeking a way to extricate himself from this predicament when Pierre's note from Paris arrived and immediately suggested a solution: true, he had created this log-jam of copying, correcting, and mailing for himself—yet why should he not deputize his bright young nephew to unsnarl it? He dashed off a reply to Pierre, confessing that the news of his intention to visit London had "arrived in the very critical moment to put me at my ease." After explaining his situation, he went on to propose the following arrangement:

> ... I must get you to superintend the publication of my work in London, correcting the proofsheets, &c. As you will be able to decipher my handwriting, and from your knowledge of languages will be able to see the quotations in Spanish, Italian, &c., are printed correctly, I need not lose time in getting it copied here. You will send out proofsheets to E. Irving as fast as they are printed, for the work to be reprinted in America. Thus you see you will really be of vast service to me.... This arrangement will enable me to forward my work by piecemeal as I get it ready, and will greatly expedite its publication, while it will make me feel easy as to the manner in which it will be brought out in London, which I should not have done had I committed it to the superintendence of strangers.[66]

In short, by sending sections of the manuscript to Pierre as he completed them, Irving hoped to dispense with the hand-copying stage of manuscript preparation while at the same time ensuring that Ebenezer would have corrected proof in hand well before publication of the London edition. Relying in this way upon Pierre, he would be able to send the manuscript to Murray in the shortest time possible, protecting his literary property into the bargain.

All of this was very well—for Irving; and yet, hasty and arbitrary as it was, Pierre willingly accepted the proposed enlistment as agent for his uncle's unfinished business. Perhaps he was pleased that his

---

[66] WI to PMI, Madrid, January 18, 1827; *LLWI*, II, 256.

bouts with foreign languages might prove useful to him as a kind of subordinate literary collaborator. At any rate, his uncle's scheme promised to mesh with his own plans, and thus as the days passed he was content to remain at Paris awaiting further instructions. On February 21, Longfellow, equipped with letters of introduction and much good advice, set out for Madrid,[67] where he was to pass several "altogether delightful"[68] months, often in company with the harried but still affable Irving. A few days later Pierre received a disconsolate letter from his uncle, who regretted to say that his expectation of having copy to forward by this time had proved inaccurate. "I had no idea of what a complete labyrinth I had entangled myself in when I took hold of the work," he wrote. He had suffered some "extremely irksome" delays—difficulty procuring documents, the necessity of extensive revision, and a scarcity of trustworthy copyists to take extracts from indispensable source material—which had badly deranged his schedule. As matters stood, he could not expect Pierre to wait any longer, and so he urged him for the time being to follow his inclinations. "I may yet require your aid while in England," he added, "but that must depend entirely upon your movements and convenience."[69] Irving need not have worried that his unrealistic planning had upset Pierre's schedule in any major way. David continued weak, and so long as Longfellow had been among them they all had passed the days pleasantly enough. Still, once Pierre was conditionally released from his literary responsibilities, he did not linger in Paris. He wrote a reply to Irving, said goodbye to the Storrows, and together with Storer and Berdan made his way toward England.

Traveling with caution and in short stages, the three did not arrive in London until about March 17, 1827.[70] Berdan, fooling no one, professed to be so pleased with the city that he preferred to remain there rather than continue with Pierre on the cross-country excursion they had talked of. He would explore the place with Storer, he said, and gather his forces for the return voyage to New York. The prospect of beginning another tour without his companions struck Pierre as so dreary, however, that he also changed his plans. After spending only two days in London he departed for "The Shrubbery," the home of his Aunt Sarah Irving Van Wart and her family near Birmingham, where he arrived on March 21.[71] The Van Warts' home had been a favourite resort of Irving's while in England, and the quiet

---

[67] Thompson, *Young Longfellow*, p. 105.

[68] Longfellow arrived in Madrid on March 7. On March 20 he wrote to his brother Stephen that WI was "one of those men who put you at ease with them in a moment" (Hilen, ed., *Letters*, I, 222). See also Andrew B. Myers, "WI's Madrid Journal 1827-1828 and Related Letters," *Bulletin of the New York Public Library*, 62 (1958), 465-70.

[69] WI to PMI, Madrid, February 22, 1827; *LLWI*, II, 257.

[70] PMI to Henry W. Longfellow, Birmingham, April 11, 1827 (Harvard).

[71] Sarah Irving Van Wart (1780-1849), the second youngest of the eleven children born to William Irving, Sr. and Sarah Sanders Irving, was seven years older than her brother WI.

family life there must have been a respite for Pierre from the often lonely routine of travel. Apparently his revised travel plans were rather vague, for he was easily induced to extend his visit beyond the few days he had at first intended to stay. Henry and Irving Van Wart,[72] his Aunt Sarah's eldest sons, proved to be genial, informative company, and he struck up a friendship with the latter cousin which was to continue over many years. Although he was separated from Berdan and Storer and still uncertain whether he would ever perform the editorial duties his uncle wished to delegate to him, he was satisfied to remain a guest of the Van Warts until the next message from Madrid should arrive.

On March 20 an exasperated Irving wrote to Pierre that in the four weeks since his last letter his efforts to save time had only caused him to commit new errors and create fresh delays for himself. He was disgusted at his failure to execute his own portion of the January plan, and he had decided that the best course was to re-adopt his original intention of preparing dual manuscript copies at Madrid. With dogged optimism he professed to be in hopes of completing the work before many more weeks; but after having experienced so many unanticipated delays, he wrote, he could not be precise about his schedule. Under these circumstances it would be unfair to expect Pierre to remain near London any longer; and so, regretfully, he urged him to abandon all thoughts of superintending publication of the *Columbus*—even of checking proofsheets for the English edition. Being uncertain of Pierre's whereabouts, he directed his letter to the Storrows at Paris; they forwarded it to London; and on April 11, after three weeks in transit, it straggled into Birmingham.[73] Pierre was not particularly disappointed to learn that the scheme for collaboration had proved impracticable, for at least having gained that knowledge he was free to spend his remaining weeks in Europe however he pleased. Writing to Longfellow on the same day as he had received his uncle's letter, he expressed an intention of exploring England and Scotland before his departure for home the following month. Yet he was by now so sybaritically at ease among the Van Warts that, despite his announced plans to undertake a strenuous tour of historical and literary shrines,[74] he was really in no hurry to begin this last leg of his European tour. He remained at "The Shrubbery" two weeks longer,[75] and so he must have modified his plans radically in order to arrive at

[72] Henry Van Wart, Jr. was born in 1807 and Irving Van Wart was born in New York on March 7, 1808 (Victor H. Paltsits, "Report on the MS Diary," with the Diary of Irving Van Wart, Jr., 1854-1855—NYPL, MS). For an account of Henry Van Wart, Sr. (b. 1783), see *Life*, I, 146.

[73] *WI and the Storrows*, p. 111; PMI to Henry W. Longfellow, Birmingham, April 11, 1827 (Harvard).

[74] He mentioned Kenilworth, Warwick, Stratford-on-Avon, Oxford, and Woodstock. PMI to Henry W. Longfellow, Birmingham, April 11, 1827 (Harvard).

[75] WI wrote in his journal for May 14 that he had that day received a "letter from Pierre M I. & from V Wart – dated 24 April" (Myers, "WI's Madrid Journal," p. 223). PMI must have remained with the Van Warts until the date on which he wrote the letter.

London before May 1, when a packet ship bound for New York was due to sail with him aboard. When he did reach the city, he learned without surprise that David was unfit to attempt the voyage. On May 1, therefore, Pierre and Storer parted with their feeble companion—who pluckily insisted that he would be sailing in another ship soon enough—boarded the ship *Hudson*, and sailed for home.[76]

On June 14, 1827, the New York *Evening Post* announced the arrival that forenoon of "E. Storer, N. York; P. Irving, do."[77] The escape to Europe, which Pierre had once envisioned as the fulfillment of all his best wishes, was behind him. He enjoyed the reunion with his three brothers and three sisters after an absence of almost two years, and in short order he was no doubt called upon by Uncle Ebenezer and his family to empty himself of impressions and anecdotes about Irving, Peter, Madrid—and indeed, the still-unfinished *Columbus*. Amidst these attentions, however, were more sober obligations. He must inform Mrs. Berdan of David's condition, and in the near future he would need to find a place to live and settle down (as Irving had urged two years before) to "making his fortune." Irving's fretful concern of 1825 that Pierre would become "permanently unsettled" by the experiences of Europe had not proved prophetic, it was true, and for his part any qualms he may have felt about his nephew had been dispelled. In February 1828 he wrote to his sister Mrs. Catharine Paris in New York that he was "highly pleased with Pierre Munroe [*sic*]" and expressed the opinion that he "has only to persevere to rise to importance and high respectability."[78] For himself, however, Pierre was uncertain what he wished to do with his life. Persevere in what, he wondered, and where? If he chose, he might easily enough secure himself a position in New York through the intercession of Judge John Treat Irving or any of his late father's influential friends—or even, like Pierre Paris, through the offices of Uncle Ebenezer. Nevertheless, as a licensed attorney he clearly had his professional options open, and he was not hunting favours. His real problem in June 1827 was one of self-knowledge. During the past two years he had been able to avoid considering his future very seriously, so that at twenty-five he was still doubtful as to his aptitudes and aims. Probably, too, this concern about his own want of direction was heightened by a sense of isolation. Despite his will to independence, Pierre felt close ties to his family and possessed a quietly social disposition toward others as well. Having lost both his parents, being about to lose his closest friend (David Berdan died aboard the ship *Cameo* on July 20, 1827, bound for home),[79] and out of contact with his New York acquaintances, he was to a degree cut off from his own past.

[76] PMI, MS Outline, Chapter 47 (1827).

[77] *Evening Post*, p. 2, col. 5.

[78] WI to Mrs. Catharine Paris, Madrid, February 17, 1828 (Yale). On April 4, 1827, WI had written a similar report to Henry Brevoort, soliciting the good offices of his friend in Pierre's behalf; see *Irving to Brevoort*, pp. 414-15.

[79] Seward, p. 126. Berdan had sailed from London on July 1.

Not long after his arrival in New York Pierre made some provisional decisions. For the time being a move away from the city was out of the question. He was already low on funds, and now that his two elder brothers Lewis and Oscar were married and raising families[80] he must expect to share the responsibility of supporting his three younger sisters, Julia, Euphemia, and Susan, and his brother Henry Ogden. The one profession in which he could hope to make his way with a measure of comfort while also setting something aside for his semi-dependents was the law. Fortunately, David Berdan's younger brother James had just received his M.A. degree from Yale College and was about to begin practice as a lawyer in New York.[81] James was willing and probably eager to take a partner in his new chambers in Maiden Lane,[82] and so he and Pierre went into business together. The latter was glad of this opportunity, not only because Berdan was intelligent and likeable but also because he owned a respectable collection of legal volumes which Pierre could not have purchased on his own account. Beginning in the summer of 1827, he applied himself to his profession, his immediate aims being to line his pockets and help provide for his family.

From this time until May 1832, when Irving returned to the United States, Pierre seems to have made no effort to stay in contact with him. Neither, for that matter, does Pierre's name occur frequently in Irving's correspondence.[83] After their meeting in Spain and the subsequent flurry of messages, they seem to have gone their separate ways. Perhaps the potential future usefulness of Pierre as a literary aide was somewhere at the back of Irving's mind, but it is less likely that such a thought would have occurred as a real possibility to Pierre. The vicissitudes of his affairs from year to year were to claim his attention so insistently that he had little leisure to speculate about the indefinite future.

Life as a fledgling lawyer was unexciting, but Pierre was determined to keep his mind occupied in areas outside the confines of professional routine. He and James Berdan shared a high opinion of the late David's literary talents, and they discussed the possibility of editing for publication a volume of his selected letters and fugitive writings. Although they delayed beginning work on this project, in the spring of 1828 they did exert themselves on David's behalf by

[80] Lewis (1795-1879) married Maria Carleton Hale at Plattsburg, New York, on June 16, 1823, and by 1827 they had two sons. Oscar (1800-1865) had married Catharine E. C. Dayton, and in 1827 they had one son (PMI, Misc. Notebook).

[81] James Berdan (1805-1884) was enrolled along with his elder brother David in the Columbia College of Physicians and Surgeons during the session of 1814-1815; he studied arts at Columbia from 1819 to 1822 (Thomas, *Columbia*, p. 137), and received his B.A. from Yale College in 1824. A sketch of his life is in Bateman, *Historical Encyclopedia of Illinois*, I, 45.

[82] *Longworth's Directory* for 1828.

[83] WI received letters from PMI on May 14 and September 10, 1827 (Myers, "WI's Madrid Journals," pp. 223, 306); he addressed a letter to him on December 20, 1828 (*WI Diary. Spain 1828-1829*, ed. C. L. Penney [New York, 1926], p. 87).

assembling some of his papers for William H. Seward,[84] now a rising New York state politician, who in July gave an "oration" on Berdan at the Union College commencement exercises.[85] Pierre often passed evenings alone in his room cultivating a new-found taste for readings in divinity. Since his sceptical days at Paris he had grown interested in Unitarianism, and he was even becoming a regular churchgoer—often in the company of his sisters and of Margaret Berdan, James' sister.[86] He exchanged letters of literary gossip and personal reminiscence with Longfellow, who in 1828 returned to the United States to assume the Professorship of Modern Languages at Bowdoin College.[87] Altogether, despite his modest professional success and his want of real direction, Pierre was not unhappy.

For reasons of economy James Berdan was living at his mother's home in Broome Street, and so as in earlier years Pierre frequently visited there. He enjoyed the company of Margaret, whose quiet temperament and cultivated habits meshed well with his own character, and presently he began to feel affection for her. She agreed with his religious views, she was a close friend of his sisters, she impressed his family, and eventually it appeared that she also returned his regard. In the summer of 1829 Pierre threw prudence aside, proposed, and was accepted. As yet he was far from being financially secure; but with an impulsiveness that throughout his lifetime periodically overbalanced his prudent circumspection, he damned the consequences and was married to Margaret on September 19, 1829.[88]

Through the ensuing winter he and his brother-in-law continued in partnership, both disturbed at their sad want of business. To help make ends meet they conceived the scheme of publishing a "Lawbook"[89]—apparently a reference work of some kind—on which they spent some of their idle hours in February and March; but nothing seems to have come of this project. Meanwhile, Pierre thoroughly enjoyed his role as uxorious husband. True to form, it took him not less than six months to announce his marriage to Longfellow; but when the latter did receive the news he wrote to James Berdan that "the lively colours in which Pierre describes his happy lot—make me very discontented with my present inglorious estate."[90] Nevertheless,

[84] PMI and James Berdan to William H. Seward, New York, January 19, 1833 (Rochester).

[85] At the time he gave this address Seward was requested by the Adelphic Society of the college to provide a copy of it for publication. He agreed to do so, but it took him eleven years to make good the promise. See below, p. 71.

[86] PMI to Henry W. Longfellow, Northampton, July 3, 1830 (Harvard).

[87] On October 15, 1829, Longfellow added the following postscript to a letter to Alexander Slidell at New York: "Remember me if you please to Irving and Berdan. They will hear from me before long" (Hilen, ed., *Letters,* I, 324).

[88] New York *Evening Post,* September 19, 1829, p. 2, col. 5. They made their home at 27 Bleecker Street (*Longworth's Directory* for 1830).

[89] Hilen, ed., *Letters,* I, 339.

[90] "How very singular that I should not have heard a word about Pierre's marriage?" Longfellow wrote to James Berdan on April 14, 1830. "I was ashamed to tell him

as spring approached the threat of penury obliged Pierre to think of other locations where he might better be able to make his way. It was clear in any case that the city atmosphere did not wholly agree with Margaret. All through the past winter Pierre's sister Euphemia had declined with a consumption, and when she died in March[91] he must have had an anxious thought that without proper care his delicate wife might also be in danger. Such a grim premonition of personal disaster would have been difficult for him to avoid, for in his early adulthood he had already been obliged more than once to look on helplessly while the persons closest to him sickened and died. Certainly he need run no unnecessary risks with Margaret when New York was too expensive a city anyway. He toiled on with James Berdan until the end of June; but then, acting on a plan he had been forming for some time, he gathered together his wife, his two surviving sisters, and Henry Ogden, and abandoned New York to take up residence in the rural town of Northampton, Massachusetts.

On July 3, 1830, installed at a bedraggled tavern in Northampton while awaiting the tardy arrival of his household effects, Pierre began a long overdue letter to Longfellow. Summarizing his unsettled circumstances, he managed to sound distinctly optimistic. He had always felt an urge for a country life, he said, and Northampton was not only situated among "beautiful scenery" but also boasted "excellent society" and that essential requisite, a Unitarian church.[92] He planned to practice law here, growing some of his own food and trusting to luck for the rest. "I entertain no rash expectation of being able to beat the Yankees on their own ground," he joked, but "I have a faint and humble hope that Fortune will not *cut* me entirely."[93] At least in the way of business, Northampton seeked likely to realize his wishes. Situated about twenty miles north of Springfield at the junction of the Connecticut River and the Hampshire-Hampden Canal, it was a minor centre for inland commerce, the site of several mills and manufacturies, and also a county seat.[94] Pierre had no real experience of life outside a city, but he believed that the quiet and privacy at Northampton would be healthful for Margaret and also agreeable to his own retiring instincts. On the whole, he had chosen wisely.[95]

so: but as he neglected to send me a newspaper, announcing the same, I cannot conceive that it was my fault" (Hilen, ed., *Letters*, I, 338).

[91] Euphemia Irving was born on November 17, 1808 and died in March 1830 (PMI, Misc. Notebook). See also PMI to Henry W. Longfellow, Northampton, June 24, 1831 (Harvard).

[92] "You will smile to hear this last circumstance mentioned as influencing in any degree my choice of a residence.... But it was not myself alone whose wishes were consulted in this particular—besides myself & *wife* (I can write this little monosyllable, but I find it an awkward mouthful as yet to speak aloud) my household consists of two sisters and a brother, and the *true church* enlists the partialities of all."

[93] PMI to Henry W. Longfellow, Northampton, July 3, 1830 (Harvard).

[94] John Bigelow, *Statistical Tables ... of Industry in Massachusetts* (Boston, 1838), pp. 79-80; John Hayward, *A Gazetteer of Massachusetts ...* (Boston, 1849), pp. 166, 222-23, 362.

[95] He had at least chosen it after much deliberation, selecting Northampton over

At last the furniture arrived, enabling him to move the family into a small house in which they all passed uneventful lives during the next few months. He was encouraged that his briefs and fees soon promised to maintain the household in physical comfort, but as time passed he was made uneasily aware of how absolutely life in Northampton tended to throw one upon his own resources for amusement. The Irving and Berdan families in New York were at two strenuous days' distance over wretched roads, and on his infrequent journeys there the requirements of business made his visits hasty and unsatisfying. Removed in this way from his accustomed haunts in the city, and pursuing a profession which he could regard only as a means to financial competence, Pierre began to wonder whether in fact he was temperamentally fitted for the law. At times the pettiness of his work rankled in him. He had continued to pursue his avocation of reading in theology, and during the winter of 1830-1831 his rather confused sense of himself came to a new hypothetical focus: might not his taste for theological studies be a sign of his aptitude as a minister? His thoughtful disposition, the sobering effect of repeated bereavements, his desire to live quietly while indulging a taste for reading and reflection, and perhaps even a memory of William Irving's not-yet-realized wish that one of his sons should be a clergyman, all pointed plausibly to this area of speculation. Probably Pierre recognized that the image of himself as a clergyman had taken shape in his mind as a response in some part to his discontentment with the law; but once having decided that he did feel a religious vocation, he was thoroughly in earnest. Setting aside his legal practice, he began to devote himself exclusively to the study of divinity in order to prepare for the Unitarian ministry. In June 1831, when he announced his change of sentiments and aims to Longfellow, he professed to have discovered a "serious and decided preference for this new field of labor" and expressed the hope that he would be able to "embark upon a new sphere of duty" within eighteen months.[96]

Pierre's intention was to live out the remainder of the year at Northampton and then remove to Cambridge, Massachusetts, to enroll in the theological seminary there. Unfortunately, like many of his well-laid plans, this one was destined to be frustrated by events he could not possibly have foreseen. After his letter to Longfellow he never again mentioned in extant correspondence his hope to enter the ministry.[97] By the fall of 1831 it had become unmistakably clear that Margaret was lapsing into a decline, and that, despite her sympathy with his aims, her health must take precedence over his ambition to

"many other" places (PMI to Henry W. Longfellow, Northampton, July 3, 1830—Harvard).

[96] PMI to Henry W. Longfellow, Northampton, June 24, 1831 (Harvard).

[97] However, he did not immediately abandon the plan. Eighteen months later, on January 23, 1833, WI wrote to Mrs. Catharine Paris from Washington, D.C.: "I had letters from Pierre Munro lately who I find has given up his idea of devoting himself to the church; and I am heartily glad he has done so" (Yale).

begin a new career. Worried and distracted, he resumed his practice in Northampton. Before the onset of winter his sisters and brother returned to New York, taking with them much of the cheer of the household. Months passed, and Margaret grew weaker. Pierre undoubtedly knew through the family grapevine that his Uncle Washington, who was now serving as Secretary to the United States Legation at London, planned to return home before many months; but on May 21, 1832, when Irving's ship was given its enthusiastic welcome at the docks of New York, he was not among the crowd of well-wishers. He was in Northampton, wondering whether by returning to the city he might save Margaret's life. As long as he could believe that the rural air might help to work her cure, he had delayed the return; but by now that fancy seemed almost fully disproved.

Under these dismal circumstances the young couple presently made their appearance in the city, where they did meet Irving. Showing the spirit of her family, Margaret rallied herself for the introduction and carried it off well. Irving was "greatly pleased with the mildness and gentl[eness] of her deportment and appearance,"[98] even though he was not deceived about her condition. Possibly he saw Margaret and Pierre again in July, when Pierre's sister Susan married Irving Van Wart in a gala New York wedding, but at other times they came together infrequently if at all. Pierre and Margaret were not in society, while Irving, still the darling of the welcoming committees, was busy renewing friendships among his early acquaintances since become the great men of the city.

Late in August, he set out on a tour of the Great Lakes to see a part of the burgeoning West he had heard his countrymen describe with such expansive enthusiasm during his long absence. In the course of the journey he fell in with Henry L. Ellsworth, a Connecticut gentleman who was bound on a mission to the Indian tribes of Oklahoma Territory on behalf of the United States government. Having ample time on his hands, he was easily induced by Ellsworth to join this more adventurous expedition; and thus during September he sailed down the Ohio River toward St. Louis, whence he proceeded overland into Oklahoma Territory.[99] Irving greatly enjoyed his extended tour of personal discovery, and in letters home he described himself as "charmed with the grand scenery"[100] along his route. The New York newspapers eventually made their way to the frontier, however, and on November 16 he wrote from Fort Gibson, a remote army outpost

[98] WI to Mrs. Catharine Paris, Montgomery's Point, Mouth of the Arkansas, November 10, 1832 (Virginia). The square brackets enclose text supplied at a point where the manuscript is torn.

[99] WI's western tour is fully chronicled not only in his own journals and letters but in those of fellow travelers. See *The Western Journals of WI*, ed. John F. McDermott (Norman, Okla., 1944); Henry L. Ellsworth, *WI on the Prairie . . .* , ed. Stanley T. Williams and Barbara D. Simison (New York, 1937); Charles J. Latrobe, *The Rambler in North America*, 2 vols. (New York, 1835); and *On the Western Tour with WI: The Journal and Letters of Count de Pourtales*, ed. George F. Spaulding (Norman, Okla., 1968).

[100] WI to Mrs. Catharine Paris, St. Louis, September 13, 1832; *LLWI*, III, 37.

near Pawnee country, that he had just read of Margaret's death. "This is another of those depredations for which we were prepared by long anticipation," he wrote philosophically.[101] Margaret had died on October 4, 1832, at the age of twenty-three.[102]

Back in New York, the harrowing months that had preceded the death of his wife left Pierre depleted in energy and fortitude. Being as yet unable to form new plans, he remained in the city among his relations. Often he visited at the home of Ebenezer, which was at this time the temporary residence of a recently bereaved cousin of his, Helen Dodge.[103] Having attended her widowed father through a protracted illness, Helen had been with him at his death in their rural home near Troy, New York, and immediately thereafter she had removed to the city. An intelligent and vivacious spinster of thirty, she had been for many years a favourite of all the family,[104] and this winter her firm good spirits were a helpful curative to her cousin's melancholy. Pierre also saw much of James Berdan, who had prospered in the past two years and now occupied chambers at a desirable location in Pine Street.[105] When Berdan offred to renew their partnership, he was readily accepted. Perhaps to create employment for himself, Pierre re-activated the old project of preparing a literary memorial to the genius of David Berdan. Various friends encouraged him, particularly since William H. Seward had never accomplished his stated intention of four years before to compile and publish a biographical memoir. Setting himself the task of gathering all David's correspondence, he became engrossed in the search, and his spirits began to revive. By mid-January 1833, he was eager to begin selecting and editing the contents of the volume. Eventually, as he and James Berdan informed a correspondent, they planned to submit the work "to the judgment of Washington Irving and other literary gentlemen"

[101] WI to Mrs. Catharine Paris, Montgomery's Point, Mouth of the Arkansas, November 16, 1832 (Virginia).

[102] New York *Evening Post*, October 5, 1832, p. 2, col. 5. The cause of Margaret's death was given as "a lingering illness."

[103] Helen (b. 1802) was the youngest of six children born to Richard Dodge (1762-1832) and Ann Sarah Irving (1770-1808), an elder sister of WI. Richard Dodge rose to the rank of Colonel in the Revolutionary War, after which he became a surveyor, settling in Caughnawaga, New York. On a trip to New York City in 1787 he convinced his friend William Irving to return with him to the Mohawk Valley and set up a trading agency there. He married William's sister Ann in 1788 (John P. Frothingham, "Genealogy and History of the Frothingham Family and its Connections: Frost, Dodge, and Irving Families," pp. 135-38—typescript, NYPL, MS).

[104] WI was especially fond of her. On November 16, 1832, he wrote of her to Mrs. Paris: "I received a parcel of letters at Fort Gibson among which was a very interesting one from you, informing me of the death of poor Dodge. All things considered we may look upon it as a happy release for him from a state of suffering from which there was no prospect of a recovery. Helen has behaved in an admirable manner and has nothing to reproach herself with. I trust you spoke to our brother E.I. [Ebenezer] and settled as to the pecuniary allowance I am to make her, which must be such as to render her situation completely comfortable. She is *my* daughter now, poor girl!" (Virginia).

[105] *Longworth's Directory* for 1831, 1832.

so as to be guided "in a final revision."[106] Thus, within only a few months of Margaret's death Pierre had recovered himself sufficiently to look with enthusiasm toward his future activities. Nevertheless, at intervals over the next few years he was to grow depressed at the memory of his late wife.

In March 1833, when Irving swept back into New York after seven months of travel, Pierre was as yet without a completed manuscript of the memorial volume to show him. There is no evidence, in fact, that he ever did complete one. During the past few weeks his interest in that undertaking had been diminishing, and by the time he saw his uncle he was impatient to begin another, more ambitious enterprise. He had fixed his eyes anew on the goal of financial independence, preferably to be achieved without performing various dull and tamely respectable duties. Infected with the contagion of fabulous rumours concerning the quick fortunes being made in the West, both he and Berdan had decided to grow wealthy as lawyers and land speculators somewhere in the still largely unpopulated state of Illinois.[107] If Irving had expected to find his nephew still sensibly affected by the loss of Margaret, therefore, he was quickly disabused, for Pierre was sanguine enough to make the best of his enforced independence as a widower. On the other hand, if Pierre had anticipated that Irving might be able to offer helpful investment advice on the basis of his own recent journey to the West, he was surely disappointed. Irving's tour had been entirely desultory, and even if it had not been so Pierre was already much more knowledgeable than his uncle about business affairs. Irving had only a single bit of advice to offer, one in which he seconded the sentiments of Pierre's sisters: that he should not stay away too long. It was bad practice, he knew from his own lonely years in Europe, for the family to be dispersed.

Following the Erie Canal to Buffalo, and thence continuing southwestward by lake and land on an exploratory tour, Pierre and Berdan decided in May 1833 to settle in Jacksonville, Illinois—at that time a town of 1,800.[108] Only three years earlier this frontier village had numbered a total of 446 inhabitants, but by the time Pierre arrived it was a bustling place which boasted five churches, a "female seminary," and even a college.[109] Like other western communities of its

[106] James Berdan and PMI to William H. Seward, New York, January 19, 1833 (Rochester). The quotation is from the portion written by Berdan.

[107] Berdan wrote to Seward in his portion of the January 19 letter (see footnote 106): "It is of the greatest importance that we should immediately if possible, receive the portions which you and your brother can contribute to the book, as Irving and I have determined to remove at an early date from this City, and to practise Law in the State of Illinois."

[108] Although Jacksonville possessed sound credentials in itself as a place favourable to their aims, PMI and Berdan may have been influenced in their choice of it by information received by James from his late father, who had visited there in 1819 (Bateman, *Historical Encyclopedia of Illinois*, I, 45).

[109] Frank J. Heinl, "Jacksonville and Morgan County: An Historical Review," *Journal of the Illinois Historical Society*, 18 (July 1925), 5, 7-9).

era, Jacksonville was rife with incongruities. Its large town square was a source of local pride, but it was overgrown in spots with jimson weeds so thick and sturdy that according to a contemporary witness, "a pig would not be able to make his way through them."[110] William Cullen Bryant, who visited there in 1832, thought the whole town "horribly ugly"; he stigmatized the town square as "dirty" and described the brick courthouse in its centre as "the ugliest of possible brick courthouses."[111] Yet, notwithstanding its motley appearance, Jacksonville was, according to a biographer of Stephen A. Douglas, "the pole star of Illinois cities" during this period, and the "ablest lawyers of the state" practised there.[112] The leading men of the community were young and ambitious: Douglas, then a rising lawyer; Murray McConnel, long afterward a warhorse in state politics; and Judge Samuel D. Lockwood, later esteemed as "the John Marshall of Illinois."[113] It was a lively, exhilarating place. Shortly after their arrival Pierre and Berdan began to mingle with these men and, suitably impressed, actually to weigh the possibility of settling there permanently.

They took rooms at the home of Isaac Israel, a struggling grain trader whose wife was active in local society.[114] The population of Jacksonville was characterized by a plurality of unattached young men, but Mrs. Israel exerted herself successfully on behalf of her tenants and introduced them into the social life of the town. Soon Pierre found himself escorting various of "the fair," as he called them—particularly a certain "Eliza"—to "dancing parties"[115] and other functions. In the daytime he argued his cases and attended to financial rumours at the courthouse—a building which also served as a forum for political debates, a hall for social events, and a tabernacle for religious gatherings. Legal practice was not at first very remunerative, but he was unconcerned, for the air was full of intoxicating news—of possible canals, incorporations, or legislative actions which would open up new vistas of quick profit. Out of his modest savings he purchased thirteen town lots, intending to dispose of them shortly without the trouble of making improvements.[116]

---

[110] Cyrus Epler, "History of the Morgan County Bar," *Journal of the Illinois Historical Society*, 19 (January 1927), 165.

[111] "Illinois Fifty Years Ago," in *Prose Writings of William Cullen Bryant*, ed. Parke Godwin (New Yor, 1884), II, 13-14. This sketch is compiled from letters Bryant wrote to his wife while on a visit to his brother John, who had settled on a farm near Jacksonville.

[112] Frank A. Stevens, "Autobiography of Stephen Douglas," *Journal of the Illinois Historical Society*, 5 (October 1912), 328. Douglas' memoir, written in 1838, affords a colourful glimpse of Jacksonville in 1834, where he arrived in March.

[113] Heinl, "Jacksonville," pp. 5, 10.

[114] PMI to Daniel Roberts, New York, January 16, 183[5] (Huntington). For information about the Israels, see Sara J. English, "The History of Trinity Church, Jacksonville," *Journal of the Illinois Historical Society*, 20 (April 1927), 111-59 *passim*; Elizabeth D. Putnam, "Diary of Mrs. Joseph Duncan," *Journal of the Illinois Historical Society*, 21 (April 1928), 26-68 *passim*.

[115] PMI to Daniel Roberts, New York, January 16, 183[5] (Huntington).

[116] PMI to Daniel Roberts, New York, March 15, 1835 (Huntington).

Meanwhile, there was little to do but enjoy himself. He joined his fellow lawyers in drinking sessions featuring impromptu outbursts of song, and once in a letter to a Jacksonville friend he recalled with ironic rapture "the de profundis bass of Gordon" and the "rich psalmody of Berdan."[117] Yet one of the most popular forms of entertainment in that frontier community—the religious revival—he spurned with disgust as "the worst of abominations." Perhaps with a lingering devotion to rational Christianity, he wrote angrily to a friend upon hearing that his "little favourite," Eliza, had been touched by the "fanatic impulse" of revivalism:

> I can tolerate with some philosophy open and undisguised wickedness, but when evil comes in the garb of good, and a system of human management and paltry trick, selfish often in its origin, miserable always in its fruits, is made to bear the name and wear the imposing sanctions of a work of omnipotence, I cannot suppress an emotion of indignant contempt towards the authors and abettors of such movements, nor refrain from the expression of a feeling of exasperated pity for the poor dupes who suffer themselves to be so egregiously gulled. I hope the little Eliza will make a better use of the reason that God has given her than to surrender it to the guidance of these religious Bacchanals.[118]

Pierre was never of so tolerant a nature as to allow what he considered moral abuses to go undenounced. Later, when he was no longer in Jacksonville, he was inclined to refer to the place as a social and cultural wasteland; but the record shows clearly that he enjoyed himself for a substantial proportion of the time he lived there.

Naturally he continued to see much of James Berdan, but he also formed a close friendship with Daniel Roberts, an 1829 graduate of Middlebury College in Vermont whose wide reading, bachelorhood, hungry acquisitiveness, and somewhat moralistic ideas of conduct gave them much in common.[119] Roberts, who was also a roomer with Mrs. Israel, had arrived in the West only a few weeks before Pierre but had quickly won a reputation as a promising lawyer.[120] He was a welcome companion, both for his own solid self and, with ominously increasing regularity, for the relief he provided from the excesses of Berdan, who was showing signs of alcoholism. James was fond of the town, was well liked, and had even acquired a certain local fame owing to his labours in compiling statistics for the Reverend John

---

[117] PMI to Daniel Roberts, New York, January 16, 183[5] (Huntington). In the same letter he alluded to his correspondent's "surpassing agility in the Indian war dance."

[118] PMI to Daniel Roberts, New York, March 15, 1835 (Huntington).

[119] Roberts (b. 1811), from Wallingford, Vermont, was admitted to the bar there in September 1832. He practised law in Jacksonville from 1833 to 1835 and then, returning home on a visit, was persuaded to open a law office in Wallingford. Thereafter he remained in Vermont, where he became known as one of the ablest lawyers in the state (M. D. Gilman, *The Bibliography of Vermont... with Biographical and Other Notes*, 2 vols. [Burlington, 1897], I, 233).

[120] See Stevens, "Autobiography of Stephen Douglas," pp. 323, 338; George McConnel, "Some Reminiscences of My Father, Murray McConnel," *Journal of the Illinois Historical Society*, 18 (July 1925), 89-100.

Mason Peck's popular *Gazetteer of Illinois*;[121] but he suffered, it seemed to Pierre and Roberts, from weakness of will. They attempted to cure him by philosophy, and they loyally concealed his periodic incompetence, but the situation was distressing to them both.[122]

Aside from the embarrassment caused him by James' erratic behaviour, after a year at Jacksonville Pierre felt quite content to remain there indefinitely. By now his legal trade was tolerably brisk, and he maintained an unshaken faith in an eventual and precipitous rise in land prices. In the summer of 1834 an immediate rise did seem unlikely, it was true, and for a time he considered making a journey home in order to visit his sisters Julia and Susan, both of whom were importunate for him to do so.[123] Weeks passed, however, and the rounds of festivities as escort to "the gentle Eliza" ran on. Pierre had set aside the notion of a trip to New York as impracticable when, in late September, he received an unexpected letter from his Uncle Washington which revived the issue.

Since his last meeting with Pierre more than a year before, Irving had been continuously active, though not in the comparatively purposeful manner of his nephew. He had traveled, visited with family and friends, and thought about buying a house—all the while reassuring Ebenezer, his anxious agent, adviser, and fiscal conscience, that he was gradually attuning himself to begin writing a volume about some American subject.[124] Despite these placating claims, however, since his return from Europe he had done nothing substantial in literature and had not given much thought to doing so. He resented the dictatorial tone being adopted by the press, and even by well-meaning acquaintances, strongly advising him to demonstrate his sympathy for the United States once for all by taking up some "native" topic. His carefully compiled observations made on the tour to Oklahoma Territory were an obvious lode to mine should he ever be inclined to undertake such a task; but as he bitterly remarked in a letter to Peter, his temperament was unsuited to writing "under whip and spur."[125] Eventually he did plan to take up his pen in earnest, but he would do it in his own time and on whatever topic appealed to him.

During the summer of 1834 Irving received an interesting literary proposition from John Jacob Astor, the wealthy mercantile magnate. Astor, an old acquaintance[126] now seventy-one years of age, had

[121] PMI to Daniel Roberts, New York, March 15, 1835 (Huntington).

[122] James Berdan's reformations and periodic relapses were a recurrent theme in the letters PMI wrote to Roberts between 1835 and 1837. In August 1837, he admitted that he had given up hope for James: "He is a doomed man – reform is utterly hopeless & the sooner he ceases to cumber the earth, the better it will be for himself & friends" (PMI to Daniel Roberts, Toledo, August 9, 1837—Huntington). Berdan overcame his infirmity, however, and became a leading citizen of Jacksonville, where he died in 1884.

[123] *LLWI*, III, 59-60.

[124] See *LLWI*, III, 54-57.

[125] WI to Peter Irving, New York, January 8, 1835; *LLWI*, III, 65.

[126] WI's early acquaintance with Astor is surveyed by Andrew B. Myers in "WI and the Astor Library," *Bulletin of the New York Public Library*, 72 (June 1968), 380-81.

recently retired from active direction of the American Fur Company, whose extensive network of trading and distributing posts he had supervised for over thirty years,[127] and he was at leisure to promote the fulfillment of a long-cherished wish. He hoped to convince Irving, the acknowledged leader among the nation's prose writers and since the publication of *Columbus* in 1828 a historian of repute, to write a history of a daring but unsuccessful commercial undertaking he had conducted on the northwest coast of America between 1810 and 1813. More than once Astor urged the author to consider assuming this task, reminding him that the story of the Pacific Fur Company's attempt to wrest control of the vast western fur-trading empire from the British-controlled Northwest Company was an episode of significance in the history of American exploration and commerce. He was so eager to secure Irving's cooperation and see the work completed that he practically offered the author his own terms. In time, the blandishments of the old merchant began to take effect. Since childhood, when he had listened with rapt attention to William Irving's stories of his own youthful exploits as a trader among the Mohawk Indians of western New York, Irving had been interested in the fur trade, the American Indian, and the history of American exploration.[128] At present he was on the lookout for just such a wide-ranging and congenial topic as the one now being urged upon him; and he knew, of course, that a work of the kind Astor proposed would go far to satisfy the clamorous demands of the American reading public.

Considering Astor's proposition more seriously, he saw only two serious obstacles to his undertaking the work. The first of these was associated with Astor's great wealth: Irving was unwilling to give justification, in fact or appearance, for the slightest public suspicion that he was compromising his integrity by forming an association with this proverbially rich man. Like Pierre, he was in some respects a quietly but firmly self-reliant individual. While he was quite willing at need to take advantage of the special favours which were his prerogatives as a gentleman—and indeed, was rather adept at doing so[129]—he would not sacrifice his self-respect nor permit his relations with Astor, should he enter into any, to be misconstrued. This delicate problem was of real moment to him, yet he was confident that with Astor's cooperation it could be solved. The second difficulty, though more mundane, was less easily disposed of. Astor's bold experiment in empire building had been a complex venture, involving scores of persons on a literally worldwide scale. As the projector, administrator, and underwriter of the entire scheme, the old merchant now had at hand a rich and unique collection of documents, memoranda, and journals relating to its rise and progress; and from these, together

---

[127] The definitive study of Astor's mercantile career is by Kenneth W. Porter, *John Jacob Astor, Business Man*, 2 vols. (Cambridge, Mass., 1931).

[128] See the "Author's Introduction" to *Astoria; or Anecdotes of an Enterprise Beyond the Rocky Mountains*, ed. Edgeley W. Todd (Norman, Okla., 1964), p. xlv.

[129] For example, see below, pp. 69-70.

with other published and unpublished material, the proposed history was to be assembled. Irving immediately recognized the enviable opportunity for research being offered him, but he was at this time becoming so deeply involved in other affairs that he could not hope to find leisure to sift unaided through all the Astor material. Previously, as for example in performing the research for *Columbus*, he had been able to rely heavily upon the capable assistance of his brother Peter to facilitate the necessary spadework. But Peter, now aging and unwell, was still in Europe, and in spite of Irving's unflagging encouragement the prospect of his soon overcoming his fears of the Atlantic crossing was remote. If Irving was to accede to Astor's entreaties, therefore, he would need to find himself a congenial and dependable new research assistant. Informed of this necessity, Astor readily agreed to pay the salary of such a person. And thereupon, on September 15, 1834, Irving wrote to Pierre.

In this letter, he first explained to his nephew something of the project as he now envisioned it. Astor's short-lived fur-trading colony on the Columbia River, he wrote, was "likely to have ... important results in the history of commerce and colonization." He believed that "a work might be written on the subject, full of curious and entertaining matter, comprising adventurous expeditions by sea and land, scenes beyond the Rocky Mountains, incidents and scenes illustrative of Indian character, and of that singular and but little known class, the traders and voyageurs of the Fur Companies." Having heard of Pierre's "inclination to return to New York," he wondered if his nephew might be interested in some temporary employment: "... it has occurred to me that you might be disposed to take this subject in hand; to collate the various documents, collect verbal information, and reduce the whole to such form that I might be able to dress it up advantageously, and with little labor, for the press." These duties would require about one year, Irving estimated, to complete. Pierre would receive ample pay for his services, and while engaged in his work at Astor's home he would have the excellent company of Fitz-Greene Halleck, the poet, who served as the old gentleman's private secretary.[130] Having thus sketched in some detail the advantages of Pierre's possible employment, Irving noted that he was entertaining the whole matter only for his nephew's sake, "having no care about it for myself." In closing, however, he perhaps betrayed some of his own interest when he observed encouragingly that "the sooner you come on the better."[131] The exact intensity of Irving's unstated desire to take up the Astor topic is of course undeterminable. On the other hand, it is safe to say that he actually was motivated in part by a wish to establish his nephew in some advantageous position. A high opinion of Pierre's talents and an awareness of his chronic bad luck thus far in life were probably among the most weighty considerations that led

[130] See Nelson F. Adkins, *Fitz-Greene Halleck: An Early Knickerbocker Wit and Poet* (New Haven, 1930), p. 253.

[131] WI to PMI, New York, September 15, 1834; *LLWI*, III, 60-62.

Irving to offer the employment to him rather than to any of several other eligible and more available nephews.[132]

Upon reading the letter from his uncle, Pierre was both pleased at so unambiguous a mark of Irving's good opinion and interested in the proposition he had made. Still, he considered the idea with cautious reserve, for an entire year's absence from Jacksonville was much longer than he had ever thought of permitting himself. Moreover, he was not yet fully clear as to the exact nature of the proffered position. After examining Irving's gift horse and discussing its points with Roberts for a few days, on October 5 he wrote a measured reply. If, he stipulated, he could be assured of being detained no longer than the period mentioned in Irving's letter and of being paid $2,000 for his trouble, he would accept the offer, and—one more bit of lawyerly detail—he would waive claim to a share in the profits from the published work.[133] In mid-November a confirmation of this arrangement arrived, in which, however, Irving urbanely reported that he had held a "definite conversation" with Astor and had fixed Pierre's salary at *$3,000.* He proceeded to give a fuller account of his conception of the Astor work and of Pierre's role in preparing it. With the glaring exception of the relatively minor part he expected to play in its creation, Irving's statement proved to be remarkably accurate:

> My present idea is to call the work by the general name of *Astoria*—the name of the settlement made by Mr. Astor at the mouth of Columbia River: under this head to give not merely a history of his great colonial and commercial enterprise, and the fortunes of his colony, but a body of information concerning the whole region beyond the Rocky Mountains, on the borders of Columbia River, comprising the adventures, by sea and land, of traders, trappers, Indian warriors, hunters, &c.; their habits, characters, persons, costumes, &c.; descriptions of natural scenery, animals, plants, &c., &c. I think, in this way, a rich and varied work may be formed, both entertaining and instructive, and laying open scenes in the wild life of that adventurous region which would possess the charm of freshness and novelty. You would be required to look over the various papers, letters, and journals in the possession of Mr. Astor, written by various persons who have been in his employ, to draw anecdotes and descriptions from him, and from Northwest traders who occasionally visit him; to forage among various works in French and English that have been published relative to these regions, and

---

[132] The most likely among these were the three eldest sons of Ebenezer: Pierre Paris, whose literary ambition WI had sought to snuff out in 1824-1825; Edgar, whom he had come to know after an unexpected meeting at the Alhambra in 1829; and Theodore, whom he had seen at least twice during the former's tour of Europe in 1828-1830. Theodore, who in 1833 had made a tour west in company with Henry L. Ellsworth, WI's companion on his own journey the year before, was a budding author. In 1835 WI helped arrange for publication of his *Indian Sketches,* an account of his observations on the western tour. There is no evidence that WI approached any of these nephews about the possibility of their assuming the duties he eventually delegated to PMI.

[133] *LLWI,* III, 62.

thus to draw together and arrange into some kind of form a great body of facts. In all this I may be able to render you much assistance. When the work is thus crudely prepared, I will take it in hand, and prepare it for the press, as it is a *sine qua non* with Mr. Astor that my name should be to the work.

By now, Astor was anticipating a busy winter to be spent rummaging among his papers, and he had expressed a particular wish for Pierre to take a room at his New York mansion. Should he accept this favourably revised offer, Irving concluded, Pierre "had better put [his] portmanteau in the first stage coach, and come on as promptly as possible."[134]

Pierre could hardly conjure up any cause for delay, and so in short order—without even waiting to collect all his books and belongings[135]—he was bound for New York. For the second time in his career he had agreed to suspend his own pursuits in order to assist his uncle in a literary undertaking. In this instance, however, the collaboration was not merely a hasty scheme caught at through happenstance but a plan carefully formulated from the beginning. Furthermore, Irving's offer was attractive to Pierre in several ways: it would afford him a welcome access to his family, a sumptuous mode of living in the expensive city, an opportunity to indulge his taste for literary compilations, and eventually a solid financial base for further speculations in western real estate. He must have felt indebted to Irving for having made available this interlude of literary occupation, but in his gratitude he felt no accompanying sense of dependence on his uncle's good offices. He was a self-reliant individual who insisted on pursuing his own aims, imperfectly defined as they had been and still were. He would invest a bit of time in his uncle's literary project and then make his way again westward. As he hurried home to New York in late November 1834, Pierre had no idea that he was about to begin an active collaboration with his uncle that would continue for twenty-five years until Irving's death in 1859, and extend beyond.

[134] WI to PMI, New York, October 29, 1834; *LLWI*, III, 62-64.
[135] PMI to Daniel Roberts, Tarrytown, June 16, 1835 (Huntington).

Chapter Two

The Beginnings of a Working
Relationship, 1834-1839

To the relief of Ebenezer Irving, by the fall of 1834 his improvident younger brother Washington was beginning to show some interest in minding the main chance. For the past two years, it seemed, Irving had devoted his entire energies to roistering with old and new cronies, traveling, entertaining a brace of nephews and nieces, or enjoying his favourite amusement, the opera.[1] He had been unable to share Ebenezer's distress at the heavy losses they were both suffering from unlucky investments. He had not even mustered much curiosity about the negotiations Ebenezer was conducting with Messrs. Carey

---

[1] In January 1834 Ebenezer's seventeen-year-old daughter Catharine wrote from New York to her elder brother William explaining how WI was enlivening the household: "Uncle Washington has got us in the habit of dancing every evening, he dances with all his ni[letter torn]. You do not know what a pet he has got to be to us all, he is very lively and is always playing with the children, he has been home ever since in the summer and we have become better acquainted with him so that we talk to him as much as [torn] you know we used to be very still in the room but we are not [torn] taken us to the opera five or six times since the new company have come out, for my part I have been perfectly delighted and could go every evening" (SHR).

and Lea of Philadelphia for an arrangement to reprint his back works. Like the commands from the press that he set about writing a "native work," Ebenezer's encouragements to return to active authorship had seemed actually to retard his progress in that direction. Quite suddenly, however, Irving was becoming all business. No doubt his discussions with John Jacob Astor in previous months had helped bring about this change of views, but the immediate incitement to literary activity had come from elsewhere. Upon learning that Charles J. Latrobe, a companion of his on the western tour of 1832, was writing an account of that journey for publication,[2] he had been shocked by the threat of competition into beginning a work of his own on the same subject. Ebenezer was not really clear about what this new book might be—it was "something about tours to the Prairies and the Indians," he informed his son William[3]—nor did he care, for he seldom looked into Irving's books. In December 1834 he was simply pleased that his brother was at work on one volume, had projected two sequels to it,[4] and was planning eventually to take up the Astorian narrative. Recently Irving had even thought to inquire what might be a proper price to ask for the right to reprint his earlier writings.

Irving's renewed attention to his own financial affairs and prospects was not limited to those associated with literary activity. Under the tutelage of knowledgeable acquaintances he was also mounting a campaign of speculations in steamboats, railroad companies, canals, western lands, and other ventures, using a large proportion of the funds he had on hand. In June 1835 he explained to John Pendleton Kennedy, a friend and financial adviser in Baltimore, that his aim in these investments was only "to secure a moderate increase"[5] of his capital; but in fact he had become infected with the zeal for speculation endemic to the United States of the early 1830's, and his anticipations were virtually boundless. His assurance to Kennedy was accurate only in the sense that all his schemes to grow rich quickly were directed at a single reasonably modest goal: at the age of fifty-two, having spent an overlong period in Europe away from his family, he wanted to settle down—to build himself a comfortable home and live there free, as he put it, from "the irksome fagging of [the] pen"[6] for a living. Shortly after his return to the United States in 1832 he had visited an old friend, Gouverneur Kemble, at his estate on the Hudson

[2] Latrobe (1801-1875) published his two-volume account, *The Rambler in North America*, in 1835. For sketches of his character by WI and others, see McDermott, ed., *Western Journals*, pp. 4-5. There is a biography by Alan Gross, *Charles J. Latrobe* (Melbourne, 1956).

[3] Ebenezer Irving to William Irving, New York, January 16, 1835 (SHR).

[4] These were *Abbotsford and Newstead Abbey*, an account of visits to the homes of Walter Scott and Lord Byron, and *Legends of the Conquest of Spain*. They were published, respectively, in May and October 1835.

[5] WI to John P. Kennedy, New York, June 9, 1835; in Killis Campbell, "The Kennedy Papers," *Sewanee Review*, 25 (January 1917), 4.

[6] WI to Mrs. Sarah Van Wart, New York, November 25, 1840; *LLWI*, III, 153.

River near West Point. Impressed with this "bachelor's Elysium"[7] of Kemble's, he had wondered at the time why he should not build one of his own. He felt deeply indebted to his brothers Ebenezer and Peter for their unselfish assistance and counsel over the years, and he envisioned his "nest," should he build one, as a place where through his hospitality he would be able to express a grateful sense of obligation to them. Besides, the years in Europe had taught him that polite society alone left unsatisfied his need of a family nearby. The thing to do was to find himself a house near New York and make of it both a permanent home for himself and a gathering place for the rest of the Irvings.

By the time he set out on his western tour, Irving had already set his sights on an area along the east bank of the Hudson about twenty miles north of New York, a region where he had made exploring expeditions as a boy. His nephew Oscar—one of Pierre's elder brothers—had purchased a plot of land in this vicinity, next to which was an old stone cottage, much in disrepair, that had caught his eye.[8] The property fixed itself so firmly in his mind that in November 1832, writing to his sister Catharine Paris from Oklahoma Territory, he announced himself "more and more in the notion of having that little cottage below Oscar's house." He was "willing to pay a little unreasonably for it,"[9] and he even projected moving into it the following spring. Of course he did not return from the West until March, and in the months afterward he was swept up into an aimless round of socializing. By the close of 1834, however, his landholding impulse had reasserted itself and he was eager to purchase the place. In January 1835 a New York newspaper announced, erroneously, that he had already bought it.[10]

When Pierre arrived in New York, therefore, his uncle's interests in the proposed cottage, his investments, and his other literary undertakings rendered it impossible for him to devote much attention to the genesis of *Astoria*. Irving had of course indicated from the first that the task of gathering and classifying the information necessary for the narrative would be primarily Pierre's, so that as the latter took up his dual tasks of sifting papers and amusing John Jacob Astor he was not surprised to find himself proceeding without overmuch consultation. From the whimsical letters he wrote to Daniel Roberts at this time it appears that any inconvenience given him by the infrequency of

[7] WI to Peter Irving, New York, July 9, 1832; *LLWI*, III, 27; see also II, 426.

[8] WI was in Tarrytown visiting James Kirke Paulding in August 1832; presumably this was when he became seriously interested in the property.

[9] WI to Catharine Paris, Montgomery's Point, Mouth of the Arkansas, November 16, 1832 (Virginia); *LLWI*, III, 30.

[10] Harold Dean Cater, "WI and SS," *New York History*, 38 (Spring 1957), 133-34; the newspaper quoted is the New York *Evening Post*, January 28, 1835. Cater's account of WI at his home is the most thorough available description of the estate and of the author's improvements to it over the years. The work was published in pamphlet form in 1957 by Sleepy Hollow Restorations, Inc. Another pamphlet describing WI's home is by Joseph T. Butler, *WI's SS* (Tarrytown, 1968).

meetings with his uncle was more than compensated by the mere return to the city. "A thousand attractions invite – a thousand tempta-tions assail," he exclaimed in January; and then he evoked for his correspondent on the frontier the glories of his transformed "domestic habits." The fare at Astor's had made of him "a devourer of oysters and regaler upon Champagne at other people's expense—an eater with silver forks, a user of napkins and washer of the hands in blue bowls, of all of which usages the unsophisticated children of Jackson-ville know nothing."[11] As yet he had managed to attend only one fancy ball, but it had realized all his libertine fantasies: "Such waltz-ing – such twirling and whirling – such clasping of female waists – such displays of female legs! tell it not in Winchester – let it not be heard in the streets of Jacksonville!"[12] With access to the "twirling and whirling" and also to more sedate enjoyments amongst Uncle Ebenezer's family in Bridge Street, Pierre spent the early months of 1835 at Astor's mansion contentedly at work.

Considering his evident enjoyment of life in New York, Pierre's determination to return to Illinois upon completing the research task assigned him seems remarkable. Almost immediately upon arriving in the city he had refused "certain overtures,"[13] as he darkly informed Berdan, which would have kept him there longer than he planned. His old friends regarded his remaining as a matter of course, affecting to make light of his words whenever he protested to the contrary; but this annoyed him, for he was serious. It is true that in March, when his sisters returned to the city from an extended visit elsewhere, he endured a sore trial of will: ". . . if ever I have felt my resolution falter," he told Roberts shortly afterward, "it has been since their arrival." Their presence gave "new life to my affections, and filled up in some degree that dreary vacancy of heart with which here, as well as at Jacksonville, I have been at times most wofully oppressed." Yet even the protestations of Julia and Susan failed at last to move him, and through most of the spring he held on to the fall months as the estimated time of his completing the Astorian chore and leaving New York. Meanwhile, his habits had settled into a routine. "I busy myself in an humble way with my pen during the day," he reported to Roberts, "and take refuge from the weariness of the flesh produced

[11] He continued: "Am I not this moment fresh from the table of a 'certain rich man'—have I not taken 5 glasses of sherry, 3 of Madeira, 4 of Champagne, and 1 of Tokay!!—think of that, Master Brooks—'imperial Tokay'!!! and yet in this self-same hour, with all my blushing honors thick upon me, with my belly full of good things, and my brain running over with the juice of the grape,—do I not stoop to exchange words with thee, thou insignificant plebeian—thou starveling attorney—thou drinker of water—thou feeder upon pot-pie—thou filler of thy belly with pawpaws, that base fruit which even the swine doth refuse! Art thou not amazed at such proof of my humility? Dost thou not feel ennobled by my condescension? But 'Halloo my fancy—whither wouldst thou go?' Rein in—rein in thy fiery Pegasus—cease thy mad frolic, – check thy headlong gait, and quit thy furious pace for a decent, sober, well-behaved trot!"

[12] PMI to Daniel Roberts, New York, January 16, 183[5] (Huntington).

[13] *Ibid.* Roberts, Berdan, and Mrs. Israel seem to have been PMI's only Jacksonville correspondents; his letters to the latter two are lost.

thereby, sometimes at the theatre, but most generally in social converse, at night."

Thus Irving's failure to take up *Astoria* as yet had only tended to clarify Pierre's ideas about his own career and fortify his determination to follow them. In response to a taunt from Roberts that perhaps he would prove *"miscreant* to the West," he wrote in March:

> The seductions of the city, the very temptations upon which you descant so eloquently, so far from *corrupting my better nature,* and producing a disrelish of the simple life at Jacksonville, constitute one of the strongest motives for my return. I cannot mingle much in the gaiety and share freely in the pleasures of this expensive city without realizing the deficiency of my income and being made sensible that I must here forego the proud attitude of independence.... I prize the feeling of independence which I could there enjoy to a partial extent at least – too highly not to regard it as a fair set-off against all the pleasures of the city.[14]

Certainly Pierre had not lost his interest in western politics nor his ready ear for rumours of fluctuations in land prices. His letters from this period are dotted with stories of speculators in western properties, such as the one about a lawyer who "had a considerable quantity of valuable land for sale at *75 cents* per acre"—land which, as he surmised in this case, was covered with water.[15] Chancing to meet Charles Fenno Hoffman, an old friend who had just returned from a tour of the West and was preparing a miscellaneous work describing it, he helpfully lent him a copy of Peck's *Gazetteer* so that he could borrow a suitable passage about Jacksonville, "the *Athens* of Illinois."[16] He passed on to Roberts reports of the "political wiseacres"[17] in New York, and he avowed his staunch support of Senator Daniel Webster, the merchant's and speculator's friend. Politics and prices aside, Pierre was at times lonely for his friends in Illinois. As a correspondent he often hid his feelings behind laboriously comic turns of phrase, but once he concluded quite soberly to Roberts: "If you knew the real pleasure I take in your letters, & the

---

[14] PMI to Daniel Roberts, New York, March 15, 1835 (Huntington).

[15] *Ibid.* The land was in the Military Tract of Illinois.

[16] *Ibid.* This work was *A Winter in the West. By a New-Yorker,* 2 vols. (New York, 1835). Passages in *A Winter in the West* which may have been owing to the good offices of PMI are I, 137-39, 184, 191, and II, 60-62.

[17] Roberts sent his in return, and a subject in them that aroused acrimony in PMI was the political success of his former colleague Stephen A. Douglas, later the candidate, against Abraham Lincoln, for the Presidency of the United States. PMI nicknamed him "Douglas of the Bloody Heart." On March 15, 1835, he responded to news of Douglas' having attained public office with jibes at his "pigmy" stature: "The Douglas is a consecrated name in martial annals, and the titular distinction of 'General' would well accord therewith. Has the man of *gaffs* betaken himself to high-heeled boots? Does he cast a longer shadow since his elevation?" (Huntington). Years after the death of Douglas in 1861, Daniel Roberts published a "Reminiscence of Stephen Douglas" in *Harper's Magazine,* 87 (November 1893), 957-59.

exhiliration of spirit produced thereby, every benevolent impulse of your nature would urge you to a speedy reply."[18]

On April 17, 1835, Irving wrote to his brother Peter summarizing the progress of his several enterprises, including the three-volume *Crayon Miscellany* (whose first volume, *A Tour on the Prairies,* was now published and "doing well"), an abridgment of his *Columbus* (sales of which were "steadily increasing in circulation"), transactions in common stocks (which "produce handsomely"), and the arrangement with Carey and Lea (he had just sold them the rights to reprint his back works for the sum of $1,150 per annum). "I look forward to have easy times in pecuniary matters for the rest of my life," he noted with satisfaction. It was under these promising conditions that he prepared to enter another phase of his financial campaign, the authorship of *Astoria.* What little he had seen of Pierre's compilations had instilled in him a degree of confidence unusual in an author ordinarily so diffident of his own productions as he. "I have not taken hold of the subject yet," he told Peter, "but have no doubt I shall be able to make it a rich piece of mosaic."[19] On May 16 he informed the same correspondent that he was "now engaged in the work," reiterating his opinion of a month before: "I am much mistaken if I do not make it a very rich, curious, and unique work. Pierre Munro makes an admirable pioneer."[20]

One more month was to elapse, however, before Irving was able to begin giving continuous attention to the project. During the remainder of May he was occupied in completing *The Crayon Miscellany.* On June 7 he paid $1,800 to purchase the stone house and the ten acres of land surrounding it which were to become the nucleus of his famous home, "Sunnyside."[21] Immensely pleased, he was eager to begin a series of renovations immediately. Nevertheless, he recognized that further delay in turning to *Astoria* would be unfair to Pierre, who expected, as agreed, to complete his assigned task within two or three months. Besides, as he wrote to Peter on June 10, he himself wanted "to get the Astor work into the rough."[22] Beginning in mid-June, then, Irving's work on his cottage—"the Roost," as it was then called—and on *Astoria* went forward together.

By this time Pierre was already resigned to a postponement of his return to the West. His progress as a researcher, he wrote to Roberts on June 16, was "necessarily affected to some extent by the divided attention which my uncle gives, and is only able to give, to the work," and he believed that after this much delay he could not hope to see Illinois again before the next spring. Actually, Irving's interference

---

[18] PMI to Daniel Roberts, New York, March 15, 1835 (Huntington).

[19] *LLWI,* III, 69.

[20] *LLWI,* III, 70.

[21] "Lands purchased and sold by WI" (typescript, SHR). Together with Ebenezer and his brother-in-law Daniel Paris, WI had owned property in this vicinity as early as 1814.

[22] He added: "Pierre M. has acted as an excellent pioneer, and, in the course of two or three months, will have gathered together all the materials" (*LLWI,* III, 72).

with his plans did not disturb him so much as did his imperviousness to repeated assurances that once the stint as "pioneer" was completed he still intended to return to Jacksonville. His uncle had "persuaded himself," he told Roberts, "(this in *strict confidence*) that he can turn my services to a valuable account, and make it for his interest as well as my own that I should remain, and hence he is bent upon keeping me." Pierre did not specify these "services," but he added that no matter how shrewd and mutually beneficial Irving's scheme might be, he had no intention of being drawn into it. "I . . . do not view the matter in the same light, and hence I am bent upon returning."[23]

He addressed this letter from Oscar's cottage, where he expected to remain for the greater part of the summer and where Irving was also residing temporarily. The primary reason for Pierre's move from New York was no doubt to facilitate preparation of a draft of *Astoria* by putting author and "pioneer" into regular contact. However, Pierre must have welcomed the change of residence as a means of escape from further embarrassments of the kind he had recently suffered in the city. Apparently Irving and Astor had agreed to maintain absolute silence about the forthcoming book, and Pierre had thus been enjoined as a condition of his employment to keep his lips sealed. Only to a safely distant correspondent such as Roberts did he feel at liberty to give some account of his activities. To others, as the following anecdote in a letter to Roberts attests, he was obliged to adopt various ruses to divert attention from his want of "an ostensible occupation":

> . . . I am often annoyed by the question—what are you driving at now-a-days, and provoked by the evasions which it forces upon me. It was only the other day that this puzzling interrogatory was *speered* at me by an old acquaintance. With a dexterity acquired by long practice I eluded a reply, and branched off upon Jacksonville—Illinois, the prairies, and any thing and every thing but what was—as sundry writers would say—*germane* to the matter. The gentleman looked bewildered, and shewed a disposition to bring me to the point—whereupon, infusing a double portion of suavity into my manner to atone for what might be deemed its abruptness, I very politely bade him good morning —leaving him no doubt in a state of perplexed speculation as to the singular character of that employment about which it was necessary to affect so much mystery.[24]

Any of several considerations may have prompted Irving to insist that *Astoria* not be discussed in public. He may have decided that a policy of discreet silence was the best way to avoid scandal about his relationship with Astor; he may have been attempting to bolster sales of the work by encouraging speculation about his activities during the period prior to publication; or he may have refused to acknowledge that he was engaged on another "American" topic out of resentment at

[23] PMI to Daniel Roberts, Tarrytown, June 16, 1835 (Huntington).

[24] *Ibid.* He prefaced the anecdote with an observation that "the secrecy I am obliged to observe with regard to my present task is any thing but agreeable to me."

the public clamour prior to the publication of *A Tour* that he do just that. On the other hand, Astor himself may have placed the embargo on public discussion of the book—though no compelling reason for him to do so is apparent. In any case it seems clear that he and Irving were agreed on the matter—and that the requirement of secrecy did not agree with Pierre.

Once Irving and Pierre set seriously to work together on the project, in mid-June, they functioned well in collaboration and made rapid progress. After almost two months at Tarrytown they returned to Hellgate, Astor's mansion just outside New York, for a second period of steady composition. By this time Pierre was somewhat jaded by the splendid mode of life in the old gentleman's bachelor hall, but Irving was full of praise for its every feature. After living and working there upwards of a month, on September 26 he wrote to Peter of his surroundings: "I cannot tell you how sweet and delightful I have found this retreat; pure air, agreeable scenery, a spacious house, profound quiet, and perfect command of my time and self. The consequence is, that I have written more since I have been here than I have ever done in the same space of time."[25] Thus far, he had easily surpassed his own hopes for expediting the work. He was already within a few chapters of completing a first draft, and by October 1, after "a long and successful fit of writing," he had finished it. He now intended to begin "enriching" the book with additional details which he would garner on his own.

In the letter to Peter announcing that he had completed the draft of *Astoria*, Irving went on to say that the cottage, after a summer's refurbishing, was also "in a considerable state of forwardness."[26] During the remaining months of the year he passed frequently from the Roost, where he was supervising the removal of outbuildings and consulting with his architect, George Harvey, to Hellgate, where he was polishing his book.[27] He had anticipated speedy completion of both projects, but as the onset of winter proved his prognostications inaccurate he was undisturbed. Progress on the cottage was at least confirming his original impression of its desirability. On November 24, returning to New York for a stint at Hellgate, he wrote happily to Peter that it was "a tenement in which a man of very moderate means may live, and which yet may form an elegant little snuggery for a rich man."[28] Even Ebenezer was moved from his impassiveness to express satisfaction with the place.[29] As for *Astoria*,

[25] *LLWI*, III, 78.

[26] WI to Peter Irving, New York, October 8, 1835; *LLWI*, III, 79.

[27] In his letters of 1835 and 1836, WI almost invariably referred to his progress on *Astoria* in direct conjunction with his progress on the new home. See, for example, *LLWI*, III, 75, 80, 81, 83, 90.

[28] *LLWI*, III, 80.

[29] On June 1 Ebenezer wrote to his son William that he himself had already selected "a capital spot a short distance from the house for a garden" (SHR). On June 30 he wrote again to William that "your Uncle [WI] and all are more pleased than ever with

during the summer Irving's unfamiliarity with his material and Pierre's long exposure to it had naturally made the latter indispensable to his uncle. This was no longer the case, since in the course of writing a first draft Irving had himself mastered his complex topic. In late November he waited with equanimity at Hellgate for the arrival of a person whose oral recollections of the Astorian enterprise he hoped to incorporate into his account.[30]

It was fortunate for Irving that at this stage of composition he was no longer dependent on the research assistance of his nephew, for through most of the fall months the latter was unavailable. By early September Pierre had virtually discharged his responsibility as "pioneer," and for the remainder of that month, while Irving was busy writing, he was himself somewhat idle. Occasionally he looked in on his uncle, but he also haunted Wall Street, exerted himself unsuccessfully to wangle a land agency for Roberts, visited friends in Baltimore, transacted what he designated as "urgent business,"[31] and called upon his charming cousin Helen at Bridge Street. Early in October these miscellaneous activities came to an abrupt halt when he contracted a case of varioloid, a mild form of smallpox, which removed him from circulation for several weeks. The disease was to pass away, as he later facetiously said, without leaving "any marks which would spoil a compliment upon [his] beauty," but for the time being its contagiousness obliged him to absent himself from Astor's house and board elsewhere. He soon grew impatient at being bedridden, and yet his illness was hardly in itself the severest of his problems. The approach of poverty, hastened by the expenses of medical care, was a more insistent concern. Almost all his funds were invested in western lands, and since he had as yet received no payments from Astor he was virtually destitute, his certain financial prospects notwithstanding. Shortly before his illness he had negotiated a loan at high interest in order to tide him over until Astor should pay up, expecting if necessary to sell a portion of his personal library in order to repay the debt. Now, it appeared, he might not be able to extricate himself even after parting with all his books, and certainly he must at least make that sacrifice. Acting in the forlorn hope that "the competition of the attorneys against the booksellers [was] sure to run them up to cost, or very nearly," he arranged for his professional collection to be auctioned at a specialty sale. But stormy weather on the night of the sale kept the buyers away, and his lawbooks went down at a heavy loss, leaving him still barely solvent.[32]

Characteristically, rather than explaining his difficulties either to Irving or to Astor and very reasonably requesting a cash advance on

the place" (SHR). WI wrote to Peter on November 24 that the cottage was "quite a hobby of the Bramin"—that is, Ebenezer, who was probably given this sobriquet in token of his Brahmin-like serenity (*LLWI*, III, 80).

[30] *LLWI*, III, 81. This individual has not been identified.

[31] PMI to Daniel Roberts, New York, August 9, 1835; PMI to Daniel Roberts, New York, September 14, 1835 (Huntington). The quotation is from the latter.

[32] PMI to Daniel Roberts, New York, September 14, 1835 (Huntington).

the strength of his nearly completed duties of a full year's duration, this hobnobber with the Croesus of the United States chose to keep silence. In late November, having regained his health, he was settling into a room at a boarding house owned by an old acquaintance, apparently intending to spend the winter there, when in the nick of time he was rescued from his own folly. Astor, a notoriously dry correspondent, addressed him a polite invitation to spend a few weeks at Hellgate in order, as Pierre later reported it, "to keep him company in his loneliness." At this unexpected summons he dismissed the thought of his "niggard necessity" and made his way to Hellgate, where on December 11, having taken up certain literary duties for his uncle, he wrote to Roberts with cheery cynicism:

> ... here I am, and here I am likely to be for three weeks longer, compassionately relieving the solitude of the rich man, eating his dinners and drinking his wine free of expense, amusing him with a game of billiards in the morning, and keeping him & myself awake by a turn at écarté in the evening. Singular proof of disinterested devotion! amazing instance of self-sacrificing benevolence to immure myself in the country amidst the rigors of this cheerless season with no other companionship than that of a rich old man!

Perhaps a certain dissatisfaction with his role as a rich man's companion accounts for the underlying bitterness of Pierre's exclamations. Nevertheless, the savour of "oysters fried with gold gridirons and swimming in pearl sauce," the company of Halleck and Irving, and the prospect of an early end to his collaboration with his uncle all made his present dependent situation more than bearable. "I have no idea... that I am permanently fixed in New York," he once more assured Roberts. "On the contrary I think I shall quit it as soon as my present engagement with my uncle W. shall have terminated. It does not suit my notions of independence nor my other views in life to make this my abiding place." However, mixed in with these familiar protestations was a new and unexplained note. As in earlier letters he continued to bandy wondrous anecdotes of town lots in Chicago rising in price from $200 to $200,000, but now he seemed to view them from a more temperate, practical perspective. He offered advice to Roberts, who had recently abandoned Jacksonville as a lost cause and was longing for more "activity and stir": "Oh thou restless and impatient spirit... give over thy vain and dissatisfied longings. Clothe thyself with a meek and quiet temper, content thee with an uneventful life... get money, get married, and murmur not that thou art doomed to live & die, 'to lie in cold oblivion & to rot,' as other folks."[33]

During December 1835, Pierre gave his final assistance to the genesis of *Astoria*. On December 25 Irving wrote to Peter that he and his nephew had been passing their days "most pleasantly and profitably"[34] at Hellgate, and that Pierre was now being called upon to

---

[33] PMI to Daniel Roberts, Hell-Gate, December 11, 1835 (Huntington).
[34] *LLWI*, III, 83.

look over the manuscript. Ostensibly this was to criticize its style and to scrutinize it for inaccuracies and inconsistencies; more pertinently no doubt, it was to assure Irving of its excellence. From evidence in the extant portions of the *Astoria* manuscript it appears that the infrequent corrections Pierre did venture to insert were limited to minor matters of syntax and verbal taste.[35] Irving respected his nephew's literary opinions, particularly in regard to a subject which he knew so well, but it is clear that he regarded Pierre not as the co-creator of *Astoria* but as an especially dependable and acute subordinate. So far as the actual act of composition determines authorship, this view was just. Pierre's role in preparing *Astoria*, important as it was in the early stages, was almost entirely limited to performing the duties of a research assistant. From this time until October 1836, when the work was published, it was in Irving's hands alone.

On December 17, 1835, a huge fire swept through New York, destroying more than six hundred buildings in the business district and inflicting heavy financial losses on many persons, including members of the Irving family. But if, as James Fenimore Cooper later portrayed it in *Home as Found*,[36] the Great Fire was a forewarning to speculators that a day of judgment was at hand, Irving failed to get the message. "I lost three thousand dollars," he informed Peter complacently on December 25; but he was "consoled at the very same moment by the rise of another kind of stock . . . which will more than make up the loss."[37] He was deaf to prophesies that the volumes of unsound paper money being circulated throughout the country would eventually bring on a financial disaster. Riding the crest of his prosperity, he continued to prosecute his old schemes and entered with zest into new ones. For example, even before completing *Astoria* he committed himself to another promising speculation in Western American literature. During the fall of 1835 he had met Captain Benjamin L. E. Bonneville, an Army man just returned from a three-year foray into the Rocky Mountains. Falling in with him again at Washington a short time afterward, and finding him engaged in re-writing his travel notes for possible publication, he had offered to purchase this mass of manuscripts for the generous sum of $1,000 and had been accepted.[38] An account of Bonneville's exploits, he had recognized, would be a fitting sequel to *Astoria*, in a manner bringing that saga of the western fur trade up-to-date. What was more, the work would be convenient to write, since the industrious Bonneville had already hammered a narrative into shape. Once *Astoria* was

---

[35] See the Textual Commentary by Richard D. Rust in *Astoria* (Boston: Twayne Publishers, 1976).

[36] *Home as Found*, ed. Lewis Leary (New York, 1961), p. 107.

[37] *LLWI*, III, 82.

[38] For an account of WI's relations with Bonneville, see the "Introduction" to WI's *The Adventures of Captain Bonneville, U.S.A.*, ed. Edgeley W. Todd (Norman, Okla., 1961), pp. xvi-xviii, xxxvii-xxxviii. According to Todd, the two struck their bargain on March 25.

complete, Irving planned to turn his attention to improving this new literary property.

As we have seen, for some time prior to the Bonneville transaction he had been eager to secure the continued assistance of Pierre once the latter had completed his duties as "pioneer" for *Astoria*. By June 1835 he had "persuaded himself," to repeat Pierre's term, that his nephew's research aid in laying the groundwork for another historical work, an account of Cortez' conquest of Mexico, would prove advantageous to them both. For himself, he was convinced that he could combine pleasure and profit in writing a narrative of the Spanish conquest—a theme which had attracted him since his stay in Spain as a gorgeous, richly picturesque topic appropriate to his tastes and talents[39]—just as he was doing with his epic of American exploration and commercial expansion. Pierre's familiarity with foreign languages would enable him to perform the research necessary for an account of Cortez' career no less meticulously and dependably than he was doing for *Astoria*; and if he could only be persuaded to remain in New York, he could be set to work on the new project as soon as he had finished the first one. In June, of course, Pierre had not "view[ed] the matter in the same light" as his uncle; but by December he seems to have modified his ideas to the degree that, if not enthusiastic about the plan, he was at least temporarily acquiescent to it. By Christmas, he was looking over the manuscript of *Astoria* and also beginning to trace out a narrative line for the Mexican book.

On December 30 he wrote to Longfellow, who was in Sweden on a second tour of Europe,[40] informing him that having finished the "Astorian task" he was now, at Irving's "urgent request," aiding him in "some of his other literary plans in an especially humble and unambitious way." Just as he had cautioned Daniel Roberts while at work on *Astoria*, he insisted that the distant Longfellow must keep this rather vague information in "strict confidence." However, he was apparently no longer so restive in the role of secret collaborator. "The hoarding propensity is strong within me," he confessed:

> ... I begin to regard it as a mark of a strange perversity of intellect for one to weigh in the same scales "solid pudding" and "empty praise." Any labor of the pen therefore, in whatever form of plodding drudgery it may come, is welcome to me, provided it will contribute to put *money in my purse*, and help me forward that great end and object of my ambition, a comfortable independence. I should be rather impatient, however, of a long confinement to such dull work, nor do I expect that my engagements with my uncle will reach beyond many months.

[39] See Myers, "WI's Madrid Journals," pp. 410-11. In his MS Outline, Chapter 64 (1834), PMI indicates that WI may have worked on a history of the conquest of Mexico during 1834.

[40] Preparatory to his taking up duties as Professor of Modern Languages and Belles-Lettres at Harvard College in 1838.

Pierre's sudden change of attitude toward his occupation would seem to have betokened some basic shift in his sense of priorities. Typically of himself, however, he offered Longfellow no explanation for his unusual docility except to say that he had a plan which, once entered upon, offered "a prospect of immediate and certain advantage." In the meantime, he said, he was content where he was; and the desultory tone of his letter confirms his statement. He relayed a stream of literary gossip to Longfellow, including mention of their old comrade Alexander Slidell's new book, *The American in England*.[41] He offered an insouciant estimate of Fitz-Greene Halleck, his companion of the past year, as "either a very lazy or a very costive genius" who "has lately come out with a new edition of his *old* poems."[42] He commented in particular on the American reception of *Outre-Mer*, Longfellow's newly published collection of essays and sketches in the manner of *The Sketch-Book*. Its mediocre sales he attributed to "its unpronounceable and non-understandable title with the great mass of readers": "What think you of the double blunder of a southern bookseller in announcing it as Ostremer by Mr. Longbody?"[43]

Pierre had hit upon his "prospect of immediate and certain advantage" on a recent trip to the city, where he chanced to meet John Berdan,[44] the elder brother of David and James. Berdan had just returned from an exploratory visit in the vicinity of Toledo, Ohio, on the western extremity of Lake Erie, and he was enthusiastic in praise of this promising town. He laid before Pierre a handsomely engraved map revealing the natural advantages of the place and showing the plots of land already surveyed and offered for sale there. He told him that James, who appeared to be reformed, had renounced Jacksonville for Toledo and proposed to grow up with the hopeful new community. John Berdan himself had returned to New York in order to purchase there "an undivided twelfth" of the entire town. Aware of Pierre's intention to return west eventually, John offered to share with him one-fifth of his interest in this prospective purchase should he be willing to invest and move to Toledo in the near future.[45] Pierre,

[41] *The American in England*, 2 vols. (New York, 1835). PMI was particularly eager to tell Longfellow of Joseph Rodman Drake's *The Culprit Fay and Other Poems*, "lately given to the world. You may have seen some of these in manuscript, as copies have got abroad, & the Culprit Fay, his most remarkable production, hastily written in a week on a singular bet, was once in my possession. It was the dying injunction of Drake that these poems should not see the light, as several of them were imperfect, & few or none had received his finishing touch. It was therefore in violation of his last request that they were published by his son-in-law. Had he been permitted to attain the maturity of his powers, he would have taken rank among the first of modern poets."

[42] *Alnwick Castle, with Other Poems* (New York, 1836). A shorter edition with the same title had been published in 1827. Another edition, slightly longer than the 1836 publication, appeared in 1845.

[43] PMI to Henry W. Longfellow, New York, December 30, 1835 (Harvard).

[44] According to PMI, John Berdan (1798-1841) had "removed to Toledo last autumn from his former residence in Ohio"—presumably meaning elsewhere in that state. PMI to Daniel Roberts, Albany, February 20, 1836 (Huntington).

[45] PMI to Daniel Roberts, Toledo, March 20, 1836 (Huntington).

impressed by the commentary of his knowledgeable brother-in-law and frankly attracted by the offer, sought to inform himself further about Toledo; and by the time he wrote to Longfellow he was confident that an investment there could not fail to yield rich profits. Opportunities for lawyers were myriad in the burgeoning state of things, he had learned, and he had been given reason to believe that upon arriving in Ohio he might secure a lucrative land-agency. These considerations—and another one which he mentioned in none of his contemporary letters—led him to decide in January that he could mark time in his uncle's employ no longer. His mood had reverted from the docile mercenary patience of December to the earlier determination to remain independent and return west as soon as possible. He had no more time to waste with the conquest of Mexico; he would collect his money from Astor, purchase his one-sixtieth interest in Toledo, and set out with John Berdan to have a look at his holdings.

In all probability the interview in which Pierre announced this determination to his uncle was quite amiable. Even though it meant the abandonment of a project which Irving had hoped to complete in the not-too-distant future, Pierre's decision came as no surprise. He was aware that his nephew had been unsettled during the past few months, and he was himself so busy this winter that the necessity of suspending one literary plan seemed of little immediate moment. Soon his faithful coadjutor Peter, who had finally decided to attempt the Atlantic crossing, would be nearby; and should he then wish to turn to the Mexican book he could rest assured of his brother's willingness to help. Certainly he felt no cause for recrimination against Pierre. Their bargain had been for the preparation of *Astoria*, and Pierre had performed his part in that still unfinished work with skill. Besides, after listening to his account of Toledo, Irving could hardly gainsay the town's promise.[46] Who knows? Perhaps he might use his "pioneer" in a new way and entrust him with a bit of cash to invest there. As co-owner with Ebenezer and Gouverneur Kemble of a substantial range of Indian land,[47] and having recently committed $4,000 for a share in John Jacob Astor's town at Green Bay, Michigan,[48] he was himself a devout believer in the merits of western land investments.

In addition to the agreed-upon $3,000 from Astor, Pierre now received an uncovenanted $1,000 from Irving—probably in requital not only of his assistance on *Astoria* but also of his patience during the

[46] On February 16 he wrote to Peter: "[PMI] sets off to-morrow for Toledo, a new town at the head of Lake Erie, where he has the offer of a share in a land purchase, which, it is thought, will turn out very profitable. Real estate, and especially lots in the vicinity of new towns at great commercial points in the interior, are great objects of attention at present, and fortunes are rapidly made" (*LLWI*, III, 88).

[47] MS Outline, Chapter 66 (1836); WI to Gouverneur Kemble, New York, March 17, 1837 (Virginia).

[48] WI to Peter Irving, n.p., February 16, 1836; *LLWI*, III, 89; Porter, *John Jacob Astor*, II, 863-64.

previous spring and his interrupted services on the Mexican project.[49] John Berdan had not as yet been able to complete his transaction for the "undivided twelfth" of Toledo, but he was impatient to return there in order to superintend other business. He urged Pierre to accompany him, and so, after securing from the coy vendor of the property an affidavit stating his willingness to part with the land at a certain price, on February 17 they sailed together on a steamboat bound for Albany. When they arrived at Toledo on March 4, Pierre had an embarrassed reunion with James Berdan, to whom he had begun several letters while in New York without being able to complete them,[50] and quickly recognized that John had been accurate in all his praises of the town. In a letter to Daniel Roberts, who was now living in Vermont, he wrote on March 20 a glowing summary of Toledo's advantages, concluding it with an implicit acknowledgement of his own boosterism: "I have my doubts, unless it should be checked midway in its progress to greatness by an earthquake, or some such small matter, whether it will not throw London entirely into the shade. Talk [not] of your Milwalkie to me—I spurn the very thought."[51] Unfortunately, he and John Berdan soon learned that their hopes of purchasing substantial holdings in this motley town of 1,500 were doomed to a long delay. It appeared that the New York gentleman with whom John had been negotiating had only been interested in ascertaining the market value of his property by learning the maximum that would be offered him. Pierre had taken care to save the supposed vendor's written agreement to sell at a stated price, but now this individual was attempting to invalidate it. Eventually, in a Court of Chancery, the document would likely hold him to his word, but it seemed unlikely that he would submit beforehand. To be dealt with in so shoddy a way was aggravating, and yet the swindle failed to make a dent in Pierre's optimism about Toledo; he would simply invest his money on his own. He told Roberts that he would "hardly . . . to speak modestly, be willing to exchange purses with [his] venerable friend of the 10 millions."[52]

Late in March, Pierre received authorization from Irving and Ebenezer to invest the sum of $20,000 for them in whatever Toledo properties he thought most promising.[53] Accordingly, he purchased a group of lots in the same sector of the town to which he had committed his own reserves, thus beginning a series of transactions on behalf of his uncles which was to continue for almost twenty years.[54] However,

[49] However, PMI told Roberts on February 20 that this money was "all in consideration of my Astorian labors" (Huntington).

[50] PMI to Daniel Roberts, Hell-Gate, December 11, 1835 (Huntington).

[51] PMI to Daniel Roberts, Toledo, March 20, 1836 (Huntington).

[52] *Ibid.* He continued: "The day of extravagant profits, however, has now gone by, and a reasonable man must be fain to content himself with some 50 or 100 per cent. To this insignificant advance I must limit my views."

[53] *LLWI*, III, 91.

[54] Some of PMI's transactions at Toledo on behalf of himself and his uncles are recorded in a manuscript volume, "Assessments & Equalization of Taxable Property

once he had made these investments he found it more difficult to secure the regular employment necessary to bring in money to live on from week to week. His hopes of securing a land agency proved, as usual with such notions, to be chimerical. The demand for lawyers was much less keen than his informants in New York had led him to believe. Provided he could beg or borrow the requisite lawbooks, he could probably rely on legal practice to make ends meet, but he was reluctant to fall back on that recourse. After spending several weeks in a fruitless attempt to locate a suitable position not already bespoken twice over by his fellow emigrants, he was unable to sustain the high spirits he had felt upon his arrival. In April he was deeply shocked to learn in a letter from New York that his youngest sister Susan, whom he had so recently left in good health, was dead of consumption. After the onset of the illness she had taken a convalescent sea-voyage south to Mobile, Alabama, but her condition had deteriorated en route and she had expired shortly after arriving there. The sudden loss of still another close relative, one whom he had loved "as brother has seldom loved sister,"[55] compounded his lonely restlessness and left him idle and depressed. Ruefully he recalled his impatient attitude toward New York when he had been there, among family and friends. The West, then so eagerly anticipated, now seemed dull, bleak, and isolated. "Without books," he wrote to Roberts in June, "with few or no means of diversion, and no congenial companion you may readily imagine to what straits I am sometimes reduced to get through the 24 hours." After three months in Toledo marked by growing loneliness and ennui, he held fast to the faith that he would be able "to effect advantageous sales before a great while, and thus raise cash for further operations";[56] but the first exciting savour of the Toledo experiment was gone.

Meanwhile, he reported to Roberts, his fellow speculators were "scouring the country in all directions, and entering all the wild lands they can lay hold of with indiscriminate rapacity." Sensing a need to bestir himself, he had decided to make an exploratory journey of his own. After traversing "a wide range of territory," he wrote, he would return to Toledo for a few days, perhaps adjust his holdings in light of what he had seen, and then return to New York for an already-deferred visit.[57] Three weeks later, on July 12, Pierre set out on this

Lands & Buildings of Lucas County," in the Toledo Public Library. In 1840 PMI owned 8 1/2 city lots, Ebenezer 4 2/3, and WI and Ebenezer jointly 2. In 1844 PMI owned 4, WI and Ebenezer jointly 3, and WI 3. On February 23, 1853, WI purchased a parcel of Toledo land from Ebenezer for $10, and over the next five years he sold it by piecemeal for a total of $6,380 (Toledo *Blade*, April 15, 1957). All of the transactions by the family in Toledo real estate appear to have been made through PMI.

[55] PMI to Daniel Roberts, Toledo, June 23, 1836 (Huntington). In a compilation of genealogical data gathered many years later, PMI wrote of Susan Anne Irving Van Wart that she "died in 1836 at the end of April or beginning of March [sic] on entering the harbor of Mobile" (Misc. Notebook).

[56] PMI to Daniel Roberts, Toledo, June 23, 1836 (Huntington).

[57] *Ibid.* He had told Roberts in March that "in all likelihood" he would visit New York during the summer; see footnote 45.

expedition and soon discovered that it was exactly what he had required. From day to day, no matter how little he noticed in the way of likely real estate, his spirits brightened magically. This was his most satisfying journey since the days in Europe ten years before, and by the time it was over he had covered an even more extensive range of country than he had planned. Skirting the western shore of Lake Erie to Detroit, he boarded the steamboat *Monroe* bound through the Great Lakes for Chicago, disembarking shortly afterward at Green Bay. After two days in this tiny settlement spent evaluating, at best rather dubiously, the soundness of his uncle's investment there, he proceeded westward by bark canoe up the Fox River to Fort Winnebago, an Army post.[58] Thence, in company with a friend he had chanced to meet at Green Bay, he passed southward across unsettled regions of Michigan toward Galena, Illinois. This portion of the journey, as he later summarized it to Roberts, was its high point: "I was beyond the limits of civilization," he recalled, "frequently camping out at night, & holding high converse with Menomenies [sic] & Winnebagoes during the day." From Galena he passed through the young metropolis of Chicago, where he and James Berdan had "missed it egregiously in not erecting our Ebenezer[59] some three years & two months ago, the period of our exploring visit through Illinois,"[60] toward Toledo.

Although no good news of improved land prices awaited him upon his return there on August 12, he was delighted to find a letter from Daniel Roberts announcing—in distinctly shamefaced terms —his engagement to be married. Possibly Roberts had been daunted by what he knew to be Pierre's stern philosophy that a happy marriage requires ample funds to sustain it; more likely, he was familiar with his friend's penchant for mocking the amours of other persons.[61] At

[58] The canoe, he wrote enthusiastically, "was manned by five merry voyageurs." Among his companions in the boat was George Catlin, the painter and interpreter of Indian culture.

[59] See I Samuel. VII. 12.

[60] PMI to Daniel Roberts, Toledo, August 20, 1836 (Huntington). If PMI's precise dating is accurate, this exploratory tour of Illinois was made three months after he and James Berdan arrived at Jacksonville in March 1833.

[61] An example of PMI's chaffing is in a letter from him to Longfellow, June 24, 1831. After complaining of his correspondent's failure to write sooner, he continued: "I waited until expectation grew more & more feeble, & at last I gave you over as one too deeply infected with the tender passion to be able to make good your engagement [to write]. You will understand from this that I was not so wholly ignorant of the sentimental relation you hold to a certain Miss P----- (I dare not be guilty of the profanity of writing her name at full length) as you seem to suppose – – but what a lover are you not to have favoured me with a description of the thousand graces that doubtless conspire to make [her] the most perfect of her sex – Nay – the merest hint – even half a line of description would have sufficed – the rest I could have done myself – and what an engaging picture of female loveliness would I have made of it – but to preserve a total silence on the subject – not to let a syllable fall upon which my imagination could have seized, & set itself to work – how in the name of wonder will you excuse such an unpardonable omission? Could you suppose a want of curiosity on my part, or were you deterred from the task by a lurking suspicion that *Cato was not a proper person to entrust*

any rate, he had made his announcement with ironic lugubriousness, edging his letter in black. But if he had expected to receive a reply in kind, he must have been taken aback as he read Pierre's solemnly sincere letter of congratulation. "From my inmost soul I give you joy of the treasure you have won," Pierre wrote. He reproached Roberts for his fear of being derided as a "lovesick ass": "I might indeed find food for mirth in the vapid effusions of sentimental effeminacy, such as I have read, but I am too painfully sensitive myself in matters where the heart is really concerned to be guilty of any unfeeling levity towards others." Then, having registered his pleasure at Roberts' good fortune, Pierre wrote out for the first time an announcement of his own. This statement reveals his thoughts at a turning point in his lifetime with such vividness that it deserves to be quoted at length:

> And now, my good fellow, in requital of your confidence let me surprise you with a small secret of my own. Know then, "among the various turns of fate below," it has happened to me also to pledge myself anew. Long and manfully did I struggle against the indulgence of feelings which prudence reproved, but the deep thirst of my heart for some object upon which its yearning sympathies could repose, some tie to fix its restless and vacant affections, some dear companion to fill the place of her I had loved and lost would not and could not be subdued. It was in January last in the city of New York that, in a moment of overpowering fullness of feeling, my resolution yielded, and I spake the words which cannot be recalled. "As deep meets deep," so were their accents met. Three syllables composed of ten letters will spell the name of my divinity, which is Helen Dodge. She is a cousin—was born and bred in the country, & is not a great deal younger than myself, having preferred thus far to abide in a state of single blessedness rather than accept overtures of an uncongenial alliance. In size she is short—in figure rather too much inclined to fulness—in complexion dark, and her eyes are of the color which the world has agreed to call hazel. The expression of her countenance is engaging, but she has no pretensions to beauty, and were the days of chivalry revived, not a knight could be found to break a lance in honor of her charms. She is consequently deficient in the most essential qualifications for the heroine of a novel. If, however, she lacks the graces of person, she is far from deficient in the higher endowments of mind. Indeed once know her as I know her —know the softness, the delicacy and purity of her disposition, the overflowing tenderness of her heart, the elevation of her sentiments, her generous disdain of all that is vulgar and mean, the invariable sweetness of her temper, the cheerful, yet ever chastened and subdued play of her humor, and you could readily overlook her want of outward attractions. Among her relatives and acquaintances she is a universal favorite. She has a great fondness for reading, and her taste is delicate and discriminating, though her education has been somewhat limited. She is an

with such a secret? You are no true knight if you do not feel ashamed of the poor compliment you have paid your Ladye-love – – –" (Harvard). Roberts had himself suffered from the epistolary teasing of PMI.

orphan, and poor in this world's goods, but her heart is a mine of wealth. I yield to no exaggerated feeling when I assert my deliberate belief that not one in a million possesses in an equal degree with her a capacity for deep and permanent affection. She has in truth "a heart of tendrils," and it would seem as if love were almost a necessary condition of her existence. In our engagement she has laid open to me her whole inward being, has confessed that she had loved me in years long gone by. On the strength of this secret and subdued attachment I cannot speak but her love for me now I know to be an absorbing and exclusive power, ardent, uncalculating and sure and steadfast as martyr's faith. For myself I have not a wish in life—I have not a hope of happiness that does not point, tend and centre to and in a union with her. To hasten this consummation I came to the West, seeking in speculation a speedier road to competence than I could hope to open for myself in any other way. Owing to the untoward character of the times, however, my competence is yet in prospect, & I fear therefore that I shall be driven to a longer delay of my wishes than I had anticipated at my departure from New York. For this place I shall set out in the course of a week or ten days to spend the month of September.[62]

Pierre's undisclosed affection for Helen goes far to account for his temporary acquiescence during the past December and January in performing the Mexican "drudgery" under Irving's direction. The engagement, and Pierre's consequent wish to secure a "competence" in order to marry Helen as soon as possible, also help to explain his sudden determination to pull up stakes and accompany John Berdan westward. And the subsequent absence from his fiancé, along with frustration that his fortune was not accumulating so rapidly as he had hoped, account for much of his depression in later months. Perverse as it may seen, it was typical of Pierre not to divulge the news of his engagement, even to a close friend, until months after it had occurred. Expansive and unreserved as he was in August, he had been totally silent in February, leading Roberts to believe that his motive for visiting Toledo was simple cupidity.[63] Possibly before departing from

[62] PMI to Daniel Roberts, Toledo, August 20, 1836 (Huntington). According to a legend in the Irving family, Helen and PMI were once engaged before PMI's marriage to Margaret Berdan, but the engagement was broken off. Having been away from home at some time during this early period, PMI is said to have gone at once upon his return to visit his fiancé. However, Helen was in the bath when he arrived. The maid told him that as soon as her mistress was dressed she would come to him, but the woman failed to mention that Helen was not yet nearly presentable. Pierre remained for some time, but at last he left, angry at having thus been kept waiting after so long an absence. Following this incident, the legend concludes, he and Helen quarreled and parted, and later he married Margaret Berdan. Unidentified note [by Mrs. Sheldon Potter?] in Frothingham, *Genealogy*, p. 145 (NYPL, MS).

[63] On February 20 PMI had written Roberts from Albany that he was bound for Toledo, "seeking among other views which I have not time to specify a profitable investment of my little capital" (Huntington). He had been equally close-mouthed with Longfellow.

New York he had let Irving know the secret, but it is unlikely that at that early date anyone else was apprised of it.

Pierre had become acquainted with Helen at least as early as 1821, when as a girl of eighteen she had visited with Ebenezer's family.[64] They met at intervals thereafter—notably in the winter of 1832-1833 when both were in New York and Pierre was mourning his loss of Margaret—but they did not begin to visit together regularly over a long period until the winter of 1834-1835. It was a notable coincidence that they were brought together that winter through the indirect agency of Irving, since it was at his instigation that Helen had decided to make another extended stay in the city at about the same time that Pierre was being lured away from Jacksonville to New York by the prospect of three thousand Astorian dollars.[65] The possibility that Irving had matchmaking intentions when he made these separate arrangements is remote, but he must have been pleased when he was informed of the engagement.

Purposely or not, in his letter of August 20 Pierre failed to inform Roberts that the leading feature of his intended visit to New York was to be his own wedding. Competency or no competency, he felt certain that his land purchases would prove profitable soon enough, and he would wait no longer. Toledo was a tolerable place in itself, but the past few months had revealed that for him it was unbearable without Helen. Happily, she was willing to come; and to have her there he was quite willing, as he put it, to "hang out [his] tin sign to an evil generation"[66] of litigants once more. He hurried to New York, where he was immersed in a stream of preparations deemed essential by his fiancé, who was a great lover and critic of all such formal festivities as balls, receptions, and weddings. Amidst the busy weeks of September he had an opportunity to congratulate Julia, his last surviving sister, on her marriage in June to Moses Hicks Grinnell, a young shipping merchant interested in politics,[67] but he managed to do little else. As he had warned Roberts in August, "the demands of business and the claims of love"[68] had made him captive. On October 10 he and

[64] Ebenezer Irving to Richard Dodge, New York, March 29, 1821 (N-YHS). In WI's will dated May 15, 1815, he had requested of Peter and Ebenezer, his heirs, "that they would contribute out of the profits or income [of his estate] to educate & maintain the daughters of my deceased Sister Mrs. Ann L. Dodge" (SHR). Helen was one of the daughters, and although it is unknown whether WI contributed to her maintenance in subsequent years, there is no doubt that through the hospitality of Ebenezer she was a member of the inner family circle.

[65] On January 16, 1835, Ebenezer wrote from New York to his son William Irving that WI "took a fancy that it would be better to have your cousin Helen Dodge this winter at No. 3 [Bridge Street], so I brought her down with me on my return from Troy" (SHR).

[66] PMI to Daniel Roberts, Toledo, December 8, 1836 (Huntington).

[67] Grinnell (1803-1877) was a partner in Grinnell, Minturn & Co., a firm which enjoyed a worldwide commercial reputation. Julia, whom he married on June 30, 1836, was his second wife. A biographical sketch of Grinnell is in *DAB*, VIII, 5-6.

[68] PMI to Daniel Roberts, Toledo, August 20, 1836 (Huntington).

Helen were married,[69] and shortly afterward they set out on a long but hopefully economical wedding tour—toward Toledo.

The month of October 1836 was a kind of watershed for the subsequent careers of both Pierre and his uncle. Coincidentally, during this same month, in which *Astoria* was published, Pierre married Helen and Irving at last rendered the Roost fully habitable, so that two of the aims they had conceived while at work on the book were realized almost simultaneously. The period of their collaboration on *Astoria* was indirectly to shape both their future lives out of all proportion to the innate importance of the collaboration itself, for Irving was to be as deeply influenced by affection for his rural home as Pierre was to be by Helen. In later years Pierre's devotion to his charming wife would help to fix him in New York and thus make possible his increasingly close relationship with his uncle. On the other hand, Irving's solicitude to make of the Roost a place of regular family resort would impel him to take special measures to ensure that Pierre and Helen remained in his vicinity. Even now, amidst his prosecution of various enterprises, Irving would probably have preferred to override the determination of his nephew and niece to abandon their home ground. As they swept away, however, he was too busy to be cast down. They would likely be back before many years, and just now he was intent upon giving a few finishing touches to the cottage. Peter, having arrived from Europe in April, was still in residence at Bridge Street; and Irving was eager for him to take up his lodgings in the Roost.

Shortly after returning to the West and settling comfortably with Helen into rented rooms, Pierre was able to turn a profit of $2,000 for his uncles by selling a few of their town lots. His own prospects continued to be "favorable," and in December he assured the still restless (and still unmarried) Roberts that Toledo, not Vermont, was the place where he should have settled down. He excused the irregularity of his post-marital correspondence by observing complacently that "one's friends should not expect too much just after one has 'married a wife.'"[70] Very naturally, the role of regular correspondent with the family in New York was assumed by the gregarious Helen. In particular, she and Peter exchanged gossip, with Peter reporting affairs at each of his two alternating addresses, "The Hive" in Bridge Street and the Roost.[71] Pierre wrote more businesslike letters to Irving, usually confining himself to observations about the market in real estate. Both his single-minded concern with land prices and his gran-

---

[69] PMI, Misc. Notebook.

[70] PMI to Daniel Roberts, Toledo, December 8, 1836.

[71] PMI, MS Outline, Chapters 66-68 (1836-1838). On December 10, 1836, Peter wrote to Helen that all were pleased with the completed Roost: "There is an air of cheeriness & elegant comfort in the new furniture and numerous sofas with their ample cushions & the Piano in the drawing room which were hardly to be expected in a Dutch country cottage." This passage, which PMI apparently intended at one time to include in *LLWI*, he copied into Chapter 66 of the MS Outline.

diose expectations of profit were at this time more extreme than his uncle's. On December 12 Irving wrote in response to a bullish message from Pierre that he certainly hoped Toledo would "grow to be a mighty city like Babylon of old," but that he was so inured to watching *"swans* turn out mere *geese"* that he had made up his mind "not to be grieved if that should prove to be the case in the present instance."[72] Still, Toledo was no goose. By the end of the year Irving had received notice of another profitable sale. "I . . . begin to think I shall yet be able to afford another weathercock to my cottage," he wrote in reply.[73]

At the outset of 1837 Irving's situation seemed to him secure and enviable. He was now closely occupied with *The Adventures of Captain Bonneville,* and he had written Pierre on December 12 that he was working "with almost as much industry and rapidity as I did at Hellgate." Taking up his recent avian metaphor in a more optimistic context, he predicted that he would "more than pay for my nest, from the greater number of eggs I shall be able to hatch there."[74] As the cottage grew to be the gathering-place he had wished it to be, Irving was aware how rapidly his incidental expenses accumulated, and he wondered at times whether he was overextending himself. But on the whole he was not disposed to fret. As he completed *Bonneville* and sent proof to Colonel Thomas Aspinwall, his trusty agent in London, consulted with Kemble about their joint investment in Indian land, performed his ceremonial duties as a bank director, and read the enthusiastic reviews of *Astoria,* he could hardly contrive to feel alarmed. Returning to the Roost after a visit to New York, he wrote to his niece Sarah Paris: "I cannot tell you how happy I was to get back again to my own dear, bright little home, and leave behind me the hurry and worry and flurry of the city."[75] Peter, despite a surpassing hunger for English newspapers, seemed to enjoy his stays at the Roost and was visibly improving in health. Irving had acquired for his estate a much-discussed pig named after Fanny Kemble, the actress, and the pond not far from the cottage now promised to be populated the year round by a flotilla of ducks. An admiring acquaintance lent him several French novels which gave him "much amusement" despite what he termed their "peculiar and perverted taste."[76] Guests, including the youthful Louis Napoleon and the feeble John Jacob Astor, were beginning to beat a track to his door, and his several nieces pampered him satisfactorily. Some of his neighbours now appeared to be willing to part with the lands adjoining his at the proper prices.[77] With so few

[72] *LLWI,* III, 91.

[73] *LLWI,* III, 98-99.

[74] *LLWI,* III, 92.

[75] WI to Sarah Paris, The Roost, December 10, 1836; *LLWI,* III, 94.

[76] WI to Samuel Ward, Jr., n.p., September 20, 1837 (Virginia).

[77] In September 1836 he had bought three acres from Oscar for $1,500, and on June 12, 1838, after disposing of one and one-half acres to George Jones for $700, he paid Isaac Lent $4,000 for fourteen more acres ("Lands Purchased"—SHR).

apparent sources of anxiety, and with his plans realizing themselves so smoothly, Irving thought he had arrived.

On May 5, 1837, the bubble burst. The United States Bank suspended specie payment on all paper notes, thereby upsetting the false financial equilibrium of the nation and precipitating a widespread panic that stultified commerce and resulted in immediate losses of millions of dollars. For a time, however, Irving failed to recognize the seriousness of his own situation. He seemed safe enough: even now he was being encouraged to declare himself a candidate for the mayoralty of New York; he was shortly to be offered the lucrative Secretaryship of the Navy by President Martin Van Buren, his former colleague at the United States Legation at London; and several of his investments were continuing to pay dividends as before. On the other hand, the effect of the monetary crisis on Ebenezer was devastating. The business of his solidly established importing agency in New York was so prostrated by the abrupt decline in international trade that in order to avoid bankruptcy he was obliged to sell and vacate his home. Naturally Irving offered a new home at the Roost to his four suddenly uprooted nieces, Ebenezer's daughters—a kindness which was gratefully accepted, even though Ebenezer and Peter were both determined if possible to pay their own way rather than accept the charity of their brother's full-time hospitality. They took rooms together in the city, but they were soon forced to capitulate.[78] Neither was in firm health, and both were rapidly expending their savings, so that the Roost was their only dignified alternative. All this activity of course meant to Irving a sharp rise in his domestic expenses at a time when, as he came to realize, he could not well afford it. By the close of 1837, with the great majority of his funds locked up in depressed land holdings and in stock that no longer yielded dividends, he saw that he must cast about for a steady source of income. "I am more and more convinced," he wrote to Pierre on May 18, 1838, "that the very best thing to be done with the Toledo lots, is to put up small buildings on some of them as speedily as possible; by this means we may soon be in the receipt of a full interest on the whole amount invested there; and, for my own part, I should be well contented to let it remain thus invested." It would be misleading to suggest that Irving's financial worries oppressed him constantly, but as the depression wore on he did find it difficult to maintain the serene demeanour he thought proper to a landed gentleman.[79]

[78] *LLWI*, III, 128. In the MS Outline, Chapter 68 (1838), PMI quoted an excerpt from a letter of Peter to Helen dated April 6, 1838: "The family hive at No 3 Bridge St is about to be broken up. The house is advertised for a tenant – & your Uncle Ebenezer with the four demoiselles C., S, J & M. contemplate a removal for the summer, with also your Aunt Paris & her Sarah to your Uncle Washington's cottage." Ebenezer's daughters whose first initials appear in the quotation were, respectively, Catharine (Kate), Sarah, Julia, and Mary.

[79] *LLWI*, III, 129. For Paulding's amused view of WI's embarrassments at this time, see *The Letters of James Kirke Paulding*, ed. Ralph M. Aderman (Madison, Wisconsin, 1962), pp. 194-95.

The Panic of 1837 proved also to be a blight upon the hopes of Pierre and Helen. Like his uncle, Pierre refused to abandon his optimism immediately; and, in fact, he never was so straitened as Irving during this barren period. On May 5, 1837—the day of the catastrophe— he confessed in a letter to Roberts that "our only topic of conversation here is the hard times." His own liabilities were few, he said, but "it does not seem improbable that what we now see is the cloudy dawn of a dark and windy day. Ill-boding prophets in the West predict a total prostration of all who are heavily indebted without available means of payment, and I confess things seem verging towards such a crisis."[80] As he saw it, his fate as an investor already hung in the balance beyond his power to affect it materially, so that what remained while waiting "with edifying resignation" for better times was to find lawful ways of earning money to cover current expenses. His tenements on Toledo lots yielded a good return, but by way of dropping anchors to windward he was undertaking two new ventures. First, he was returning to the law, that old recourse in times of uncertainty. He had postponed this step until recently, but now, together with the seven other attorneys of the city—all of them "mediocre," he judged—he was in general practice, pleading at the courthouse in Toledo and in nearby counties as well. Second, at the beginning of May he became at the instigation of friends "a kind of volunteer by compulsion" to edit the Toledo *Blade,* a Whiggish newspaper.

The *Blade* was an unabashedly political organ and was regularly embattled with other weeklies espousing either the cause of the Democrats or the mercantile ambitions of nearby towns. Pierre's genuine interest in editing the work was at first qualified by distaste for the necessity of becoming a target for the "vulgar marksmen" who conducted these competing papers. Nevertheless, as he told Roberts with dignity, "where a reasonable civility will not serve the turn, I must even do violence to my nature & try the efficacy of pungent retort."[81] During the summer, in recognition of his efforts thus far he received an offer to continue editing the *Blade* for one year at a salary of $500, which he willingly accepted. "I do not believe I have increased my chances for immortality," he reported to Roberts at that time, "though the folks tell me I have won some honor by my labor of love."[82] Shortly after the first wave of public consternation at the nationwide financial disaster, then, Pierre bid fair to weather the storm. Helen enjoyed life in Toledo, a stream of letters kept them in contact with the family in New York, and the future, to Pierre's rose-tinted eyesight, still seemed to be so promising that he urged Roberts once again to move west.

---

[80] PMI to Daniel Roberts, Toledo, May 5, 1837 (Huntington).

[81] With at least one of his friends PMI seems to have commanded respect as a coiner of cutting phrases. In a letter to James Berdan, Longfellow wrote on January 4, 1831: "Giving you the information you desired, too late for you to avail yourself of it, is what Pierre would call *shabby treatment*" (Hilen, ed., *Letters,* I, 352.

[82] PMI to Daniel Roberts, Toledo, August 9, 1837 (Huntington).

Pierre performed his duties as editor of the Toledo *Blade* with real credit. Owing to the slowness and capriciousness of transportation on the Ohio frontier, the *Blade* devoted a considerable proportion of its space to items gathered from journalistic sources along the Ohio River and as far west as St. Louis. But Pierre set the paper apart from other Ohio Valley weeklies by including a regular feature "For the Ladies" and reprinting contemporary fiction (Hawthorne's "The Shaker Bridal" appeared—attributed, however, to Mrs. Sedgwick) and poetry (Holmes and Bryant were favoured).[83] Removed as he was from the haunts of his uncle, he did his part to promote the Whig candidacy for Congress of Irving's friend John Pendleton Kennedy.[84] In July 1837, when Senator Daniel Webster stopped at Toledo for a testimonial dinner—a "cold collation" at the local hotel—Pierre was on hand to record the orator's remarks and testify to their "deep sincerity and lofty patriotism":

> No person that listened to Mr. Webster but felt himself to be in the presence of one whose severe love of truth would never permit a base or mischievous use of his powers; whose voice would never be raised to sway the public mind to aught unworthy . . . . His quivering lip, when he rose, testified to the force of his emotions, and he spoke throughout with an earnestness and energy, and at times with a vehemence of gesticulation which formed no part of our previous conceptions of his delivery and was the very reverse of that calm sobriety of tone and gesture which we are accustomed to associate with his declamations in the senate.
>
> Mr. Webster closed with the following sentiment: "The continued prosperity of the four beautiful Towns—may I say Cities—of the Maumee River."[85]

Pierre frequently counselled his townsmen to persevere in working for Toledo rather than succumb to "faint hearted misgivings"[86] over a brief pause in the city's growth, but on some occasions he used his

[83] "The Shaker Bridal" was published in the *Blade* for December 5, 1837, p. 1, cols. 1-3; its source was given as *The Token for 1833*. Each issue of the Toledo *Blade* consisted of four six-column pages. Page one included advertisements, fiction, and poetry; page two an editorial and local, national, and foreign news; page three a continuation of the news, and advertisements; page four advertisements and the ladies' section, featuring anecdotes and recipes. A general account of the Toledo *Blade* during this period is given by Douglas C. McMurtrie, "The First Ten Years of the Toledo *Blade*," *Ohio Archaeological and Historical Quarterly*, 43 (1934), 428-40; for a detailed account of PMI's contributions to the newspaper, see Wayne R. Kime, "PMI and the Toledo *Blade*," *Northwest Ohio Quarterly*, 47 (Fall 1975), 131-50.

[84] PMI may have been influenced by his uncle's good opinion of the Baltimore gentleman's business sense. After referring to Kennedy's literary works, *Swallow Barn* (1832) and *Horseshoe Robinson* (1835), he added that the author "is said to be as much at home in matters of finance as he is in works of fiction" (*Blade*, May 30, 1837, p. 2, col. 5).

[85] *Blade*, July 18, 1837, p. 2, col. 5. Toledo was located on the west bank of the Maumee River near its embouchure into Lake Erie.

[86] *Blade*, August 15, 1837, p. 2, col. 5.

editorial column to discuss issues of national import. In January 1838, during the brief Patriot's War, he angrily denounced as hypocritical the American invasion of Upper Canada to "liberate" its citizens —and its desirable farm land—from "tyrannical" British control.[87] On the previous July 4 he had moralized over the depths of corruption to which certain persons in the United States had sunk under the spoils system enacted under the Democratic administrations of Jackson and Van Buren:

> Let corruption continue to invade the mass of the community, as it has within the last eight years, let its strides be as rapid, and what security have we for the permanence of our free institutions. We know that it is fashionable for the mere tools of power, the cringing and abject slaves that glory in their degradation to resolve all political integrity into a contest for *spoils*, and because they have no experience in themselves of the ennobling sentiments of true patriotism, to laugh in utter derision at the idea of public virtue, as if it were some fine-spun notion fit only for the heated fancy of a visionary moralist. Yet who would have dared to breath [*sic*] such language—who could have polluted his lips with the motto—*to the victor belong the spoils,*—in the presence of Washington, and stood erect before the withering scorn of his rebuking glance? Was public virtue regarded as a chimera, a bulky and gigantic phantom when he and his high-hearted band of self-devoting patriots perilled their all for conscience and liberty's sake?
>
> The language of caution is not the language of fear, yet it cannot be denied that our danger is not altogether imaginary. As a people, we have sunk far, far below the level of our high position; as disciples of Washington, we have deviated sadly and widely from the inviolable rectitude of his principles. Disguise it as we may, for the last eight years we have been treading the downward path which leads to the great sepulchre of nations, and if we still continue to prostitute our minds to the low purposes of vulgar ambition, and the corrupting influence of party strife, the clouds which have now gathered upon our horizon will be as nothing to the thick darkness which must hereafter settle upon our prospects.[88]

Except for a month's absence in April 1838, when his legal duties took him out of town,[89] Pierre performed his editorial charge attentively and without interruption. He acquitted himself so well, in fact, that he rapidly rose to local prominence.

---

[87] "Trouble Brewing," *Blade*, January 10, 1838, p. 2, col. 5; "American Volunteers," *Blade*, January 17, p. 2, col. 5. PMI's letters to Daniel Roberts during this period were full of wrath against the American invaders. See those of January 16 and March 14, 1838 (Huntington).

[88] *Blade*, July 4, 1837, p. 2, col. 5.

[89] From various statements in the *Blade* it is clear that the issues of April 4 through May 2, 1838, were prepared under the editorship of another person. See also *Blade*, May 9, 1838, p. 3, col. 1.

Along with John Berdan, who was elected the first mayor of Toledo when it was incorporated as a city in April 1837, Pierre worked energetically on behalf of the community in other ways than as its editorial spokesman. He was elected Vice-President of the Educational Society of the Maumee Valley; he was instrumental in founding a Young Men's Association; and in the spring of 1838 he was named a member of the Central Committee to organize and concentrate the Whig forces in Lucas County for the forthcoming state elections.[90] Meanwhile, he looked after his investments and those of his uncles. It was common rumour in Toledo that he had come there to act as Irving's deputy.[91] Through his civic exertions, his own investments, and his agency for his uncles, in short, Pierre was associating the family name with the early history of this western community.[92] Yet even before his arrival the literary influence of Washington Irving had made its way to Toledo: one "Dedrick Knickerbacker" is listed in a contemporary account-book as having purchased property in the place on June 16, 1834.[93]

Pierre had managed to live so successfully during the year following the Panic that he and Helen were beginning to think of residing permanently in Toledo. They were "perfectly happy" here, he told Roberts in March 1838 upon learning that his friend was starting a family; so happy, indeed, that they could afford "to dispense with those added luxuries" for a time. One reason Pierre gave to explain their restraint was that raising children in Toledo would entail a maddening effort (as Mrs. Trollope had found in Cincinnati a few years before)[94] to hire good servants. In fact, to avoid all the perplexities of setting up housekeeping in this rough-edged locale they were still "very pleasantly situated at board," which made up in conve-

[90] Charles E. Bliven, *Maumee Valley and Pioneers* (Fort Meigs, Ohio, 1880), p. 25; Clark Waggoner, ed., *History of the City of Toledo and Lucas County, Ohio* (New York and Toledo, 1888), pp. 611, 669, 851; Toledo *Blade*, March 28, 1838, p. 3, col. 1. Waggoner also states that PMI was a prominent lawyer "in the early sessions of the Courts in Lucas County" (p. 514).

[91] PMI did of course have control over substantial portions of land owned by the Irvings; see footnote 54. But the historians of the Toledo vicinity are unanimous in claiming incorrectly that the reason for his presence in the city was to supervise the landed investments of WI.

[92] Years after his residence in Toledo, a legend grew up that PMI, "inspired by his uncle's 'Astoria,'" gave the name "Oregon" to a nearby township (Waggoner, *History*, p. 851). In fact, PMI is even mentioned in local histories as having suggested the name *Toledo* for the young community; see Bliven, *Maumee Valley*, p. 25, and Charles E. Slocum, *History of the Maumee River Basin* (Defiance, Ohio, 1905), p. 592. However, that he did not name the town is shown not only by the fact that it was known as Toledo before he arrived there, but also by a passage in his letter to Daniel Roberts of February 20, 1836, when he was on his way there: "At the western extremity of Lake Erie, on the North side of the Maumee River, in the territory in dispute between Michigan & Ohio, stands a town which some with a modest & inventive taste in names have called Toledo" (Huntington).

[93] Account Book of Edward Bissell, p. 13 (MS, Toledo Public Library).

[94] Frances Trollope, *Domestic Manners of the Americans*, ed. Donald Smalley (New York, 1949), pp. 52-58.

nience whatever it wanted in comfort or splendour. Of their amusements Pierre had little to say, except that they were regular and sufficiently varied to satisfy them both. Early in 1838 they became interested in "animal magnetism," a phenomenon just achieving the popularity it was to sustain in the United States over the next twenty-five years. Pierre reported to Roberts in March that they had seen "some strange experiments performed by a Mr Russell, a very honest and sensible merchant of Buffalo." Mr. Russell had executed one of his feats upon a "modest young lady of this place who professed an obstinate incredulity" as to his powers:

> In less than ten minutes she was brought into the magnetic state, and could not speak or move a limb except at his bidding. While in this condition, a stranger came in, and Mrs. I. turned to her abruptly with the exclamation – "Come, come, Miss L., rouse up, rouse up, here's a stranger in the room." Vexed and mortified at the consciousness of her singular exhibition, the tears came trickling down her cheeks, but she could not stir or raise her hands to wipe them away. Observing her agitation, Mr R. inquired the cause, and then she entreated him convulsively to relieve her from her awkward predicament, which he did.

Although Pierre avowed that his faith in animal magnetism was "like that of the doubting Thomas," he was impressed enough to begin familiarizing himself with the body of pamphlet literature being written about it. It was "not to be disposed of by a sneer and a scoff,"[95] he believed.

After almost two years away from New York, he and Helen planned to visit there for a few weeks this summer, perhaps leaving Toledo in June. Their announcement of the intention came as a real source of pleasure to Irving at a time when he had few to enjoy. With studied indifference to money matters, he wrote to them on May 18 that he looked forward to showing them "what a capital florist and horticulturist and agriculturist I am becoming." Spring was "coming out in all its beauty," he went on, and the residents of the Roost were all "cosily quartered" and "very comfortable."[96] Behind his bold facade, Irving was feeling the financial pinch which was to inspire his heartfelt proposal a few years afterward for an addition to the litany: "From all inventors, projectors, and other devisers of sudden wealth, Good Lord deliver us!"[97] To make ends meet he had been considering a new literary project, but he knew his own nature well enough to doubt that his health and spirits would hold up under the strain of forced composition. His brother John Treat had died of overwork in March,[98] and now it was difficult to keep himself from falling prey to periodic depressions. The arrival of Pierre and Helen would brighten these overcast skies somewhat.

[95] PMI to Daniel Roberts, Toledo, March 14, 1838 (Huntington).
[96] *LLWI*, III, 129.
[97] WI to Mrs. Sarah Van Wart, Greenburgh, February 26, 1841; *Life*, II, 356, note 15.
[98] *LLWI*, III, 125.

Their visit was rudely postponed, however, when early in June Helen became ill with bilious fever, an often fatal disease epidemic in the West that year. After weeks of slow recovery interrupted by a series of minor fevers, in August she suffered a relapse that almost killed her. "I have rarely witnessed prostration more entire," Pierre recalled a few months later. "For four days it seemed as if nature were constantly verging nearer and nearer to her last struggle." Gradually, though, Helen regained strength, until by mid-September it was possible to move her. Relieved, yet shaken himself by "suspense and worry of mind,"[99] Pierre decided to take her immediately to New York, where she could complete her convalescence. His tenure as editor of the *Blade* was over,[100] his property was dormant on the market, and his legal and civic enterprises could wait; and thus they set out together. Unhappily, they had not passed Buffalo before Pierre himself was stricken with a case of the fever which, though comparatively mild, kept him bedfast for several days. After a protracted and cheerless journey of eight hundred miles, the couple finally arrived in New York at the end of September.

Once she had arrived in the city, Helen quite understandably refused even to consider setting foot in Toledo again. As Pierre put it, "an impression was riveted indelibly upon her mind that another summer at that place would lead to a permanent derangement of health, if not expose her to imminent hazard of a premature grave." Of course he could sympathize with her distaste; yet it was difficult to set aside so abruptly his thoughts of settling down in Toledo, now that his position there had become so much more than that of a mere speculator. "I was in a dilemma, & knew not what to do," he later explained to Roberts. "I could not disregard misgivings so serious & possibly so well-founded, and yet I was loth in the extreme to cast myself anew upon the world for a home." As he might have expected, Helen's friends raised a cry against her return. Distraught, he sought by way of compromise to convince her that in the following summer she might stay away from Toledo while he returned there to conclude his western operations in some semblance of orderliness. But he had not properly estimated the intensity and inclusiveness of his wife's ideas. In Helen's view the miasmal West was a threat to them both, he told Roberts, and "she would not acquiesce for a moment in such an arrangement. She would share the sickly season with me, or both must leave." Confronted with this non-negotiable position, Pierre resigned himself to a lengthy absence from Toledo. Whatever his future financial triumphs there might be, he would not soon be witnessing them at first hand.

Having spent "many anxious and perplexing thoughts" before sacrificing what had promised to be a bright future in the West, Pierre

[99] PMI to Daniel Roberts, New York, December 24, 1838 (Huntington).

[100] His editorship of the *Blade* probably continued until the issue of August 1, 1838. A new editor announced his arrival in the issue of August 8, p. 2, col. 4, and the newspaper immediately assumed a more contentious tone.

now addressed himself anew to the problems of deciding where and how to live. In light of his actions at similar times in the past, and of Helen's present sentiments, the determinations he made are not surprising: on December 24, 1838, he informed Roberts that he intended to "resume the practice of law in [his] native city." Indeed, he wryly added, for the past two weeks he had been sitting in a solitary law office "without a single client to molest me or make me afraid." He had made his decision, and if it entailed regrets at least the turmoil of the whole episode was behind him. "I begin now to feel a different & happier man," he wrote after summarizing the harrowing history of the past few months, "though I cannot help looking forward to the future with some anxiety."[101] As he sat awaiting clients in his Nassau Street office,[102] Pierre may have surmised that at thirty-six, with a wife who was closely attached to her (and his own) family here in New York, his travels were about over.

Although he certainly did not plan it that way, his return to New York had come at a fortuitous time to bring him rapidly into a much closer relationship with his Uncle Washington than heretofore. During the fall of 1838 the proximity of Pierre and Helen was extremely important to Irving. As we have seen, his personal situation had been uncomfortable the previous spring, pressed as he was for ready money and concerned as to his ability to produce it by his pen. On June 27, however, his anxiousness was overwhelmed by deep sorrow when he suffered what Pierre was to describe as "one of the severest blows of his life":[103] the sudden death of Peter. For many years, both in America and in Europe, Irving's closest companion and counsellor had been his sensitive elder brother. He had always been able to rely on Peter for intelligent perception of his changing moods as well as for generous assistance of all kinds. "Every day, every hour I feel how completely Peter and myself were intertwined together in the whole course of our existence," he wrote in September to his sister Sarah Van Wart. "My literary pursuits have been so often carried on by his side, and under his eye—I have been so accustomed to talk over every plan with him, and, as it were, to think aloud when in his presence, that I cannot open a book, or take up a paper, or recall a past vein of thought, without having him instantly before me, and finding myself completely overcome." He told Sarah that the loss of Peter left what seemed an irreplaceable void: "A dreary feeling of loneliness comes on me at times, that I reason against in vain; for, though surrounded by affectionate relatives, I feel that none can be what he was to me; none can take so thorough an interest in my concerns; to none can I so confidingly lay open my every thought and feeling, and expose every fault and foible, certain of such perfect toleration and indulgence."[104]

---

[101] PMI to Daniel Roberts, New York, December 24, 1838 (Huntington).
[102] *Longworth's Directory* for 1839.
[103] *LLWI*, III, 129.
[104] *LLWI*, III, 130.

Perhaps in this grief-inspired testament to his brother's memory Irving was slightly magnifying Peter's importance to him over the years; yet whatever the exact objective basis of his claim, it was subjectively true to him at the time he wrote it. That was on September 22, when Pierre and Helen were making their painful way from Toledo to New York.

In his emotional letter to Mrs. Van Wart, Irving wrote that he hoped during the fall months to "regain something of [his] usual vigor of body, and with it a healthier tone of mind." To realize that aim as well as to supplement his income, he planned to take up by himself the project for which he had enlisted Pierre as his temporary "pioneer" three years before—a history of the conquest of Mexico. Between the spells of depression this past summer he had attempted to put his papers on the topic in order,[105] and now he was resolute to push on with the task of sifting his authorities and winnowing the material which would become the substance of his narrative. Although when writing *Astoria* he had been too busy to handle such minute and tedious necessities as this unaided, now he entered upon it willingly, growing more pleased with his subject as the weeks passed. Perhaps sorting through Las Casas, Herrera, and Sahagun helped calm his emotions; certainly by December he had shaken off his lethargy. With a rough draft of his first volume already complete, he was busy consulting reference works in the New York Society Library one afternoon when he received an entirely unexpected bit of news. In conversation with his friend Joseph Green Cogswell, the librarian, he learned that William H. Prescott, an admirer and reviewer of his Spanish volumes and recently himself the author of a three-volume *History of the Reign of Ferdinand and Isabella the Catholic,*[106] was engaged at present on precisely the same subject as he. This was a shock; and yet immediately, and in a manner so exemplary for its courtesy that it became legendary in his lifetime, Irving relinquished his claim to the topic. He asked Cogswell to convey his good wishes to Prescott and volunteered to the latter whatever assistance he might be able to offer on the basis of his previous research in Spain and his respectable private collection of Spanish historical literature.

Irving's impulsive gesture delighted Prescott, who had long been frankly apprehensive that the more popular author might usurp the theme he hoped to claim as his own,[107] and the conversation with Cogswell soon led to the beginning of a cordial correspondence between the two historians. Nonetheless, the loss of an opportunity to

---

[105] *LLWI,* III, 131, 138.

[106] See Prescott, "Irving's Conquest of Granada," in *Biographical and Critical Miscellanies* (Philadelphia, 1845), pp. 82-113. Prescott studied WI's histories with care and in some respects adopted them as models for his own work. His *Ferdinand and Isabella* was published in 1838.

[107] See, for example, *The Papers of William Hickling Prescott,* ed. C. Harvey Gardiner (Urbana, Illinois, 1964), p. 67; *The Correspondence of William H. Prescott, 1833-1847,* ed. Roger Walcott (Boston and New York, 1925), pp. 48, 204.

complete his book rankled in Irving. He had understood from Cogswell that Prescott had already begun writing his history, but he
learned afterward that such was not actually the case.[108] A few years
later he expressed to Pierre his doubt that Prescott had been aware of
what a sacrifice he had made. First, he said, this "was a favorite
subject, which had delighted my imagination ever since I was a boy. I
had brought home books from Spain to aid me in it, and looked upon
it as the pendent to my Columbus." Second, when "I gave it up to
him, I in a manner gave him up my bread, for I depended upon the
profit of it to recruit my waning finances. I had no other subject at
hand to supply its place."[109] By a single courtly gesture Irving had in
December 1838 discarded his own plans for the somewhat critical
immediate future. In the Life and Letters Pierre recalled that on the
same day Irving recounted to him the interchange with Cogswell, "he
mentioned... that he had been looking over some papers in the
morning, and had come across his commencement of the Conquest of
Mexico; that he read over what he had written, and , in a fit of vexation
at having lost the magnificent theme, destroyed the manuscript."[110]

At the beginning of 1839, then, both Irving and Pierre found
themselves regretfully set free from the activities they had proposed to
continue, and both were confronted with the necessity of adjusting
rapidly to their new circumstances. Pierre's best hope seemed to be
through the good offices of his brother-in-law Moses Grinnell, who
was newly elected to Congress. Grinnell still controlled a large shipping business and had promised to shunt "considerable" legal trade
in his direction.[111] By January 18, however, the flow of patronage had
not yet begun. "A cipher would chronicle what I have done in the way
of business during my five weeks' apprenticeship," he reported to
Roberts, although "in the way of study I have wearied the flesh
considerable."[112] As for Irving, within a few weeks of writing a letter
to Prescott stepping aside in his favour, he had decided to enter upon
a new phase of his literary career. On February 6, in the professional
presence of Pierre, he signed an agreement with Lewis Gaylord Clark,
editor of the Knickerbocker Magazine, to write monthly contributions
to the periodical for a $2,000 annual fee.[113] By setting aside his long-

[108] LLWI, III, 134.

[109] LLWI, III, 143.

[110] LLWI, III, 134.

[111] PMI to Daniel Roberts, New York, December 24, 1838 (Huntington). Grinnell
was a member of Congress for one term (1839-1841).

[112] PMI to Daniel Roberts, New York, January 18, 1839 (Huntington).

[113] In an account of this interview, Lewis Gaylord Clark referred to PMI as WI's
"favorite nephew and confidential secretary" ("Recollections of WI," Lippincott's Magazine, 3 [May 1869], 552). However, PMI held no such position at this time. In light of his
enforced idleness early in 1839, it seems possible that he accompanied WI simply for
something to do. WI and PMI also saw Clark socially. On April 3, 1839, the editor wrote
to Longfellow, who had recently departed from New York after a visit there: "T'other
day, Irving, Halleck, Pierre, Dakin [Clark's business partner] and your 'umble servant,
(& wife) sat down to a nice 'swarry,' which was, 'on the table' seasonably; and I assure

standing dislike of periodical publication, with its onerous requirement of regular productivity, he had quickly carved out for himself a
literary niche which, if irksome at times, would at least be dependably
remunerative. This was a satisfactory interim arrangement. Yet in
regard to a more long-range plan, Irving was apparently not so interested in himself just now as in himself and Pierre.

Almost a month before he signed the agreement with Clark, he
had addressed a short letter to Stephen Whitney and John A. Stevens,
prominent merchants who were Directors in a newly-chartered New
York bank, the Bank of Commerce, soliciting their interest in behalf of
his nephew, Pierre Munro Irving, who was a candidate for the office of
Notary to the institution.[114] Early in February he broadened his attack
on the same front by addressing a similar letter to another Director,[115]
and on February 13 he besieged two more.[116] Naturally, his ritual
praise of Pierre's "high moral character, his talents and his scrupulous
good faith" must be discounted somewhat as an expression of his
private thoughts about his nephew; but his explanation to one addressee that "I take very deep interest in procuring this appointment
from a wish to fix my nephew near me, in this his native city,"[117] is
more to the point. In short, Irving was determined to keep Pierre and
Helen by him. They had both given him much comfort the previous
fall, even amidst their own confusion, and he had come to recognize
their unique importance to himself. In a letter to his niece Julia
Grinnell a few years afterward, he recalled that "they both seemed to
take the place of others dear to my heart, whom I had lost and deplored":

> Pierre came to my side when I was grieving over the loss of my
> dear brother Peter, who had so long been the companion of my
> thoughts; and I found in him many of the qualities which made
> that dear brother so invaluable to me as a bosom friend. The same
> delicacy of feeling and rectitude of thought; the same generous
> disinterestedness; and the same scrupulous faith in all confiden-
> tial matters: while Helen in the delightful variety of her character,
> so affectionate, so tender; so playful at times, and at other times so
> serious and elevated; and always so intelligent and sensitive
> continually brought to mind her mother, who was one of the

you it was 'in flow of soul,' that knew no returning ebb, until, after coffee up stairs we
sojourned to my sanctum, and Scotticised over punch de glenlivet. Halleck says, he
never saw Irving in such spirits or so incessantly entertaining in his life" (*The Letters of
Willis Gaylord Clark and Lewis Gaylord Clark,* ed. Leslie W. Dunlap [New York, 1940],
p. 153).

[114] WI to Stephen Whitney or John A. Stevens, Greenburgh, January 12, 1839
(NYPL, MS).

[115] WI to Russell H. Nevins, New York, February 3, 1839 (Yale).

[116] WI to Jonathan Goodhue, New York, February 13, 1839 (New York Society
Library); WI to T. W. C. Moore, New York, February 13, 1839 (New York Society
Library).

[117] WI to Jonathan Goodhue, New York, February 13, 1839 (New York Society
Library).

tenderest friends of my childhood, and the delight of my youthful years.[118]

No longer simply as a literary apprentice, but as a trustworthy and congenial companion, Pierre had won a place in Irving's private life. Irving was fully prepared to seek favours from his acquaintances among the gentleman-merchants of New York in order to keep his nephew and niece at hand.

Interestingly, Pierre seems to have suspended his usual attitude of quiet independence so far as to follow with active interest the progress of his candidacy for the Notaryship. Now that he was in New York, he probably thought, why should he not do as well as he could? He would tend to his practice, and if Grinnell and his uncle wished to help him secure something more substantial, so much the better. On January 18 he confided to Roberts that while he had several competitors for the position at the Bank of Commerce, his chances seemed "quite encouraging." The bank, whose primary function was to finance the current undertakings of large manufacturers and merchants, would begin with a capital of $5,000,000.[119] He judged that the office of Notary "might not yield more than $500 the first year, but after that it would be worth one or two thousand dollars, and eventually . . . little short of $5000." "Besides," he added, "it leads to other business." As he had told Longfellow at the close of 1835, just prior to his move to Toledo, "the hoarding propensity was strong" within him once again. Obtaining the position, he admitted to Roberts, would make him "the happiest of men."[120] During the next five weeks he closely observed his own campaign for the Notaryship, noting with anxious concern the activities on behalf of two rivals —one a nephew of an influential Director and the other a protégé of the President. On March 3, "to the great amazement of the aforesaid President & Director," his uncle's determined efforts prevailed and Pierre swept to victory by a wide margin.[121] When the bank opened for business on April 3—his thirty-seventh birthday—the Notary-elect was on hand to assume his responsibilities. On April 20, when he grandiosely announced his victory to Roberts, he confessed that he had not yet fastened his "Notarial fangs" on a single document: "I am waxing a little weary of the sinecure, and my feelings are somewhat akin to those which Byron so wickedly ascribes to the widows of forty at the storming of Ismail—'They wondered when the ravishing was to begin.'" Yet since he was permitted to retain his legal practice, conducting it in conjunction with his official duties in the bank, through

[118] WI to Julia Grinnell, Madrid, December 29, 1843 (Yale); see LLWI, III, 313.

[119] PMI to Daniel Roberts, New York, January 18, 1839 (Huntington); see also National Bank of Commerce in New York: A Great American Bank (New York, 1921), pp. 12-16.

[120] PMI to Daniel Roberts, New York, January 18, 1839 (Huntington).

[121] PMI to Daniel Roberts, New York, April 20, 1839 (Huntington). PMI won on the second ballot by a vote of 11 to 3.

his mere presence he was beginning to see tangible results from his victory. "Lo! I have taken a fee!" he exulted on this same day, after collecting $2 for drawing up a simple document. "How pleasant an accession to one's consequence to have taken a first fee!"[122]

Thus giddily, Pierre celebrated his arrival in a steady and promising position. The idea of himself in a "sinecure" was perhaps a bit difficult to swallow, but with Helen content, with rooms to return to after an undemanding if uninspiring day's occupation, and with his uncle's cottage as a ready haven from city life, Pierre made himself at home. In April he offered to use his influence with Lewis Gaylord Clark to publish Roberts' "Ode to Poverty";[123] a few months later he probably had a hand in seeing William H. Seward's "Memoir of David Berdan" published at last in the *Knickerbocker*;[124] and with an income beginning to accumulate he no longer found it so necessary, as he once had, to "eschew Delmonico's." While there is no evidence that Pierre and Helen thought of living anywhere else than in New York once they had decided not to return to Toledo, it is clear that Irving had employed precisely the surest means possible to secure them in his vicinity. By helping to secure the Notaryship for Pierre he had held out before him and Helen the prospects of financial security, of city life with access to the country, and of proximity to their relatives. Four years before, as Pierre had reclined at Astor's mansion with the possibility of marriage to Helen occupying his secret thoughts, he had counselled Daniel Roberts to give over his restlessness and "be humble, be submissive & unresisting to the decrees of fate, emulate the ox in thy patience & the ass in thy ambition."[125] After his abortive foray into the West, he was back in New York to take his own advice. Fate had frustrated his plans, had brought him to the city at a time when his uncle was in particular need of his presence, and had thus made Irving keenly aware of his merit. By April 1839, the role of fate in determining the course of their relationship was over.

[122] *Ibid.* Irrepressibly, he continued: "Especially comfortable is it to think, oh greedy and unscrupulous Daniel, that this same two dollar bill, now snugly ensconced in my pocket book, is but the welcome herald and forerunner of thousands that are to come after."

[123] "Clark, the editor, would no doubt be very glad of the favor, & to your many titles to distinction as Justice of the Peace, great gun of abolition & junior wrangler on temperance, why not add the wider renown of the Manchester bard?" (PMI to Daniel Roberts, New York, April 20, 1839—Huntington). Roberts was living in Manchester, Vermont.

[124] Although there is no direct evidence of this, PMI's friendship with Clark and his eagerness several years before to see a memorial of David Berdan published render such an inference plausible. On December 21, 1838, PMI addressed a letter to Seward introducing Dr. Ebenezer Storer, the comrade of David Berdan and himself during the European tour, but he made no reference to the Berdan memoir (Historical Society of Pennsylvania).

[125] PMI to Daniel Roberts, Hell-Gate, December 11, 1835 (Huntington).

Chapter Three

Attorney and Adviser, 1839-1848

Contrary to Pierre's heady expectations, the summer of 1839 proved to be, in his words, a time of "waxing poor." After a brief period during which he signed up to eleven documents daily at the rate of seventy-five cents apiece, his business as Notary declined to the abysmal rate of one per week.[1] Having taken modest rooms in order to conserve funds, he and Helen both suffered relapses of the fever and ague, their nemesis at Toledo, which resulted in expenses that further reduced their savings. By early September Pierre was back

[1] On April 20, 1839, PMI explained to Daniel Roberts the sources of a Bank Notary's business: "His emolument comes mainly from the protest of bills & notes deposited by city Merchants, Brokers &c. with the Bank for collection, or transmitted from country institutions when made pay-able in New York. The paper discounted by such an institution as the Bank of Commerce is generally met at maturity, save in times of pressure. In such seasons I have known a Notary to have 70, 80 & sometimes 100 notes to protest in a day, which at 75 cents a piece is a tolerably fair business. In ordinary times, however, the amount rarely exceeds 10, and perhaps 7 would constitute a fair daily average; but it is supposed by the knowing in such matters that the Bank of Commerce will eventually take precedence of every other institution in the city, and yield a larger emolument to the Notary. Should such be the case, I will do my utmost to be resigned" (Huntington).

behind his desk at the Bank of Commerce, but with his signature in little demand and his investments unproductive, he was without a source of ready cash. When by coincidence he received from Daniel Roberts an unsolicited remittance of $150 in repayment of an old Jacksonville loan, he was frankly relieved. "Alas," he lamented, "the days are gone by now when I could lend to a friend! The iron grasp of the times is hard upon me." He had not as yet been forced to accept credit, he informed Roberts; but, with cavalier unconcern for metaphorical consistency, he predicted that "the hateful burden of debt" was awaiting him "if the notes do not make haste and descend in a golden shower." To acknowledge the receipt of Roberts' repayment he had pencilled an appropriate notation on a newspaper, partially erased it, and then sent it to him at a low postal rate—"a knowing trick to cheat the P.O."[2]

His contacts with Toledo since his hasty departure thence had been so consistently unpleasant that now he actually professed relief at being quit of the place. This past summer, for example, he had requested a "particular friend" there to collect a debt of $500 owed him, but after securing the money the man had refused to send it along. More recently another individual, once a Jacksonville colleague but since become a notorious philanderer, religious hypocrite, and embezzler, had boldly written him from Toledo with an overture regarding certain questionable legal business.[3] The presence of persons such as these in his former home made him feel fortunate, he remarked to Roberts, to have escaped the West suffering from no worse a malady than the fever and ague. "There is a moral contamination in the atmosphere there far more infectious than its miasma. If my wife had not got sick and driven me away, who knows but that I might have become a very respectable rascal by this time."[4] Perhaps this protestation betokened something of a sour grapes attitude in one who, having thrived at Toledo, had been separated from it against his will, yet it was not insincere. Now and afterward, Pierre was content to remain in New York.

Once he and Helen had weathered the fall of 1839, their fortunes began to improve steadily. His notarial business picked up as the Bank of Commerce increased its financial reserves, and presently his legal services also came into greater demand. In January 1840 he celebrated his brightening prospects by purchasing a large black ledger for use in keeping a record of his legal transactions,[5] and the ledger shows that in the following year, besides performing minor lawyerly duties, he argued four cases on behalf of New York mercan-

[2] PMI to Daniel Roberts, New York, September 7, 1839 (Huntington).

[3] This was one Charley Jones, whose scandalous behaviour had often been a theme in PMI's letters to Roberts during the past three years.

[4] PMI to Daniel Roberts, New York, September 7, 1839 (Huntington).

[5] On the first page of the Legal Register he wrote: "*Register/* January 13, 1840./ Pierre M. Irving."

tile firms in the city Court of Common Pleas.[6] In February he and Helen—"like the birds," as Irving put it in a letter to his nieces—were "looking out for a new nest at the approach of Spring time";[7] and after a bit of conjugal debate they settled into fashionable rooms near the centre of town. They were in no position to purchase a house, but for reasons of convenience as well as of finance they still did not care to own one. At thirty-eight, after all, neither was interested any longer in the "expensive luxury" of a family.[8] Both were fond of children, but the sons and daughters of their own fecund relations provided them with an ample opportunity to gratify that sentiment.[9] During 1841 Pierre's notarial income grew to a respectable annual rate of $1,300, and the income from his law practice rose correspondingly.[10] He was clearly making his way on his own merits by November of that year, when he encountered a windfall that went far toward assuring him further prosperity under a load of work less demanding than his present one.

In August 1841 the Bank of Commerce enjoyed a sudden boost in prestige when it was designated by the United States government the sole depository of public monies in the city of New York.[11] A further distinction came in November, when John A. Stevens, the president of the bank, was formally named the sole agent for the dispensation of federal pensions in the city.[12] In practical terms, the latter appointment meant that the duties and emoluments of the Pension Agency routinely devolved upon the bank's notary, Pierre. In addition to a steady new source of income, the position of Pension Agent entitled him to a full-time secretary and a handsome new office in the bank supplied with various amenities at the public expense. In light of this revolution in his circumstances, he was understandably expansive when, in July 1842, he summarized for Roberts the "*striking changes*"[13] in his life since he had begun to occupy what his uncle

[6] All were claims for damages on behalf of Fearings and Hall, shipping merchants. In the city directories PMI's business address was listed as 9 Nassau Street, that of the Bank of Commerce. His cousin Irving Paris, a lawyer, also had an office at that address.

[7] *Letters from Sunnyside and Spain by WI*, ed. Stanley T. Williams (New Haven, 1928), p. 5.

[8] PMI to Daniel Roberts, New York, July 26, 1842 (Huntington).

[9] For example, Helen's elder sister Jane Ann (1799-1875), who lived in Johnstown, Pennsylvania, had ten children in her family; PMI's cousin Pierre Paris Irving, who lived on Staten Island, eventually had ten in his (Frothingham, Genealogy—NYPL, MS).

[10] The amount of PMI's income is from PMI to Daniel Roberts, New York, September 26, 1842 (Huntington). He continued to argue in the New York Court of Pleas before William Inglis, a classmate of his at Columbia College; once he was retained by his cousin William Paulding to argue a case before the New York State Supreme Court (Legal Register).

[11] *National Bank of Commerce in New York*, p. 16.

[12] PMI to Daniel Roberts, New York, July 26, 1842 (Huntington).

[13] Actually, his complete characterization of his activities, as "*striking* changes & many-coloured adventures," suggests that he was mocking his own burgher-like stability.

referred to as the "nest at the bank."[14] He had every expectation, he said, of prospering "better than a certain ass of whom the fable telleth." As if to typify his expanding fortunes, his formerly slim frame had filled out to a respectable 143 pounds. If he was admittedly "getting to the down-hill side of life," he vowed that "the path before me looks as bright & cheery and promises as much enjoyment as that I have left behind." Spending five or six days weekly at the bank denied him freedom, but it gave him and his wife many comforts in return. The inveterately social Helen was busily occupied with visits to Julia Grinnell at her fine mansion in College Place, excursions to and from the Roost, or journeys to the homes of relatives even farther afield.[15] "[N]ever," Pierre concluded to Roberts, "were there two happier or more undivided hearts than 'Wife & I.'"[16]

Irving's assiduous wirepulling in 1839 had thus helped bring his nephew into a position of comfort and into unquestioned, if unexciting, prospects of sustained prosperity. Unfortunately, even though he attempted to overcome his own financial embarrassments with just as much energy as he devoted to seeking favours for relatives and friends,[17] his fiscal woes proved more persistent. In January 1840, the same month in which Pierre purchased his black ledger, Irving took up the unaccustomed task of keeping his own accounts. The entries in the small black notebook he employed for the purpose from that time until August 1841 reveal that he made a serious and for him unprecedented attempt to keep a close watch over his affairs. He even made notes of such minor expenditures as those for poultry feed and carriage equipment. Summarizing his records at the end of the twenty-month period, he calculated that his income had exceeded his outlays by $1,795.94; his total assets, including common stock, land, unpaid loans, uncollected debts, copyright property, and the cottage, he estimated at the healthy sum of $72,240.[18] Ostensibly these were good

[14] WI to PMI, Paris, June 26, 1842; *LLWI*, III, 210. On November 19, 1841, WI estimated to Sarah Storrow that PMI's new office "will make an addition to his means of about twelve hundred dollars a year besides office rent, fuel, light stationary [*sic*] &c so that he is getting up in the world" (Yale).

[15] Helen had a large circle of relatives among the Dodge family in and around Albany. She and her sister Eliza (1801-1885) also visited with their sister Jane Ann Dodge Frothingham and her family. Eliza, with whom Helen was especially close, married PMI's brother Oscar at Sunnyside on April 3, 1844; it was the second marriage for them both.

[16] PMI to Daniel Roberts, New York, July 26, 1842 (Huntington).

[17] Even before Irving Paris, the son of his sister Catharine, had passed his bar examination, WI wrote to Governor William H. Seward asking that the young man be designated Commissioner of Deeds, "to assist him in his first launch into business" (WI to Seward, Greenburgh, October 27, 1839—Rochester). In December 1839, he discovered to his embarrassment that he had requested Seward's good offices on behalf of a neighbour who was a candidate for the same county office as Lewis Irving, the eldest son of PMI's father. See WI to William H. Seward, Greenburgh, December 19, 1839, and December 20, 1839 (Rochester).

[18] This was an overliberal estimate. For example, he set a value on his Green Bay land of $4,000, which had been the purchase price four years before, prior to the

results, yet he was quite properly uncomfortable with them, since his modest cash surplus amounted to virtually his entire working capital. The rest, tied up in languishing investments or owed him by persons without means of payment, was out of reach. Necessarily living on a "cramped and diminished"[19] income while attempting to support his augmented family circle, he often found it difficult to retain his equanimity. Informing Mrs. Van Wart in December 1840 of Ebenezer's recent abandonment of his efforts to keep the importing agency afloat, Irving wrote that he had admired and envied his brother's "genial and cheerful" mood amidst those protracted trials. He himself was temperamentally unable to endure the financial pressure with such philosophy.[20] When a distant niece urged him to think of making a tour of Europe, his reply in October 1841 was abrupt: "My deal Girl *it is out of the question. I cannot consult my own wishes in this matter.*"[21] By his own wish, after all, he had assembled a group of dependents for whom he must find means to play the breadwinner.

Irving was of too mercurial a temperament to succumb to a dark mood for many days at a time, however, and the daily pleasure he took in his country estate went far to offset his anxieties. "What a lucky hit it was," he wrote in September 1842, "my building that little mansion which proves such a precious family retreat for old and young. It was indeed a real blessing scratched out of the midst of insubstantial speculations."[22] Appropriately, in 1841 he had re-christened the Roost "Sunnyside,"[23] the name by which it was to be known thereafter. The vicinity of the cottage was rapidly altering in character from a sleepy rural community to an exurban colony of well-to-do New York families. Irving thought it "one of the most agreeable neighborhoods" he had "ever resided in." His own nieces faithfully attended the "delightful little parties" given by his elegant neighbour Mrs. Colford Jones and her flighty daughters; but, he assured Mrs. Van Wart, we "have picnic parties also"[24] along the river bank. He found the means to maintain a handsome carriage for morning calls, and he was active

depression. "Copyright property," the disposal of which he was to bungle the following year, he held at $15,000. An accurate valuation of WI's assets at this time would have been nearer $40,000 than $72,400 (WI, Account Book, 1840-1841—NYPL, MS).

[19] WI to Mrs. Thomas W. Storrow, New York, October 3, 1841; *Letters from Sunnyside and Spain,* p. 38.

[20] WI was speaking more particularly of Ebenezer's religious faith, "that indwelling source of consolation and enjoyment, which appears to have a happier effect than all the maxims of philosophy or the lessons of worldly wisdom" (*LLWI,* III, 156-57). Following the retirement of Ebenezer, the business was taken over by Irving Van Wart, who restored it to prosperity.

[21] WI to Mrs. Thomas W. Storrow, New York, October 3, 1841; *Letters from Sunnyside and Spain,* p. 37.

[22] WI to Mrs. Catharine Paris, Madrid, September 2, 1842 (Yale).

[23] Cater, "WI and SS," p. 140.

[24] WI to Mrs. Sarah Van Wart, [SS], November 25, 1840; *LLWI,* III, 154. "Mrs. Colford Jones" is mentioned frequently in WI's letters describing life at SS during this period. See *Letters from Sunnyside and Spain,* pp. 12-14, 18-22.

in devising plans for future vegetable gardens, stables, and refinements of landscaping. He had mixed feelings in May 1841, when his niece Sarah Paris married Thomas W. Storrow, Jr., and removed with him to live in France. She had been a favourite, and he likened his sentiments upon her departure to those of a parent separated from one of his children by her marriage.[25] "But this is a world of changes,"[26] he reflected. Besides, in Helen and "Julia Sanders," the delicate wife of his nephew Sanders Irving,[27] he had two other charming nieces who understood his ways, and of course Ebenezer's quiet daughters were devoted to him. A few months after Sarah's departure he wrote to her that during a recent illness his occasional fears of ever becoming a burden to others had been dispelled: "I feel that I have affectionate, tender-hearted beings about me, that would be to me like children, and love and cherish me the more for my very infirmities." Thus in September 1841, having lived at "the dear little cottage" for five years, he was awkwardly at a loss for money but nonetheless "in the happiest of moods."[28]

The arrangement with Lewis Gaylord Clark to contribute regularly to the *Knickerbocker* had been convenient as providing a steady source of funds, but Irving had not been surprised to discover that the "monthly recurring task"[29] of producing copy for the magazine did not agree with him. Besides, for all his geniality Clark tended to be behindhand in his quarterly payments.[30] In April 1840, after a year's connection with the publication, Irving told Pierre that he believed he could earn more money by suspending this work on ephemeral items of article length and "taking [his] time to collect [his] writings into volumes."[31] He failed to act on this belief for an entire year, however.

[25] Sarah and her mother moved into the Roost in 1836. Apparently they returned each winter to the home of Ebenezer in Bridge Street (MS Outline, Chapters 66, 67 [1836, 1837]).

[26] WI to Sarah Van Wart, n.p., n.d.; *LLWI*, III, 160; see also *Life*, II, 98.

[27] Julia Granger ("Sanders") Irving (1822-1897), a wealthy, delicate blond from upstate New York, married Sanders (1813-1884), the fourth son of Ebenezer, in 1840, and quickly became a favourite of WI. (Compilation of Information obtained through interviews with Catharine Ann [McLinden] Richardson on April 9, 18, 1957—typescript, SHR; cited hereafter as McLinden Interview.) She was called "Julia Sanders" to distinguish her from "Julia Irving," one of Ebenezer's daughters, and from "Julia"—that is, Julia Irving Grinnell, PMI's sister. Similarly, WI sometimes referred to PMI's wife as "Helen Pierre" in order to distinguish her from "Helen Treat," the wife of John Treat Irving, Jr. (1812-1906), and various other Helens in the family. The tendency among the Irving, Paulding, Paris, Sanders, Dodge, Storrow, and Van Wart families to name their children from only a small budget of names created an acute need for nicknames.

[28] WI to Sarah Storrow, SS, September 1, 1841; *LLWI*, III, 171, 172.

[29] WI to PMI, n.p., April 1840; *LLWI*, III, 152.

[30] *LLWI*, III, 152. Reckoning his assets in August 1841, WI included $1,000 owed him by Clark (Account Book, 1840-1841—NYPL, MS).

[31] *LLWI*, III, 152. No doubt WI was regularly in touch with PMI concerning his contributions to the *Knickerbocker*. Late in 1839 he mentioned in a letter to Clark that "The Bermudas: A Shakespearian Research," an article of his to be published in the

During that period he did scribble a brief biographical volume on Oliver Goldsmith for Harper's voluminous Family Library, but he also allowed himself to be sidetracked into writing a short life of the tubercular poetess Margaret Miller Davidson. The task of preparing this cloying feast of sentimentality gave him much personal satisfaction, for he found the story of Miss Davidson's short life "most affecting";[32] but since he transferred the copyright on the work to the girl's mother, the rewards he derived from its publication were spiritual only. When he severed his relationship with the *Knickerbocker* in the spring of 1841, he thus felt redoubled pressure to earn money by his writing. Owing to spells of moodiness and inertia, it was not until October that he resumed work on two pet projects which for several years past he had been considering as possibilities—a life of George Washington and an interconnected series of "legends" dealing with the Moorish conquest of Spain; but once he began to busy himself in preliminary operations with these, his depression and worries disappeared. In December 1841, he wrote to Sarah Storrow at Paris apologizing for the desponding tone in his letters of recent months and expressing relief that his "mental force and buoyancy" had returned: "Thank God, the very pressure of affairs has produced reaction; a stout heart, not yet worn out, has rallied up to the emergency, and I am now in a complete state of literary activity." Tangible results from this activity would not be forthcoming very soon, but he was willing to bide his time. "I shall keep on without flagging or flinching," he said, "as long as health and good spirits are continued to me."[33] At the close of 1841, therefore, he was sanguine about the future. At just about this time, of course, Pierre received his appointment as the federal Pension Agent for the city of New York. The Christmas celebration at Sunnyside, enlivened by "music and dancing," was one of the best in years. "It does not take much to make a fete in our simple little establishment,"[34] Irving observed in a letter to Sarah Storrow.

Between the time when Pierre took up his duties at the Bank of Commerce and December 1841, he and Irving saw each other only at intervals—ordinarily on Irving's irregular visits to the city, when he often stopped at his nephew's office, or on holidays, when Pierre and Helen came to the country. The most regular communication between the two was at second-hand—by correspondence, or else through messages carried by Helen and other commuters between the cottage and New York. Although their relationship had grown rapidly closer in the first few months following Pierre's return from Toledo, thereafter it was to develop at a slower pace over several years. Pierre con-

Knickerbocker for January 1840, "must be at the lodgings of my nephew Pierre, as I left it with his wife just before departing from town" (Clark, "Recollections," p. 553).

[32] WI to Sarah Van Wart, [SS], n.d.; *LLWI*, III, 157. The *Biography and Poetical Remains of the Late Margaret Miller Davidson* appeared in the spring of 1841.

[33] *LLWI*, III, 175.

[34] WI to Sarah Storrow, SS, December 26, 1841 (Yale).

tinued to supervise certain of his uncle's landed investments—those in Toledo and Milwaukee—but Irving was managing his other holdings by himself. He did put faith in Pierre's business judgment and he also confided in him about his literary plans, but he clearly valued his own views more highly than advice solicited from his nephew or volunteered by him. As the seven-year agreement with Messrs. Carey and Lea (now Lea and Blanchard) for the copyright to his published works neared its termination in April 1842, he discussed with Pierre the possibility of negotiating a new contract wherein he would undertake to produce a thorough revision of his works. These consultations were not extensive, however, and he did not see fit to inform his nephew of the intentions he at length formed in the matter. Almost pointedly, it would seem, he was maintaining a posture of independent reliance on his own counsel. When he did begin negotiations with the publishers, he did so entirely on his own, thus tacitly relieving Ebenezer of the duties as his agent which the latter had ably performed for over twenty years. For some reason, even though he knew that the American literary market was still depressed,[35] he regarded Pierre's suggestion that he ask a correspondingly modest sum from Lea and Blanchard as timorous. Instead, he boldly demanded $3,000 per year for the copyright—and was quickly refused. He then moderated the figure to $2,500—and was again refused.[36] In short, acting as his own agent Irving proved a dismal failure as a negotiator; and once his contract with the publishers expired it went unrenewed.[37]

During the winter of 1841-1842 Irving made an extended visit to New York in order to pursue research for his biography of George Washington. Ordinarily he worked at the New York Society Library, and since this was located within a short stroll of the Bank of Commerce he often stopped at Pierre's office for a morning's chat. When he entered the office on February 10, 1842, however, he had more on his mind than a few minutes' casual conversation, for less than an hour before he had been informed of his appointment by President Tyler as United States Minister to Spain. He was excited at this sudden and entirely unexpected opportunity, yet also disturbed, and he needed to discuss it with someone. His mind was deeply divided. As Pierre recalled him, pacing "up and down, revolving the prospect of a separation from home and home scenes, he appeared less impressed with the distinction conferred, than alive to the pain of such an

[35] For a discussion of literary economics during this period, see "American Romanticism and the Depression of 1837," in *The Papers of William Charvat*, ed. M. J. Bruccoli (Columbus, 1968), 49-67.

[36] WI to Messrs. Lea and Blanchard, SS, February 26, 1842 (Harvard); WI to Messrs. Lea and Blanchard, New York, March 10, 1842 (Harvard).

[37] It was not until December 31, 1846, that WI admitted to PMI the reason for his failure to strike a bargain, or even confided to him the amounts he had asked. By that time he was prepared to confess that he had demanded a sum "much higher than they [Lea and Blanchard] could have afforded to give with advantage" (*LLWI*, III, 396).

exile."[38] Accepting the appointment would not merely remove him from home; it might also interfere with the progress of his two literary projects. Ironically, the offer of the Ministership and its handsome salary had come at a time when, though still constrained as to expenses, he was confident of his ability to extricate himself from financial difficulty singlehanded. Yet the position would have undeniable advantages. Its annual salary of $9,000 would be a princely supplement to his present meagre income. Then, too, to hold the post of Minister in a country where he had won reputation as a literary man would be a distinct honour.[39] Of the countries of Europe he had visited, none had engaged his imagination so deeply or given him so much pleasure as Spain, and he would be glad to revisit it. As for the pains of absence, he was too familiar with the spoils system in the United States to suppose that his tenure as Minister would be unduly long. All told, he decided that the advantages of the proffered Ministership warranted his leaving home. "It is hard—very hard," he thought out loud to Pierre—adding with ironic acknowledgment of his good fortune, "yet I must try to bear it. *God tempers the wind to the shorn lamb.*" The decision to suspend his literary plans had not, however, been either immediate or easy. Pierre later expressed the view that Irving "would have declined [the appointment], but for a confident belief that a diplomatic residence at Madrid need work no interruption to his Life of Washington, the literary task upon which he had now set his heart."[40]

As Pierre's retrospective judgment suggests, Irving accepted the Ministership assuming that he would enjoy ample leisure amidst his official duties to continue writing. Consequently, prominent among his preparations after returning a letter of acceptance to President Tyler on February 18 were gathering together his notes on Washington, hurriedly dispatching inquiries to elderly individuals who might supply him with first-hand recollections of the Revolutionary era,[41] assembling his notes on the conquest of Spain, and even hunting up copies of his published works for possible revision abroad. Yet as he hurried back and forth between Sunnyside, New York, and Washington, he was already discovering that the position of Minister-designate carried with it a set of obligations and problems which

[38] *LLWI*, III, 176.

[39] PMI wrote in *LLWI*: "At a later period, and in a different mood, he spoke of this appointment to me as 'the crowning honor of his life'" (III, 176).

[40] *LLWI*, III, 176-77. According to Stanley T. Williams, on the day when WI received notice of his appointment as Minister there "was no struggle in his mind" whether to accept it (*Life*, II, 113). Basing his view on a statement by Thurlow Weed in his *Autobiography* (Boston, 1884), pp. 626-27, Williams goes so far as to contend that the Ministership came as no surprise to WI and even to speculate that his influential son-in-law Moses Grinnell helped procure the position (II, 112).

[41] For example, on April 10, 1842, he wrote to General Morgan Lewis (1754-1844), a Revolutionary officer, requesting assistance with the task which he proposed to "finish while in Spain." He was especially eager, he said, to receive "personal recollections" and "interesting documents" concerning Washington (SHR).

exacted much time and thought. For example, he encountered difficulty in assembling his staff. First disappointed at his failure to secure
Joseph Green Cogswell as Secretary of Legation, he recommended
Alexander Hamilton, Jr., nephew of his neighbour Colonel John C.
Hamilton, for the position; but it was only after protracted wrangling
necessitated by Hamilton's unsuitable political sympathies that he
succeeded in having him confirmed.[42] Once achieved, this appointment was very satisfactory. "It will be like taking a bit of home with
me," he said to Hamilton's mother.[43] Probably from similar motives
he secured as attachés two sons of old friends: Carson Brevoort, son of
Henry Brevoort, Jr., his comrade of *Knickerbocker* days, and Hector
Ames, son of the New York industrialist Barrett Ames.[44]

Before he would be free to leave, of course, Irving must also
delegate the responsibility for his home affairs. On February 17 he
wrote to Ebenezer that he would need to re-assume the role of
paterfamilias, as at Bridge Street, and add to it that of country gentleman. "You will find, in my little library, books about gardening,
farming, poultry, &c., by which to direct yourself. The management of
the place will give you healthful and cheerful occupation, and will be
as much occupation as you want."[45] However, Ebenezer's role as
substitute "laird of Sunnyside" was to be titular only, for on April 6
Irving entrusted the purse-strings to Pierre, giving him a full power of
attorney during his absence.[46] Now, with his preparations complete,
he looked forward to an interlude of diplomacy that promised to be an
advantageous investment toward an untroubled old age. Having
amassed a fund of literary capital while in Spain, he hoped to return
"with money in both pockets, be able to 'burn the candle at both
ends,' and put up as many weathercocks"[47] as he pleased. On
April 10, 1842, shortly after his fifty-ninth birthday, he sailed from
New York to begin his diplomatic career.

[42] At the eleventh hour Cogswell was induced to remain in New York by John
Jacob Astor, who indicated willingness to proceed with plans to establish a public
library in New York provided the bibliographer would remain to superintend it; see
below, pp. 109, 227. However, in a letter to Daniel Webster, the Secretary of State, WI
wrote on April 2, 1842, that Cogswell had not been his first choice. Hamilton, he
claimed, was "the person I had originally in view, when I was induced to give the
preference to Mr. Cogswell in compliance with the wishes of Mr. Legare" (Virginia). See
WI to Hugh S. Legare, New York, March 28, 1842 (Maine Historical Society); WI to John
Tyler, New York, March 28, 1842 (SHR).

[43] *LLWI*, III, 182.

[44] Hamilton proved to be the favourite among WI's three assistants. On June 24,
1843, he wrote from Madrid to Sarah Storrow: "Hamilton & myself get on very easily
together. He is an excellent companion; cheerful, animated, amiable and full of intelligence & information" (Yale). See also WI to Sarah Storrow, Madrid, March 8, 1844
(Yale); *Irving to Brevoort*, pp. 451-52.

[45] *LLWI*, III, 179.

[46] This document is at the University of Virginia. On April 7 WI wrote to
Ebenezer's daughter Sarah informing her that he had made arrangements with PMI for
money to be advanced to the girls as necessary (*LLWI*, III, 192).

[47] WI to Ebenezer Irving, n.p., February 17, 1842; *LLWI*, III, 80.

Irving did not formally assume responsibility for the embassy at Madrid from his predecessor, Aaron Vail, until August, and in the interim before taking up his duties he sought to amuse himself in travel and visits with his relatives in England and France. During this period he dispatched a steady stream of letters to the family in New York, in which messages he established a pattern of ambivalence toward his presence in Europe that was to remain essentially unaltered throughout his stay. He had been eager to revisit his old haunts, but upon arriving there he found them changed, barren of the human associations they had once possessed for him. They were no longer novel, and repeatedly they put him in mind of Peter. "There is one little, quiet, conventual garden, with shady walks, and shrubberies, and seats, behind the old Gothic church of St. Ouen, at Rouen," he wrote to his sister Sarah early in June, "which used to be his favorite resort during his solitary residence in that city, and where he used to pass his mornings with his book, amusing himself with the groups of loungers and of nursery maids and children."[48] With such memories crowding upon him, he was glad to spend weeks with the Van Warts at Birmingham and with Sarah Storrow and her handsome husband at Paris. And yet, even as he was welcomed to these households he could not help remembering Sunnyside. Once he wrote to Helen that it "seems to me as if I did not half enough appreciate that home when I was there."[49] Upon returning to Spain his feelings were divided, and for a time the ancient land failed to capture him as it had done years before. He was comfortable in his elegant quarters, with three bright, admiring assistants to enliven the household, but most of his old Spanish friends were dead or gone away. Upon unexpectedly hearing from Prince Dmitri Dolgorouki, a former fellow-campaigner in Madrid, he wrote back in October that "either I am or the place is greatly changed, for we seem to be quite strange to each other."[50] Yet as he became more fully occupied with the duties of his office, his interest in the volatile state of Spanish politics and his pleasure at forming a new circle of acquaintances frequently made him forget his moods. He held firmly to only one sentiment: he was determined to "open a literary campaign"[51] as soon as his arrangements would allow.

In the first letters he addressed to Pierre and Helen from Europe Irving also set thematic patterns which persisted in his correspondence with them throughout his four-year stay there. To Helen he wrote of domestic affairs at Madrid, gossiped about events and personages at Sunnyside, and gave narrative reviews of Spanish history or of the official functions he had attended; to Pierre he ordinarily dealt with his business affairs and his literary aspirations. On occasion, as in a letter dated June 26, 1842, he enclosed two such diverse

---

[48] WI to Sarah Van Wart, Paris, June 8, 1842; *LLWI,* III, 204.

[49] WI to Helen Irving, [Madrid], September 4, 1842; *LLWI,* III, 245.

[50] *LLWI,* III, 252.

[51] WI to PMI, [Madrid], September 5, 1842; *LLWI,* III, 245. See also III, 224.

messages within a single cover. In this instance, the body of the letter began with an expression of appreciation to Pierre for his "kind attention to my pecuniary affairs," and the postscript to Helen began with an avowal of the "avidity and relish" with which he had read her "merest gossip about home."[52] From time to time he sent his nephew general instructions as to the ways in which his investments should be managed. For example, upon learning that his last hopes of an arrangement to reprint his works had been extinguished, on September 5 he wrote that Pierre should supervise the "home resources" with caution: "Get all my funds, as soon as you can judiciously, out of these fluctuating stocks, and invest them safely, even though at less interest."[53] Notwithstanding the firm tone of this directive, he of course left all the details of implementing it to Pierre's discretion. Pierre was the only member of the family to whom he regularly wrote, not in sentimental terms of his lonesomeness for "sweet little Sunnyside,"[54] but in terms of the tactics through which he hoped to maintain the place. In order to learn more of his "Madrid concerns," he once wrote, Pierre might want to read the letters received from him by other persons: "I have little to say to you on that head, not being able, like Paganini, to play a thousand variations on one string of my fiddle."[55]

Pierre and Helen received news of Irving in the letters sent home from Madrid by Alexander Hamilton,[56] and also in those of Sarah Storrow, who relayed the substance of her uncle's frequent messages to her. Regular visits to Sunnyside enabled Helen to become one of Irving's most dependable retailers of news from that quarter. On November 12, 1842, he wrote to Sarah Storrow that he had just received a "long letter" from Helen, "two sheets full, closely written. I have just read a page and a half and put it by as a bonne bouche after I have dispatched my letters by the courier."[57] At about this time Pierre confessed to another correspondent that his "growing aversion to letter-writing" stamped him as "the shabbiest of mortals,"[58] but at least he managed to keep his uncle informed of the transactions that concerned him. Meanwhile, although his routine as Pension Agent was as yet somewhat unfamiliar and time-consuming,[59] he had re-

[52] *LLWI*, III, 210, 211.

[53] *LLWI*, III, 245. Ebenezer had conducted further negotiations in WI's absence, but apparently not as a person empowered to make any arrangements he thought best; see III, 228.

[54] WI to Sarah Irving, Paris, May 29, 1842; *LLWI*, III, 205.

[55] WI to PMI, Madrid, September 5, 1842; *LLWI*, III, 245.

[56] Conversely, WI had news of PMI and Helen and the inhabitants of SS from the letters sent to Hamilton by his sister Mary. A file of correspondence between members of the Hamilton family during the Ministership of WI is at SHR.

[57] WI to Sarah Storrow, Madrid, November 12, 1842 (Yale).

[58] PMI to Daniel Roberts, New York, July 26, 1842 (Huntington).

[59] Apparently it made inroads on the time PMI devoted to his legal practice. His entries for 1842 in his Legal Register show only two cases argued before the New York Court of Common Pleas and one before the State Supreme Court.

cently acquired a sturdy iron safe, a "convenient fixture"[60] for his office and probably also something of a private symbol of his prosperity. Often during the summer he and Helen visited Julia Grinnell at her rented home at Throgg's Neck, on the Hudson a few miles north of the city. Moses Grinnell, no longer a Congressman but still an active partner in Grinnell, Minturn & Co., had taken this estate as a place of resort for his irregular intervals of leisure, and in the afternoons Pierre and Helen accompanied him in his shipping magnate's recreation of sailing the river in a well-appointed yacht.[61] Pierre was no longer in contact with most of his friends in the West except when they chanced to be in town. He did hear occasionally from James Berdan, who was now thoroughly reformed and prospering, but prolonged separation and his own lax habits of correspondence were causing him to lose touch with Roberts and Longfellow.[62] In June 1842, even Irving found it necessary to urge him to "write often."[63]

In granting a temporary power of attorney to Pierre, Irving had given him a broad mandate to conduct all his financial and legal affairs. However, Pierre apparently interpreted his responsibilities as extending beyond the strict duties of his office, for in September 1842, confronted with what he thought was an outrage against his uncle's good name, he strode forth as the defender of his reputation. Reading in *Graham's Magazine* a review of Walter Scott's *Critical and Miscellaneous Writings* written by the Reverend Rufus W. Griswold, recently the editor of an influential anthology entitled *The Poets and Poetry of America* and in a few years to win fame as the posthumous nemesis of Edgar Allan Poe, Pierre encountered a passage wherein Griswold remarked sarcastically upon the "modesty" of Scott's puffing reviews of his own writings, and then added: "Washington Irving has done the same thing, in writing laudatory notices of his own works for the reviews, and like Scott, received pay for whitewashing himself." Disingenuously, Griswold softened the accusation by disclaiming any "great injustice" in Irving's act of self-praise—except, of course, that he had demanded and received money for his contributions.[64]

---

[60] See WI to PMI, Madrid, June 26, 1842; *LLWI*, III, 210. WI quotes the phrase as from a letter of PMI's dated May 31, 1842.

[61] See *LLWI*, III, 248-49. During the 1840's the Grinnells regularly rented a summer residence in the vicinity of SS. See WI to Sarah Storrow, SS, May 25, 1841 (Yale).

[62] PMI's letter to Daniel Roberts of July 26, 1842 (see footnote 58), prompted by a business inquiry from Roberts, was the first he had written to his friend in almost three years. Appropriately, he began his reply: "Did you ever hear of a Ghost weighing 143 pounds? Then am I no ghost, but a living breathing, corpulent piece of flesh & blood . . . beating as kindly & loyally towards you as ever. It must be confessed, however, that I have given no great proof of any very tender recollection of late, & if I be not deceased myself, a strong savour of mortality has gathered around our correspondence" (Huntington). It took six years for PMI to write Roberts again; and again the letter was to be prompted by the necessity of business.

[63] *LLWI*, III, 211.

[64] *Graham's Magazine*, 21 (October 1842), 218-19. Griswold may have been influenced in his view of WI by hostile comments in a letter he had received from James Fenimore Cooper, dated August 7, 1842. See *Passages from the Correspondence of Rufus W. Griswold* (Cambridge, Mass., 1898), p. 114.

Upon reading this "coarse aspersion,"[65] as he later termed it, Pierre was incensed. He immediately wrote to the reviewer with the following stern challenge:

> As Mr Irving is not in the country to meet so degrading a charge with the instant denial it would otherwise receive at his hands, permit me, as his nephew, before I communicate with him on the subject, to ask from you your authority for the statement, with a specific reference to the number, title and page of the Reviews containing the laudatory notices in question.[66]

A flurry of correspondence ensued in which Griswold held forth as evidence the report of an unnamed English gentleman that "Mr. Irving wrote the articles in the *Quarterly Review*, on the Life of Columbus, and the Chronicles of Granada." After completing a hasty bit of research, Pierre replied with dignity that the *Quarterly Review* had never published a review of Columbus, "'laudatory' or otherwise," and that its review of *Granada*—in the issue for May 1830—"had not a commendatory expression of the work or its author, or a single sentence that might not have come from the pen of Mr. Irving without the slightest impeachment of his delicacy." Pierre was in fact uncertain at this point whether Irving actually had written the article, let alone been paid for it. He presented a bold face, however, insisting that even if it was a self-review "it was not, at any rate, a self-eulogy," and appealing to Griswold's "sense of equity"[67] whether he should not therefore reconsider his slur against Irving's character. On October 13 Griswold concluded the interchange by promising, on the whole falsely, to retract his statement in the next possible issue of *Graham's*.[68]

In the midst of his correspondence with Griswold, Pierre sent to Irving a letter summarizing the affair thus far, enclosing a copy of the offending excerpt from the magazine and also of the editor's first reply, and requesting a brief statement of the facts for possible publication, should that step prove necessary. His letter did not arrive in Madrid until November 12, weeks after the dispute had been resolved, but upon receiving it Irving immediately wrote out a reply stoutly vindicating himself from Griswold's implication that he was the corrupt creature of a European journal.[69] Five days later he wrote again, pointing out occasions when for reasons of personal honour or

---

[65] *LLWI*, III, 265.

[66] PMI to Rufus W. Griswold, New York, September 29, 1842 (Historical Society of Pennsylvania).

[67] *LLWI*, III, 265-66.

[68] In the December issue of *Graham's* Griswold recalled his "allusion to reviews of various publications of Mr. Washington Irving, which we had good reason for believing were written by that gentleman himself. We learn with pleasure, from one who speaks on the subject with authority, that Mr. Irving is guiltless of the imputed self-laudation. He did indeed write the article in the London Quarterly on his 'Chronicles of Granada,' and received for it the sum we mentioned; but, like so many of the modern 'reviews,' it had very little relation to the work which gave it a title, or to its author" (334).

[69] *LLWI*, III, 267-69.

national allegiance he had refused to associate himself in any way with journals hostile in policy toward the United States. He did not deny writing the essay on *The Conquest of Granada* and receiving payment for it, for he did not believe that these facts were in any sense dishonourable. He suggested to Pierre that it might be prudent to reprint the essay in the *Knickerbocker* so as to allow the public to judge whether he had actually puffed himself. Yet, despite the prompt and careful attention he gave to the short-lived Griswold affair, he was not in fact particularly shocked or worried by such a "paltry attack."[70] Recently, he had learned, his frankness in acknowledging dependence on secondary sources in *Columbus* had publicly and falsely been challenged.[71] "I must expect attacks of this and other kinds now," he wrote Pierre in a postscript to his letter of November 17. "I have been so long before the public, that the only way to make anything now out of me is to *cut me up.*"[72]

On November 12, the day when he received and first replied to Pierre's account of the Griswold embroilment, Irving opened a second letter, from Helen, which contained more agreeable news. "I cannot suffer your long, delightful letter to remain unacknowledged," he replied to her on the same day. "It fills my heart to the very brim, and with the very best of good feelings; and then, your details about sweet little Sunnyside—God bless my dear little cottage!—what a treasure of comfort and enjoyment it is to me!" He had just been reading his nephew's "indignant" message, he said: "Don't tell Pierre, but absolutely he had put himself in such a passion . . . that I found all the indignation appurtenant to the matter was done to my hand, so I retained the smoothness of my temper without a wrinkle." His own allegedly unsavoury past as a writer merely supplied him with material for self-mockery. Now that he was standing among kings, he wrote, "I begin to think I'll give out that I am not the Washington Irving that wrote that farrago of literature they are occasionally cutting up, and that I have never followed any line of life but diplomacy, nor written anything but despatches."[73]

Fortunately for Pierre's equanimity, in the next three years no further "aspersions" rose up requiring his attention. His own life also followed an even routine. Late in 1842 the Bank of Commerce moved its offices to larger quarters in Wall Street,[74] and in the following year

[70] *LLWI*, III, 272. On November 12, 1842, WI wrote to Sarah Storrow: "I enclose a letter from to [*sic*] Pierre M. Irving, in reply to a long one about a paltry attack on me in an American magazine, which put honest Pierre in a great rage; but never ruffled my tranquillity, as I happened to be able to give a complete contradiction" (Yale).

[71] For a summary of the challenge and of subsequent publications in the controversy it excited, see Anon., "Mr. Washington Irving, Mr. Navarrete, and the Knickerbocker," *Southern Literary Messenger*, 8 (November 1842), 725-35.

[72] *LLWI*, III, 269.

[73] *LLWI*, III, 270-71; see also III, 269.

[74] From this time until 1854 it was located at 32 Wall Street, near the corner of Nassau Avenue (*National Bank of Commerce*, p. 15). For a time the United States Pension Office was at 15-1/2 Wall, but presently it was moved into the main bank building.

he and Helen took a new residence in a still more fashionable boarding house, one in Broadway.[75] He saw to it that his name was listed in the city directory among the practising attorneys-at-law, but he was not very busy as a lawyer. Such cases as he did accept were usually on behalf of the bank, or its president, John A. Stevens, or close acquaintances such as Henry Holdrege, Jr., a near neighbour to Sunnyside.[76] His duties as Pension Agent, which consisted primarily of determining the eligibility of claimants and of dispensing appropriate amounts to them, were dull and dry,[77] and the essential requisite of his Notaryship was only the most modest of talents, the ability to write his signature. Yet he had been under no illusions that this was the line of work he had been hoping for, and besides, it was not uniformly sterile. While as a minor officer of the bank he played no part in directing its policies,[78] he did enjoy access to commercial information that was useful to him personally. Under tow by Helen, he made periodic calls on the Grinnells and the group at Sunnyside and also frequented more pretending circles of New York society. One summer he and Helen traveled south to Yadkin County, North Carolina, where they visited her brother James Dodge at his country residence.[79] More regularly, however, Helen paid calls on her own or accompanied by her sister Eliza. In September 1843, for example, she was on an extended visit to Sunnyside[80] and was busy attending ice-cream "sociables" with Kate, Charlotte, and Sarah.[81] A few

[75] The New York City Directory for 1844 & 1845, p. 181.

[76] In 1843 he represented his elder brother Lewis in a damages suit before the State Supreme Court; in 1844 and again in 1845 he represented John A. Stevens, President of the Bank of Commerce, before the Court of Common Pleas; in 1845 he defended Henry Holdrege, Jr., in a large damages suit before this court; and in 1847 he represented his cousin, Thomas W. Storrow, Jr., in the same court (Legal Register). Only a small proportion of PMI's legal practice seems to have been devoted to court cases.

[77] A few examples of PMI's work as Pension Agent survive. On June 2, 1845, he wrote to A. Carrington, the Controller at Hartford, Connecticut, requesting him to certify the service of one James Weed in the United States Coast Guard during 1781 and 1782. His object was "to prove the duration of the service" in order to determine the pension owing to Weed's widow. On June 19, he wrote again to Carrington complaining that the documents forwarded to him pertained to a Lieutenant Weed rather than to the person in question, who had been a private. PMI requested either a corrected record or a statement that the record had been lost (Virginia). See also PMI to Henry M. Morfit, New York, August 10, 1844 (Yale); Pierre M. Irving to Henry M. Morfit, New York, November 27, 1844 (Library of Congress).

[78] PMI was not a member of the Board of Directors, but he was one of the three officers listed under the Bank of Commerce in the annual city directories. The other two were the President and the Cashier.

[79] Dodge (1795-1880) was a prominent lawyer in this vicinity and a gentleman of letters. In 1836 he married Susan Williams, a daughter of a prominent resident of Huntsville, North Carolina, and despite regular visits to New York he made his home in North Carolina afterward (Frothingham, Genealogy—NYPL, MS). See also John W. Moore, History of North Carolina (Raleigh, 1900), II, 135.

[80] SS thrived under the watchful eye of Ebenezer. After a visit with the Irvings their neighbour Mary Hamilton wrote to her brother at Madrid on December 24, 1843, that she had never seen "a house more neat & orderly than theirs is, silver bright" (SHR).

[81] Mary Hamilton to Alexander Hamilton, n.p., September 14, 1843 (SHR).

months later she was obliged to suspend her socializing in order to undergo surgery to correct a long-standing and bothersome condition of an at present undeterminable kind. The operation, at any rate, was a total success; and as Pierre reported to Irving shortly afterward, his ebullient wife was "so elated" at its result "that she can scarce think of anything else."[82]

Irving repeatedly expressed appreciation to Pierre for his various good offices. Upon learning early in 1844 that his nephew had salvaged approximately one-half of the capital from the ill-fated investment in Green Bay—that "sanguine speculation"—he was delighted to see even this shrunken remnant. "It is so much money," he wrote with satisfaction, "that will yield me interest during my lifetime, instead of producing a possible profit after my death."[83] At about this time he reported to Mrs. Paris that Pierre had handled his affairs with "great judgment," adding that he was "an invaluable friend and standby, on whom I feel that I can rely with the most entire confidence, as he serves me through affection, not interest. He comes next to my dear brothers in that full communion of heart and soul which is the invincible bond of kindred."[84]

The steady inflow of funds was especially welcome to Irving during 1843 and 1844, for he was finding himself unable to realize the literary aims he had been resolute to pursue. For almost the whole of 1843 he was incapacitated by a painful inflammation of the ankles, a nervous condition which precluded the mental strain of composition. As late as March 1844 he wrote to Pierre that he was still obliged to "exercise the pen sparingly, as I find literary excitement produces irritation in my complaint."[85] Then, too, his official duties would have left him scarcely any free time even had his health enabled him to work. Upon accepting the Ministership he had failed to realize that the result of the precarious state of Spanish politics would be his preparing official dispatches to weariness. In the spring of 1844, as his health showed signs of returning, he wrote beseechingly to Moses Grinnell asking whether he might not be transferred to some diplomatic post which placed lighter demands on his time,[86] but nothing was to come of this forlorn wish. On May 15 he felt himself ready "to resume the occasional exercise of my pen," yet only three days later, swept up into the duties of his office, he wrote bitterly to Sarah

[82] WI to Sarah Storrow, Madrid, April 27, 1844 (Yale); WI is reporting news received from PMI. In his response to PMI's announcement, WI invoked a blessing upon all surgeons: "I am rejoiced to find . . . [Helen] is completely recovered and was to receive but one more visit from Dr. Mott. I can easily conceive the sufferings she has derived from the late operation. God bless these Surgeons and Dentists! May their good deeds be returned upon them a thousand fold; may they have the felicity in the next world to have successful operations performed upon them to all eternity!" (WI to PMI, [Madrid], June 14, 1844; quoted in PMI, MS Outline, Chapter 77 [1844]).

[83] WI to PMI, Madrid, March 24, 1844; *LLWI*, III, 332-33.

[84] WI to Mrs. Catharine Paris, Madrid, March 23, 1844 (Yale).

[85] *LLWI*, III, 333.

[86] *Life*, II, 198-99.

Storrow that he was "wearied and at times heartsick of the wretched politics of this country."[87] His disillusionment with Spanish politics was of course compounded with frustration that it interfered so tyrannically with his own inclinations. Late in April he had confessed to Sarah that even though the letters from Pierre were "encouraging as to the influence the return of 'good times'" would have on his means, he was pessimistic about the prospect of financial security:

> I fear . . . it will be a good while before I can realize much income from my property, and I do not see any likelihood of realizing sufficient to enable me to return home and be independent of the fagging of the pen. Bachelor as I am, I have too large a family now to provide for: and, if it were not for *diplomacy,* I do not know what would become of us. However, as Theodore [Ebenezer's son, now a minister in the Protestant Episcopal Church] says, 'the Heavenly Father' has ordered things wonderfully for us; so I am humbly thankful—and bless *Uncle Sam* into the bargain.[88]

He was to take up his life of Washington at intervals during this year and again in 1845, but he made no significant progress on it until after he had returned to the United States.

Irving's failure to supplement his income through literary production had little moderating effect on his expenditures while in Europe. On the contrary, the bullish reports he received from Pierre impelled him toward prodigality extending even beyond his generous Ministerial allowance, until this tendency became a source of amusement between him and Helen. In April 1844, fresh upon learning of the funds reclaimed from the Green Bay fiasco, he informed her that Pierre's "flourishing accounts" had impelled him to give "a succession of diplomatic dinners" and that he was searching for a pretense to offer more. "I am terribly afraid my purse will get ahead of me under Pierre's accumulating management, and I shall grow rich and stingy. However, I'll have a 'hard try' for the contrary."[89] On July 18, responding to Pierre's news that some formerly moribund shares of stock had been sold at a profit, he wrote: "Tell Helen this new and unlooked-for influx of wealth makes it indispensable for me to hurry to Paris, to prevent a plethora of the purse."[90] He was exaggerating the facts somewhat in these pleased self-caricatures, but it was true that his relative prosperity had helped him to feel justified in giving free rein to his instinct for liberal spending.[91] At times he grew so improvident that Pierre was obliged to draw upon Grinnell in order to meet current debts.[92] At last, late in 1844, Pierre's awareness that his uncle

---

[87] *LLWI,* III, 343.

[88] WI to Sarah Storrow, Madrid, April 27, 1844 (Yale).

[89] *LLWI,* III, 340.

[90] *LLWI,* III, 355.

[91] For example, only four months after leaving New York he had revised his annual allotment for each of his nieces at SS from $100 to an unlimited amount (WI to Catharine Irving, Madrid, August 15, 1842—SHR).

[92] See PMI to Moses Grinnell, New York, July 2, 1844 (NYPL, MS).

was nearly oblivious to the state of his cash account drove him to perpetrate the heresy of suggesting that to make ends meet Irving might consider renting out the cottage for a time![93] He can hardly have been surprised at the response to this proposition. The notion of having to part with Sunnyside even temporarily seems to have achieved a desirable effect, however, for Irving immediately stinted his spending. A few months later he insisted that there be "no more talk of abandoning the cottage." It was "having such an object to work for," he said, "which spurs me on to combat and conquer difficulties."[94] Pierre had wished for him to recollect precisely those difficulties amidst his Ministerial revellings.

By the spring of 1845 Irving had become rather weary of the Ministership.[95] He knew that Sunnyside and its neighbourhood was changing materially in his absence,[96] and he begrudged the accumulating days away from home. "The evening of life is fast drawing over me," he wrote wistfully more than once, and "Heavens! how do I feel at times the narrowness of my means, which continually cramps my efforts to do what I would wish to do."[97] Thus, despite his not-yet-realized financial security, it was with no regret that in November he learned from Pierre the rumour of his imminent replacement as Minister.[98] Not to be behindhand, he immediately transmitted his

[93] MS Outline, Chapter 79/XX (1844). As WI indicated in a letter to Sarah Storrow on December 29, 1844, other considerations than economy alone had prompted the suggestion of PMI, and it was not his alone: "I received a few days since a letter from Pierre M. Irving on the same subject mentioned by your Mother [Mrs. Catharine Paris], the renting of the cottage &c. That must be left entirely to the wishes of the inhabitants of the cottage. If they find it lonely to be so many months of the year shut up in the country, and if your uncle E.I. would like it, they may remove to the city; but it must not be through motives of economy, and at the sacrafice [sic] of inclination. . . . I have considered the cottage as a quiet retreat for your mother & your uncle, and do not like to hear it disturbed" (Yale). The idea of renting the cottage was abandoned, but in the early months of 1845 the girls at SS did visit their relatives in town; see WI to Sarah Storrow, Madrid, March 6, 1845 (Yale).

[94] *LLWI*, III, 394. Apparently PMI renewed the suggestion in 1846, for in *LLWI* he dates this quoted reply of WI's a "month or two before his official mission closed at Madrid," which was in July of that year.

[95] On May 24 he wrote of his office to Sarah Storrow: 'I am heartily tired of all its forms and ceremonies and solemn humbug, and nothing would retain me for a moment in office if it were not that I have 'a family to provide for,' a consideration which bends the neck to all kinds of yokes" (Yale).

[96] And not in all ways for the better. The George Jones family, near neighbours to the Irvings, had returned in 1844 from a tour of Europe full of aristocratical notions, and had made social life in the neighbourhood much less unpretending than before. On December 29 of that year WI expressed the hope that their "bewigged and bepowdered coachman has been snowballed" (WI to Sarah Storrow, Madrid, December 29, 1844—Yale). See also WI to Sarah Storrow, Madrid, July 25, 1845 (Yale).

[97] WI to Eliza Romeyn, Madrid, April 2, 1845 (SHR); WI to Sarah Storrow, Madrid, March 6, 1845 (Yale).

[98] *Life*, II, 193. The topic of WI's possible replacement had been a fairly regular feature of PMI's letters for over a year past. On June 9, 1844, WI wrote to Sarah Storrow that PMI had just informed him of "rumors of recalls of the foreign ministers; myself included among the number" (Yale). See also WI to Sarah Storrow, Madrid,

resignation to Washington, effective as soon as a successor could be appointed and installed. Nevertheless, several months of miscellaneous activity were still to pass before he would be released from his official responsibilities. He had received Pierre's boding letter while at Paris, visiting the Storrows and awaiting the arrival of Louis McLane, the United States Minister to England, who was then engaged in the tense negotiations going forward between those two nations concerning the disputed northern boundary of the United States, and who was eager to consult with him about this complex affair. Irving was more than willing to cooperate, for he was knowledgeable on the topic and firmly believed in the importance to the United States of securing the Pacific Northwest as an outlet for its expanding trade.[99] When McLane arrived he soon became convinced that his fellow diplomat could be of material assistance in the negotiations by coming to London and preparing for publication a pamphlet setting forth the United States' view of the border controversy. The two men returned to England together in December, and within a month Irving had virtually completed his pamphlet.[100] Although to his annoyance McLane now failed to make good his stated intention of publishing the work—which never did appear—Irving was satisfied, as he wrote to Sarah Storrow on February 2, that he had "been of service to Mr. McLane in facilitating some of his diplomatic affairs; at least he said he thought my coming quite a god send."[101] Later in the month he left London and returned to Madrid, where he awaited the arrival of his successor, who, as he learned from Pierre in April, was to be Romulus P. Saunders.[102] Pierre believed that Saunders was to depart for Spain shortly, but to his uncle's chagrin the prediction proved inaccurate, for the Minister-designate failed to arrive until mid-July. Then, at last, Irving was able to resign his credentials before the Queen, hurry back to London, embark thence on a steamer for Boston, catch a train to New York, and from there a steamboat to Tarrytown, where, after an absence of four and one-half years, on September 19 he hired a carriage and rode home.

On the whole, his years in Europe had been pleasant and rewarding. The combination of nervous illness and distraction by the duties

December 6, 1844 (Yale). On June 13, 1845, WI reported to the same niece: "My letters from home give me reason to think that I shall not be displaced for the present. Such Pierre M. Irving writes me, is the opinion expressed by Mrs. Polk, in presence of several persons, one of whom reported it to Treat [John Treat Irving, Jr.]: and Mrs. P. is supposed to be acquainted with affairs of state" (Yale).

[99] He had emphasized this view in *Astoria* and *Captain Bonneville*, and in an anonymous contribution to the *Knickerbocker* in 1840 he had even waxed vehement on the subject. See Wayne R. Kime, "WI and 'The Empire of the West': An Unacknowledged Review," *Western American Literature*, 5 (Winter 1971), 277-85.

[100] Not surprisingly, while at London WI commented at length in his letters to PMI on the ideas which he had formulated ten years before, while the two were at work together on *Astoria*. See *LLWI*, III, 380-82, 390.

[101] WI to Sarah Storrow, London, February 2, 1846 (Yale).

[102] According to PMI, Saunders had been "long an assured expectant of the post." Quoted in WI to Sarah Storrow, Madrid, April 7, 1846 (Yale).

of his office had of course frustrated his hopes to ensure his financial future through literary activity, so that he would need to write for money longer than he had intended. "In the early part of my career I used to think I would take warning by the fate of writers who kept on writing until they 'wrote themselves down,' and that I would retire while still in the freshness of my powers," he had remarked to Sarah Storrow in 1845; "but you see circumstances have obliged me to change my plans, and I am likely to write on until the pen drops from my hand."[103] Upon his arrival home, however, the notion of beginning a literary campaign was far from his mind. For several weeks he stayed close about the cottage, visiting neighbours and entertaining friends and relatives up from the city. Declining an invitation to visit New York, he wrote on December 24 that his visits there had been "few and very brief" since his return.[104]

In the months following his return to private life, Irving's relationship with Pierre and Helen rapidly grew closer. He had always valued Helen for her bright disposition, and when she came to Sunnyside, with or without her husband, he always sought to detain her as long as he could. "She is such a delightful companion," he wrote to Sarah Storrow in February, "so full of *conversation*; which, in general, is the one thing wanting in my quiet domestic fireside."[105] As we have seen, prior to his departure for Spain Irving had learned to value Pierre as a literary assistant, a financial agent, and occasionally an adviser on other topics. Pierre now began to assume the roles of domestic companion, general sounding-board, and even literary counsellor and critic—the roles which Peter had filled during his lifetime—and also those of literary agent and fiscal conscience regarding the necessity of a campaign of writing—the roles formerly filled by Ebenezer. On December 31, 1846, Irving wrote to him explaining why his absence from the family gathering at Christmas had been such a disappointment: "I wished much to talk to you about my literary affairs. I am growing a sad laggard in literature, and need some one to bolster me up occasionally."[106] At the turn of 1847, however, the primary service Pierre regularly performed for his uncle was still the superintendence of his investments.[107] The power of attorney of 1842 was no longer formally valid, but by tacit agreement it remained in force, so that Pierre was now the unofficial comptroller of Irving's estate. As in the five years previous, he continued to render accounts periodically. On January 6, 1847, he informed his uncle that the Screw Dock Company, one of the corporations in which Irving owned com-

---

[103] WI to Sarah Storrow, Madrid, February 27, 1845 (Yale).

[104] WI to the Reverend Robert Bolton, SS, December 24, 1846 (SHR).

[105] WI to Sarah Storrow, SS, February 20, 1847 (Yale).

[106] *LLWI*, III, 396-97.

[107] For some reason WI neglected to inform PMI of three outstanding debts until January 1847, but upon doing so he assured him that he had now learned "the full extent" of his indebtedness (*LLWI*, III, 397). From the context of WI's remarks it appears that the debts were not recent.

mon stock, had just paid a fat dividend. The name of this firm became a byword between them. "In faith," Irving replied, "the Dock deserves its name. I fancy there must be a set of Jews at the windlasses to screw the ships so handsomely. Tell them to screw on, and spare not!"[108] Presently all Pierre's financial manoeuvrings were to be dubbed by his uncle as "screwing."

That Irving should have expressed great pleasure at the returns from his investments was particularly fitting at this time, for he had devised grandiose plans for home improvement which would require a substantial outlay of funds. In a manner recalling his use of anticipated profits from *The Crayon Miscellany*, *Astoria*, and other works as a basis for the purchase and first improvement of the Roost, Irving proposed to enlarge the house at Sunnyside and to finance his improvements by the income from sales of an edition of his revised works. Also, just as he had done before, he plunged with enthusiasm into planning and building his addition before he became engaged in the literary project which was to pay for it. Within a month of his return from Europe he had secured from George Harvey, the architect who had assisted him previously, a plan which would harmonize with the rest of the building and would not, he claimed, "be expensive enough to ruin me."[109] Designed to accommodate his resident family in greater comfort and to provide lodgings for guests, the addition was to be a three-storey tower connected to the house by a closed archway and containing a guest room, servant's quarters, and a basement for storage. Work on the "Pagoda" was begun before the end of October, and in the months afterward this and other improvements occupied the primary place in Irving's mind. At the same time—"whenever he could find mood and leisure," as Pierre tactfully put it in the *Life and Letters*[110]—he attempted to busy himself in his study with revising his back works. Although the refusal of Lea and Blanchard to republish the works at a suitable premium had enforced upon him a suspension of payments from the sale of copyright for almost five years, the complexion of affairs in this regard was brightening. While at London in 1845 he had become acquainted with George Putnam, the energetic junior partner in the New York publishing firm of Wiley & Putnam, and had responded favourably to an inquiry from this person concerning a possible revised edition. As yet nothing had come of the preliminary flirtation, both because Irving had made no progress in providing a saleable product and because Putnam's partner doubted that an arrangement with the author would prove profitable. Irving had assured Putnam that there was no firm "with which [he] would be more happy to deal,"[111] but by the close of 1846 generous offers from

[108] WI to PMI, SS, January 6, 1847; *LLWI*, III, 397.

[109] WI to Sarah Storrow, n.p., October 18, 1846; *LLWI*, III, 395. As before, WI was in active consultation with the architect. See WI to George Harvey, SS, October 16, 1846 (SHR).

[110] *LLWI*, III, 395. WI was probably at work revising *A History of New York*.

[111] See WI to George Putnam, Madrid, August 13, 1845; in George Haven Putnam, *George Palmer Putnam: A Memoir* (New York, 1912), pp. 85-86. This work is a condensa-

other concerns were turning up unsolicited.[112] The time was propitious for him to win his comfort in old age by making a solid bargain.

In his influential account of the years following Irving's return to the United States in 1846, Stanley T. Williams has claimed that, regrettably, the author at this time "bartered the changeless world of literature, which had inspired his youth, for the ideal of the prosperous American who wrote occasionally." Certainly Irving's intention of attaining financial independence by revising his works and marketing them as a unit does seem to provide a basis for Williams' contention. Other facts may also be adduced which seem to support the further views of Williams that after 1846 "not only the creative power but the curiosity about literature was dead or dying"[113] in Irving, and that fear of poverty alone kept him writing. It is undoubtedly true that early in 1847 he was in so unproductive a state that, as he wrote to Sarah Storrow on February 15, "I cannot even bring myself to the literary task of preparing my works for republication; much as I need an addition to my income from that source."[114] As late as June 6 he confessed to Sarah that, altogether against his will to write, he had been "idle and inert"[115] for the past few weeks. Contrary to the ideas of Williams, however, this settled indisposition was by no means the sign of a growing disinterest in literature. What left Irving "inert" was not literary activity itself but rather what he denoted as a "literary task"—the arduous undertaking of revising the extensive canon of his writings. As a matter of fact, during March and April he had been able temporarily to overcome his inertia by tinkering with the life of George Washington and the medley of Spanish narratives, projects that had engaged his interest before he ever seriously entertained the idea of a thorough revision. It was "fagging" at the revision, the merchandise to be exploited by "bartering," that Irving found so distasteful.

Nevertheless, it was impossible for him to ignore the necessity of amassing new funds. Pierre was reporting advantageous sales and large dividends more regularly than ever, but Irving's notions for new improvements to the cottage were also multiplying. In March he urged Helen to "tell Pierre to make money for me as fast as possible, as my expenses will break out anew with the blossoms of spring, and will

tion of the same author's *A Memoir of George Palmer Putnam*, 2 vols. (New York and London, 1903), but the earlier memoir does not include the letter. In their treatment of the WI-Putnam relationship, the two works are in most respects identical. At subsequent points, information duplicated in both versions is cited from the revised text —abbreviated as *Putnam*—as being more readily accessible than the earlier one, which is abbreviated as *A Memoir of Putnam*.

[112] *LLWI*, III, 396. No doubt WI's disappointment at not seeing PMI at Christmas in 1846 was owing in part to a wish to discuss some of these. Apparently Wiley and Putnam was among the firms wooing him. See WI to Messrs. Wiley and Putnam, SS, January 30, 1847 (NYPL, Berg).

[113] *Life*, II, 197.

[114] WI to Sarah Storrow, SS, February 15, 1847 (Yale).

[115] WI to Sarah Storrow, SS, June 6, 1847 (SHR).

need all his *screwing* to keep pace with them."[116] Jolly as the prediction was, Irving knew that it was soberly accurate. He did not really believe his assurance to Pierre in April that by completing his two pet projects he would "more than pay the expense of [his] new building,"[117] and he was disturbed by his failure thus far to finance his improvements by his own exertions. When he received from Sarah Storrow an invitation to make a promised return visit to Europe, his reply was unqualified: "*I cannot afford it.*" However, he was never one to solve a problem immediately when he could set it aside temporarily and pursue more congenial pastimes. What occupied him most regularly was not his revisions but the work on his house. "The additions and alterations have turned out beyond my hopes, both as to appearance and convenience," he wrote to Sarah on June 6. As for the revisions, "I hope . . . before long, to get again in the vein."[118]

One person did counsel Irving consistently at this time on the importance of bartering his literary wares: Pierre. It was he, after all, whose duty it was to dispense his uncle's money with such prodigality. Irving repeatedly professed to Pierre his awareness that the cash was flowing too swiftly, reported his progress on any and all literary work, and avowed his eagerness to "get [his] literary property in a productive train" as soon as possible. Pierre should not be "frightened at [his] extravagance, and cut off supplies,"[119] he joked. Meanwhile, even though his nephew reminded him that the times were right to make his bargain and set to work, Irving was not to be started from his own track, no matter how "strongly urged"[120] he might be. Thus, much as Ebenezer had done after Irving's return from Europe in 1832, Pierre gradually grew impatient to see his uncle in productive activity. At last, in April 1847, he sought to turn Irving's attention definitively round to the revision, and a *contretemps* occurred.

Early in the month Irving reported with satisfaction that he had overcome his literary inertia in recent weeks by "working up some old stuff which had lain for years lumbering like rubbish in one of [his] trunks."[121] Pierre saw that his uncle was pleased to have made progress on this congenial task, yet it distressed him to see "rubbish" placed before Irving's best interests. He wrote in reply that while any activity was of course to the good, he was chiefly anxious that Irving should begin his revisions, "for which there was an expectation and demand." He made a delicate yet telling appeal:

> You lost the Conquest of Mexico by not acting upon the motto of
> *Carpe diem;* and I am a little afraid you may let slip the present
> opportunity for a favorable sale of a uniform edition of your

[116] *LLWI,* III, 399.
[117] *LLWI,* III, 402.
[118] WI to Sarah Storrow, SS, June 6, 1847 (SHR).
[119] *LLWI,* III, 397, 401.
[120] *LLWI,* IV, [13].
[121] *LLWI,* III, 402.

works, by suffering your pen to be diverted in a new direction. A literary harvest is before you from this source, on which you could reckon with confidence *now*, but which might turn to barrenness under a future pressure in the money market. . . . Therefore "Now's the day and now's the hour."

Irving replied to Pierre's letter in a tone of strained tolerance. After a single rebuke ("Don't snub me about my late literary freak"), he explained fully the history of his renewed interest in the early wars between the Spaniards and the Moors. Fatigued with the drudgery of "muddling" over his printed works, he said, he had turned for occupation to a series of Moorish chronicles begun at Madrid in 1826 and 1827. Selecting one, he "took it up, was amused with it, and . . . went to work and rewrote it, and got so in the spirit of the thing, that I went to work, *con amore*, at two or three fragmentary Chronicles." The result of this activity was that he had both completed the frame for a new publication and put himself "quite in heart again, as well as in literary vein." The task of poring over his works had been making him feel "as if the true literary vein was extinct," he said. "I think, therefore, you will agree with me that my time for the last five weeks has been well employed."

On the same day as Irving was writing this explanation, Pierre learned from a Sunnyside resident then in New York that the subject which had been occupying his uncle was his "old Moorish Chronicles." At this time the project of a revised edition was so predominant in his mind that upon hearing the news he immediately—before receiving Irving's letter—dispatched to him a second note. Borrowing the word "rubbish" from his uncle's original reference to the fragmentary narratives, but employing the term to refer to the manuscripts in which Irving now took such satisfaction, he coined another unhappy phrase—"literary 'skimmings'"—to denote the same improved works. He had an "agreeable though indistinct" recollection of these "skimmings," he blandly wrote, and had no doubt they would prove creditable; but he still suggested that the public might not be content with works of this kind in place of "a uniform edition of his works now out of print." Closing the "ill-starred epistle," as he correctly termed it in the *Life and Letters*, Pierre conjured up a grand vision of authorial independence: "Make all despatch with the preparation of your uniform edition, and then to work to complete your Life of Washington, and take your ease forever after." In this statement Pierre had formulated Irving's wishes to a tee, but his unconscious slighting of his uncle's new material was soon to cause him consternation.

Irving received Pierre's second note on April 15, the day after writing the reply to his first one, and he immediately wrote another reply, roundly informing him that he could "know nothing of the work" he claimed to recall. "The whole may be mere 'skimmings,' but they pleased me in the preparation; they were written when I was in the vein, and that is the only guide I go by in my writings, or which has led me to success. Besides," he added, "I write for pleasure as well as profit; and the pleasure I have recently enjoyed . . . has been so great, that I am content to forego any loss of profit it may occasion me by a slight postponement of the republication of my old works."[122] He then announced his intention henceforward to take his own counsel in literary matters—a resolution which, even if he was to observe it rigidly for only a few weeks, reveals the degree of his pique at Pierre's lack of interest in his recent efforts and his impatience with the narrowly materialistic conception of literary rewards that his nephew seemed to be advocating. His first letter of explanation, prompt delivery of which would have obviated this entire confusion, did not reach Pierre until April 17, two days after the discussion had been abruptly and unilaterally closed. Realizing the probable effect of his ill-advised remarks on his uncle's spirits, Pierre quickly wrote out a recantation, but to no avail; Irving had been thrown out of his writing mood and could not be coaxed into resuming work on the Chronicles. He was supervising the completion of the Pagoda.

Irving's anger passed away quickly, as it usually did, and two weeks later he joked to Helen about the misunderstanding. In response to her report that Pierre was still distressed lest any "'thoughtless word of his should have marred [Irving's] happy literary mood,'" he assured her that Pierre should not feel uneasy. But then, alluding to Gil Blas, he administered a good-natured rebuke in a Spanish double-entendre not to be overlooked by his lettered nephew. The slurs against his work had not really bothered him, he said: "Like the good archbishop of Granada, that model and mirror of authorship, I knew 'the homily in question to be the very best I had ever composed;' so, like my great prototype, I remained fixed in my self-complacency, wishing Pierre 'toda felicidad con un poco de mas gusto.'"[123] Irving was already eager to see his nephew again to talk over his affairs with him. He urged Helen to come to Sunnyside for a long stay so that he could lure Pierre there on Sundays. "Tell him I promise not to bore him about literary matters when he comes up," added this genially devastating satirist. "I have as great a contempt for these things as anybody, though I have to stoop to them occasionally for the sake of a livelihood; but I want to have a little talk with him about stocks, and railroads, and some mode of screwing and jewing the world out of more interest than one's money is entitled to."[124] By this absurd self-characterization Irving concluded the episode. Despite his precarious finances, he would not be prodded into a narrowly profit-oriented conception of writing. While he knew that Pierre was hardly so philistine as the incident had made him appear, he rejected any interference with a course of action he thought successful in itself. He had invited Pierre's counsel, of course, and he

[122] LLWI, IV, 14-17.

[123] LLWI, IV, 18-19. Literally translated, in English the Spanish word gusto is taste; but PMI would have read it to suggest tact as well.

[124] LLWI, IV, 19.

knew that it was in some measure just. Eventually he must turn his full attention to the revisions.

Pierre was disgusted that his well-meant interference with his uncle had placed him in a false position, but he realized that the disagreement was a coincidental misunderstanding rather than a deep-seated difference of views. In any case, events had clearly shown that expressing anxiety over his uncle's irregular habits was wasted trouble, and now that Irving projected a serious attack on the revisions once work on the cottage was complete, nothing was to be gained by attempting to budge him from that schedule. Pierre was so fully occupied with his own affairs that he would have few opportunities to consult with Irving anyway. After eight years of re-settlement in New York, his only serious complaint about his mode of life was in fact that he wished for more leisure. "I am eating and sleeping like any other mortal at 697 Broadway & holding out a sign to a perverse generation, as of yore, at 32 Wall Street," he informed Daniel Roberts at about this time. "I hop about as usual in this 'cage of life,' now and then beating my wings against the bars, but in the main eating my crumbs with quiet satisfaction."[125] This summer Helen was planning to take rooms at the Franklin House in Tarrytown,[126] and Pierre was not altogether satisfied at the prospect of her absence. He valued her, he told Roberts, as a "choicer blessing" than his own sturdy health (he now weighed "154 pounds of 'too solid' material"),[127] but Helen was not to be denied her visits. One topic that occupied a prominent place in Pierre's mind at this time, if his correspondence with Roberts may be taken as a measure, was not personal but national. In language which recalled his editorial columns in the Toledo *Blade*, he professed concern for the moral fibre of the nation now that slavery was threatening to be extended into the western territories. "Every right feeling within me rises up in solemn protest against it," he wrote. "The soul of the nation will be dead if it consents to have that accursed institution cast its baneful shade over one foot of free soil. 'I can die, but I cannot do wrong,' was the saying of an illustrious martyr, & I have something of this feeling when I think of being called on to participate in an act of such flagrant wickedness." Comfortable man of the world as he had become, Pierre had not lost his moralistic streak. He was pleased, he wrote, to see evidence that "for once the North is not willing to sacrifice conscience & right to the pretended danger of a dissolution of the Union."[128]

[125] PMI to Daniel Roberts, New York, May 31, 1848 (Huntington). In 1846 and part of 1847 PMI and Helen lived at 97 West 13th Street; then they returned to 479 Broadway (*Doggett's New York City Directory* for 1845, 1846, 1847, 1848). Apparently they moved to 697 Broadway in 1848.

[126] WI to Sarah Storrow, SS, June 6, 1847 (Yale). Helen and her sister Eliza were planning to take a room together.

[127] PMI to Daniel Roberts, New York, May 31, 1848 (Huntington).

[128] PMI to Daniel Roberts, New York, July 31, 1848 (Huntington). In this letter PMI also wrote that, because he was "opposed tooth and nail to the extension of slavery," he

The remainder of 1847 passed strenuously for Irving—so strenuously, indeed, that he was repeatedly obliged to call for assistance from his nephew. During part of the summer he proceeded, in his own words, "to enclose a kitchen yard, to enclose the stable, and make a large farmyard, poultry yard, outhouses, &c."[129] This was taxing work for a man of sixty-four, and by September 9, having just completed construction of a new ice pond, he was exhausted. "I would not undertake another job, even so much as to build a wren coop,"[130] he wrote to Mrs. Paris. At odd times he had also scratched away at his life of Washington, which often preyed on his mind. He wondered whether all his exertions on it had been worthwhile, and he was uncomfortable at the thought of the sheer range of research still to be completed. To relieve his mind on both issues he asked Pierre to give a critical estimate of the fragmentary manuscript he had completed thus far and to assist in gathering further materials.[131] Pierre assented, and presently he returned the manuscript with encouraging comments. Later in the summer Irving laid another burden on his nephew. He was so busy with the cottage and George Washington that he simply could not attend to anything else. Would Pierre kindly look over the enclosed proposals from various publishers for the republication of his works?[132] Pierre did so, and undoubtedly the two discussed these offers while Irving was in New York later in the year. His round of "mornings in the libraries, and frolicking in the evenings" did not abate until Christmas Eve, when he returned home accompanied by Pierre and Helen for the annual family festival.[133]

In January 1848 Irving returned to New York to immerse himself again in research, composition, and socializing. His evening dissipations "rejuvenated" him, he claimed, so that in the long forenoons he was able to work with "greater alacrity and success."[134] For a time he was the houseguest of John Jacob Astor, now eighty-four years of age and failing, and while there he succeeded both in buoying the old man's spirits and in making progress on the biography. Once Pierre called at Astor's before breakfast and found him already at work.[135] On March 29, however, the old merchant died, and Irving's attention to the life of Washington was thereby to be suspended for many

planned to vote in the forthcoming Presidential election for Martin Van Buren, the candidate of the Free Soil Party.

[129] WI to Sarah Storrow, SS, August 23, 1847; *LLWI*, IV, 24.

[130] *LLWI*, IV, 26.

[131] "Sends to me in August [1847] manuscript chapters of his Life of Washington – with a request that I should aid him in compiling materials" (MS Outline, Chapter XXIV [1847, 1848]).

[132] *LLWI*, IV, 31.

[133] WI to Catharine Irving, New York, December 20, 1847 (SHR); *LLWI*, IV, 32. Also expected for the Christmas celebration were Miss Mulhollin, a neighbour, Irving Paris, Sanders and Julia, and PMI's brother Ogden.

[134] WI to Sarah Storrow, New York, February 27, 1848; *LLWI*, IV, 34.

[135] *LLWI*, IV, 35.

months. Astor had designated him an executor of his will and, "as a token of respect," had also named him a trustee for a public library to be funded by monies from his estate.[136] As the tedious meetings of the executors and the trustees began in April, he was left with little time for literary work. To complicate matters further, early in the same month George Putnam reactivated his campaign to secure an agreement to republish the back works.[137] Having separated from his conservative partner, Putnam was eager to seize an opportunity to make good his belief that the works of Washington Irving were still desirable literary merchandise.

In light of the heavy demands being made on his time, it is virtually certain that Irving found it necessary to rely on the assistance of Pierre in responding to Putnam's new overture. Writing from "Pierre's law shop" on April 10, he informed his niece Kate that "I am now negotiating an arrangement with Mr Putnam for the republication of my works, which promises to be a very satisfactory one."[138] Irving was a regular visitor in Pierre's office this spring, and any further "negotiation" he may have done on his own behalf was punctuated by regular consultations with his nephew. As we have seen, he was not a skilful bargainer himself; and even had he been one, the pressures of his other operations precluded his handling these discussions unaided. In fact, it was probably Pierre who took the most time and pains in hammering out the final terms of the contract. We know that Irving and Putnam signed their agreement on July 26, 1848, and that one week later Pierre left town for a "holiday visit" to Sunnyside.[139]

In his earliest letter to George Putnam, that of December 1845, Irving had suggested how "in the hands of an extensive publishing house" his writings might be marketed in many formats other than as complete sets in themselves, such as "series of tales, of essays, of sketches . . . series of similar writings by other authors, etc."[140] Putnam had in mind not only these innovations, but more particularly an edition of Irving's writings produced in a variety of fine bindings; individual works richly illustrated and bound; and the possibility of

[136] Porter, *John Jacob Astor*, II, 1285.

[137] It is doubtful whether Putnam's campaign was ever absolutely dormant. For example, in the MS Outline, Chapter XXIV, PMI includes the following notations under September 1847: "Overtures from the publishers for a re-publication of his works – Expecting proposals from Wiley & Putnam – Their letter of proposals – Not so advantageous in his view as their previous propositions in London – Send him a copy of these –."

[138] WI also referred to his responsibilities as executor and trustee, and then added: "All these things detain me in town, and may oblige me hereafter to visit town frequently, – but they all contribute to increase my pecuniary means, and of course to advance the well being of the cottage and its inmates; so I trust you will not scold me for being such a truant" (WI to Kate Irving, New York, April 10, 1848—SHR).

[139] *LLWI*, IV, 40. On July 31 PMI wrote to Daniel Roberts that three days hence he planned to "go to the country . . . for three weeks" (Huntington).

[140] Putnam, *Putnam*, p. 85.

publishing any new titles which the author might produce. As summarized by his nephew George Haven Putnam, however, his proposition to Irving of early 1848 specified none of these options. Putnam merely proposed to pay Irving a royalty on all his works sold, guaranteeing him a remuneration of $1,000 during the first year of the agreement, $2,000 during the second, and $3,000 during the third —after which, presumably, a new contract would be drawn up on the basis of developments to that date.[141] Evidently Irving was pleased with these first terms,[142] although he was, as he told Kate in April, negotiating. By the time he signed the agreement he must have been more fully satisfied, for the term of the contract had been lengthened to five years and the association between author and publisher much more carefully specified. In return for exclusive rights to publish Irving's revised works and such additional writings as he might produce, Putnam was to bear the full cost of publication, pay a royalty of 12-1/2 per cent on the retail price of each volume sold, and guarantee Irving payment of $8,500 in graduated sums over the period. This was a heavy risk for Putnam to take, but the Irvings made a stipulation in his favour: namely, that he was free to prepare illustrated editions of the works and to pay only the usual royalty on the ordinary edition for each copy of these more expensive volumes sold.[143] No matter how well Putnam might fare, the arrangement was clearly favourable to Irving. Eventually, as Pierre observed in the *Life and Letters*, it "redounded to the advantage of both."[144]

Having played his part in shaping this important compact, Pierre made his visit to Sunnyside purely for relaxation. Irving, however, was hard at work. His pact with Putnam might imply a life of sybaritic ease a few years hence, but for the duration of the publishing project it meant sheer toil. Journalists were responding enthusiastically to the news that an edition of his revised works was imminent, and Putnam was understandably eager to begin the undertaking. By the time he signed the contract Irving had already completed his thorough revision of *A History of New York*, and only three weeks after that date he returned to Sunnyside from a visit in the city with an advance copy of the revised *History*, the first of the series. Pierre, who was still at the cottage, turned over the pages of the volume and remarked "that there appeared to be considerable additions... written expressly for this new edition"; to which Irving replied that he had indeed altered the

---

[141] *Ibid.*, pp. 127-28.

[142] According to George Palmer Putnam, the "suggestion was made in a brief note, written on the impulse of a moment; but (what was more remarkable) it was promptly accepted without the change of a single figure or a single stipulation" ("Recollections of Irving," *Atlantic Monthly*, 6 [July 1860], 603). Putnam's recollection that WI "promptly" accepted his offer is clearly in error, and his suggestion that the offer was made on "impulse" is inconsistent with the evidence that he had been interested in this matter for three years previous.

[143] The contract is summarized in *LLWI*, IV, 40-42, 50.

[144] *LLWI*, IV, 42.

work—"chastened the exaggerated humor of some portions—the effect of age and improved taste combined."[145] Pierre's casual observation about the *History* suggests that while he was familiar enough with earlier editions of the work to recognize deviations from them, he had not previously been informed of the reshaping to which Irving had subjected this spritely publication of his youth. Apparently Irving had decided to "ride [his] hobby privately, without saying a word about it to anybody,"[146] just as he had expressed an intention to do at the close of the exchange over the Spanish chronicles. Similarly, in the months that followed he informed his nephew from time to time of his progress on a book or of his ideas about it, but he did not seek his criticism or employ him as a co-reviser. Pierre's duties in assisting the actual production of revised texts were few, consisting only of acting as a liaison between Irving and Putnam—transmitting copy from one to the other—and as an informal auditor of the publisher's rather casual accounts. His most substantial contribution to the genesis of Irving's revised works, once the author became seriously interested in the idea at all, had been his assistance in defining the terms of the contract.

When he returned to New York at the end of August, therefore, Pierre's long struggle to get his uncle into harness was over, so that he could learn of Irving's impulsive promise to donate $100 to the local Episcopal church without wondering where the money was to come from.[147] As the revised *Sketch-Book* appeared in September, and in the next month *Columbus*, the journals and newspapers heralded their arrival with formulaic praise. Calling upon Irving in October, Pierre found him "evidently somewhat fagged" from exertions on an entirely new work, the *Life of Mahomet*, which he was struggling to complete in time for its advertised date of publication, January 1. He could not understand why his uncle should be taxing himself to turn out volumes at so rapid a rate. "I told him the uniform edition was doing so well," he wrote in the *Life and Letters*, that "he could afford to take his ease, and not to drudge." But Irving knew that Putnam expected early delivery of the texts, and he was not a man casually to renege on his agreements. Moreover, as he replied to Pierre, he was anxious to complete the work of revision so as to take up his labour of love, the life of Washington. "I must weave my web," he said, "and then die."[148]

As he pushed forward, administering a quick brush-up to *Bracebridge Hall* and attempting futilely to bring *Mahomet* to a conclusion, Irving's social life was severely curtailed, his life at home hectic,

[145] *Ibid.*

[146] *LLWI,* IV, 17.

[147] PMI's note of this incident in the MS Outline, Chapter XXIV (1847, 1848)—"Promises Dr Creighton 100 dollars for an organ!"—may indicate amusement at his uncle's propensity for spending freely as soon as his pockets became full. In the fall of 1848 WI joined the Protestant Episcopal Church.

[148] *LLWI,* IV, 47-48.

and his mind continually occupied. He had no time for anything but this "fagging of the pen," and not surprisingly, on November 1, 1848, he signed a new power of attorney to Pierre, granting him "full power and authority to do and perform all and every act and thing whatsoever"[149] to conduct his affairs. While in this document he was only formalizing a role which Pierre had begun to assume several years before and had actually been performing for the past two years, the permanent power of attorney stands as Irving's open acknowledgment of the degree to which he had become dependent upon the cooperation of his nephew. Without Pierre's willingness to look after his interests, it is unlikely that he would have made so rapid and advantageous a bargain for republishing his works as he managed to do, and it is clear that he could not have completed his revisions at the rate he was able to do in the closing months of 1848. It was no secret within the Irving family that Pierre was acting as his uncle's comptroller, nor that Irving enjoyed his company, valued his advice, confided to him his uncertainties, and at times sought his judgment as a critic of his writings. By the time Irving signed the power of attorney, Pierre had superintended the resurgence of his personal fortune and had helped manoeuvre him into a position in which, by a single period of exertion, he would go far toward assuring himself a comfortable old age. In performing these offices he had not imposed a strictly utilitarian point of view upon Irving's attitude toward writing, nor, his uncle's telling caricatures notwithstanding, had he really intended to. Rather than attempting to set aside Irving's interest in the embryonic life of Washington, he had wisely presented it to his uncle as the reward for preliminary labours on the revisions. Having read the manuscript one year before and been enlisted at that time as a deputy researcher for the remainder of the Washington project, he was already set down as collaborator in its production. While he kept at his own professional life, then, and thought himself within a few years of that often-formulated aim, "a moderate competence," Pierre must have recognized how thoroughly he had become involved with the present and future affairs of his uncle. Yet he no longer felt any cause to "beat his wings against the bars" of the close family relationship he had once seemed to eschew. The years had taken away his restless energy and given him the security he so valued. At forty-six, he had become toward Irving less a dependent nephew than a peer. Indeed, by and large the dependency now lay on the other side.

[149] "Power of Attorney to Pierre M. Irving, November 2, 1848" (SHR).

Part II

Washington Irving at
Sunnyside, 1848-1859

Chapter Four

The Author and His Nephew, 1848-1858

Irving persevered manfully in the long chore of revising his works, but gratifying as public praise and his publisher's brisk sales might be, he was unable to regard his exertions as anything but a necessary evil, "fagging of the pen" to be dispatched as rapidly as possible. In July 1849 he wrote to Sarah Storrow that in the past months he had endured more "toil of head . . . than in any other period" of his life, and that he was rather surprised at his sturdy ability to write on from week to week.[1] No doubt his stamina was owing in some measure to the decision he had made in the spring to indulge himself, as a hopefully therapeutic respite from the monotonous work of revision, in the more creative labour of preparing a full life of Goldsmith. As he had told Putnam at the time, the topic "was a favorite theme of his," and he was pleased to exercise his literary talent for the mere pleasure of doing so. His plan was to use his own 1842 sketch of Goldsmith as a general frame, supplementing the earlier work with new material taken primarily from John Forster's recent biography of the author. The interlude of original authorship began

---

[1] *LLWI*, IV, 52.

auspiciously, but it failed at last to prove so refreshing as he had hoped. In August, with only two or three more chapters to write, he complained to Pierre that his "literary freak" had "taken him more time than he could afford—had plucked the heart out of his summer; and after all he could only play with the subject. He had no time to finish it off as he wished."[2] A habit of hurry developed under the pressures of an unrelenting schedule had made even so attractive a topic as this one merely more "fagging" work. He concluded his unsuccessful experiment in September; but then, in order to make good his obligations to Putnam, he turned again to the *Life of Mahomet*, another jerry-built effort which he had abandoned with impatience several months before; and after *Mahomet* he grimly saw awaiting him the revision of two more back works, *The Alhambra* and *The Conquest of Granada*. While the *Life of Goldsmith* was going through the press, he told Pierre that he was almost exhausted and feared "that his talents might be flagging."[3] He did not manage to complete his uninspiring but remunerative jobwork until the summer of 1850.

Throughout the two-year period during which he revised his works, Irving was acutely aware of the rapid passage of time—the more so since his foremost literary interest was necessarily being held in suspension. Even before the publication of the revised *Conquest of Granada* in June 1850, he ignored his physical depletion and according to Pierre "expressed the most earnest desire to begin anew upon his Life of Washington."[4] It was frustrating to be so inclined to write yet held month after month to one's dreary obligations,[5] and what made his impatience excruciating was that he felt unusually confident of his own skills. In a shrewd bit of self-analysis he told his nephew: "I might not conceive as I did in earlier days, when I had more romance of feeling, but I could execute with more rapidity and freedom." If only he were able to devote himself at his leisure to work on the biography! "All I fear," he said, "is to fail in health, and fail in completing this work at the same time. If I can only live to finish it, I would be willing to die the next moment."[6]

[2] Putnam, "Recollections of Irving," p. 605; *LLWI*, IV, 53.

[3] *LLWI*, IV, 54.

[4] *LLWI*, IV, 54.

[5] This, and the avowal that he had never felt more like writing, was the burden of his complaints to Charles Augustus Davis (1795-1867), his friend and frequent host in New York. (Davis to PMI, New York, June 1863—NYPL, Berg) Davis, an iron merchant and financier, won modest literary renown by a series of thirty-one satirical letters he published in the New York *Daily Advertiser* between June 1833 and February 1834. These letters, similar to the "Jack Downing" letters published by the Maine journalist Seba Smith in 1830-1831, were published as a volume in 1834: *Letters of J. Downing, Major, Downingville Militia, to his Old Friend, Mr. Dwight, of the New York Daily Advertiser*. During the last decade of WI's life Davis was one of his closest friends. WI referred to him familiarly as "Major Downing" or "Jack Downing."

[6] *LLWI*, IV, 64, 65.

During the greater part of the period when he was enmeshed in the toils of the revisions Irving was occupied as well with his responsibilities in connection with the estate of John Jacob Astor. As we have seen, in his celebrated will Astor had designated Irving one of twelve unsalaried trustees charged with investing a bequest of $400,000 to purchase and house a collection of books suitable for a public library in the city of New York. Probably the news of this delegated duty had come as no surprise to Irving, for as early as 1840 he had joined Joseph Green Cogswell and other persons in the old gentleman's confidence in urging him to endow such an institution within his own lifetime—a suggestion which he had entertained sympathetically but had never acted upon.[7] In any case, beginning May 20, 1848, Irving attended bi-weekly meetings of the trustees at 587 Broadway, just down the avenue from Pierre's rooms. A few months later he was unanimously elected President of the Board, and thereafter he assumed a guiding role in assembling the collection. In the spring of 1850, when preliminary plans for the Astor Library were completed and the cornerstone of its permanent home was laid, Irving's duties became more routine. His contributions to the welfare of the library were by no means finished, however, for throughout the remainder of his lifetime he served as the working president of this public trust.[8]

A second duty growing out of his friendship with Astor was serving as an executor of the old man's will. By appointing him to this office Astor had doubtless intended to give testimony to his regard, but he probably meant something more than that. He had felt deep appreciation to Irving for the latter's cooperation in writing *Astoria* and for his attentive friendship in the years since, but despite his unwonted eagerness to reward him in some tangible way, Irving would never hear of it. The closest Astor had come during his lifetime to sharing his wealth with the author was in 1836, when he convinced him to purchase a share in the then promising town of Green Bay. When that speculation failed, the old merchant wished to refund him his purchase price, but this offer was refused.[9] Astor was fertile in expedients, however, and he at last managed virtually to force money on Irving: for by naming him as an executor of the will he delegated to him a task—and a remuneration—which as a gentleman he could scarcely refuse. That Irving was apparently unaware for a time of just how generous his late friend had contrived to be is revealed in a letter he wrote to Sarah Storrow on July 7, 1848, three months after he had begun attending conferences with his co-executors. Summarizing his financial prospects at that time, he wrote:

[7] The history of WI's contribution to the formation and administration of the Astor Library is summarized by Myers, "WI and the Astor Library," pp. 382-96. See also Clark, "Recollections," p. 553.

[8] Myers, "WI and the Astor Library," pp. 391-95. See also WI to Mary M. Hamilton, SS, September 20, 1852; *LLWI*, IV, 119.

[9] Porter, *John Jacob Astor*, II, 863-64, 867.

> I trust through my arrangement with the bookseller [Putnam] and
> further exercise of my pen in completing works now nearly
> finished, I shall make my income adequate to my support. The
> executorship of the Astor estate is by no means so lucrative a post
> as you seem to have heard; but must yield some tolerable profit,
> and with me every little tells.[10]

"Tolerable" indeed: in July 1849, having discharged his duties as an
executor, he received for his services the sum of $10,592.66.[11] Collect-
ing so large an amount all at once—a larger sum, after all, than Putnam
had been able to guarantee him over a full five-year period—he must
have thought for a moment that his long captivity in New York had
been purchased at very nearly a satisfactory rate. Certainly he understood that, except to fulfill his agreement with Putnam, he need give
no further attention to literature as a livelihood. Literally against his
will he had been assisted munificently by Astor toward becoming an
independent gentleman of means.

To the suspicious and cynical, notably the porcupinish James
Finimore Cooper, Irving's cordial relationship with the elderly merchant during the past decade[12] had been an unmistakable sign of his
sycophancy and greed. Upon learning that his fellow author had
been designated an executor, Cooper wrote to his wife that rumour
spoke of a $50,000 legacy for Irving. "What an instinct that man has for
gold!" he scoffed. "He is to be Astor's biographer! Columbus and
John Jacob Astor. I dare say Irving will make the last the greatest
man."[13] For his part, Irving was aware that bits of unflattering misinformation such as Cooper's were abroad, just as they had been after
the publication of *Astoria*. To some persons, even physical proximity
to Astor was somehow reprehensible, no matter how honourable to
either party it might in fact have been. Had not Irving closeted himself
with the rich man on many occasions since 1835, and were not his
visits especially frequent in the months just preceding Astor's death?
The inevitable stories spawned by such ruminations as these naturally
disturbed him, but he chose to make no public statement on the
matter until a suitable tale should surface in public, lest he should
appear overeager to explain himself.[14] The first slur about his relations

[10] WI to Sarah Storrow, SS, July 7, 1848 (Yale).

[11] Porter, *John Jacob Astor*, II, 1055.

[12] On October 10, 1846, three weeks after his return from Europe, WI wrote to
Sarah Storrow that he had recently seen Astor: "He expressed great satisfaction on
seeing me and pressed me to pass the winter with him in town. I had to promise to make
him a visit as formerly" (Yale). Between this time and Astor's death, WI visited him
often (MS Outline, Chapter XXIV [1847, 1848]).

[13] *The Letters and Journals of James Fenimore Cooper*, ed. James F. Beard (Cambridge, Mass., 1968), V, 330.

[14] He had a natural opportunity upon publication of the revised edition of *Astoria*,
but in that work he made no allusion to the personal relations between himself and
Astor. He confined himself to pointing out that since the first publication of the work in
1836, the territory of Oregon had been declared by treaty a possession of the United
States, so that Astor had died with his vision of the nation's expansion partially
realized. See *Astoria*, ed. Todd, p. 505.

with Astor to reach print came in 1851, when Henry Rowe Schoolcraft's *Personal Memoirs* appeared. In that prosy work the anthropologist, ironically a long-time admirer and correspondent of Irving, recounted an "instructive" conversation he had held in 1838 with Albert Gallatin, wherein the statesman had made the following statement:

> Several years ago J[ohn] J[acob] A[stor] put into my hands the journal of his traders on the Columbia, desiring me to use it. I put it in the hands of Malte Brun, at Paris, who used the geographical facts in his work, but paid little respect to Mr. Astor, whom he regarded merely as a merchant seeking his own profit. . . . Astor did not like it. He was restive several years, and then gave Washington Irving $5,000 to take up the MSS. This is the history of 'Astoria.'[15]

Upon reading Schoolcraft's allegation, Irving acted swiftly. He wrote out a 1,000-word rebuttal and sent it to Evert A. Duyckinck for insertion in the influential *Literary World*, which he edited; and when galley proofs were returned he corrected them with unusual care, elaborating his statement at several points.[16] This considered vindication of his conduct, in the form of a letter addressed to Schoolcraft, began with a narrative of the genesis of *Astoria* and moved on to a discussion of his personal relations with Astor. In rather stern tones he affirmed his admiration of the late merchant and denied the rumour that he was himself Astor's hack. Their intimacy, he wrote, "was sought originally on [Astor's] part, and . . . was drawn closer when . . . I became acquainted . . . with the scope and power of his mind, and the grandeur of his enterprises." But as to a financial arrangement, he stated categorically that Astor "was too proverbially rich a man for me to permit the shadow of a pecuniary favor to rest on our intercourse."[17]

For the remainder of his lifetime, at least, Irving's dignified rebuttal achieved its desired effect, putting to rest public speculation about his relationship with Astor. It is interesting to note in this light that Schoolcraft's airing of the venal rumour seems to have had no adverse effect whatever on Irving's regard for him. On the contrary, the author wrote cordially to him in May 1852, six months after the letter of rebuttal had appeared, remarking that he had been "glad to avail myself of the opportunity which the statement gave me of setting the public right as to the circumstances and conditions under which that work [*Astoria*] was undertaken and published and as to the whole of my intercourse with Mr. Astor; about which I found there had been

---

[15] *Personal Memoirs of a Residence of Thirty Years with the Indian Tribes on the American Frontier . . .* (Philadelphia, 1851), pp. 624-25.

[16] He then sent the corrected proofs to PMI to be delivered to Duyckinck. WI to PMI, SS, November 4, [1851] (SHR); MS Outline, Chapter XXVIII (1851).

[17] *Literary World*, 9, no. 251 (November 22, 1851), 408; reprinted in [Evert A. Duyckinck, ed.] *Irvingiana: A Memorial of WI* (New York, 1860 [1859]), p. xvii.

much misapprehension."[18] Considering that the years in which he had known Astor most intimately were the same years in which he had struggled hardest to keep Sunnyside afloat, Irving must have thought it bizarre to hear rumours of the comfort he had supposedly won himself by forming a useful attachment to the great man.

In July 1850, having at last completed the revisions, he turned eagerly to work on his mammoth labour of love, the life of Washington. He was looking forward to an intense, relatively undisturbed period of literary application, but he soon learned how heavy a toll his journeyman-work had exacted from him. Following a brief visit with Helen to the home of his friend Barrett Ames in Orange County,[19] on July 20 he was aboard the morning train to New York, intending to work in the city libraries, when he was seized with a severe case of chills and fever that was to prostrate him for the next several days. When he returned to Sunnyside that afternoon his condition was so poor that both he and his family actually feared for his life. After a frantic but unsuccessful search for a physician in the vicinity, Pierre, who was visiting the cottage, was dispatched as a last resort to row across the broad expanse of the Hudson to the village of Nyack, on the western shore; and after a few hours he succeeded in returning through the summer darkness with a doctor.[20] Under constant attention Irving gained strength in the next few days, but the sudden onset of illness had reminded him anew of his advancing age, and on July 28, while still feeble, he made his will.[21] A few more days proved this precaution premature, but all the same his illness had taught him a necessary prudential lesson. While his intention to resume activity on the biography remained unshaken, he resolved to trim his sails henceforward; and at least for a time he was as good as his resolution. Although by May 1851 he had fallen back into the habit of writing in his study long after others were asleep, he was still determined "not to overtask" himself.[22] He planned to work steadily through the winter of 1851-1852, but when in the event he was plagued by a nervous condition that forced him to forego all study and take to horseback for exercise, he was philosophical about it. He had actually hoped to complete the Life of Washington by the spring of 1852, but in May of

[18] WI to Henry R. Schoolcraft, SS, May 27, 1852 (Library of Congress). WI greatly admired Schoolcraft's achievements as a collector of information about the American Indian. See WI to Henry R. Schoolcraft, SS, October 27, 1853 (Library of Congress).

[19] WI to Sarah Storrow, SS, July 10, 1850 (Yale).

[20] MS Outline, Chapter XXVI (1850); see also LLWI, IV, 74.

[21] "Last Will and Testament of WI, Tarrytown, July 28, 1850"—typewritten copy (NYPL, MS). In this will he made a generous bequest to PMI: "I give to Pierre M. Irving, who for many years has managed my pecuniary concerns, gratuitously Five Thousand Dollars and I bequeath to him the manuscript of my Life of Washington, should it not have been published before my decease, and I leave it to his discretion to do with it what he may think fit, for his own pecuniary benefit...." See also p. 252, note 51.

[22] WI to Sarah Storrow, SS, May 6, 1851; LLWI, IV, 85.

that year he wrote to Sarah Storrow that he had "renounced all further pressing myself in the matter."[23]

Meanwhile, the activities of Pierre remained much of a piece with what they had been in the past decade, as did his ambitions. "I long for enough to break the chain that binds me to uncongenial drudgery," he wrote to Daniel Roberts in January 1851. "I 'want but little here below,' but 'I want that little' soon. At 48 one may be excused for craving repose; and I value the base drop only as it brings that consummation nearer." His stores of the "base drop" were steadily increasing. In November 1849 he had been designated Pension Agent for the entire southern district of the state of New York, and the emoluments from that enlarged responsibility, combined with his other salaries, now earned him over $4,000 annually.[24] Steadfast in their financial conservatism, he and Helen contented themselves with their parlour and bedroom as of old, although Pierre now allowed himself the luxury of a business assistant in the person of his nephew Pierre Leslie Irving, an 1848 graduate of Columbia College who was planning to take up the law.[25] He no longer troubled himself with court cases,[26] spending the greater part of his time in business "dispensing the favors of government" in Wall Street; and in the summer months he often turned over that function to Leslie. His occupations were so profitable that in August 1852 he made a cautious prophecy to Roberts: "I begin to entertain the hope of being able one of these days to retire to that quiet enjoyment of life for which I am best constituted, and which my spirit craves more than all the world's honors & wealth."[27] Until then, a correct, slightly rotund figure tipping the balance at 155 pounds, he made his way back and forth daily between Mrs. Lowe's elegant boarding house in 15th Street and the Bank of Commerce a few blocks away.

The phrase "quiet enjoyment of life" no longer implied to Pierre a country residence; he and Helen wished for no more than the regular access they enjoyed to such rural spots as Sunnyside.[28] In contrast,

[23] WI to Sarah Storrow, n.p., May 29, 1852; *LLWI*, IV, 105.

[24] PMI to Daniel Roberts, New York, January 22, 1851 (Huntington).

[25] Pierre Leslie Irving (1828-1891), the eldest child of Pierre Paris Irving, lived on Staten Island. In *Doggett's Directory* for 1850-1851, p. 257, he is listed as a notary public at 32 Wall Street, the address of the Bank of Commerce.

[26] The last case recorded in PMI's Legal register as having been argued before the New York Court of Common Pleas was in 1848. For his services in this case, the Bank of the State of Missouri vs. William W. Woodworth, he collected his largest single recorded fee, $309.28.

[27] PMI to Daniel Roberts, New York, August 25, 1852 (Huntington). Two weeks before he had written to Roberts on the same theme—that he was "living very comfortably and continuing every year to lay up something of the shining dust" (PMI to Daniel Roberts, New York, August 12, 1852—Huntington).

[28] The diary for 1854-1855 of Irving Van Wart, Jr. (b. January 20, 1841), twin son of Irving Van Wart and Sarah Craig Ames, affords several glimpses of the social life PMI and Helen led in the city. They took Sunday dinner quite regularly at the Van Warts' fine

Irving's predilection for his home was growing more pronounced. It is true that he still found much to enjoy in the city, particularly after days of drudgery in official duties. When in New York he regularly attended the opera,[29] and despite his usual dislike of mere vocal recitals he came so deeply to admire Jenny Lind, the "Priestess of Nature," that he was often among her audiences during her triumphant stay in the city beginning in September 1850.[30] Still, somewhat to his own surprise, he found himself "indisposed to cope with the bustle and confusion of the town, and more and more in love with the quiet of the country." An instance of this shift of identification occurred in November 1850, when Helen had arranged for the entire Sunnyside household to attend an evening concert by Jenny Lind. Irving went along, but upon arriving in the city he discovered that another person had been added to the party, which would thus be complete without him, and thereupon he suddenly returned home alone. The next morning Helen wrote expressing her concern and regret at his unannounced departure, but in his reply he assured her that he had left simply to avoid putting others to inconvenience: "While tossing about . . . on the troubled sea of the city, without a port at hand, I bethought myself of the snug, quiet little port I had left, and determined to ' 'bout ship' and run back to it." He had, he said, "led a life of single blessedness" until the next afternoon, when his nieces returned "to put an end to my dream of sovereignty."[31]

It had been many years since Irving had regarded New York as his home. In 1849 he and Pierre went together to see for the last time the house in William Street where he had been born and raised; shortly afterward it was pulled down.[32] More recently, in response to a re-

home in Lafayette Place. For example, on February 11, 1855, Irving Van Wart, Jr. recorded that they had all dined on "a little roasting pig." As well, either PMI or Helen stopped in for tea every few days, and sometimes they went on outings with members of the family. On December 10, 1854, "Cousin Pierre sat some time and then as Mama and Ames [the twin brother] and I were going to the Brevoort House to see Mrs Hoge he took us down there." March 1, 1855, "Cousin Eliza and Helen and Cousin Oscar came around and we all went (again) to the panorama (moving) of the seat of war (Sebastopol[)] we got home at 10 o clock and had tea and all went home" (NYPL, MS).

Helen and her sister (and sister-in-law) Eliza were still frequent companions. Catharine Frothingham (1832-1914), a daughter of their sister Jane Ann, spent much time at both their homes and recalled years later that she "was to them like an own child." Catharine Frothingham married Dr. Welding Dennis and named one of her daughters, Helen Irving Dennis (1854-1926), after her Aunt Helen. PMI was also close to the Frothingham family: John Pierre Frothingham (b. 1869), a grandson of Helen's sister Jane Ann, was named after him (Frothingham, Genealogy, pp. 42, 141, 146—NYPL , MS).

[29] Moses H. Grinnell rented a double box together with the Hamiltons and the Schuylers, and this was always at WI's service (WI to Sarah Storrow, SS, February 27, 1848—Yale). WI's correspondence includes frequent allusions to operas and performers. See, for example, WI to Sarah Storrow, SS, January 13, 1853, and November 23, 1854 (Yale); LLWI, IV, 76, 102, 163, 171, 181.

[30] LLWI, IV, 75-77.

[31] WI to Helen Irving, SS, November 17, 1850; LLWI, IV, 77-78.

[32] LLWI, I, 22.

mark by Charles A. Davis about the improvements daily to be seen in the city, he was moved to ask, "are all these changes and alterations *Improvements?*":

> Many of them to me are coupled with memories that make me sad – take for example, the hospitable mansion of our late friend, *Honble Philip Hone*—all his household Gods divided up and scattered among "his next of kin." – I felt all this as I passed the door one day and saw workmen busy altering the mansion into a banking house and the Library into a den for money changers. *Going, going, Gone!* may indeed be the motto of our changeful country, and especially our changeful city, where once a man is *gone,* he is too soon apt to be forgotten.[33]

To his long-absent sister Sarah Van Wart, Irving compared contemporary New York to a year-round fair.[34] "Even the opera does not draw me to town so often as formerly,"[35] he confessed to Sarah Storrow in 1852. He enjoyed visiting with nearby friends, or taking short excursions to his cousin Eliza Gabriel's home on Long Island[36] or to Kemble's at Cold Spring, up the river. Early in 1852 he summarized his sentiments: "I draw more and more into the little world of my country home as the silver cord which binds me to life is gradually loosening; and, indeed, I am so surrounded here by kind and affectionate hearts, and have such frequent visits from one or other of the family, that I feel no need and but little inclination to look beyond for enjoyment."[37]

Given the conception he had evolved of a desirable mode of life, Sunnyside fully merited his complacency. With its flourishing flower gardens, a greenhouse, an icehouse, a coach-house, doghouses, dovecotes, a "capacious hennery," stables for horses and cows, pens for sheep and pigs, and several vegetable plots—all of these looked after by hired men, it was fully fitted out as an estate where he could play the gentleman farmer.[38] Once, returning after a two-weeks' absence, he confessed quizzically: "I really believe more had been done in my absence than would have been done had I been home."[39] One unwelcome feature of his fourteen-acre property was that at regular intervals the cottage was shaken by the rumbling of locomotives on

[33] Charles A. Davis to PMI, New York, June 1863 (NYPL, Berg). Philip Hone (1780-1851), mayor of New York for one year, 1825-1826, was active in Whig circles and in civic and charitable undertakings.

[34] WI to Sarah Van Wart, n.p., August 29, 1847; *LLWI,* IV, 25.

[35] WI to Sarah Storrow, SS, January 13, 1852; *LLWI,* IV, 102.

On October 31, 1850, WI wrote to Sarah Storrow that he had enjoyed a recent visit there: "Eliza has refitted her house and made it a very cheerful residence; and she has the enviable talent of diffusing happiness around her" (Yale).

[37] WI to Sarah Storrow, SS, January 13, 1852; *LLWI,* IV, 101-02.

[38] Cater, "WI and SS," pp. 154-55; McLinden Interview (SHR). A diagram of the grounds at SS is in Butler, *WI's SS,* p. 31.

[39] WI to Mrs. John P. Kennedy, SS, March 11, 1853; *LLWI,* IV, 136.

the Hudson River Rail Road, whose right-of-way ran athwart his property along the river shore.[40] A captive to progress, he bore this affliction stoically, consoling himself that at least through expostulation he had convinced the engineers to discontinue blasting their steam whistles in friendly salute as they passed. Another redeeming point was that through the cooperation of Moses Grinnell, a Director of the company, it had become possible at certain times to hail passenger trains to stop directly alongside the cottage so as to accommodate himself and his family.[41]

In the summer of 1851 the vicinity of Sunnyside became even more a place of family resort than previously when Moses and Julia Grinnell moved into a palatial home they had built immediately to the north.[42] Prostrated by overwork, Grinnell had been commanded by his physician to relocate away from New York to a community where he could live at a more deliberate pace. He complied at least so far as to build his country residence, although once he had moved into it he could not be kept from plying back and forth in his private boat between it and the city. Grinnell expended some of his surplus energy in landscaping his grounds,[43] and the result was a parklike expanse of lawn between his house and Irving's. By mutual pact the two men had no fences or barriers separating their properties, and the gravelled walks of each ran without interruption into those of his neighbour. The consequence, Irving wrote in January 1852, "is a continual outpouring of one house into the other; the [Grinnell] children are sporting about our walks and lawns, sometimes with their pet pony and a troop of pet dogs." During the summer of 1851 Pierre and Helen stayed at the Grinnell mansion, and, to use Irving's words, "there was a perpetual jubilee."[44]

An increasingly important resident of Sunnyside following his arrival there in 1849 was Irving's "Prime Minister," Robert McLinden. Shortly after emigrating from Ireland during the Potato Famine, Robert drifted into Tarrytown, where he met and married Maria Nevins, then Irving's assistant cook. Hired as a gardener, he rapidly ascended in his employer's favour until he became the chief caretaker of the gounds. Except for the chambermaids, Robert and Maria were Irving's only employees who were permitted to live on the premises.

[40] Construction of the Hudson River Rail Road along the east bank of the river in WI's vicinity had begun in 1848. See *LLWI*, IV, 36-38.

[41] MS Outline, Chapter XXVI (1850); *LLWI*, IV, 67-68, 87.

[42] It was "in a state of progress" when WI wrote to Sarah Storrow on July 10, 1850 (Yale), and was habitable early in 1851. See WI to Thomas W. Storrow, SS, February 27, 1851 (Harvard). The Grinnell property, just east of the Albany post-road, was about a quarter of a mile from the cottage. See "Map of Irvington, 1867" (SHR) and Newell S. Brown, *Map of West Chester County, New York, from Actual Surveys . . .* (Philadelphia, 1851).

[43] WI to Sarah Storrow, SS, January 13, 1852 (Yale); Helen Irving to WI, New York, February 5, 1853 (Yale).

[44] WI to Sarah Storrow, SS, January 13, 1852 (Yale). Oscar and Eliza were among the summer visitors to SS.

Irving thought the vivacious Maria "handsome," and he often called on her in the afternoons to take tea. Late in 1853, upon learning that she had just given birth to twins, he built a six-room cottage for the growing family a short distance from the main house,[45] and he even helped to furnish it. Robert amply repaid the kindnesses of his employer by faithful service as a viceregent. For example, on occasions when Irving was absent overnight, he slept in the main house in order to assuage the timorous fears of Ebenezer's daughters, who were unable to sleep when they heard the drum and patter of squirrels and birds on the tin roof over their bedroom. Among Robert's other duties were carrying surplus fruit and vegetables by the wagonload to widows in nearby Dearman and Tarrytown, and leaving wood, coal, linen, bedding, and clothing with the poor and sick in the vicinity.[46]

In order to perform charitable errands Robert must have needed to drive at least a mile or two, for in the 1850's the near neighbourhood of Sunnyside was hardly a depressed area. In fact, most of Irving's neighbours possessed much larger fortunes than he. As we have seen, twenty years earlier Tarrytown had been a sleepy farming community; but in the interim it had become virtually a showplace,[47] dotted with baronial residences owned by what N. P. Willis called a *"class who can afford to let the trees grow."*[48] Irving was on friendly terms with many of the wealthy families living near him.[49] Two miles to the north was "Rockwood," home of the independently wealthy Edwin C. Bartlett, whose wife was a particular admirer.[50] Others among his familiar acquaintances in that direction from Sunnyside were Richard M. Blatchford, a New York banker and city officer; William Hoge, another banker; Henry Holdrege, Jr., whose wife Mary was a niece of Grinnell; and "General" James Watson Webb, the controversial editor of the New York *Courier and Enquirer*, a man toward whom Irving had for many years held a rather cautious regard.[51] To the east lived other

[45] It was this cottage rather than his own which prompted WI's *bon mot* in a letter to Mrs. Kennedy, November 11, 1853: "A pretty country retreat is like a pretty wife—one is always throwing away money in decorating it" (*LLWI*, IV, 167). The date of the letter is from PMI, MS Outline, Chapter XXXII (1853).

[46] McLinden Interview (SHR). Catharine Anne (McLinden) Richardson (b. SS, March 6, 1865), was the tenth of thirteen children born to Robert and Maria McLinden. Named after Ebenezer's daughter Catharine (Kate), she began to work at SS as a maid at the age of twelve.

[47] The fine homes in the vicinity were accorded generous coverage in descriptive works, such as Benson J. Lossing, *The Hudson from the Wilderness to the Sea* (New York, 1866), pp. 340-64. See also N. P. Willis, *Out-Doors at Idlewild . . .* (New York, 1855); Edgar M. Bacon, *The Hudson River, from Ocean to Source, Historical, Legendary, Picturesque* (New York, 1910).

[48] *Out-Doors at Idlewild*, p. 47.

[49] Information concerning the whereabouts of particular residences in WI's vicinity is from "Map of Irvington, 1867" (SHR).

[50] For an account of the Bartlett home, see Allison Albee, "The Case of the Missing Castle," *Westchester Historian*, XLV (Fall 1969), 78-86. See also J. T. Scharf, *History of Westchester County, New York . . .* (Philadelphia, 1886), II, 310; and *LLWI*, IV, 107-08.

[51] An account of Webb (1802-1884) is given by James L. Crouthamel in "James Watson Webb, Mercantile Editor," *New York History*, 41, no. 4 (October 1960), 400-22.

contemporary personalities now forgotten, such as Edward S. Jaffray, a potent merchant prince and a frank admirer;[52] George D. Morgan, brother of Edwin D. Morgan, the governor of New York from 1858 to 1862; and John E. Williams, another independently wealthy man who often walked to Sunnyside from his home, "Strawberry-Hill," one-half mile away. Irving's closest and most intimate neighbours lived to the south. These included Robert Bowne Minturn, Grinnell's business partner; George L. Schuyler, grandson of Philip J. Schuyler, the Revolutionary general; and James A. Hamilton, son of Alexander Hamilton and father of Irving's former secretary of Madrid. Hamilton's daughters Mary and Angelica, who in 1850 struck the visiting Swedish novelist Fredrika Bremer as resembling "types of two female characters which are often introduced in Cooper's novels,"[53] were Irving's favourites among the local young ladies, and they were frequent visitors to Sunnyside. Mrs. Schuyler, who was a sister of the Hamilton girls, also paid regular calls. In fact, carriages bound on social missions over the surprisingly ill-kept roads of the small community were a common sight. Irving's nieces had a large circle of friends and went visiting punctually once a week.[54]

Aside from visiting, playing host, or tending to his grounds, Irving's favourite extra-literary pastime seems to have been amusing himself with children, relatives or no. In 1879 Irving Grinnell, one of Julia's three children, wrote in recollection of his own childhood that his Uncle Washington had "delighted in gathering some of his little nephews and nieces on his knees, & in telling them stories by the hour." Afternoons and evenings he was "constantly at our house," Grinnell wrote. His earliest memory of Irving was of being told a story:

> My little sister & I sat, one on each of his knees, while his arms were about us, & he told us a favorite story called "Hempen House" of which we never tired & which was as well known among the younger members of the Irving family, as was, in later years, any one of his charming books.[55]

Webb's title of "General" was conferred on him in recognition of his diplomatic services, not as a result of military activities (*DAB*, XIX, 574-75).

[52] Jaffray's daughter Florence was the neighbour to whom WI dedicated his poem, "The Lay of the SS Ducks," written after the failure of Jaffray's attempt to dam up the small brook that ran past SS. The poem was first printed in Scharf, *Westchester County*, I, 239-40.

[53] *The Homes of the New World*, trans. Mary Howitt (New York, 1853), I, 58.

[54] McLinden Interview (SHR). On January 25, 1854, WI wrote to Sarah Storrow: "Our neighborhood has filled up very much of late. Villas are springing up in all directions, and some of them are very tasteful and picturesque. Some of our new neighbors are very agreeable people, and live through the whole year in the country. We have had several public lectures this winter, not a mile distant from Sunnyside, and very well attended. So you see this part of the country is quite looking up" (Yale).

[55] Irving Grinnell to Charles Dudley Warner, New York, November 10, 1879 (Trinity College). Grinnell's claim about the younger members of the family seems to have had some foundation. On April 24, 1856, WI recalled in a letter to Sarah Storrow

The children of Edgar and Amanda, Pierre Paris and Anna, and Theodore and Jane—all nephews of Irving and their spouses[56]—made visits to Sunnyside, where they were entertained by their great-uncle and watched over closely by their aunts.[57] As many anecdotes attest, Irving's enjoyment of children was returned in kind. According to Lewis Gaylord Clark, "the little children of the neighborhood . . . used to bring him fresh flowers, and often put them in his pew before he came to church on Sunday."[58] One summer afternoon as he stood chatting with a group of children a woman standing nearby mistakenly assured him that he must surely be "a kind father of a big family."[59] He enjoyed to sit and watch children, and he was pleased to have made of Sunnyside a common playground for his dozens of young relatives.[60]

From time to time Irving improved his rural leisure by a stint at the life of Washington, that "long task."[61] He was careful to maintain a casual attitude toward the project, and his progress on it was slow and erratic. Even though he had not called upon Pierre for serious literary assistance on the biography since 1847, he was confident of his nephew's interest in its eventual publication.[62] In his will of 1850 he had bequeathed to Pierre the manuscript of the work, should it be incomplete at his death,[63] and he had kept him generally apprised of

the days at Paris when her daughter Kate "used to take such possession of me and oblige me to *put away my spectacles* and give up my book and entertain her for the hundredth time with the story of little Miss Muss and Hempen House" (Yale).

[56] Two of WI's favourites were Hatty and Nelly, daughters of Pierre Paris Irving. In 1847, shortly after the departure from SS of Charlotte Irving, who was married in that year to William R. Grinnell, he wrote to Sarah Storrow that he had been entertaining the girls at the cottage: "I have been much pleased with them and hope to have them frequently at the cottage. I intend to have others of the children with me in the autumn . . . I must keep up my supply of nieces" (Yale). The exact date of this letter is lost. See also WI to Sarah Storrow, SS, November 23, 1854 (Yale). Another favourite was Kate Irving, daughter of WI's nephew William, who until his sudden death in August 1854 was employed at the United States Census Office in Washington, D.C.

[57] Most of WI's young relatives enjoyed their visits at SS, but not all. On one occasion Helen Irving took her niece Catharine Frothingham there, and the latter recalled years afterward that "it was a constant case of: 'Hush, children, your uncle is taking his nap.' Or, 'Children, you must keep quiet, your uncle is writing' " (Frothingham, Genealogy, p. 158—NYPL, MS).

[58] Clark, "Recollections," pp. 558-59.

[59] Charles A. Davis to PMI, New York, June 1863 (NYPL, Berg); LLWI, IV, 115.

[60] LLWI, IV, 29.

[61] WI to Sarah Storrow, SS, January 13, 1852 (Yale); LLWI, IV, 102.

[62] That he was giving at least occasional assistance on the biography is indicated by a manuscript, entitled in PMI's hand "Memoranda of Hiram Paulding, son of John Paulding, sent to P.M.I. July 17th 1851" (Yale). On the three folio pages of this document Hiram Paulding had written out an account of the capture of Major John André near Tarrytown in 1777. He began: "This is the revelation that I heard my father often repeat when a child." John Paulding had been one of the captors of André. Marginal notes to this account in the hand of PMI indicate that he compared the Hiram Paulding version with a deposition on the same subject given by John Paulding, published in Peleg Chandler's *American Criminal Trials* (Boston, 1841-1844), II, 232.

[63] "Last Will and Testament of WI, July 28, 1850," typewritten copy (NYPL, MS).

his progress since. Meanwhile, Pierre devoted a substantial proportion of his time to performing the favours and delegated chores which had become his ordinary exertions on his uncle's behalf. He looked after Irving's finances, submitted periodic reports of his accounts,[64] lent a confidential ear to his ruminations on all subjects, accompanied him on excursions of various lengths and purposes, and was, in general, his patient and capable factotum.[65]

In fact, the reliable assistance of Pierre went far in itself toward making possible for Irving the state of easeful gentlemanly retirement which he had awaited so long. After 1848, Pierre's superintendence of his uncle's affairs was so all-inclusive that Irving was free virtually to forget financial matters, except routinely to ratify or occasionally to modify courses of action submitted for his approval. How clearly he recognized this opportunity and how unreservedly he seized it is suggested by the character of his association with George Putnam, the man with whom of all persons he might plausibly be expected to hold primarily contractual relations. Whatever Pierre might report as Putnam's shortcomings as a man of business, Irving liked him personally and thought him "amiable, obliging, and honorable."[66] From time to time the elderly author was to be seen sitting at his ease in the back corner of Putnam's bookshop in Broadway, glancing through new arrivals from London or chatting with friends.[67] Occasionally he even spent a night as a guest at Putnam's home on Staten Island. At Christmas, 1852, he wrote to the publisher that he had "never had dealings with any man, whether in the way of business or friendship, more perfectly free from any alloy."[68] On his side, Putnam felt "proud satisfaction" at the author's good opinion and set a high value on his status as one of the select circle who were welcome at Sunnyside whenever they came; but he did not presume upon the friendship. In a memoir of Irving he described him as "a man who would unconsciously and quietly command deferential regard and consideration . . . emphatically a gentleman, in the best sense of that word."[69] It seems evident that Irving had so completely delegated the business end of his association with Putnam to Pierre that his own relations with the publisher were, except in special circumstances, more social than commercial.[70]

[64] The jokes between WI and Helen prompted by these reports still flourished. On February 28, 1853, having just received from PMI a summary of his accounts, WI wrote to Helen from Washington that he was "in constant dread of growing rich in spite of myself" (NYPL, MS).

[65] On one occasion, PMI was employed as a lowly courier of spinach seed for the use of Robert. See WI to Kate Irving, New York, September 14, 1852 (SHR).

[66] WI to George Putnam, SS, December 27, 1852; LLWI, IV, 120.

[67] Putnam, "Recollections of Irving," pp. 605, 608; note also the return address of WI's note to James Fenimore Cooper, November 11, 1850: "Putnam's Desk" (Yale).

[68] Putnam, "Recollections of Irving," p. 605; WI to George Putnam, SS, December 27, 1852—LLWI, IV, 120-21.

[69] Putnam, "Recollections of Irving," p. 603.

[70] In an appreciation published in A Memoir of Putnam, the publisher's daughter Minnie commented on the affinity of her father's character with WI's. The association

Of course, on financial grounds alone Putnam had every reason to feel cordial toward this leading light among his authors. In 1853, at the expiration of their five-year agreement, Irving authorized a renewal of the arrangement probably with the terms substantially unchanged, even though with the popularity of his works so clearly re-established he might reasonably have demanded a higher royalty rate than before.[71] By 1855, Putnam claimed sales of 255,000 volumes from Irving's revised works.[72] However, while he tallied up his profits and felicitated himself on his access to the author's good company, Putnam was rather negligent as a businessman and was steering his firm into desperate straits where he was to find in Pierre a more useful if less glamourous colleague. Always an optimist, in 1856 Putnam over-extended his ready resources on credit, and when one of his agents failed he found himself unable to take up the man's debts. In order to weather the storm, he found it necessary to arrange with Pierre a deferred schedule of royalty payments.[73] Yet even this narrow escape was insufficient warning to bring him round to sound business principles. According to his son, George Haven Putnam, he "preferred to believe . . . that 'things would come out right.' He found it very difficult indeed to convince himself that . . . any men with whom he had direct personal relations, would fail to do what they had promised."[74] Within a year Putnam had precipitated himself into a more serious crisis from which, but for the intercession of his friends, he could not possibly have escaped.

On July 4, 1857, a young man whom he had recently taken into partnership and placed in charge of the firm's accounts mysteriously drowned. Purely as a matter of routine, following the accident Putnam hired an accountant to audit his ledgers before some other person should begin to maintain them; and within a few days he was informed that his late partner had embezzled thousands of the firm's

between the two men, she wrote, "was much more than the ordinary relations between a publisher and author who share each other's success. . . . [Putnam's] divination of Irving's possibilities for success, to whose external conditions he largely contributed, was not the mere insight of a man of business trained to detect what will succeed. It was rather that joyful perception of a person who meets in another the full and graceful and adequate expression of what he would like to say himself, and said in just the way in which he would wish to say it. . . . Irving was, indeed, his hero, his ideal in the world of letter [*sic*] in which he lived, his type of the region of that world which he most preferred" (II, 405-06).

[71] No evidence concerning the terms of the 1853 agreement survives, but the facts that PMI seems to have intended his summary of the arrangement of 1848 to be understood as defining the financial relations between WI and Putnam until 1857, when they were put "on a different footing" (*LLWI*, IV, 42, 237), and also that in 1857 Putnam urged a higher royalty rate upon WI (*Putnam*, p. 245), suggest that the agreement of 1853 was a renewal of the earlier one, perhaps with the guaranteed annual payment equal to that in the final year of the period covered by the 1848 contract.

[72] PMI, MS Outline, Chapter XXXV (1856).

[73] "Has strained himself of late to take up the paper of an agent who had failed—am arranging with him & Leslie" (PMI, MS Outline, Chapter XXXV [1856]).

[74] Putnam, *Putnam*, p. 235.

dollars to finance a series of disastrous private speculations. Notes authorized by this person but not recorded in the firm's books soon began to be presented for payment. Putnam was for a time despondent, but within a few weeks he was his plucky self again, engaged in a narrow but hopeful struggle to save his firm from bankruptcy.[75] Had the year 1857 been a normal one financially, his property in copyrights, plates, machinery, and printed stock would have been adequate as collateral to warrant a loan in an amount sufficient to discharge the notes. Early in September, however, a monetary crisis similar to the one of 1837 swept across the United States, forcing an immediate suspension of credit and swiftly wiping out thousands of merchants. Putnam's sudden inability to borrow money or even to sell his assets at decent prices rendered it impossible for him to pay his debts. Without some unforeseen reversal of fortune, he would have no choice but to abandon his lately thriving business.

In this situation he assigned ownership of his entire property to Lowell Mason, a still-solvent fellow publisher and old friend, who undertook to realize enough out of the assets to satisfy the creditors and allow resumption of the business on a reduced scale. Meanwhile Irving, who through Pierre had been kept informed of Putnam's difficulties, was not at all inclined to defect from his associate even though the rumours of the publisher's failure had stimulated offers to take over publication of the revised works.[76] On the contrary, he wished to come to Putnam's aid, and he asked Pierre what he might do. Pierre re-examined the books of the firm, consulted with Putnam and Mason, and decided that the best measure for all concerned was to purchase from Mason, the assignee, Putnam's most valuable former asset, the stereotype plates of Irving's revised works.[77] In this transaction Irving would simply be providing Putnam, through Mason's intermediation, the capital he needed to resume operations in return for the title to the plates. Irving assented to the proposal, but once the exchange was made, legend has it that he came to the relieved publisher with this surprising remark: "Now, Putnam, I want you to be the owner of these plates for me." In response to Putnam's natural disclaimer that he had no money to pay for the property he had just sold, Irving is said to have spelled out more clearly the terms of a new arrangement between them: "I will sell you [back] the plates and receive payments from you by instalments. . . . You, being the owner of the plates, will then pay me royalties at the same rate as before."[78] In

[75] Putnam, *Putnam*, pp. 236-39.

[76] Putnam, *Putnam*, pp. 242-43; PMI, MS Outline, Chapter XXXVI (1857).

[77] Putnam, *Putnam*, pp. 243-44.

[78] Putnam, *Putnam*, p. 244. The exact date of the agreement between WI and Putnam is unknown, as are the precise terms. In his summary of the "literary statistics" of WI's career, PMI wrote that the "stereotype and steel plates" received from Putnam were worth "about $17,000" (*LLWI*, IV, 411). On December 31, 1857 he reported to WI that, "taking a business retrospect of the year . . . you have received from Mr. Putnam . . . what is equivalent to twenty-five thousand dollars," but in this report he

effect, this meant that Irving was loaning a large sum of money to Putnam without penalty of any kind. However, while it is barely possible that the two men may actually have held some such conversation as this, the probabilities are against it, for both the sale of the plates and the new arrangement with Putnam as "owner" were negotiated with Putnam by Pierre.[79] If Irving did accost Putnam in the way described above, as the publisher's son claims he did, he did so purely in the way of friendship, to seal a compact already arranged on his behalf between Putnam and his nephew. He may well have mentioned to Pierre his wish to spare the publisher the burden of paying interest on his debt, or of paying a higher royalty rate in exchange for the use of the plates, but he played no other substantial part in the matter.

Rescued at the brink of disaster, Putnam set up renewed operations with all his customary gusto. He focused his attention on aggressively marketing Irving's revised works in a new uniform edition, and with a surer eye for personnel than formerly he hired an imaginative new agent, Charles T. Evans, to supervise a house-to-house campaign selling the complete works in a bewildering variety of sizes, qualities of paper, bindings, and degrees of illustration—ranging from the unillustrated plain duodecimo on ordinary paper bound in plebeian green cloth to an extra-illustrated octavo on cream paper bound in full morocco.[80] A new contract went into effect between Irving and Putnam on April 1, 1858, specifying that the publisher was to act as agent for the sale of the author's works until the debt on the plates was repaid, and in the meantime was to pay royalties as before. Under this agreement Putnam managed to repurchase all of the plates

did not specify how much of the total was from royalty payments. Early in 1858 PMI advised WI that a new contract with Putnam, to take effect April 1, 1858, had been executed. In *LLWI* he summarized the arrangement: "Mr. Putnam, who had made a full settlement of their present business, was to act as his agent, Mr. Irving purchasing from him the stereotype plates of all his works" (IV, 238). Putnam was eager to regain ownership of the plates, however, and he made payments to that end on account. According to George H. Putnam, by 1859 "the plates were again fully under the ownership of the publisher" (*Putnam*, p. 245).

[79] The evidence supporting this statement is circumstantial only, but strong. PMI's long-established role as WI's financial administrator; his function for ten years as the superintendent of WI's interests with Putnam in particular; and his letters to WI of December 31, 1857 and early 1858 summarizing for his uncle's information the state of the Putnam account, all suggest the unlikelihood that in 1857 WI broke precedent and formulated the new arrangement with Putnam by himself. On February 15, 1858, WI wrote to Sarah Storrow that despite some misgivings he had managed to survive the crisis of 1857 quite comfortably: "I have experienced but a very moderate loss in my investments and my relations with my publisher have been placed on a different footing, which I trust will prove advantageous to us both" (Yale). As much as any other evidence, the indefinite passive voice in his reference to the new arrangement with Putnam suggests that he was not himself its formulator.

[80] See Putnam's advertisement in the New York *Tribune*, August 30, 1859, p. 1, col. 2. The plainest available copies of the new, twenty-one-volume "Sunnyside" edition were at this time priced at $27.50; the most costly at $68.

except those for the *Life of Washington* within two years.[81] Thus, the crisis of 1857 eventually redounded to Irving's advantage by putting his works into wider circulation and to Putnam's by placing him in a position where he soon more than recovered his losses. Both had benefitted from the assistance of Pierre, through whose acumen the good feeling between them had been translated into a new, mutually profitable business relationship.

As the list of Irving's plutocratic neighbours suggests, during the 1850's he was the friend of many businessmen more prominent (and provident) than Putnam. Without exception, however, his relations with them were those of a fellow gentleman rather than of a professional colleague. The degree to which his reliance on the good offices of Pierre enabled him to form associations with men of the commercial and political worlds on the terms most congenial to himself is perhaps best indicated by the character of his friendship with John Pendleton Kennedy, the lawyer-politician-financier-litterateur from Baltimore. The two men met first in 1834 and again at irregular intervals afterward, but their acquaintance did not grow close until the summer of 1852, when they chanced to meet at Saratoga Springs, a fashionable watering-place in upstate New York. Irving had decided to visit the Springs in order to quiet a nervous condition that was interfering with his intermittent attentions to the *Washington*,[82] while Kennedy, who had just been designated Secretary of the Navy, was on a pleasure excursion with his family prior to taking up his official duties. Upon being obliged to return to Washington, Kennedy asked Irving to pay his wife "some small attentions" in his absence; and Irving, who had secretly been anxious that he might become lonely for the domestic life at Sunnyside, readily agreed. He confided to his niece Mary at home that he was relieved to have found "a little domestic party to attach [himself] to."[83] He immensely enjoyed his three-week "social outbreak"[84] at Saratoga Springs, and at the close of his stay there Mrs. Kennedy urged him to pay the family a visit at their new home in Washington. The following January Irving made good his promise to do so, and during his sojourn of over a month among this accomplished family he became a close friend of theirs. He enjoyed hobhobbing with Kennedy—"Horseshoe," as he called him[85]—and he took

---

[81] Putnam, *Putnam*, p. 245. PMI's initial entry in his account book as executor of WI's estate is as follows: "This book was originally used by Mr G.P. Putnam for W.I. but finding no further occasion for it I have cut out 2 leaves of his entries of no value—& adopted it for my own use as Executor of Washington Irving" (Account Book). It is tempting to speculate that the two missing leaves included a list of Putnam's payments on the stereotype plates, which by the time of WI's death he had completed, thus obviating the necessity of a running account of them.

[82] See *LLWI*, IV, 106.

[83] WI to Mary Irving, Saratoga Springs, July 21, 1852; *LLWI*, IV, 109.

[84] WI to Kate Irving, Saratoga, July 24, 1852; *LLWI*, IV, 110.

[85] After Kennedy's work of fiction, *Horseshoe Robinson* (1835), which was dedicated to WI.

an interest in several relatives whom he had met as well.[86] In all, Irving spent fully five months during 1853 and 1854 in the company of the Kennedys, and in the intervals of his absence from them he addressed a steady stream of pleasant, chatty letters to one family member or another. In the years after 1854, he saw the Kennedys less frequently, being caught up with his own concerns, but he always looked forward to meetings with them, and to the end of his life he maintained a correspondence with them.[87]

Taking note of this most intimate friendship formed by Irving during his last years of life, Stanley T. Williams has explained its development on the basis of the elderly author's supposed interest in business affairs. In Williams' view, Irving was attracted to Kennedy because the latter embodied for him the "commercial standards" for literature and life which he had recently adopted himself. Their talk, according to Williams, "was forever of insurance companies, Wall Street, railroads, and the building of houses," and in general "they were now just prosperous American business men, hobnobbing together." About literature "they exhibited no curiosity whatever," viewing authorship merely as a gentlemanly avocation for men of the world who had more substantial matters to concern them. "Kennedy crystallized for Irving an attitude toward literature" which he espoused "unashamed."[88]

In light of Irving's conscious and virtually complete dismissal of his own business affairs to the supervision of Pierre, this characterization of him as a full-bellied, philistinic old man full of talk about cent.-per-cent. is clearly erroneous. At least once during the 1830's, when he was hoping to multiply his fortunes by speculating in common stock, Irving had written to the knowledgable Kennedy asking his opinion of certain proposed investments.[89] Yet now when Kennedy wrote to him on business topics he had nothing to reply. For example, when Kennedy asked his opinion in October 1854 about the financial difficulties under which George Putnam was then rumoured to be labouring, he responded: "I am not sufficient of a man of business to give you the kind of information you require. . . . My nephew Pierre M Irving looked into the matter on my part; and found it much better than he had expected."[90] Far from emulating or even

---

[86] In particular, with Kennedy's niece Mary, to whom he addressed a series of letters. See Stanley T. Williams and Leonard B. Beach, "WI's Letters to Mary Kennedy," *American Literature*, 6 (March 1934), 44-65. WI was also pleased by Mr. Gray, Kennedy's father-in-law. See WI to Edward Gray, SS, April 24, 1853; *LLWI*, IV, 143-44. He thought Mrs. Kennedy "a lovely woman" (WI to Sarah Storrow, SS, October 27, 1856—Yale).

[87] On October 27, 1856, WI wrote to Sarah Storrow that he was glad she had taken care of the Kennedys during their recent stay in Paris: "They are friends that I value very highly and with whom I have been especially intimate of late years" (Yale). See also WI to John Pendleton Kennedy, New York, October 29, 1858 (Virginia).

[88] *Life*, II, 208, 212.

[89] See WI to John P. Kennedy, New York, June 9, 1835; Campbell, "The Kennedy Papers," p. 4.

[90] WI to John P. Kennedy, SS, October 5, 1854 (Peabody).

approving of Kennedy's periodic preoccupation with investments, he counselled him at second-hand to give them over in favour of writing. "Your Uncle John," he wrote to Kennedy's niece Mary Kennedy in December 1853, "I understand is occupying himself very much with rail roads. I wish he would put his mind on a better track and leave his every day concerns to every day people."[91]

Contrary to the allegation of Stanley T. Williams, Irving did not share Kennedy's view of literature as only a gentleman's avocation.[92] Writing was not an exercise he could take or leave casually, but his profession, and at best his pleasure. The two men differed radically in their ideas of a satisfactory mode of living. For example, Kennedy thrived in the political arena, a sphere of activity which Irving had long since eschewed. In February 1854, upon receiving from his friend an invitation to accompany him and President Fillmore on a tour of the South, he replied to Mrs. Kennedy: "Heaven preserve me from any tour of the kind! . . . To have to listen to the speeches that would be made, at dinners and other occasions, to Mr. Fillmore and himself; and to the speeches that Mr. Fillmore and he would make in return! . . . No, no." Neither businessman, politician, nor willingly even a celebrity, Irving valued his comfort and privacy too highly to travel "among the million."[93] He respected Kennedy's ability to get things done, as he had always admired that trait in men of affairs; he enjoyed his wealth of anecdote and consistent good humour; and he felt at home with his family. On the whole, Irving's friendship with Kennedy stands as proof of his happy ability to get along with men much different from himself. While Kennedy toured the country and helped direct the course of the empire, Irving occupied himself on a narrower scale. Writing "has become a kind of habitude with me," he wrote to Mary Kennedy in March 1854, "and unless I have some task in hand to occupy a great part of my time I am at a loss what to do."[94]

During his first visit at the Kennedy home in Washington, in January 1853, Irving attempted to make headway in his research for the *Life of Washington* by spending his days rummaging through the Archives at the Department of State. He was taken aback by the mass of material to be examined, particularly since he knew that Jared Sparks had already surveyed these same collections in preparing his standard edition of Washington's writings.[95] His labours at the Ar-

[91] WI to Mary Kennedy, SS, December 17, 1853; Williams and Beach, "WI's Letters to Mary Kennedy," p. 59.

[92] According to Charles H. Bohner, *John Pendleton Kennedy: Gentleman from Baltimore* (Baltimore, 1961), p. 236, Kennedy did regard writing in this way and showed a patrician "indifference to public taste."

[93] WI to Mrs. John P. Kennedy, SS, February 21, 1854; *LLWI*, IV, 170.

[94] WI to Mary Kennedy, SS, May 27, 1853; Williams and Beach, "WI's Letters to Mary Kennedy," p. 50.

[95] *The Writings of George Washington . . .* , 12 vols. (Boston, 1834-37). WI told Charles Lanman that among "the Washington Papers in the Department of State . . . he had found very little in them worth printing which had not already been published" ("A Day with WI," *National Intelligencer*, March 20, 1857, p. 2; see also *LLWI*, IV, 228.

chives were lightened somewhat by the assistance of their curator, the prolific painter and literary jack-of-all-trades Charles Lanman,[96] but the new material he managed to unearth was really of trifling importance. Sometimes, he told Lanman, all his work on the biography seemed sheer wasted effort.[97] When he returned to Sunnyside on March 11, he had resolved to put the whole troublesome subject out of his mind indefinitely. Within a month, however, his authorial instinct reasserted itself. As he celebrated his birthday among relatives on April 3, he enjoyed a high sense of well-being, noting that in spite of his years he seemed still to possess good health, and he looked forward to intensified bouts with the biography. In this hopeful mood he began anew, but after a few days of study and writing he fell ill with a severe nervous irritation that dispelled any false notions he might have harboured about his physical condition. He was seventy years old, and he was unable to write a page.

Prostrated once again in consequence of his devotion to this task, Irving was regretful and confused. He could not hope to write and remain healthy, and yet he could not remain inactive and be content. Early in May, as he sat at home with these gloomy thoughts, he received from Mary Kennedy the information that a relative of George Washington living not far from the Kennedy's regular residence near Baltimore owned unpublished letters and diaries written by the first President.[98] Would Irving consider coming south in order to see these manuscripts? The invitation had arrived at an opportune time, and he had no difficulty rationalizing his wish to accept it. Why should he not make this journey, he thought, and so combine his research responsibilities with his pleasure? He might even hope to uncover material that would place his biography in an entirely new perspective. The very thought of the visit almost renewed his optimism about the book. Yet, after all, he was unable to wish away his fear that as it stood the narrative amounted to a wasted effort. If it really was as lifeless as at times it seemed, he should trouble himself with it no longer. Before setting out for Baltimore he asked Pierre to read carefully through the entire manuscript and to give him his candid opinion of it.[99] Since he and Helen were to "mount guard" at the cottage during his absence,[100] Pierre would have the leisure and the quiet surroundings

[96] Lanman (1819-1895) dedicated to WI his *Adventures in the Wilds of America* (Philadelphia, 1854); see also *LLWI*, IV, 30.

[97] Lanman, "A Day with WI." This account, in the form of a letter to Peter Force, was dated February 20, 1853.

[98] *LLWI*, IV, 148; WI to Mary Kennedy, SS, May 27, 1853—Williams and Beach, "WI's Letters to Mary Kennedy," p. 50. The relative of Washington was Mr. Washington Lewis; see Henry T. Tuckerman, *The Life of John Pendleton Kennedy* (New York, 1871), pp. 358-59.

[99] *LLWI*, IV, 148.

[100] They were willing, but a change of plans was necessary to enable them to do so. On June 26, WI wrote to Helen from Cassilis, the Kennedys' home: "I hope you find the sojourn at the Cottage pleasant enough to indemnify you for being kept from Staten Island" (NYPL, MS).

necessary for him to arrive at a sound critical estimate. Pierre was of course willing to accommodate his uncle in a matter which was obviously causing him anxiety. Thus, on June 13 Irving began his journey to Baltimore, his feelings about the Washington at their lowest ebb ever.

In the days immediately following his uncle's departure Pierre spent long hours, sometimes accompanied by Helen, going over the considerable body of manuscript entrusted to him. He found himself becoming engrossed as he reviewed the account of Washington's youth and military career— struck, in his words, that "so much of freshness and new interest could be thrown about a subject so often gone over."[101] On June 19, still in the midst of reading, he communicated this reaction to his uncle. Irving was delighted and wrote back that he was beginning "to hope that my labor has not been thrown away."[102] During the next two weeks Pierre read on, relaying further favourable impressions; and on July 5 he pronounced as his verdict that the work, which in its present form concluded with Washington's accession to the Presidency in 1789, was essentially complete as it stood, requiring only a few refinements of style. "Familiar as I am with the story," he reported, "I have been equally surprised and gratified to perceive what new interest it gains in your hands. I doubt not the work will be equally entertaining to young and old."[103] To Irving, the value of this opinion far exceeded that of the other benefits he had derived from his journey. His visit to the relative of Washington had turned up scarcely anything worth notice, and during his stay with the Kennedys he had failed to overcome his nervous ailment. Nevertheless, as he replied to Pierre on July 8, he was "prodigiously relieved."[104] If he half-consciously suspected that his nephew's high opinion of the book could not possibly be accurate in his own eyes, and if he was unable as yet to give it "the toning up which a painter gives to his picture,"[105] with luck his time to sit down to work would come soon enough. When he returned home in mid-July he had actually convinced himself that his task was almost finished. "I feel," he wrote with satisfaction, "that my working days are over."[106]

By 1853, too, Pierre had almost arrived at his own long-envisioned goal. After spending the entire summer at Sunnyside, in October he was, according to Ebenezer, "actively in use"[107] of his office at the bank. Early in the following year, however, he resigned his position as Pension Agent, retaining only that of Notary. After thirteen years' tenure in his federal post he had naturally become a

---

[101] LLWI, IV, 151.

[102] WI to PMI, Cassilis, June 25, 1853; LLWI, IV, 151.

[103] PMI to WI, SS, July 6, 1853; LLWI, IV, 153.

[104] WI to PMI, Ellicott's Mills, July 8, 1853; LLWI, IV, 154.

[105] WI to Helen Irving, [Cassilis], June 26, 1853; LLWI, IV, 152.

[106] WI to PMI, Ellicott's Mills, July 8, 1853; LLWI, IV, 154.

[107] Ebenezer Irving to William Irving, SS, October 24, 1853 (SHR).

familiar figure to the pensioners whom he served, and after his resignation they continued to call at his office for routine assistance. Unfortunately, his successor, a Mr. Livingston, was not only inexperienced in work of this nature but was vocally disgruntled at having been assigned to a post he had not applied for. Mr. Livingston also became a regular applicant for Pierre's instruction and counsel.[108] Pierre had of course bargained for none of this harassment when he resigned the agency. As ever, he had been seeking freedom to pursue his interests unmolested, and if these interests had ever included the dispensing of federal pensions, they did no longer. Early in the spring of 1854, to escape the besiegements and perhaps to celebrate his partial coming-to-independence, he left the Notary's office in charge of Leslie[109] and made his way south with Helen for a few weeks' relaxation.

Protracted escapes from the city—to North Carolina, Johnstown, Staten Island, Craigsville, Albany, or Sunnyside—had in recent years become a regular feature of life for Pierre and Helen. In 1852 Pierre had hoped to visit James Berdan and his family at Jacksonville, but a commitment to Helen for a jaunt north into Canada had temporarily postponed fruition of the plan.[110] The following summer they spent closer to home, at Sunnyside, but apparently even that holiday demanded elaborate preparations. Irving was in town late in May 1853, and reported seeing Helen "preparing for her annual hegira to the country. The Hall outside her door was full of large black trunks containing all her earthly effects, which I believe are to be stored for the summer in Pierres office."[111] Now in 1854, after a short visit to Sunnyside, they began a leisurely journey toward the home of James Dodge, Helen's brother in North Carolina.[112] After calling at the Kennedy home in Baltimore[113] they spent a few days in Washington amidst the spring social season. On the basis of a letter received from Helen, Irving summarized to Julia Sanders some of their activities in the capital city:

> Helen had been at the height of . . . grandeur and felicity, passing several days . . . visiting presidents, dining with senators and dancing at Brazilian ministers balls. The last heard of her, she was

[108] Ebenezer Irving to William Irving, SS, March 20, 1854 (SHR).

[109] Leslie still kept a law office at the new address of the Bank of Commerce, 18 William Street, as did PMI. *Trow's New York City Directory* for 1854-1855, p. 374; Appendix, pp. 13, 95.

[110] PMI to Daniel Roberts, New York, August 25, 1852 (Huntington).

[111] WI to Julia [Mrs. Sanders] Irving, SS, May 26, 1853 (SHR).

[112] Ebenezer Irving to William Irving, SS, March 20, 1854 (SHR). According to Ebenezer, they expected to be absent only a month.

[113] On June 29, 1854, WI wrote to John P. Kennedy: "My nephew Pierre M Irving and his wife came home perfectly delighted with the visit they had paid your family . . . during your absence. Pierre was especially pleased with a long conversation he had with Mr. Grey [*sic*], who had quite won his heart. I am glad they were able to look in on the family during their brief sojourn in Baltimore. I like that good people should know one another, especially good people in whom I take especial interest" (Peabody).

at the Brazilian ministers fete at one o'clock on Friday morning and was to set off for Richmond at 5 o'clock in the morning in the steamboat. How was she to pack up her trunk in the interim! Pierre did not intend to go to bed. Had I been there I would have advised him to pack up Helen in a trunk in her ball dress—it would have saved a world of time and trouble and arrangement and disarrangement of toilette. It might however have damaged a stupendous dress cap with which she took the field; and in which she had figured to great advantage at a dinner party of Julia Grinnells before her departure. It surpassed, for glory of ribbands, any cap in her wardrobe, and was of unquestionable taste—French my dear![114]

Presumably Pierre rescued his vivacious wife in time to board the steamboat. In any case, they did not return to New York from their more placid entertainments in North Carolina until mid-June.

Shortly after his arrival home, Pierre received from Irving a generous gift which was obviously motivated by a desire to encourage his immediate retirement from his lightened professional duties as Notary and lawyer. The gift was a six-acre plot of land directly adjacent to the cottage at Sunnyside and eminently suitable for a country home.[115] Irving had probably made no secret of his wish to secure Pierre and Helen as his near neighbours, but now that Pierre's retirement seemed imminent he had decided to hasten his nephew's decision. Over the past few months his steady labours on the *Washington* had impressed upon him the great potential usefulness of Pierre's assistance, and no doubt he made the gift of land with an eye toward fixing his nephew beside him for the duration of the project. He was well acquainted with Pierre's wish to secure "a moderate competence" and then to do as he pleased. Presuming in his usual way that, since his own plans would so obviously benefit both himself and his nephew, the latter would certainly be in agreement with them, Irving took it for granted that he would soon have Pierre as a near neighbour. On August 31 he wrote to Mrs. Kennedy that Pierre was "about to build a cottage in my immediate vicinity."[116] Apparently the prediction was not without foundation, for on August 27 Helen's sister Jane Ann had passed on the same information in a letter to her husband. Pierre and Helen, she wrote, "expect to build a house so as to enter by spring. If they are prospered in their calculations, they expect to live together, Oscar and Eliza, Ogden and the owners. It is a happy prospect."[117] However, the prospect was not to be realized. Pierre was not yet satisfied that his savings warranted sacrificing his regular income and building a house into the bargain, and hence the idea of a supplementary family residence was abandoned. Once again Irving

[114] WI to Julia [Mrs. Sanders] Irving, SS, April 3, 1854 (NYPL, Berg).

[115] PMI, MS Outline, Chapter XXXII (1854). The deed was dated August 10, 1854.

[116] WI to Mrs. John P. Kennedy, SS, August 31, 1854; *LLWI*, IV, 179.

[117] Jane Ann Frothingham to John Frothingham, n.p., August 23, 1854; Frothingham, *Genealogy*, p. 158 (NYPL, MS).

had failed to reckon seriously enough with Pierre's circumspectness in financial matters and his unrelenting determination to follow his own lights. He was as powerless in 1854 to bend his nephew's will by a generous gift as in 1847 Pierre had been in his attempt to sway his uncle toward literary activity by wise admonitions.

With his hopes to secure Pierre's full-time proximity and literary collaboration temporarily balked, Irving undertook during the closing months of 1854 to complete the first volume of the *Washington* on his own. Pierre was unfailingly encouraging about the quality of the biography, but his assurances were insufficient to overcome his uncle's renewed doubts, and by the time the volume was ready for the press, early in 1855, Irving was virtually disconsolate. As the date of publication drew near, he was tormented by a series of petty problems demanding immediate attention. He had intended for the work to appear in an imposing octavo format, symbolically to range with the stately historical tomes of Bancroft and Prescott; but Putnam preferred to issue it in duodecimo, to stand alongside the uniform edition of the revised works of Washington Irving. After consultation a compromise was agreed upon: the volume would appear in both formats.[118] This arrangement was reasonable and satisfactory, except that it entailed the doubly tedious burden of correcting proof sheets for each edition. Irving plowed through the proofs and managed to complete the corrections, but labour of that minute, exacting kind was always poison to his delicate nerves. Moreover, quite aside from his sheer dislike of mechanical jobwork, the experience of seeing his brainchild in print distressed him so much that for weeks after completing the corrections he could not bear to set eyes on the book again.[119] When in April he received a letter from John Murray at London with the warning that Putnam's tardy forwarding of proof sheets to him might result in piracy of the work in England, Irving was beyond concern over such a minor misfortune. He had so far forgotten his unassailable reputation in the United States as seriously to fear that his book would be panned. He forwarded Murray's letter to Pierre with the comment that if "my work be well received by the public, I shall be content, whatever be the pecuniary profits."[120]

The Life of George Washington, volume one, was published with great fanfare in mid-May, 1855. At the end of the month George Bancroft, having read the work through, wrote its author a letter of solid, discerning praise.[121] Other letters followed; neighbours hurried to

[118] *LLWI*, IV, 189. PMI seems to have played a part in making this arrangement. In his MS Outline, Chapter XXXIV (1855), he wrote: "Letter to Pierre M. Irving relative to terms of publication of the Life of Washington. First intention to publish only in the octavo form." Unless otherwise noted, subsequent citations of the *Washington* refer to the first impressions in the duodecimo format.

[119] *LLWI*, IV, 193.

[120] WI to PMI, [SS], May 20, 1855; *LLWI*, IV, 192-93.

[121] George Bancroft to WI, n.p., May 30, 1855; *LLWI*, IV, 194. While much of the critical response to the first four volumes of the *Washington* was no more than *ad*

Sunnyside with their congratulations; Putnam's sales boomed; until at last, bolstered by the popular and critical success he should have taken as a certainty, Irving was himself again. A few days after receiving Bancroft's note he met him at a social gathering at the home of Fernando Wood, the Mayor of New York. General Winfield Scott, another guest, advanced to the dinner table with Irving on one arm and Bancroft on the other—wishing, he said, to "honor [himself] by being sandwiched between the two historians."[122] Flattery such as this was balm to Irving's soul. No less than at twenty, at seventy-two he was a creature of whims and moods, easily influenced by the opinions of others. The enthusiastic reception of his first volume speedily dissolved his intention to continue working on the biography only at intervals. It even made him wonder whether he might not revise his present plans and carry the work through Washington's Presidential administration and last days at Mount Vernon. As he had often remarked to Pierre, the final period of Washington's life seemed barren of "personal or picturesque detail";[123] yet possibly, with assistance, he might succeed in piecing together something presentable and thus truly complete the work, which he had anticipated for so long as "the crowning effort"[124] of his career. In the final preparation of this first volume Pierre had given him some assistance as critic and courier, but if he should decide to attempt a full life of Washington his nephew must play a considerably more important role in its production. Irving knew that convincing him to put so large a proportion of his energies at his own disposal might be difficult, but in his relief and excited pleasure at his book's success he decided to try.

Determined to avoid a repetition of his failure the year before, early in the summer of 1855 Irving devised a new plan of attack and laid full siege to his nephew. Could not Pierre assist him somewhat as he had done for *Astoria*, by attending to the research that remained and then preparing a kind of brief or précis of Washington's later life, so that Irving could concentrate on the task of writing alone? If he was set against a move from town, that need not be necessary; it might in

hominem adulation, WI had been heartened by the intelligent perception of his aims displayed by some persons. H. T. Tuckerman, for example, wrote praising his "careful avoidance of rhetoric" and "calm, patient, and faithful narrative of facts" (*LLWI*, IV, 206). An anonymous reviewer of the first volume wrote in *Putnam's Monthly Magazine* a sensitive analysis of the strengths and weaknesses of the "semi-historical species of biography" WI was attempting (6 [July 1855], 1-7; the quotation is from p. 1). F. S. Cozzens delighted WI with the information that he had read the work to his children and they had understood it. "Ah, that's it: that's what I write for," the author replied (Arthur D.F. Randolph, "Leaves from the Journal of Frederick S. Cozzens," *Lippincott's Magazine*, 45 [March 1890], p. 741). Perhaps the surest sign of his success came late in 1856 when he discovered that Ebenezer, who for fifty years had been flatly uninterested in his younger brother's scribblings, had picked up the *Washington* and was reading it with enthusiasm (PMI, MS Outline, Chapter XXXV [1856]).

[122] A. Oakey Hall, "A Dinner at the Mayor's," *Harper's New Monthly Magazine*, 21 (October 1860), 654.

[123] *LLWI*, IV, 195.

[124] *Life of Washington*, V, v.

fact be more useful for him to stay within easy reach of Putnam and the Astor Library in order more conveniently to solve problems of detail as they arose. Filled with the idea of expanding his work with Pierre's aid, Irving put his case as attractively as he could. Pierre was not unwilling to entertain such a proposal, nor was he disturbed that his uncle wished to rely on him more heavily than either had originally planned. The only question at present—a vexatious one—was whether he could afford to give up the amount of time his uncle was requesting. Sensing Pierre's uncertainty, Irving sweetened the proposal by offering to pay him a monthly salary of $135 to compensate for the fees he would necessarily sacrifice; and with this added provision he managed to overcome his nephew's hesitancy.[125] By the end of June, Irving's pertinacity and Pierre's own inclination to take up an occupation more congenial to him had resulted in his decision to retire from business. Turning over the Notaryship to Leslie and vacating his office,[126] Pierre entered a new era in his lifetime by putting himself entirely at his uncle's disposal. He subsequently opened another office in the city, but it was to be given over to his private uses, to tasks associated with the *Washington*, and to other projects growing out of his relationship with his uncle. After twenty years of increasing dependence on his nephew's talents, Irving had thus at last secured his full-time assistance. Now, assured of a competent hand to lighten his remaining labours, he was all eagerness to set to work on the second volume. "I live only in the Revolution," he told Pierre in September. "I have no other existence now—can think of nothing else."

In the years since 1825, when he first seriously entertained the possibility of writing the biography, Irving had kept abreast of the material published about George Washington and had gradually formed a clear notion of the work he hoped to compose. By 1855 the field of Washington's life and times had been so minutely examined that he almost despaired of saying anything new on the subject; but at least, he believed, he could write a life characteristic of his own talents and yet different in conception and style from its predecessors. More specifically, as he told Pierre in September of that year, he had decided to "avoid all melodramatic effect" by including "no hubbub of lan-

[125] PMI, MS Outline, Chapter XXXIV (1855). On February 16, 1856, WI wrote out a statement of the terms of the arrangement: My nephew Pierre Munro Irving having for some years kindly and gratuitously attended to the management of my pecuniary affairs, and being still in need of his assistance in my literary researches, I prevailed on him last year to give up his office business and put his time at my disposal; offering to give him an equivalent, in monthly payments, to the profits of the business so given up. I now continue the arrangement, and authorize him to pay himself out of any funds of mine which may be in his hands at the rate of an hundred and thirty-five (135) dollars per month" (SHR).

[126] The *Trow New York City Directory* for 1856-1857 lists as the Notaries of the Bank of Commerce "Leslie Irving and Otis D. Swan" (Appendix, p. 13). The directories continued to list the two men as co-holders of the office until 1860, when Leslie Irving became its sole occupant. During this period he also maintained a law office at 2 Hanover Place.

guage, no trickery of phrase, nothing wrought up."[127] Familiar with
the florid rhetoric of such performances as Edward Everett's spread-
eagle oration, "The Character of Washington,"[128] or the lifeless
periods of John Marshall's early *Life*, he was resolved to adopt a
subdued tone of dignified calm, along the lines of his own *Columbus*.
He wanted the work to be a popular biography—not so much a showy
tour de force constituting a "performance" of his own as an unpretending narrative placing no obstacles before a ready understanding of its
action. "I want the action to shine through the style," he told F. S.
Cozzens. "No style, indeed; no encumbrance of ornament."[129]

Within the limits of historical fidelity Irving proposed to shape
and modulate his narrative as he would a work of fiction. As he had
done with his other historical works, he planned to present it as far as
possible as a kind of narrative pageant, a series of verbal portraits and
scenes. Thus when Pierre complimented him on his account of the
Battle of Princeton—part of the second volume which he was then
completing—he replied as if he were painting a historical panorama.
His procedure, he said, was "to seize the strong point, then dip my
brush in the paint, and color up for that."[130] In light of this characteristically visual approach to his subject, it is not surprising that, feeling
reasonably confident of rendering the external action satisfactorily,
Irving was anxious in writing the *Washington* to give interest to more
abstract matters such as the evocation of character and the presentation of affairs of state.[131] Rather than a narrowly focused study of its
primary character alone, the biography was to be a broad portrayal of
revolutionary times, and keeping this breadth of coverage in mind,
Irving was unceasingly on the lookout for striking details or personal
anecdotes relating to Washington, his colleagues, and his countrymen. He planned to include sketches of Washington's close as-
sociates, to draw upon his own childhood memories of New York,
and—at the risk of overloading the work with curious minutiae—to
include anecdotes of relatively unsung figures in the American
Revolution.[132] In November 1855, having received from a correspondent a collection of unpublished Hessian journals compiled in 1777,
he recalled proofs of the second volume in order to incorporate mate-

[127] *LLWI*, IV, 196.

[128] He heard Everett give this popular speech on March 3, 1856. PMI, MS Outline,
Chapter XXXV (1856).

[129] Randolph, "Leaves from the Journal of F. S. Cozzens," p. 741.

[130] *LLWI*, IV, 196.

[131] In light of this concern, Edward Everett Hale's compliment after reading the fifth
volume of the *Washington* pleased him particularly. Hale said that he "had the power,
which few people have, of giving to diplomacy and matters of state the interest which is
supposed to belong to adventure and battle." WI replied, according to Hale, that
" 'rub-a-dub' and 'roro-toro' were more apt to catch the ear than the quiet discussions
of the Cabinet and the Senate" (Hale, *Memories of a Hundred Years* [New York, 1902], II,
74-75).

[132] *LLWI*, IV, 198, 227, 254.

rial from this new source.[133] As he told Henry T. Tuckerman, he wished "to step down occasionally from the elevated walk of history, and relate familiar things in a familiar way; seeking to show the prevalent passions and feelings and humors of the day, and even to depict the heroes of Seventy-six as they really were—men in cocked hats, regimental coats, and breeches; and not classic warriors, in shining armor and flowing mantles."[134]

As he completed each volume, Irving found himself more and more impressed with the character of George Washington and hence increasingly tempted to wax oratorical, but he persisted in his determination to include a minimum of evaluative comment. As he explained in the conclusion to the fourth volume, he "endeavored to place [Washington's] deeds in the clearest light, and left them to speak for themselves." In a sense, of course, his technique of "avoiding comment or eulogium"[135] was that of creating an illusion of detachment—for he did have distinct ideas about Washington, and by his selection and arrangement of details he composed the book so as to enforce these views. For example, to compensate for the heavy emphasis of earlier biographers on the great man's inflexible dignity, he searched out anecdotes revealing his sense of humour. On the other hand, he played down a contrary strain wherein Washington had been portrayed as irascible and violent. True to his instinct, as an interpreter of Washington's character he pursued a middle way, seeking to restore to him the ordinary humanity that earlier biographers had seemed to ignore or deny.[136] Rather than writing from a distinct political viewpoint, he was careful to avoid the appearance of partisanship whenever possible. He told Pierre that he wished "to stand in my history where Washington stood, who was of no party."[137]

As he composed his serial biography, therefore, Irving was writing with a clear set of aims in mind in regard to tone, narrative style, and theme. It is true that without the encouragement of Pierre he might never have published even a single volume of the *Washington*, and also that without securing his nephew's agreement to lend assistance throughout the remainder of the project he would probably not have decided to write a narrative of Washington's entire career. Pierre had no discernible influence on his uncle's conception of the work, however, and with the exception of the final volume he played no part whatever in its actual composition. In fact, he was sometimes uncertain about Irving's rate of progress on a particular volume and was

[133] *LLWI*, IV, 199.

[134] WI to Henry T. Tuckerman, SS, January 8, 1856; *LLWI*, IV, 206-07.

[135] *Washington*, IV, 478.

[136] Allibone echoed a familiar contemporary formula in praising WI's portrayal of Washington's private life: "Marshall and Sparks have made Washington familiar in the legislative assemblies and Council Hall; but you have brought him into the parlour" ("A Day with WI, June 12, 1855—Huntington).

[137] *LLWI*, IV, 250.

obliged to ask.[138] At many other points in the bookmaking process, of course, he rendered his uncle signal services. He assisted him by consulting and copying documents in published works owned by the Astor and New York Society Libraries but not in the respectable working collection at Sunnyside.[139] He accompanied him on the re-connoitering expeditions necessary for him to form pictorial concep-tions of events he must describe.[140] When Irving was too busily engaged to seek out oral testimony from descendants of persons who had figured in Washington's life history, Pierre acted as his deputy interviewer.[141] He was asked to give his imprimatur to the manuscript of each volume before Irving released it to the printer; and when, even after this stage, Irving insisted on making revisions, he was called upon for confirmation of the improvements. Irving denoted him his "elbow critic"[142] and took his advice seriously, but there is no evi-dence that in volumes one through four of *Washington* Pierre ever recommended drastic revisions or vetoed a single mooted passage. He was not at all diffident of expressing unfavourable views; he was simply more easily satisfied than Irving, who remained, except at the times of his greatest self-distrust, his own best critic. During the composition of these volumes Pierre was probably most valuable as a sounding board for Irving's ideas and a rallier of his spirits during periods of depression and lethargy.

Once Irving had completed the manuscript of each volume, the literary duties of Pierre became more regular and demanding than in the weeks immediately preceding, for it was he who assumed the principal burden of seeing the works through the press. Passing between Sunnyside and New York at short intervals, he was the liaison man between the author and Putnam. When he was at the cottage, as he usually was when the manuscript of a volume was nearing completion, Irving gave him copy a few chapters at a time to look over and then pass on to the printer. As the proofs of these chapters became available Pierre received them from Putnam and returned to Sunnyside, where Irving was ordinarily at work touching up a new portion of copy. The two then sat in the study together collating the proofs against the corresponding copy and checking quoted material against the original sources; and when this step was completed Pierre returned to New York with the corrected proof and a new installment of manuscript copy, beginning another cycle.[143] In

---

[138] *LLWI*, IV, 252.

[139] *LLWI*, IV, 227.

[140] For example, in October 1855 the two went together to nearby Chatterton Hill for WI to study the setting of the battle known by that name, an account of which he was then about to write (*LLWI*, IV, 197; see *Washington*, II, 367-70).

[141] On November 17, 1856, PMI conducted an interview with Thomas C. Amory, grandson of James Sullivan, who was a brother of Washington's colleague Major General John Sullivan (1740-1795) (MS Outline, Chapter XXXV [1856]).

[142] WI to Charles C. Lee, SS, July 31, 1857 (Virginia).

[143] This summary description is based primarily on PMI's passing references to the process of preparing the biography for publication in *LLWI*, IV, 196-99, 209, 227.

the labourious process of dispatching, reviewing, collating, correcting, and receiving copy and proof, Pierre's methodical ways were
most helpful in causing operations to run smoothly. For the same
reason, he was extremely useful in checking the proofs for accuracy of
quotations and documentation. His meticulousness came to him
naturally, but Irving could emulate it only by an effort of will and at the
risk of nervous attacks that incapacitated him for writing. "Writing
history is a very different thing from writing fiction," he once informed S. Austin Allibone. "You have such trouble with dates and
facts."[144] By exercising his talent for analysis and his habit of clerkly
accuracy, Pierre complemented his uncle's gifts for conception and
composition.

Still, Pierre's services as a co-corrector and courier were probably
a welcome convenience to his uncle rather than an absolute necessity.
Just as the copy and proof could have been sent back and forth
between Sunnyside and New York by post, Irving could perhaps have
handled by himself the various chores connected with seeing his
volumes into print. Had he done so, however, he would certainly not
have been able to make the steady progress he did, and he almost
certainly would not have made these volumes so factually dependable
as they are. In short, Pierre relieved Irving from certain of the burdens
of authorship which he was better prepared to shoulder than his
uncle, and in doing so he both facilitated the process of serial publication and helped preserve Irving's energies.[145] In June 1855, shortly

[144] Allibone, "A Day with WI, June 12, 1855 (Huntington).

[145] One variety of work which PMI performed almost entirely on his own was
supervising the printers' correction of factual errors discovered in previously published
volumes of *Washington*. Even here, however, he was to some degree subject to the
orders of WI; for ordinarily the author decided on the form which the necessary
alterations of the printed text should take. Upon encountering information that seemed
to suggest the need of a correction, WI first delegated PMI to ascertain its propriety. For
example, on June 15, 1859, WI received from Joshua J. Cohen of Baltimore a letter
including the following remarks on the *Washington*, "the minute accuracy of which has
been so generally noted": "In the third volume, p. 110, in speaking of the active part
taken by André in the Mischianza in Philadelphia, it is said 'Miss Shippen, afterwards
Mrs. Arnold, being the lady whose peerless charms he undertook to vindicate.' This is
not exactly so. It was not Miss Shippen, but Miss Peggy Chew, in whose behalf he
'figured as one of the Knights Champions of Beauty.' This lady afterwards became the
wife of Col. Jos. E. Howard. . . . A full account of the entertainment is also found in
Lossing, II, p. 99." First noting to himself that WI's account of the Mischianza, an
entertainment held in honour of Sir William Howe in May 1778, was in the fourth
volume of *Washington* rather than the third, as Cohen claimed, PMI consulted Benson J.
Lossing's *Pictorial Field-Book of the Revolution* (New York, 1851-1852), II, 97-100, and
verified the correction. "This is a minute point," he commented to himself. "The error
may probably be explained in this way: Miss *Peggy* Chew was a daughter of Chief
Justice Chew of Pennsylvania, & Miss Peggy Shippen was the niece of the daughter of
Chief Justice Shippen of Pa., and both were heroines at the Mischianza" (PMI, 1859
Journal). The following day PMI wrote in a list of corrections he had ordered in the
octavo and duodecimo plates of the biography, this entry:
     June 16. 1859
     for Vol. IV. Life of Washington.
     Gave Putnam the following correction

after securing Pierre's full-time assistance, Irving was asked by Mrs. Allibone "whether he employed an amanuensis in his literary labors." "Oh no!" he replied. "I prepare every thing for the press myself. No one could do it for me, because I correct so much, and strike out whole sentences, and add new scraps of paper."[146] Pierre never did become his amanuensis, but two years and three volumes after his conversation with Mrs. Allibone Irving could not have answered her question with so ready and sweeping a negative. By 1857 it was no longer possible for him to affect total independence as an author. By then he admitted that his health was too uncertain for him to presume "on the indulgence of nature";[147] and while heretofore his nephew had merely facilitated the realization of his aims by clearing petty concerns from his path, assistance of that kind had become more a necessity than a luxury.

Irving was naggingly doubtful whether, even with Pierre's aid, he possessed strength enough to complete the *Washington* creditably to himself. At the time he enlisted his nephew's continuous assistance he believed that the completed biography would fill three volumes; but by early 1856, as it became evident that no less than five would be required, he was dismayed at the expanse of toil that lay before him. After the appearance of the third volume in July of that year, he wondered out loud about the cumulative effect this extended, intense occupation might exert upon his health. "I am constantly afraid that something will happen to me," he told Pierre.[148] He had fallen into a habit of writing late at night and then rising early the next morning to resume work, and the long hours of sedentary concentration were depriving him of exercise, straining his eyes, and bringing on nervous headaches. In March 1857, as the fourth volume was beginning to go through the press, he felt "fagged and a little out of order,"[149] and he decided to take a rest. By the time the work was published, in May, he seemed to have recovered much of his fitness, although in answer to a congratulatory letter from F. S. Cozzens he confessed that he was still "a little weary."[150] With the whole history of Washington's ad-

12mo. Vol. IV p 101. 8th & 9th lines from the top—
for "the lady whose peerless charms he undertook to vindicate" put "a belle whose peerless charms were maintained in the lists."
Make the same correction in the octavo Vol. IV. p. 110
6th and 7th line from the bottom (NYPL, Berg)
As volume followed volume, these corrections—usually of misprints, misspellings, or minutiae such as the one above, but sometimes of passages up to fifty words in length—naturally grew numerous. PMI compiled lists of the alterations to be made in each format and passed them on to Putnam every few months, carefully noting the dates on which the publisher had been given them.

[146] Allibone, "A Visit to WI, June 12th, 1855" (Huntington).
[147] WI to F. S. Cozzens, SS, May 22, 1857; *LLWI*, IV, 230.
[148] *LLWI*, IV, 209.
[149] WI to PMI, SS, Tuesday evening [late March 1857]; *LLWI*, IV, 228.
[150] WI to F. S. Cozzens, SS, May 22, 1857; *LLWI*, IV, 231.

ministration before him—and Pierre—in the fifth volume, he thought it best to stop work temporarily. In July he told S. Austin Allibone that he had on hand unfinished works on other topics than the *Washington* which he meant to take up presently,[151] but if he really believed this jaunty claim he was to be disappointed. The preparation of the fifth volume was to prove such an ordeal that, once having completed it, he would never consider writing another work. Meanwhile, having produced four substantial volumes in a little over two years, he deserved a rest.

Even though a succession of minor complaints denied him real relaxation, and neither the financial crisis in September nor the subsequent negotiations with Putnam were conducive to repose, through the remainder of 1857 Irving was reasonably at ease. In February 1858 he wrote to Sarah Storrow that in the previous year he had not spent more than a dozen nights in the city. "I have a very pleasant social neighborhood," he commented, "and it has been more social than usual this winter."[152] The Hamiltons had entertained several distinguished visitors, including the loquacious Charles Sumner; James Watson Webb had wined and dined Colonel John C. Fremont, the unsuccessful Presidential candidate in the national election of 1856; and Moses Grinnell had continued to justify his renown as a host at lavish dinner entertainments. Irving had attended these festivities or else, probably with equal enjoyment, heard all about them in visits with Mrs. Schuyler, the Hamilton girls, or Mrs. Holdrege. He was disappointed when the Grinnell family embarked in May 1858 for a year's tour of Europe,[153] yet he hardly stood in danger of being ignored by his other neighbours. William Hoge called and presented him with a cane, and a few months later with a specially designed invalid's chair.[154] H. S. Smythe, a director of the Hudson River Rail Road who lived in the vicinity, sent him wren boxes for the cottage.[155] Gouverneur Kemble dispatched his gardener down the river with roots and cuttings to stock a recently built hothouse where he hoped to grow grapes.[156] All these tokens of friendship or homage Irving accepted with tranquil appreciation. "Perhaps it is the effect of gathering years," he reflected, "to settle more and more into the quiet of one's elbow chair."[157]

[151] "Another Visit to WI, June 2, 1857" (Huntington). I have supplied this title for clarity of reference. Allibone's account of his visit to WI in 1857 is filed in the Huntington Library with his account of the 1855 visit, under the common title "A Visit to WI, June 12th, 1855."

[152] WI to Sarah Storrow, SS, February 15, 1858 (Yale); *LLWI*, IV, 240.

[153] WI to Julia Grinnell, SS, September 2, 1858; *LLWI*, IV, 251.

[154] WI to George D. Morgan, SS, July 4, 1856 (SHR); PMI, 1859 Journal, March 16, 1859; Myers, "WI and the Astor Library," p. 390, note 34.

[155] WI to H. S. Smythe, SS, March 30, 1858 (SHR); PMI, 1859 Journal, June 15 and 25, 1859. Earlier Smythe had sent ducks for roasting, and a Stilton cheese.

[156] WI to Gouverneur Kemble, SS, April 23, 1856; *LLWI*, IV, 211.

[157] WI to Sarah Storrow, SS, February 15, 1858 (Yale); *LLWI*, IV, 240.

Work on the biography had thus far imposed more rigourous day-to-day demands on Irving than on Pierre, and accordingly, to occupy himself when his assistance was not required, the latter had taken up a research project independent of the *Washington*. Now that his uncle was resting temporarily, he continued to devote time to this avocation—the gathering of information about the history of the Irving family. His curiosity about the topic had been aroused quite by accident and in a roundabout way. In 1850, several years before the thought of taking up genealogical studies occurred to him, the redoubtable London literary pirate Henry G. Bohn began to include the newly revised works of Irving in his cheap "Popular Library" series.[158] This constituted an infringement of the copyrights on the works owned by Irving's publishers in England, John Murray III and Richard Bentley, but in response to their threats Bohn alleged that as an American citizen the author held no claim whatever to the copyright protection extended to British subjects. Thereupon Murray, who stood to lose a large amount if Bohn were to have his way, resolved to institute legal proceedings against him. As part of his case Murray proposed to advance the rather equivocal claim that, in consideration of Irving's English ancestry, he was properly to be considered English himself. To secure the necessary proof that the authors father, William Irving, Sr., was born within British dominions, Murray applied to the island of Shapinsha, in the Orkneys, for documentary evidence to that effect.[159]

In this way the fact of Irving's Orcadian ancestry became known in that remote district and impelled a local antiquarian, James Robertson, Sheriff Substitute at Kirkwall, to trace out for his own pleasure the pedigree of the Irving or Irvine family.[160] Meanwhile Pierre, who was acquainted with the issues involved in Murray's litigation[161] but had apparently given no further thought to the topic of the Irving ancestry since the suspension of the case in 1851,[162] was unaware of this continuing transatlantic interest in his family's origins. It was not

[158] The enterprises of Bohn are described in F. G. M. Cordasco, *The Bohn Libraries* (New York, 1951).
[159] Murray had learned the location upon making inquiry of WI. See McClary, *WI and the House of Murray*, pp. 191-202.
[160] PMI, Irving Genealogy, p. 7.
[161] PMI witnessed a power of attorney sent by WI to John Murray III on August 19, 1850. This was at the request of the latter, whose counsel believed that the power of attorney might prove useful in presenting his case. PMI had also assisted his uncle in this matter by performing research to ascertain facts pertaining to the writing and publication of his works. WI incorporated the results of this research in a memorandum he sent to Murray on September 22, 1850 (McClary, *WI and the House of Murray*, pp. 194-200, 217-20).
[162] It was brought before the Queen's Bench on May 27, 1851, and suspended the same day, when it appeared that Bohn's solicitor was willing to bargain. On August 27, 1851, the matter was closed when Bohn purchased the copyrights and printed stock of WI's works from Murray for two thousand guineas (McClary, *WI, and the House of Murray*, p. 200).

until 1855 that he happened to read a newspaper extract from an English review of James Dennistoun's *Memoirs of Sir Robert Strange*[163] and noticed the following passage: "I guess, that if Irving knew his pedigree could be traced, step by step, to John de Erwyn of 1438, he would readily claim and vindicate his Orcadian descent." Curious, Pierre immediately wrote to London for a copy of the journal from which the extract was taken, and presently he ascertained that the published review was the work of one James Robertson. He then addressed an inquiry to this stranger, beginning genealogical research of his own which was to occupy him at intervals over almost twenty years.[164]

In March 1856 Robertson obligingly replied to Pierre, tracing the Irving lineage back to 1438 and adding that he would send further information after checking certain records and consulting two colleagues, Mr. George Petrie, County Clerk of Supply, and Mr. Balfour, the present owner of Shapinsha.[165] Before Robertson was unable to complete his additional researches, however, another Irving from New York joined the search. In the summer of 1856, at the close of a European tour, the Reverend Pierre Paris Irving called upon Robertson, armed with a letter of introduction from Pierre Munro. He was entertained lavishly, shown the house where William Irving, Sr. was born, and introduced to Mr. Balfour, who demonstrated by reference to a chest full of documents and deeds how the landed property of Shapinsha had gradually passed from the Irving family to his own. When Pierre Paris took his leave in August, Mr. Balfour presented him with some of the oldest of these documents, bearing the name of an Irving ancestor and the Irving family emblem of the three holly leaves. To that gift Robertson and Petrie added a genealogical table incorporating all the information they had succeeded in gathering thus far.[166] Pierre Paris arrived home triumphant with the news —particularly satisfying to his Uncle Washington—that the family was descended from the same "Irving of Bonshaw" who was renowned for having given shelter to the great Scots hero Robert Bruce.[167] Still more information was forthcoming when, on December 30, 1856, Mr. Petrie sent directly to Irving, "in token of the great

---

[163] James Dennistoun, *Memoirs of Sir Robert Strange . . . and of his Brother-in-Law Andrew Lumsden*, 2 vols. (London, 1855).

[164] PMI, Irving Genealogy, p. 10.

[165] The bound manuscript volume entitled "The Genealogy of the Irving Family . . ." (SHR)—cited hereafter as "Irving Genealogy"—includes letters and documents received between 1856 and 1859 from each of these persons.

[166] PMI, Irving Genealogy, pp. 12-16.

[167] On October 27, 1856, WI wrote to Sarah Storrow of the family's derivation from Irving of Bonshaw, and added: "The whole story of Pierres visit to the Orkneys is interesting, and the genealogical research in question, which had been going on for several months before his arrival, is a curious instance of Scottish antiquarianism and the national propensity to trace up pedigree" (Yale).

pleasure he had taken in connecting him so closely with Orkney,"[168] a new, expanded table showing the family ancestry.

With all these digests of the Irvings' history at hand, Pierre compiled in narrative form a survey of the information he had unearthed by himself together with that which he, Pierre Paris, and Irving had received. "The names of our more remote progenitors . . . having recently been traced out," he began, "it seems a desideratum that some member of the family should record the history of this curious discovery, and arrange & elucidate the memorials of a descent equally ancient & honourable. For such, therefore, as desire to be certified 'through whom/ Their life-blood tastes its parent lake,' . . . I undertake this task."[169] Shortly after Pierre had completed the narrative, his cousin Irving Van Wart uncovered further family lore that rendered it obsolete. In July 1857, while on a visit to his childhood home in England, Van Wart made an excursion to the village of Drum, where through the agency of Colonel Jonathan Forbes, the author of *Eleven Years in Ceylon* (1840), he managed to open communications with a family of *Irvines* whose ancestors had lived in the area for centuries. Presently Pierre entered correspondence with Colonel Forbes, who proved to be as cooperative as Robertson and Petrie; and between April and August, 1858, the two exchanged letters concerning a genealogical sketch of the Irvines of Drum which Forbes had drawn up.[170] On the basis of this new material Pierre was enabled to complete a five-chapter manuscript, interspersed with "historical and illustrative sketches" drawn from his private research,[171] surveying the Irving family and its lineage. In October his other duties obliged him to suspend these pleasant studies, but Irving Van Wart and Pierre Paris continued their inquiries in his absence.[172]

In the past few months the demands on Pierre's time both as a collaborator on the *Washington* and as Irving's companion-nurse had been mounting steadily. On December 14, 1857, Irving had written to him that he was "in the vein, and anxious to complete the rough draft of his final volume."[173] He was so severely troubled by an obstinate

[168] PMI, Irving Genealogy, p. 16. PMI indicates that the phrases are Petrie's.

[169] PMI, Irving Genealogy, pp. 5-6.

[170] PMI, Irving Genealogy, pp. 19-23. The letters from Forbes to PMI are bound together with PMI's genealogical narrative.

[171] PMI, Irving Genealogy, p. 23. The account was in six parts, the first of which was a summary of the recent researches on both sides of the Atlantic. Succeeding sections were: "Of the name of Irving," pp. 24-27; "Of [Crinus?] Irvine," pp. 28-37; "Of Sir William de Irwyn," pp. 38-57; "Of the Irvines of Drum," pp. 56-79; "Of the Irvines of Orkney," pp. 80-115. A modern work treating in depth a portion of this subject is by Alastair M. T. Maxwell-Irving, *The Irvings of Bonshaw: Chiefs of the Noble and Ancient Scots Border Family of Irving* (Bletchley, England, 1968).

[172] In 1859 or 1860 the Rev. Pierre Paris Irving wrote at the beginning of PMI's genealogical narrative the following notation: "Written first in 1857. Afterwards in 1859 corrected & enlarged, after receipt of fuller examinations from the Orkneys & of the letters of Col Forbes. The original or first draft was copied by Mr Irving Van Wart & myself. I now copy the *revised* history as follows: P. P. Irving" (Irving Genealogy, p. 2).

[173] *LLWI,* IV, 239.

cough, however, that he placed himself under his physician's supervision, and during February Pierre became so concerned about his health as to pass a few precautionary days with him at Sunnyside.[174] By the end of the winter Irving was able to work regularly, if slowly, and in July he completed a rough draft. Irritatingly, Putnam had advertised by mistake that the volume would be published in the fall, but at this point Irving was so tired and unable to concentrate that, according to Pierre, he was "half dubious whether he would ever publish" it. Trying to be helpful, Pierre reminded him of Dr. Johnson's dictum that a man can write at any time if he will only set himself doggedly to it, but Irving dismissed the idea. For "*the effects*" he was seeking, he said, he must "bide his time."[175] Pierre stayed in close contact with his uncle through the summer of 1858, encouraging him in his distress when the special effects would not come. Returning on September 12 from a visit elsewhere, he learned that Irving had "taken things to pieces, and could not put them together again."[176] On some days in September Irving was so troubled with cough and laboured breathing that he was unable to write at all. "I have to watch for a flaw—," he observed in that vein of stoic humour which left him so rarely, "a little breeze, then spread my sails, and get on." On September 18 he gave Pierre a few of the dismantled and reassembled chapters to read, and when his nephew recommended rejections, he acceded. He could see how the work should be "dress[ed] up," he said, but he "lacked the power to do it." Pierre could only assure him that "*he* saw what effects might be given, but others would not."[177]

By October 11 Irving had given Pierre the final chapters of the volume to read, yet almost six months were to elapse from that date before the work was published. Harassed by asthma and nervousness, both of which he was aggravating by his dogged determination to complete the book in proper style, Irving could neither satisfy himself with what he had completed nor trust the revisions he made. On October 20 Pierre discovered that he had apparently forgotten to mention Washington's consent in 1793 to serve a second term as President; upon being queried the next day, Irving located the missing pages among his papers.[178] In the following months he reworked several chapters, adding material and rewriting passages in all parts of the volume, copying over some sections, and as he accurately termed

[174] *LLWI*, IV, 238. On February 15 WI wrote to Sarah Storrow: "I am endeavoring to accomplish a fifth volume, wherewith to close the Life of Washington, but I work more slowly than heretofore. For two or three years past I have been troubled by an obstinate catarrh, but this winter it has been quite harassing; at times quite stupifying me. Recently I have put myself under medical treatment and begin to feel the benefit of it" (Yale).

[175] *LLWI*, IV, 249-50.

[176] *LLWI*, IV, 252.

[177] *LLWI*, IV, 252-54.

[178] *LLWI*, IV, 255-56.

it, "muddling"—and then submitted the results to Pierre. Fighting his nervousness and a haunting idea that he would be unable to sleep when he tried to rest, on January 19, 1859, he released the first three chapters of manuscript copy to be sent to the printer. Pierre passed back and forth between Sunnyside and the city in his usual fashion until February 1, when he returned to find his uncle engaged in re-writing his summary discussion of Washington's character. That evening, completely unstrung by the mental exertion, Irving gave him the entire draft and declared, to Pierre's great relief, that he was determined to bother no more with it. It was impossible to hold him to his word, however, and within a few days he had resumed his tinkering. When, on March 17, Pierre informed him that the work was fully printed, he replied: "Well, I never got out a work in this style before, without looking at the proof sheets. In better health, I could have given more effect to parts; but I was afraid to look at the proofs, lest I should get muddling."[179] He clearly had no reason to reproach himself for inattention to the work; he had almost prostrated himself in his efforts to perfect it. When he wrote his preface to the volume two weeks later, he acknowledged the assistance and "kindness" of Pierre, adding that he was able to lay the work before the public only through the assistance of his nephew.[180]

In the preparation of the concluding volume of the *Washington* the role of Pierre had obviously extended beyond the tasks he had performed for its three predecessors. For this volume alone he was responsible for synopsizing testimony from the major authorities on Washington's later life and supplying a preliminary outline. While as usual he played no part in writing a draft, he was a more than usually influential critic, not only as a corrector of factual errors and oversights but as an evaluator of proposed revisions and additions. Finding his own aesthetic sense less sure than formerly, Irving placed heavier reliance on his nephew and submitted to his judgments more docilely. On April 4, having just sent his preface to the printer, he wrote to Charles A. Davis that Pierre had in fact performed all "the labor of revising the volume and getting it through the press."[181] Although the latter part of his claim is probably accurate, the former, perhaps written out of a fresh sense of gratitude and relief, is misleading. Pierre did correct the proofs, checking them against the manuscript and collating quoted material with sources, but he did not revise Irving's text in a substantive manner. Extant manuscripts reveal that the few corrections he did make were almost invariably limited to minor points of phraseology,[182] and in his own words, the sole in-

[179] *LLWI*, IV, 270-76; the quotation is from pp. 275-76.
[180] "Preface," *Washington*, V, vi.
[181] WI to Charles A. Davis, SS, April 4, 1859 (Yale).
[182] Of the fifth volume of the *Washington* I have examined the manuscript of chapters 5 (NYPL, MS), 12 (Buffalo and Erie Public Library), 16-25 (NYPL, Berg), and 31 (NYPL, MS); in all of these the editorial influence of PMI is small or negligible. His emendations of the text were limited to refinements of diction, correction of obvious

stance of his more extensive editorializing occurred when he "improved . . . by omissions" Irving's revised summary of the character of Washington.[183] The only consistent manuscript evidence of Pierre's hand in completing the final volume is that for each chapter he wrote a synoptic headnote summarizing the topics to be covered, then pasted it onto the first sheet of Irving's manuscript. Thus, contrary to Irving's statement to Davis, the record shows that the real labour of revising the final volume was his own. Considering his feeble health, it is clear that the assistance of Pierre was indispensable to his completion of the biography; but it is equally clear that the final volume was written and revised not by his nephew but by Irving himself.

Since the winter of 1857-1858, Irving's health had been undermined by a chronic asthmatic condition. On October 12, 1858, the day after he had completed a thorough revision of the first draft, a reaction to his exertion set in and he was stricken with intermittent fever. He told Pierre, who had come to Sunnyside with him, that he was afraid "he might have injured himself seriously in his endeavors to finish this fifth volume; that the pitcher might have gone once too often to the well."[184] Within a few days his apprehension seemed dispelled, and, though still troubled by his cough, he was able to resume the bracing routine of a morning carriage-ride. Seeing his condition improve, Pierre and Helen returned to New York and took rooms for the winter at the Clarendon Hotel. During the next few weeks Irving visited them there on his visits from the country, and when relatively free from symptoms of his various maladies he was his old self. Beginning in mid-November he remained in New York, sleeping at the Clarendon or at Irving Van Wart's and calling frequently at his physician's clinic, but he failed to overcome his laboured breathing, nervousness, and fear of sleeplessness. On December 18, he decided to disobey his physician's strong advice and return home. As he prepared to leave, he earnestly requested of Pierre and Helen that they give up their rooms in town, accompany him to the cottage, and stay there with him indefinitely; and sensing his need of them, they assented. At last, Irving had succeeded in bringing his nephew and niece into as close physical proximity to himself as for several years he had wished. "From this period," Pierre wrote in the *Life and Letters*, "to his death, we were, by his desire, inmates of Sunnyside."[185]

oversights, and verification of quoted passages. Ordinarily PMI wrote his suggested alterations of diction, using pencil, above the words in question, and WI then confirmed the changes in ink. The manuscripts reveal no instance wherein WI rejected PMI's suggestion. The text of chapters 16-20 reveals no marks in PMI's hand whatever.

PMI's additions to the extant manuscripts were of two kinds. First, he wrote all the chapter headings pasted onto the first sheet of each manuscript chapter. Second, he added documentation. The printed results of the latter variety of additions are in *Washington*, V, 7, 191, 260, 261, 262.

[183] See below, p. 183.

[184] *LLWI*, IV, 255. This is given by PMI as an indirect quotation.

[185] *LLWI*, IV, 263.

Chapter Five

The Elderly Author, in Public
and in Private

As we have seen, the permanent presence of Pierre and Helen at Sunnyside beginning in December 1858 culminated a trend toward interinvolvement between Irving's life and theirs which, owing largely to his sponsorship, had been developing over the past twenty years. In order for us to view the relationship between the elderly Irving and his nephew and niece in a broader perspective, it is now necessary to trace briefly the progress of another trend which was reaching its culmination at about this time, one which he regarded with much less complacency. His strenuous efforts to improve Sunnyside and make of it a family gathering-place had proven successful, but they had wrought corollary effects which threatened to interfere seriously with the patriarchal retirement he had envisioned for himself. While the revised edition of his works had produced an ample stream of royalties which had gone far toward financing life at Sunnyside, concomitantly the edition had placed his name into more extensive public circulation. Beginning in 1848 his already-established literary reputation had broadened rapidly, so that throughout the 1850's he was known throughout the United States as a presiding genius of the national literature, almost a culture hero—in a common phrase, "the Patriarch of American Letters."[1] In themselves, of course, the testimonials of affectionate respect he received from his public were harmless enough—a source of embarrassment, to be sure, but gratifying nonetheless. What complicated matters for Irving was that Sunnyside, the "snuggery" he had planned and perfected as a rural retreat, was also achieving wide fame and becoming a kind of literary shrine. Whether he approved or not, in the years after 1848 Irving became a beloved public figure, and his home became a popular place to visit.

Naturally he had been initiated into the stresses of being a public personality long before 1848. For example, the rigorous weeks of gratulatory ceremonies following his return to New York from Europe in 1832 had taught him some of the disadvantages of fame and confirmed his dislike of biding in the public eye. Following the publication of the revised works, however, his inconveniences began to assume more alarming proportions, until eventually he found it impossible to set foot in a public place without running serious risk of being accosted by a flock of admirers.[2] More particularly, his recuperative visit to Saratoga Springs in the summer of 1852—the visit during which he chanced to meet the Kennedy family[3]—seems to have been a turning point in his career, the last occasion when he was able to appear in public for any length of time and escape the threat of capture by the celebrity-hunters. As we have seen, he thoroughly enjoyed his three-week stay at the resort. Besides the Kennedys he fell in with Charles A. Davis, John A. Stevens, Edwin Bartlett, Gouverneur Kemble, his young admirer Donald Grant Mitchell, and other cronies,[4] and he presently took an opportunity to meet new people. He played squire to ladies of all ages and origins, took carriage-rides with matrons and sometimes with their husbands, danced a bit, and twice daily sauntered along the gravelled walks to and from the baths, always in conversation with friends. "One sees society here without the trouble, formality, late hours, and crowded rooms of New York," he reported happily to his niece Kate after a week.[5]

True, it was only through careful circumspection that he was able to avoid tiresome scenes of tribute from utter strangers. Mitchell and Davis, both of whom wrote accounts of his activities at Saratoga, concurred in observing that, in the words of the former, he made himself "utterly incapable of being lionized." Time and again, Mitchell continued, "under the trees in the court of the hotel, did I hear him

[1] George Ripley, "WI,"*Harper's New Monthly Magazine,* 2 (April 1851), 580.

[2] He was not insensible to the advantages of his popularity, of course. See, for example, WI to Sarah Irving, New York, September 29, 1853; *LLWI,* IV, 162-63.

[3] See above, p. 124.

[4] WI to Kate Irving, Saratoga Springs, July 17, 1852; WI to Mary Irving, Saratoga Springs, July 21, 1852; *LLWI,* IV, 107, 109.

[5] WI to Kate Irving, Saratoga Springs, July 27, 1852; *LLWI,* IV, 113.

enter upon some pleasant story, lighted up with that rare turn of his eye, and by his deft expressions, when, as chance acquaintances grouped about him,—as is the way of watering-places—and eager listeners multiplied, his hilarity and spirit took a chill from the increasing auditory, and drawing abruptly to a close, he would sidle away with a friend and be gone."[6] He much preferred walking alone or with a single acquaintance, such as the deferentially inquisitive Mitchell, to the demands of celebrity; and at Saratoga he still had some choice in the matter.

A few months later, while on his first visit to the Kennedys at Washington, Irving discovered that his hopes of combining a long period of biographical research with a temperate round of socializing in the national capital were simply impossible of attainment. For a short time after his arrival all went smoothly enough. On January 20, after a bit of dissipation in New York and Baltimore, he was "comfortably fixed" at the Kennedys, glad to learn that several of his friends were in the city, but nonetheless resolved "to keep out of the whirl as long as I can, that I may get among the archives of the State Department."[7] Only three days afterward he described himself to his niece Kate as having been "assailed with invitations of all kinds" which he could not refuse. Just the night before, he reported, he had attended a levee given by President Fillmore, and also a ball, both of which were potentially agreeable enough. To his irritation, however, he had found it impossible to enter into conversation with any of the interesting persons he met at either function. At the levee, "I had to shake hands with man, woman, and child, who beset me on all sides, until I felt as if it was becoming rather absurd, and struggled out of the throng." At the ball, where he was delighted to come upon his friend Madame Calderon, wife of the Spanish Minister, he was driven from the field by a similar attack just after he had begun to chat with her. Today he had been installed as an honorary member of the Smithsonian Institution.[8] The time and energy he spent in these ceremonies and social excursions left him depleted on the days when he was free to pursue his research, and more than once he was at the point of hurrying home. "I cannot keep my spirits up," he wrote in exhaustion on January 27. "Playing the lion has killed me."[9]

Nourished by the journalists' adulatory comment on the revised works and on himself as well, Irving's reputation grew apace, and the signs of his fame multiplied ominously. In November 1852 an extremely popular volume appeared with great fanfare, entitled *Homes of American Authors*[10] and avowedly intended by its editor, Henry T.

[6] "A New Preface," *Dream-Life: A Fable of the Seasons* (New York, 1863), pp. v-vi, x-xii; see also *LLWI*, IV, 114.

[7] WI to Sarah Irving, Washington, January 20, 1853; *LLWI*, IV, 126.

[8] WI to Catharine Irving, Washington, January 23, 1853; *LLWI*, IV, 126-27.

[9] WI to Sarah Irving, Washington, January 27, 1853; *LLWI*, IV, 128.

[10] *Homes of American Authors* (New York, 1853 [1852]), p. iv. Despite the date on its title-page, the work was published on November 26, 1852 (New York *Times*, p. 5,

Tuckerman, to show the American public "how comfortably housed many of their favorite authors are."[11] A leading feature of the work was Tuckerman's essay on Sunnyside, which was accompanied by a steel engraving of the cottage. In private, Tuckerman was frank to admit that this bland confection had "few points"[12]—a just estimate, since it consisted of nothing more than a quick review of Irving's career, an appreciative description of the scenery near his home, and, ironically in light of its indirect effect upon Irving, a comment that the "repose," "retirement," and modest "seclusion" of Sunnyside were precisely in line with the author's most cherished tastes. However few its intrinsic merits may have been, Tuckerman's sentimental tribute to the nation's "literary pioneer" helped swell the rising tide of what he called the "national pride and affection"[13]—a tide which was already threatening to overwhelm Irving's peace and seclusion. By 1853, steel engravings of Sunnyside scenes or of Irving himself were coming into vogue. In April of the following year, the village of Dearman, within whose boundaries Sunnyside was situated, was given a new name. Predictably, the name was "Irvington."[14]

It was flattering to be informed of his election to honorary memberships in literary unions, historical societies, and young men's associations—many of them named after him—and it was also satisfactory to receive solemn tributes from younger writers testifying to his influence on their careers. Yet, having received an honorary doctorate from Oxford University as early as 1831, and having had a street in New York named after him only two years later, in the years since then Irving's palate for honours and accolades had understandably grown a bit jaded. He had become so accustomed to finding books dedicated to him that once to his embarrassment he forgot that his friend Professor Francis Lieber's *The Stranger in America* (1834) fell into that category.[15] He recognized that most of the praise for himself and his works in the newspapers and magazines was simply formulaic, yet at the same time he knew that it symptomatized a widespread esteem. For example, once in 1854 when a train was stopped with mechanical trouble near Sunnyside, N. P. Willis, who was aboard, overheard this exchange: "One man announced that we were but a stone's throw from Washington Irving's. 'Well,' said a rough-looking fellow from the

col. 5). Less than a month later, on December 23, Putnam was advertising a second edition (New York *Times*, p. 5, col. 5). It was produced in a lavish format and sold in various bindings, the least expensive copy at $5.

[11] "Preface," *Homes of American Authors*, p. iv. For an elaboration of this theme, see the anonymous article-review, "The Homes of American Authors," *Putnam's Monthly Magazine*, I (January 1853), 23-30.

[12] H. T. Tuckerman to George Putnam, Newport, R.I., August 13, 1852 (Virginia). The essay appeared on pp. 35-61 of *Homes of American Authors*.

[13] *Homes of American Authors*, pp. 46, 50, 51.

[14] Scharf, *Westchester County*, I, 182.

[15] Allibone, "Another Visit to WI, June 2, 1857" (Huntington). When first published, this work was entitled *Letters to a Gentleman in Germany, Written after a Trip from Philadelphia to Niagara*. The dedication to WI appeared in the first edition.

corner, 'I would rather lay my eyes on *that man* than any man in the world.' 'I've seen him,' said another; 'he looks like a gent—, I tell you!'"[16] If Oliver Wendell Holmes' remark that by 1859 Sunnyside had become "next to Mount Vernon, the best known and most cherished of all the dwellings in our land"[17] implied a comparison of personalities and places which Irving could never have sanctioned, it suggested how literally the cottage was an unofficial national shrine.

Heartfelt as the tributes from admirers often were, Irving was preoccupied with, among other things, his family, his writing, and his health, and at times the role of celebrity threatened to overtax his sturdy patience. "Look at that!" he once said to F. S. Cozzens, pointing to a sheaf of little notes stuck onto a candlestick in his study. "What are they? Requests for autographs. Sometimes I have a whole boarding-school at once." "Do you answer them?" "Oh, yes, I endeavor to. It is a great tax; but, still, it gives young people pleasure to have their letters answered."[18] As a rule, he sought to write replies to the queries and comments of all his correspondents, no matter how trivial they might be. For example, thanking a Miss Hannah North of Wilmington, Delaware, for offering to send him a manuscript letter by George Washington, he politely informed her that the text of the letter had been published more than twenty years before in Jared Sparks' collection of Washington's writings.[19] More tersely he informed a gentleman from St. Louis (an autograph hunter?) that he was *not* planning to write a biography of Kit Carson.[20] He answered enquiries about his writing habits, sometimes complied with petitions for financial aid, firmly declined offers to cure him of real and imputed illnesses, and faithfully signed hundreds of autographs. Yet, as he told S. Austin Allibone in 1855, it was impossible for him to answer even the mail to which he would like to respond. To Allibone's suggestion that he establish a private Dead Letter Office modelled on the one at Washington, he replied: "I have in my study a dead letter office." The study was in such disarray from manuscripts, research notes, and unanswered mail lying about, he said, that when his nieces came to put the room in order "they look around, and leave it in despair."[21] Irving joked about his heavy mail, but it was a blight upon his peace of mind. According to George Putnam, few of his correspondents "had any idea of the *fagging* task they imposed on the distinguished victim. He would worry and fret over it trebly in anticipation, and the actual task itself was to him probably ten times as irksome as it would be to

[16] *Out-doors at Idlewild*, p. 325. The sketches comprising this work first appeared as articles in Willis' *Home Journal* between April 2, 1853, and October 7, 1854; the one from which the quotation is taken is cited as from the issue of March 11, 1854.

[17] "Dr. Holmes' Remarks," *Proceedings of the Massachusetts Historical Society, 1858-1860* (Boston, 1860), p. 419.

[18] Randolph, "Leaves from the Journal of F. S. Cozzens," p. 744.

[19] WI to Miss Hannah North, SS, September 10, 1857 (University of Delaware).

[20] WI to Jesse B. Turley, SS, November 9, 1857 (Missouri Historical Society).

[21] Allibone, "A Visit to WI, June 12th, 1855" (Huntington).

most others."[22] With characteristic gallows humour he once said to
Pierre that answering trivial letters tore his mind from him "in slips
and ribbons."[23] One notices in the replies he did manage to write that
he often mentioned the severe strain being placed upon him by loads
of correspondence.

Several persons who knew Irving well claimed that, as G. W.
Curtis put it, there "is not a young literary aspirant in the country,
who, if he ever personally met Irving, did not hear from him the
kindest words of sympathy, regard, and encouragement."[24] This may
well have been true, but it should be added that if the aspirant
attempted to communicate with the author by mail he was not likely to
receive prompt or helpful attention. Osmond Tiffany fared relatively
well when in December 1855 Irving wrote him the vacuous critical
advice that his plan of writing a "work of fiction embracing scenes in
the Ancient Dominion one hundred years since . . . cannot fail if well
executed of commanding general attention."[25] He added, however,
that he distrusted his own judgment, had been extremely busy of late,
and recommended that Tiffany send his completed manuscript to
Putnam. To send one's manuscript to Irving was literally to take a risk,
for even if he did read it he might lose it. "I have been very much
troubled about a MS. sent to me by a young man," he told Mrs.
Allibone in 1855, "requesting my advice whether it was worthwhile to
continue the story. I saw he knew nothing about book making, but
there were some excellent things in it, and I meant to write and tell him
so; but I forgot it, until some months after he wrote again, asking me to
send the MS. to New York. But I have lost *that letter,* and don't
remember the address in N. York, or the name of the man."[26] When
authors forwarded complimentary copies of their newly published
works to him he usually tried to write a suitable reply. For example,
upon receiving from Joseph Worcester a copy of his *Dictionary* in a
new edition, he returned a note prophesying widespread use of it "to
supply the wants of common schools."[27] On occasion, however, even
the price of an acknowledgment was too steep for him to pay.

While he was at least able to set aside temporarily the piles of
letters and other tributes that lay on his desk, it was not so easy for

[22] Putnam, "Recollections of WI," p. 607.

[23] *LLWI,* IV, 209. PMI dates the conversation February 23, 1856. On October 27 of
the same year WI complained to Sarah Storrow of the "incessant interruptions" to his
work on the biography of Washington; and on February 15, 1858, explaining his failure
to answer her letters so promptly as before, he wrote that besides being wearied by his
literary undertaking he was "unable to cope with the additional claims of an over-
whelming correspondence" (Yale).

[24] "WI," *Harper's Weekly Magazine,* 3 (December 17, 1859), 803; see also *Irvingiana,*
p. lxvi.

[25] WI to Osmond Tiffany, SS, December 15, 1855 (Virginia). Tiffany later published *Brandon; or, A Hundred Years Ago. A Tale of the American Colonies* (New York,
1858).

[26] Allibone, "A Visit to WI, June 12, 1855" (Huntington).

[27] WI to Joseph Worcester, SS, October 3, 1855 (Massachusetts Historical Society).

Irving to ignore another oppressive symptom of his fame, the incursions of uninvited visitors. Some of his guests addressed him notes of self-invitation in advance, but most others came unannounced, as did the young man he once met while on a stroll through the garden, who asked him whether Washington Irving lived hereabouts.[28] "I consider him national property," another individual is said to have remarked cheerily, "and being near Sunnyside lately, *I called to get my dividend.*"[29] In 1854 the enterprising owner of a carriage at Tarrytown began driving crowds of sightseers to Sunnyside during the summer months.[30] One of these passengers, who published an account of his visit in a New York newspaper, expressed a rather surprised disappointment in the reception given him at his destination. Immediately upon entering the house, he wrote, he noticed that Irving's parlour bespoke "repose and contentment. The author was sitting, or rather reclining in an easy chair, his legs extended on another in front of him, and a magazine which he had been reading when I entered, lay open on the table beside him." Oddly, he recalled, though "I expected him to say something which would remind me of his 'Sketch Book' and 'Knickerbocker's History of New York,' ... there was none of that quiet humor in his conversation . . . . There is a slight tinge of reserve in the expression of his kind and benevolent countenance."[31] Considering Irving's frequently unwilling exposure to the merely curious, it is not surprising that "a slight tinge of reserve" should have marred his communion with a few of them.

"They come at all hours, without ceremony," he lamented. "Mr. Smith of Texas walks in . . . and when I shake hands I find myself gazed at like a show."[32] In order to protect their privacy when they wished to sit outside on the piazza, his nieces directed Robert to plant a bed of tuberoses to act as a concealing wall. Irving himself found it expedient to order white roses planted near the front porch in order to shield himself from boorish visitors who attempted to peer through his study window in order to catch a glimpse of him at work.[33] In a sketch regretting the tendency among famous Americans to turn their popularity to a profit, N. P. Willis ironically asked in 1854: "Could not Sunny-side 'pay' to be got ready for a boarding-house?"[34] Irving might well have asked himself the same question. At times, recalling James Fenimore Cooper's legendary rage upon discovering that the

[28] Allibone, "A Visit to WI, June 12, 1855" (Huntington).

[29] John Esten Cooke, "Irving at SS in 1858," *Hours at Home*, 1 (October 1865), 509. Cooke misremembered; he visited SS in 1859. See below, p. 204.

[30] Viator, "A Visit to WI," New York *Herald*, May 2, 1855, p. 1, col. 1. See also John Esten Cooke, "A Morning at SS with WI," *Southern Magazine*, 12 (July 1873), 712.

[31] *Ibid.* "Viator" did manage to engage WI in conversation on the subject of international copyright, but his remarks seem almost to have duplicated those in his published letter on the matter in the *Knickerbocker Magazine*, 15 (January 1840), 78-79.

[32] Cooke, "Irving at SS," p. 509.

[33] McLinden Interview (SHR).

[34] Willis, *Out-doors at Idlewild*, p. 127.

populace of Cooperstown had appropriated his land at Three-Mile Point for a picnic-ground, he must have felt a certain spirit of kinship with his old detractor. Like locusts in a field of grain, casual visitors almost denuded the ivy plant covering much of the cottage by each helping himself to a few sprigs as a memento of the occasion. Even invited guests did not scruple to relieve him of his household possessions for souvenirs. On behalf of his daughter, N. P. Willis "begged the possession" of Irving's desk-blotter, duly autographed.[35] Standing beside his desk, Allibone coyly observed: "How valuable one of these pens would be! I am almost tempted to ask for one."[36] One unidentified guest was discovered attempting to pry the silver presentation plate off this same desk, which Irving had received as a gift from Putnam. In light of freedoms such as these, the report of a former servant in the house that the girls grew especially nervous when visitors penetrated into the study is readily understandable.[37]

Irving often invited his friends to visit Sunnyside and welcomed them when they came, but he shrank from the attentions of idly curious strangers. One day in June 1859, Evert Duyckinck and John Esten Cooke, the Virginia novelist, were walking up the little slope before the cottage intending to pay a surprise call, when Cooke, who had never met Irving, noticed "a gentleman of low stature, clad in black," standing near the house with his back to them, gazing intently across the river and apparently unaware of their presence. However, upon being accosted by Duyckinck the individual whirled around, exclaiming: "*Why*, Mr. D[uyckinck]! I am very glad to see you!" Being introduced to Cooke and assured that he was not "a mere lion-hunting stranger," Irving admitted that he had noticed the two men at a distance but had sought to avoid an interview by looking in the opposite direction. "I thought you were some of those people from New York," he sighed with relief. He then proceeded to win over the Virginian with his pleasant, unassuming manner and easy politeness. "Mr. Irving's voice was firm and cordial," Cooke recalled; "his smile bright, his walk easy and unlabored, and he resembled any elderly gentleman strolling quietly through his grounds."[38] When he was free from asthma and otherwise in good health, as he was this day, Irving delighted guests with his varied conversation. In a diary entry summarizing his visit Duyckinck remarked that the elderly author spoke in a quiet voice but was "fond of expressions and gesticulations in telling a story, which he manages with considerable mimetic force."[39] Irving was not always able to perform so well as he did for Cooke and Duyckinck, but even when illness kept him from entertaining guests with stories he usually managed to send them away fully satisfied

[35] Willis, "Visit to SS," *Home Journal*, no. 601 (August 15, 1857), p. 1.
[36] Allibone, "A Visit to WI, June 12, 1855" (Huntington).
[37] McLinden Interview (SHR).
[38] Cooke, "A Morning at SS," p. 713, 715.
[39] Evert A. Duyckinck, Diary, June 24, 1859 (NYPL, MS).

with their reception. N. P. Willis attributed this success to the deferential attitude he adopted: "He gives to all that is said, the mood of attention which is most flattering to it . . . so that the sayer, at its return to him, is more pleased than when he said it."[40] Others agreed; and George Putnam summed up a near-consensus among those who wrote of Irving as a host when he remarked that "no one, however dull, and however uncertain his claims, would fail to be pleased with his visit."[41]

It is quite unlikely that as they "yielded to the spell" of their host's pleasing manner—to borrow a phrase from Willis—[42] Irving's uninvited visitors and even some of his casual acquaintances recognized that they were being administered something rather like a guided tour. Several of his guests wrote detailed reports of the occasions in diaries or journals, or else published them in magazines or memoirs, and a comparison of these various accounts reveals a striking consistency among them. For example, certain topics were broached with notable regularity. The engraving of "Sir Walter Scott and his Contemporaries" which hung above the fireplace in Irving's parlour was a fertile conversation piece, repeatedly provoking questions about his memories of such old familiars as Scott, Campbell, Jeffrey, Moore, and Rogers. To guest after guest Irving reminisced fondly about his first meeting with Walter Scott in 1817 and, sadly, about his last one fourteen years later, shortly before the death of the broken old man.[43] Having entertained Allibone with these two anecdotes in 1855, on the bibliographer's second visit two years later he ran through them both again. Moreover, on the latter occasion Allibone could not help noticing that in his description of the parting with Scott Irving used "nearly the same words which we find in his 'Abbotsford.'"[44] Was he reciting from memory? From the frequent recurrence of this and other anecdotes which Irving seems at the least to have reduced to formulae, one infers that in order to provide satisfactory conversation he very sensibly trotted out the same dependable stock-in-trade. He told of an interview with Robert in 1853 when, responding to a question whether Maria had just borne a boy or a girl, the caretaker had

[40] Willis, "Visit to Sleepy Hollow," *Home Journal*, no. 602 (August 22), 1857), p. 1.

[41] Putnam, "Recollections of Irving," p. 605. This article was published in revised and expanded form under the title "WI" in *Harper's Weekly Magazine*, 15 (May 27, 1871), Supplement, pp. 491-96. See also Clark, "Recollections of WI," p. 560; T. Addison Richards, "SS, the Home of WI," *Harper's New Monthly Magazine*, XIV (December 1856), 1-21.

[42] "Visit to Sleepy Hollow," p. 1.

[43] See Allibone, "A Visit to WI, June 12, 1855" (Huntington); Cooke, "Irving at SS," p. 509; Putnam, "Recollections of Irving," p. 605; Theodore Tilton, "Half an Hour at SS," *Irvingiana*, pp. l-liii—acknowledged as from *The Independent*, November 24, 1859; James Grant Wilson, "A Day with WI," *Irvingiana*, pp. lviii-lix—acknowledged as from the *Church Record*, December 15, 1859, and reprinted in Wilson's *Bryant and His Friends* (New York, 1886), pp. 157-76; Willis, "Visit to SS," and "WI at Home," *Home Journal*, no. 719 (November 19, 1859), p. 2.

[44] Allibone, "Another Visit to WI, June 2, 1857" (Huntington).

exclaimed, "It's twins, Sir!"[45] He drew attention to the portraits that hung around the house showing him at various ages, giving special notice to one which he called "the green man."[46] Again and again he answered questions about his "literary habits."[47] Perhaps slyly, he sometimes lamented his inundation by visitors.[48] Then, after these few pleasantries inside his home, Irving often took favoured guests on a placid carriage drive through the vicinity, commenting on points of historical or legendary interest along the way.[49] Upon returning, he conducted a tour of his grounds, pointing out their manifold improvements,[50] and finally he invited the curious into his study,[51] where he regaled them with more small talk before they took their departure.

Irving had excellent reasons for adopting this ritualistic procedure as a host. He was aware that, by virtually everyone except close acquaintances, he was regarded in a distinctly formulaic way. To quote John Esten Cooke as a representative example, Irving was of interest as a "Nestor of literature . . . famous in the Old World and the New. He had outlived the generation which witnessed his early struggles, and those who thus looked to him [now] as the head of our literature were a sort of posterity."[52] Essentially, that is, to the public he was a relic of the past and a source of vicarious contact with famous bygone personalities and events. The journalists agreed that his home was a beautiful "retreat," that a visit there was a temporary escape from the turmoil of contemporary affairs to a more benign, polite realm hedged round by graceful wit and sentiment.[53] People certainly did not seek out Irving as a prophet of the present, nor, indeed, to see

[45] Duyckinck, Diary (NYPL, MS); Cooke, "A Morning at SS," p. 714.

[46] Duyckinck, Diary, December 1, 1859 (NYPL, MS); [Frederick Saunders], "WI: His Home and His Works," *New York Quarterly*, 4 (April 1855), 76; Tilton, "Half an Hour," p. liii; Willis, "Visit to SS" and "WI at Home."

[47] This topic was taken up in virtually every published account of a visit to WI. The following other topics were also popular: WI's own writings; WI's interest in the historical associations of the nieghbourhood; the ivy at SS; WI's recollections of Napoleon III and the Empress Eugenie; WI's nieces.

[48] Clark, "Recollections of WI," p. 553; Cooke, "Irving at SS," p. 509; Putnam, "Recollections of Irving," pp. 603, 607; Willis, "Visit to SS."

[49] Clark, "Recollections of WI," p. 554; Putnam, "Recollections of Irving," p. 605; [Saunders], "WI," pp. 70-71; "Viator," "Visit to WI"; Willis, "Visit to Sleepy Hollow."

[50] Asahel Davis, *A Visit to SS in the Lifetime of the 'Father of American Literature'* (Buffalo, 1860), p. 12; Putnam, "Recollections of Irving," p. 604; Osmond Tiffay, "A Day at SS," *Irvingiana*, p. liii—acknowledged as from the Springfield (Mass.) *Republican*; Willis, "Visit to SS."

[51] Putnam, "Recollections of Irving," p. 608; [Saunders], "WI," p. 73; Tilton, "Half an Hour," p. lii; Willis, "Visit to SS."

[52] Cooke, "Irving at SS," p. 511.

[53] The legendary and historical associations in the vicinity of SS were consistently dwelt upon in accounts of visits to WI, as was the journey from New York to the cottage. This material and the repeated claim that the calmness of WI's life was in harmony with that of his surroundings created together the impression that a journey to the cottage was a journey into the past or a region of fable.

him as he actually was; they came to Sunnyside because they wanted to cast eyes upon the "Nestor of literature" in America. Irving recognized this, and accordingly he confirmed the popular fables about himself by playing out a role as gentle Geoffrey Crayon grown old.

A more personal motive also impelled Irving to conduct these prepatterned entertainments. He was jealous of his privacy, and the oversimplified image of himself which he projected for admiring strangers was in fact an artful device to shield a portion of his identity from the public stare. Some of his guests recognized that in return for his hospitality he implicitly required of them a degree of respect for his private life, but not all were so considerate. Ordinarily, when a visitor published an account of his call at Sunnyside he followed the precedent of Frederick Saunders, who in 1855 declined to recount his host's conversation on the ground that to do so would be an invasion of privacy and constitute a "serious injustice to both their author and the reader."[54] Others, however, notably N. P. Willis, had fewer scruples.[55]

In July 1857, after spending a day at Sunnyside, Willis published an article in the weekly *Home Journal* setting forth the history of his dilemma whether he should discuss the event in print. Adopting the form of a personal letter to G. P. Morris, his co-editor of the magazine, Willis explained that he had already written an account of the day for his "own private public"—that is, Morris and the thousands of subscribers to the *Home Journal*. "I wrote of it," he recalled, "a long happy morning of shirt-sleeves and glowing spontaneity"; but once he had finished, a doubt had beclouded his memories:

> It was written too confidingly to you—as if on the same axis revolved Morris and "the world"—you with your overflowing heart and the world with its volcano of misconception—and both "craters" are not equally to be trusted! I had seen Irving that day, too, with a certain privilege—in the unguardedness of a holiday among relatives—and, more delightful as of course this was to me, and more valuable as it makes the description for the reader, I am, in a manner, more restricted by its confidingness. It is a question somewhat mooted, just now, you know, how far may be thus used, if at all, the privileges of hearth, friendship, and relationship.

The thought that the very art of biography would be impoverished without access to intimate information had failed to convince him of his right to render Irving's privacy public, Willis professed, and thus he had torn up his account. Since then, however, he had decided to set

---

[54] "WI," p. 77. See also Holmes, "Dr. Holmes' Remarks," p. 420; Putnam, "Recollections of Irving," pp. 606-09; Tuckerman, *Homes of American Authors*, p. 52.

[55] In 1852 Willis asked Thackeray after the latter's genial interview with WI why he had overlooked to take notes of their conversation. "I was about to answer what I thought of such a liberty," the novelist later told F. S. Cozzens, "when I remembered that he had done such things himself, and was silent" (Randolph, "Leaves from the Journal of F. S. Cozzens," p. 743).

aside his strict reserve, for he had re-read "Abbotsford," which he designated as "Irving's answer to the same question, for himself." Claiming to discern a happy parallel between Irving's former dilemma and his own, Willis must have dismissed as immaterial the facts that Irving's account of his visit to Walter Scott in 1817 was not published until 1835, three years after Scott's death and eighteen after the event itself, and even then was tactfully done and virtually devoid of new material about the author. For Willis, the important point was that Irving had "used his privilege of guest to share with the world his nearer view of such a man; and posterity, without it, would be poorer by a much-prized memorial. Who has not laid away in his heart, like a sweet-scented flower, Irving's portraiture of SCOTT AT ABBOTTSFORD [sic]?"[56] Thus, freed from his scruples by Irving's example, Willis had reconstructed his account, and his report of the visit duly appeared in the two subsequent issues of the Home Journal.

Invasions of privacy justified by such sentimental chicanery as this were bound to put Irving on his guard, making him resolute to deny everything but a carefully regulated budget of anecdotes and insights to potential merchandisers of his casual talk. As to Willis himself, he had set him down as a bustling gossip well before the 1857 visit, and the "glowing spontaneity" of the interview was purely an illusion of the journalist. Commenting after Irving's death about his storied reserve, F. S. Cozzens wrote: "Halleck could never get him to talk of his acquaintances in England, although he knew the greatest and best of them intimately. Did Willis ever get anything out of him? Not one word."[57]

Irving was often urged during the 1850's to share his personal history with his public by preparing an autobiographical memoir. When Allibone suggested that he do so, he added that Edward Everett had also expressed a wish that Irving would take up the task, since "no American had mingled with so many distinguished persons."[58] George Putnam, a privileged listener to whom he confided recollections of his early life, ventured more than once to suggest—"not professionally," he claimed—"I hope you have taken time to make a note of these." Irving's only reply was a humourous negative shake of the head.[59] Tantalizingly, he alleged to Allibone in 1857 that he simply had too many memories at command to fit them all into a book. When Theodore Tilton broached the subject in 1859, the author dismissed

[56] "Irving and Sleepy Hollow," Home Journal, no. 600 (August 8, 1857), p. 2. In this article Willis spoke frankly of WI's approaching death. Comparing the personalities of WI and Walter Scott, for example, he wrote: "Irving at Sunnyside, will be as sweet a dream to posterity as Scott at Abbottsford—two 'great hearts' (in fact, I think) set, as nearly to the same tune by Nature, as their two monuments mark the same height for their genius. Thank God the monument for Irving is a cenotaph—built but unoccupied as yet." See also below, p. 180.

[57] Randolph, "Leaves from the Journal of F. S. Cozzens," p. 748.

[58] Allibone, "Another Visit to SS, June 2, 1857" (Huntington).

[59] Putnam, "Recollections of Irving," p. 604.

the idea altogether.[60] Unlike Cooper, who, according to Cozzens, was "all open, spoke out all he felt and all he knew,"[61] Irving was reserved, and the autobiographical recollections he was to leave behind after his death were almost all to be left with Pierre. He respected the privacy of other persons, living or dead, as he coveted his own. While he believed that the claims of history warranted thorough examination of a public figure's life, he distinguished between the rights of a living man and the rights of the public after the man's death.

His reluctance to be lionized also led Irving in his later years to refuse requests that he pose for portraits, photographs, and busts. He did not wish to have his image hung on parlour walls throughout the nation any more than he wanted to see his own home crowded with admirers. Visitors were welcome to sketch their impressions of the buildings at Sunnyside, and trusted acquaintances such as Benson J. Lossing were even permitted to sketch the study,[62] but Irving himself was out of bounds. In January 1859, upon being requested by his friend T. W. C. Moore to permit a photograph to be taken of himself and distributed for sale on behalf of the Mount Vernon Fund to restore George Washington's home, he "definitively" refused. "I have declined everything of the kind for a long time past," he added. "It would be deemed a great piece of vanity and presumption on my part to consent to such a thing."[63] It was impossible for him to resist the inevitable, however. During the previous summer W. H. Bidwell, the editor of the *Eclectic Magazine,* had prevailed upon the popular painter John Sartain to attempt a portrait of Irving from memory which would then be engraved and published in the magazine. Accordingly, the two paid a call at Sunnyside and waited on the author in his study. After only a few moments' conversation, Sartain's scrutiny of his host's habitual positions and characteristic expressions became so obvious that Irving divined his general intention. Sartain recalled that as they took their leave, the resigned author "gave me a note to a relative in Lafayette Place, New York, requesting him to lend me a small portrait of him painted in his youth."[64] This portrait proved to be "of no use" to the artist since "years had wrought too great a

---

[60] Tilton, "Half an Hour," p. lii.

[61] Randolph, "Leaves from the Journal of F. S. Cozzens," p. 748.

[62] Lossing's sketch is reproduced in Butler, *WI's SS,* p. 22.

[63] WI to T. W. C. Moore, SS, January 12, 1859 (New York Society Library). WI's unwillingness to be photographed or sketched was by this time common knowledge in New York, but for some reason T. W. C. Moore believed he might prevail by perseverance. However, when a second note from Moore arrived within a week after WI had written his reply, PMI, who was attending to the most pressing of his uncle's correspondence, wrote a letter of his own, expressing "in the most emphatic manner [WI's] positive and unqualified repulsion to your suggestion in any form or shape in which you or the ladies of the Mt Vernon enterprise can present it" (PMI to T. W. C. Moore, SS, January 18, 1859 [New York Society Library]). Moore dropped the matter.

[64] This was Irving Van Wart, who had at his home John Vanderlyn's drawing of WI made in 1805. See below, p. 210.

change,"[65] but he completed a likeness of his own, and a much-praised engraving from it appeared in the *Eclectic* for October 1858.[66]

By discouraging the sketchers, portraitists, and daguerreotypists, by declining to write an autobiographical memoir, and by entertaining his visitors in a calculatedly formulaic manner, Irving sought to protect his privacy at the same time as he projected a satisfactory public image of himself. His manner with strangers and casual acquaintances was of course not so much a deliberate falsification of his character as a carefully controlled and limited expression of it. In many ways his behaviour when alone with his family was not significantly different from that when he was playing the elder literary statesman. As a rule he actually was of a gentle, tolerant temper; he did enjoy telling stories about Maria and her swelling brood of children; and he did take an antiquarian interest in the historic spots he pointed out to visitors on the carriage rides. The essential distinction between his public manner and his private one is simply that when among his family he expressed himself more fully and freely in every way than when not.

Naturally he did not regulate his conduct according to a black-and-white distinction between his co-residents at Sunnyside and all "outsiders." Knowledgeable, discreet friends, or acquaintances whom he happened to like were more privileged than strangers or merchants of gossip such as Willis, and to favoured visitors he behaved with a degree of openness. To them he felt free to range outside his standard repertoire of topics and sentiments and to alternate his whimsical humour and equable good nature with a crustier, more partisan self. For example, speaking to Duyckinck of Charles Dickens, with whom public lore had established him as a cordial friend, he declared himself "so provoked by his wanton ill treatment of the country in his American book after the unprecedented attentions he had received" during his visit to the United States in 1842, that while in London three years later he "would not accept an invitation to be present at one of [Dickens'] private theatricals."[67] Irving also possessed a supply of satiric stories about various dignitaries. In 1857 he related to Putnam and Allibone a tale of Henry Hallam, the legendarily captious historian, who "went to bed one night, feeling dissatisfied because he had contradicted no one that day. Directly, the watchman passed under his window, and called the hour. Hallam threw up the sash, and contradicted him." During the same interview he quoted from memory passages in the "lost" diary of Lord Byron—passages which, as Allibone noted in his record of the visit, were "not fit certainly for me to record."[68] Occasionally, too, Irving vented his

---

[65] Sartain, *The Reminiscences of a Very Old Man, 1808-1897* (New York, 1899), pp. 185-86.

[66] Vol. 45, opposite 145.

[67] Duyckinck, Diary, June 24, 1859 (NYPL, MS).

[68] Allibone, "Another Visit to WI, June 2, 1857" (Huntington).

pique at targets close to home. Mitchell, who called at Sunnyside on several occasions, recalled that "at times—rare times, it is true—I have seen this most amiable gentleman manifest a little of that restive choler which sometimes flamed up in William the Testy... impatience at something gone awry in the dressing of a garden border, in the care of some stable-pet—that was all gone with the first blaze, but marked and indicated the sources of that wrathy and pious zest (with which he is not commonly credited) with which he loved to put a contemptuous thrust of his sharper language into the bloat of upstart pride, and of conceit, and of insolent pretension."[69] Neither, in the proper company, did Irving hesitate to draw on a store of blue jokes.[70]

Nevertheless, if he gave freer rein to his temper and offered a wider range of anecdotage when among select company than when not, we have the testimony of Pierre that

> ... it was only in the easy familiarity of domestic life, that he could be seen to the greatest advantage. It was here that the riches of his conversation were most apparent. His forte in this respect, was his humor; much of which, however, was of a kind of which language can give no idea; it was not more in what he said, than in the way he said it; the play of feature, the eye, the tone, the gesture. There was a natural, easy, delightful sportiveness about his conversation when under no restraints of form or ceremony, a mixture of wit, whim, fun and drollery, of which few could resist the fascination.

Pierre recalled that even during his bouts with illness in 1859, Irving's conversation in the evenings was filled with "the interesting scenes of his life [which] seemed to pass before him—a thousand anecdotes of persons and things of which you had never heard, related in the most graphic manner, and filled, at times, with all his old fun and humor."[71] Just as he entertained the family when in good spirits, he vented his anger before them at incidents which raised his hackles, and he revealed thoughts about himself which he kept hidden from outsiders. Fearing the onset of senility, he repeatedly expressed the wish that he should not live so long as to become a burden to others. Occasionally, on days when nervousness, anxiety, or depression beset him, he would fly out at Pierre or someone else, presently to apologize. At times he was moved to tears of gratitude for the solicitous kindness shown him by his family. Meanwhile, even though he

---

[69] *Washington Irving. Commemoration of the One Hundredth Anniversary of His Birth...* (New York, 1883), p. 41. Putnam remarked of WI in his "Recollections of Irving": "His characterization of a... functionary, who had once served in the State Department, was more severe than I ever heard from him of any other person; and severity from a man of his judicious and kindly impulses had a meaning in it" (p. 610).

[70] On the last page of PMI's 1859 Journal, among miscellaneous and fragmentary entries, is an undated example: "Editor of John Bull–Complained to land lady of weak tea–'Sir–when I make water I make water–& when I make tea I make tea"–"not in the same pot, Madam I trust."

[71] *LLWI*, II, 200; IV, 268.

could not conceal his physical condition, he did his best to put up a good front for visitors. When John Pendleton Kennedy called at Sunnyside on October 31, 1859, he wrote in his journal for that day that Irving "looks wretchedly altered since I saw him last. But he receives us with his usual cheerfulness and we have lunch. . . . Irving is full of kindest remembrances and tells me he will get down to New York. . . . I fear he is too weak to accomplish this, but he persists in saying he will do so."[72] Irving had no wish to elicit sympathy from Kennedy, much less from strangers, and he managed with considerable success to conceal from view the weaknesses and fears which he divulged within his own household. To Pierre, Helen, and his nieces he was neither "The Patriarch of American Letters" nor a genial host and friend, but an aging member of an affectionate family circle.

Alluding to his advanced age and poor health, Irving remarked to G. W. Curtis in 1859: "I am getting ready to go; I am shutting up my doors and windows."[73] Melancholy as the figure was, it aptly typified many features of his character during his last years of life. He still presided over the board meetings of the Astor Library, occasionally took in an opera or attended a dinner party given by some New York grandee, and regularly glanced over the popular weekly and monthly miscellanies of the United States and England. Through conversation with neighbours and visitors he kept apprised of literary, political, and other gossip, and owing to the omnivorous journalistic appetite of Ebenezer he was daily exposed to the newspapers of New York. In short, he was not at all ignorant of contemporary affairs, and yet for the most part they interested him less and less. His formerly hardy social instincts were now erratic: at times he was vivaciously gregarious, but at others he would sit silent in company. He often expressed a desire to meet persons whose activities he thought interesting, yet at other times he wished to see no new faces. He was solicitous to keep his family around him, and in 1859 he became so eager to see Sarah Storrow that he offered to pay her expenses should she be able to make the passage from Paris.[74] The delights of New York had lost all their savour. Although he was animated in discussing the 1857 opera season with Duyckinck, in the same conversation he observed that the changes to the city made him feel "three or four hundred years old."[75] On his visits there he preferred quiet dinners and evenings with Davis and his spritely wife, or with Pierre and Helen, or Irving Van Wart and his family, to the rigours of public entertainments. The Grinnells' letters detailing their progress across Europe called up

[72] Kennedy, Journal, vol. XI (March 15, 1857 to December 6, 1859), pp. 353-54 (Peabody).

[73] Curtis, "WI," p. 803.

[74] WI to Irving Paris [Sarah's brother], SS, July 28, 1859 (SHR). On September 7 he wrote again to Irving Paris expressing disappointment that Sarah would be unable to accept his offer (SHR).

[75] Duyckinck, Diary, June 24, 1859 (NYPL, MS).

memories of the more than twenty years he had lived on the Continent, but they failed to render attractive the possibility of making a final visit to his old haunts. He was chiefly concerned to learn when his neighbours planned to arrive home.

Similarly, the drama of international politics and the bustle of mid-century progress left him largely unmoved. During his Ministership at Madrid the machinations of Spanish political intrigue had excited his imagination, and in 1851 and 1852 he had eagerly awaited details of Napoleon's dramatic *coup* in France. The Crimean War of 1854-1856 seems to have made little impression on him, however, and at the outbreak of the brief Franco-Austrian War in June 1859 he was much less concerned about the conflict itself than about the safety of the Grinnells, who happened to be not far from the action when fighting began. The previous September he had been unmoved when the laying of the Atlantic Cable provoked a prodigal display of civic celebrations in New York.[76] After spending a day looking on at these "paroxysms of excitement" among the citizenry, he wrote to his grandniece Julia Grinnell that he did "not know what would have become of us all, and whether we should not have sunk into the spell-bound oblivion of Sleepy Hollow, if we had not been suddenly roused from our apathy" by the Cable.[77] His mind was still active and alert, but he was no longer receptive to new patterns of thought. He continued to pursue the interests which he had formed decades before.

Irving's contentment in indulging long-formed tastes was evident in two of his most frequent pastimes, conversation and reading. As a conversationalist, for example, he clearly took great pleasure in talk of plays and players, a favourite topic of his for many years. He recalled to Allibone the days he had spent in the British Museum reading in early English drama, and he still impressed his auditors, as he had done in the 1820's, with his encyclopaedic knowledge of early plays.[78] He spoke of his acquaintances with the great tragedians George Frederick Cooke and John Philip Kemble, anatomizing their styles and comparing their performances in various roles. He told of performances by his favourite actress, Mrs. Siddons, and of plays he had seen as a youth at the Park Theatre in New York.[79] His interest in the drama ran to personalities and performances rather than to works; and as to personalities, he seems to have been a generation out of date. There is no record of his having read a single play during this period.

As a reader, his predilection was for authors of his own generation or before. When James Grant Wilson asked him in 1857 for his opinion of the modern poets, he replied bluntly: "I ignore them all. I

---

[76] Only a few years before he had been excited at the engineering successes of John Ericsson (1803-1889), later the designer of the ironclad ship *Monitor*. See WI to Sarah Storrow, SS, January 13, 1853 (Yale).

[77] WI to Julia Grinnell, SS, September 2, 1858; *LLWI*, IV, 251-52.

[78] Allibone, "Another Visit to WI," June 2, 1857" (Huntington).

[79] *LLWI*, IV, 241-42.

read no poetry written since Byron's, Moore's, and Scott's."[80] Two years later he assured John Esten Cooke that "a man at my time of life makes few acquaintances with the poets. I read but little of them; and that among the friends of my youth."[81] Ordinarily his appetite for verse was well satisfied by dipping into Vicesimus Knox's compilation of excerpts, *Elegant Extracts*.[82] He was a wide reader in fiction, however, and was conversant with the work of contemporary novelists. He claimed to have read Scott's *The Antiquary* a hundred times,[83] and he also professed to admire Cooper's Leatherstocking Tales.[84] One of his standard sentiments for public consumption was that in the Leatherstocking series Cooper had done honour to his country, however true it was that his later works had best be forgotten. Yet, he told Putnam privately, it was impossible to consider this American novelist without contrasting "Scott's genial humor with Cooper's *want* of it."[85] Similarly, he found it impossible to dissociate the works of Dickens from the memory of his unsavoury personal traits. His judgment of Thackeray was much more favourable, and when he once confessed to Cozzens that he had not yet read *The Virginians* he added that he knew he would enjoy it: "Ah, Thackeray understands our character. He is a better judge of character than Dickens. It must be good."[86] He praised the work of Kingsley and of Hawthorne, but he dismissed the novels of Bulwer-Lytton as being "like music with false notes."[87]

Not surprisingly, Irving's generic preferences lay outside the drama, verse, and the novel, and within the forms which he had practised with success in his own career. He respected the compilers of formal biographies and histories on topics related to the United States—Bancroft, Prescott, and Motley—with whom, as the author of *Columbus, Astoria,* and *Washington,* he shared a common practice, and among whom he was recognized as both pioneer and peer. Perhaps for similar reasons he admired the biographical memoir as written by Henry T. Tuckerman, the personal essay and the miscellany as variously practised by Longfellow, Cozzens, and Mitchell, and the amateur nature study as done by Charles Lanman. He continued to enjoy brisk wit and humour such as he found in Holmes' spritely *Autocrat of the Breakfast Table* or Leland's *Meister Karl's Sketch Book,* although he had come to feel strongly that polite literature must not give offense. His rather severe conception of literary propriety had led him, in fact, to regret that he had ever published his own breezily

[80] Wilson, "A Day with WI," p. lix.

[81] Duyckinck, Diary, December 1, 1859 (NYPL, MS).

[82] See below, p. 205.

[83] Putnam, "WI [1871]," p. 495.

[84] See below, p. 231.

[85] Putnam, "WI," p. 495.

[86] Randolph, "Leaves from the Journal of F. S. Cozzens," p. 744.

[87] Allibone, "A Visit to WI, June 12, 1855" (Huntington).

whimsical early works, the "Letters of Jonathan Oldstyle" (1802-1803) and the *Salmagundi* papers (1807-1808), and to refuse permission to republish them. He was galled that, after he had scoured his unciti- zenly levity from the *History of New York* for the revised edition of 1848, the popularity of the book caused his errors of decades past to continue haunting him. He habitually spoke of the *History* in slight- ing terms,[88] and when the actor-playwright James H. Hackett sent him a dramatic adaptation of it for comment in 1857, he damned its original as "the thoughtless work of a young man who had no idea of the grave offense that might be given by a heedless joke" and strongly advised against performing it.[89] To his chagrin, Hackett produced the play with great success.[90] Perhaps Irving's rather stern conception of the popular author as properly a guardian of good taste proceeded from his consciousness that the reading public looked to him as a kind of gentle sage. In any case, if his notions of decorum militated against his admitting the lively merits of his own early works, others were more liberal, and their opinions eventually prevailed.[91]

While the elderly Irving did continue to cultivate tastes he had formed long before, to regard him as a man wholly cut off from the concerns of his contemporaries during the 1850's would be seriously to misinterpret both his character and that of the age; for in some respects he was unmistakably a man in touch with his times. For example, his lifelong amateur's interest in painting continued to flourish during this vital period in the history of American art, and he entertained at Sunnyside several of the foremost painters and illus- trators of the day, including Thomas Hicks, Thomas P. Rossiter, Frederick E. Church, and F. O. C. Darley. The congruency between his established interests and some of the most popular contemporary pastimes is also evident in his fascination with the pseudo-science of spiritualism. Although he and the other members of the Sunnyside household were only dabblers in this field of experimentation, had they wished they could have joined any of several thriving clubs devoted to the advancement of the study. They could have subscribed to a newspaper, *The Spiritualist Telegraph,* or attended lectures in New York by such personalities as the "celebrated" Mrs. Cora Hatch, or Mr. Lewis C. Walsh, "a ripping, splitting, and speaking medium," or even joined the purposeful people of Boston in advocating a third political party, "The Spiritualist Ticket."[92] By 1859 spiritualism was so

---

[88] See, for example, *LLWI,* IV, 244.

[89] WI to James H. Hackett, New York, January 3, 1857 (Virginia).

[90] WI suffered another twist of the knife in October 1859, when a much-publicized *History of the Colony of New Plymouth* appeared, "written after the manner of Diedrich Knickerbocker" by his admiring friend in Yonkers, F. S. Cozzens. The *History* was purportedly the work of "I.B., A Descendant of Anne Bradstreet" (New York *Tribune,* October 4, 1859, p. 1, col. 3). It was serialized in the New York *Ledger,* and there was speculation for a time about its authorship.

[91] See below, pp. 249-51.

[92] New York *Tribune,* March 17, 1859, p. 1, col. 2; September 16, 1859, p. 5, col. 1. New York *Times,* March 8, 1859, p. 3, col. 3; March 12, 1859, p. 3, col. 3.

widespread a fad that in August a "National Convention of Spiritualists" was held at Plymouth, Massachusetts, to which the press gave generous and on the whole sober coverage.[93]

For many years Irving had been ambivalent toward his own curiosity about spiritualistic phenomena. His amusement at credulity in such matters had more than once taken memorable form in his fiction, but in the author himself it had always co-existed with a disposition to regard spiritualism as a legitimate subject for inquiry. The latter inclination is attested to by his well-known pact with the dying John Nalder Hall in 1828 to wait at an appointed time and place after Hall's decease for a communication from him. Irving kept the rendezvous, but Hall did not; and twenty years afterwards he told Pierre that he "had been hardly treated by the ghosts . . . [having] invoked the presence of the dead more than once, but in vain."[94] During his visit to Washington, D.C. early in 1853, he received from Helen the information that the family had been engaged in experiments with "moving tables," which she thought "one of the most wonderful discoverys [sic] in nature."[95] In his reply he denounced the pastime as "hocus pocus" but added that he had himself attended a party the night before where the same experiments had been conducted.[96] For all his scoffing, he admitted to Allibone in 1857 that "unaccountable facts" were connected with the spiritual manifestations. "They tried moving the tables here," he said, "and they did move and the girls . . . would not do it any more."[97]

Notwithstanding the timorous caution of Kate, Mary, and Sarah, communication with the spirits was a topic often broached at Sunnyside. Experiments witnessed in company with Daniel Dunglas Hume, the flamboyant medium who was then the most prominent practitioner of his art in the United States, were discussed, and Pierre made knowledgeable reference to the writings of John W. Edmonds, a leading apologist and theorist of spiritualism. Helen had no taste for analysis nor any wish, she said, to "meet a spirit," but she was so fond of virtually any other social gathering that despite hesitations she attended the sessions held periodically by members of the family or by persons living near Sunnyside.[98] On April 28, 1858, a seance was held at the cottage, and Pierre, who was present, wrote out a transcript of interchanges between a human questioner and a garrulous spirit voice. His transcript appears below:

[93] New York *Times,* August 6, 1859, p. 4, col. 5; August 9, 1859, p. 2, cols. 1-2.

[94] *LLWI,* II, 359-60; IV, 36. The quotation is from the latter page.

[95] Helen Irving to WI, New York, February 5, 1853 (Yale).

[96] WI to Helen Irving, Washington, February 10, 1853; *LLWI,* IV, 131.

[97] Allibone, "Another Visit to WI, June 2, 1857" (Huntington).

[98] Recounting to WI the events of a large family party, Helen wrote on February 5, 1853: "As usual of late, at all small parties, the amusement of the evening was 'moving tables' . . . . The whole city is full of it. Every house you go into in the evening you find a table trying the experiment" (Yale).

Q. Have you still the powers of sight, hearing, touch, taste[,] smell—as in earth—

A. All these we have more acute than ever, but they are not like the mortal organs.

Q. In what light do you regard Jesus?

A. We regard him as an advanced spirit—If you ask us as regards our ideas of his life on earth, that is altogether different. *On earth.* He *was* a reformer—a social advocate of what he believed true principles—though personal—and he refuted the many attempts of the Jews to make a God of him—

Q. Give me a brief message in *Spanish*

A. I cannot—if you will excuse me this I will touch thee 5 times—(then came 5 touches below the knee on the right leg.) It makes me feel not only happy—but full of inexpressible joy that I *can* give thee something to help thee in this great cause—...

Q. Have you passed thro' more than one form of spirit life since your body was committed to the deep?

A. No. I first entered 2d sphere—but I did not remain long—I soon began to expand in mind and open my own ideas of life- xxx

Q. Is the writing or reading of books among the pursuits & enjoyments of the spirit world?

A. We do not *read* books in spirit life—but we often read their synopsis in the spirit of the authors.

Q. Did you not give me an opinion of Longfellow's Hiawatha

A. Indeed I did—& am familiar with the work & the *Author* who is as much interested in these truths as thee.

Q. What are your pursuits & employments?

Ans. Our chief employment is to compare our various developments that we may more freely progress and also to open more widely the gates of science and religion to the world. In 100 years man shall not be as now—he shall be more free with the spirit and more open mentally—

Q. Can you go now to Savannah—

[A.] Yes

Well—the child has just taken *some good* and appears to be a little more comfortable—but looks very ill—& I shall be sent for again *soon*—I shall remain with the child tonight— x I will touch & *push* thy leg as I go—[99]

Was Irving the questioner in this extraordinary dialogue? Internal evidence in the transcribed text and other considerations suggest that he was almost certainly present at the seance.[100] Evidently, however,

[99] PMI, Holograph Notes (NYPL, Berg). The references to "Savannah" and "the child" at the end of the transcript raise a tantalizing question as to the identity of the child being referred to—and indeed, about the identity of the visiting spirit, who seems to be associated in some way with the child. This latter person, referred to as "ill," may possibly have been Leslie Irving, PMI's former assistant, who had recently been ill and was probably in Savannah on a tour for recuperation at the time the seance was held. See Ebenezer Irving to Katrina Irving, SS, March 4, 1858 (SHR).

[100] The probability that WI was at SS at the time of this interview is established by the facts that in the spring of 1858 he did not often venture away, being in poor health and also busy with the final volume of the *Washington,* and further that as a rule—until 1859—PMI did not visit SS unless WI was there, too. The possibility that WI was the

even this experience failed to win him over to faith in the manifestations. During the remainder of his lifetime he seems to have regarded
the topic of spiritualism with something of Helen's non-committal,
semi-serious good nature rather than with the single-minded sobriety
of Pierre. During 1859 "the spirits" provoked some of his best witti-
cisms, and yet amidst the family's animated discussions of mediumship he seems more than once to have fallen asleep.

Out of all proportion to his other interests, of course, the elderly
Irving's most engrossing pastime was work on the biography of
George Washington. Paradoxically, in pursuing this project which he
had long regarded as an occupation for his years of retirement from
public life, he was devoting himself to one of the most prominent
topics of contemporary interest in the United States. Perhaps, indeed,
in partial response to his example as the biographer of Washington, an
unusual amount of scholarly and artistic attention was being lavished
at this time upon the entire Revolutionary period. Even in the neighbourhood of Sunnyside several devoted amateurs were at work on
historical studies: John C. Hamilton was writing a multi-volume
paean to his father, the statesman; G. W. Greene was engaged on a life
of his grandfather, General Nathaniel Greene; Benson J. Lossing from
White Plains was collaborating with the Schuylers on a life of their
grandfather, General Philip Schuyler.[101] Professional authors were
mining the lode of popular interest in the early history of the nation,
including Mrs. Lydia Minturn Post, who dedicated to Irving her
Domestic Annals of the Revolution (1859), and Rufus W. Griswold, who
before his death in 1857 began a series of pamphlets collectively
entitled Griswold's Illustrated Life of Washington.[102] The historical painters were extremely active. In October 1857, for example, Thomas P.
Rossiter began his famous "Washington and Lafayette at Mount Vernon, 1776," which he completed in 1859.[103] Edward Everett was exercising himself in major cities with his well-worn oration, "The
Character of Washington," and less well remembered persons were

questioner in the dialogue is based on two considerations. First, of the regular occu-
pants of the cottage only PMI and WI could, probably, have understood a message from
the spirit in Spanish. Second, there is no extant record of PMI's compiling a transcript
of any conversation wherein WI was not a participant.

[101] Hamilton, History of the Republic of the United States of America ... as Traced in
the Writings of Alexander Hamilton and his Cotemporaries, 7 vols. (New York, 1857-1864).
The third volume was published in May 1859 (New York Tribune, May 27, 1859, p. 1,
col 2). Greene, The Life, Letters, and Despatches of Major General Nathaniel Greene, 7 vols.
(New York, 1859). Lossing, The Life and Times of Philip Schuyler (New York, 1860). For
WI's opinion of Schuyler, see WI to Benson J. Lossing, SS, March 15, 1856 (Virginia).

[102] Griswold lived to complete only four of the forty-five pamphlets eventually
comprising this work. At his death it was taken up by Benson J. Lossing, who completed it in 1860. It was then published in book form under his name: The Life of
Washington; A Biography Personal, Military, and Political, 3 vols. (New York, 1860). See
below, pp. 318-19.

[103] In 1860 Rossiter moved from New York to Cold Spring, New York, where he
continued to produce Washingtoniana, including "Washington in his Library at Mount
Vernon" and "Washington's First Cabinet" (DAB, XVI, 182).

available to declaim on similar topics.[104] Patriotic feeling ran high. On March 4, 1859, when Everett spoke at the New York Academy of Music, he was escorted to and from the building by a regiment of militia to the accompaniment of appropriate music.[105] By 1859 the volume of testimony to the virtues of the founding fathers—George Washington in particular—was becoming so great that the editor of the New York *Tribune* dubbed the fad "The Washingtonian Mania."[106]

Whatever other motives might be advanced to account for this abundance of attention to the American Revolution and its most eminent figure, it seems plausible to regard it as a means of affirming, despite insistent sectional tensions, the identity of origins and political sentiments between North and South. Certainly Irving regarded his portrayal of Washington in that light. As we have seen, in February and March, 1859, he devoted much care to preparing the concluding remarks for the work, wherein he affirmed that the memory of Washington was a unique possession of all Americans:

> The fame of Washington stands apart from every other in history.... With us his memory remains a national property, where all sympathies throughout our widely-extended and diversified empire meet in unison. Under all dissensions and amid all the storms of party, his precepts and example speak to us from the grave with a paternal appeal; and his name—by all revered —forms a universal tie of brotherhood—a watchword for our Union.[107]

Amidst the Civil War four years later, Pierre wrote pointedly in the *Life and Letters* that his uncle had been "[e]minently national in his feelings, a lover of his whole country," but that he "was not without foreboding at the signs of the times."[108] Unlike his obliviousness to political upheavals in foreign countries, Irving's attitude toward the impending crisis in the United States was one of attentive anxiety. He conceived of his final published work as an indirect plea to preserve a political system which, as he wrote in the conclusion to the *Washington,* had fostered "'purer civil liberty ... than [had] hitherto been the portion of mankind.'"[109] Yet even as he wrote these sounding phrases he must have perceived their glaring irony. How could he talk of "civil liberty" in the United States when half the nation practised Negro slavery, an institution which he denounced in private as "accursed"? He could not reconcile his plea for national unity with his

[104] For example, on November 22, 1859, one William W. Badger advertised in the New York *Tribune* his availability "to lyceums, &c." to deliver a poem he had written, entitled "Washington, or the Vision of Liberty" (p. 1, col. 1).

[105] New York *Times,* March 5, 1859, p. 4, col. 5.

[106] New York *Tribune,* May 19, 1859, p. 4, col. 4.

[107] *Washington,* V, 301.

[108] *LLWI,* IV, 299-300. See also Randolph, "Leaves from the Journal of F. S. Cozzens," p. 744.

[109] *Washington,* V, 301. WI is quoting a statement by George Washington.

belief that slavery was a blot on the national conscience which must be removed at any cost. Like many Americans, North and South, he was committed to two mutually exclusive positions. Little wonder that he thought the times portentous.

The irreconcilability of his views on slavery and national unity was paralleled by the inconsistency of his attitudes toward Negroes. Apparently without any disturbing sense of self-contradiction, however, he could denounce the dehumanizing system of slavery while he balked at enforcing even an appearance of racial equality on his own property. He could be moved to tears of sentimental benevolence by the "negro anecdotes" in the Reverend W. H. Milburn's *Ten Years of Preacher Life* (1859), yet he enjoyed recounting anecdotes of various amusing darkies he had encountered.[110] His humanitarian sympathies co-existed with a strong strain of condescension toward Negroes, and when in high spirits he was capable of what now seem breathtaking *gaucheries*.[111] A small room above the kitchen at Sunnyside was affectionately named "Old Mammy's Asylum."[112] Yet in the disjuncture between his uncompromising theory and his equivocal practice relating to Negroes, Irving was once again thoroughly a man of his time, and perhaps rather better. For example, in September 1859, when a petition against permitting continuation of the slave trade out of New York was placed before his brethren at the Diocesan Convention of the Protestant Episcopal Church, it was received with suppressed laughter. A proposed resolution to that effect was then rejected by a decided majority, and the reporter for the New York *Tribune* noted that "only the sacredness of the place kept the applause from breaking forth at this result."[113] Like his curiosity about mediumship and his anxiety about the immediate future of the nation, the discontinuity between Irving's reformist attitude toward Negro slavery and his condescending views of Negroes themselves placed him squarely among his American contemporaries.

In the years since the publication of his revised works, his growing celebrity had threatened to deprive him of the retired mode of life

[110] For example, Charles A. Davis related the following anecdote of WI: "Walking with him in Broadway one fine day—a dashing looking negro—(black as the ten of spades which is nine times blacker (he said), than the ace) passed by us—dressed in all sorts of finery and fashion—Even to *kid gloves*—and bearing a new silk umbrella over his head—'that Gentleman' said he—is more cautious than we are – against being *'tanned' –*" (Davis to PMI, New York, June 1863—NYPL, Berg). See also below, p. 225.

[111] On April 27, 1851, WI expressed this thought to John P. Kennedy: "I wish to heavens nature would restore to the poor negroes their tails and settle them in their proper place in the scale of creation. It would be a great relief to both them and the abolitionists, and I see no other way of settling the question effectually" (Peabody). See also below, p. 214.

[112] McLinden Interview (SHR).

[113] New York *Tribune*, September 30, 1859, p. 8, cols. 1-2. Although the slave trade out of New York was outlawed in 1808, the regulation was virtually ignored, and in 1859 the city was "generally acknowledged" as the centre of the trade in America (Basil Lee, *Discontent in New York City, 1861-1865* [Washington, D.C., 1943], p. 131).

among his family which he had coveted for many years. Recognizing the threat, he evolved a response to it by developing a public manner which enabled him to satisfy the needs, or demands, of his admiring audience while at the same time preserving for himself a degree of privacy. By his gravious behaviour and his standard repertoire of amiable, retrospective anecdotes he tacitly confirmed for visitors to Sunnyside the accepted folk-characterization of himself as a gentle, placid relic of a less troubled age; yet even as he delighted his visitors he was withholding aspects of his personality. No matter how satisfactory he may have been to his fellow citizens as a cultural symbol—"The Patriarch of American Letters"—seen in private the Washington Irving of the middle and late 1850's was an appreciably more varied, believable, and interesting human being than one might suppose on the basis of the bland public image he projected. This was the man whom, over a thirty-year period, Pierre had come to know more intimately than any other person knew him. With Pierre, in whose daily (and often nightly) company he was to pass the closing months of his lifetime, Irving was unaffectedly himself. Fortunately, during 1859 Pierre kept a journal in which he faithfully recorded the details of his uncle's life at Sunnyside. This journal, which is extant, affords us an opportunity to view more closely the elderly author at home.

Chapter Six

A Private Journal, 1859

For several weeks after his decision in December 1858 to return from New York to Sunnyside, Irving paid dearly for ignoring the contrary advice of his physician, Dr. John C. Peters. His condition grew so poor as to preclude the possibility of his returning to the city for treatment, so that the alarmed Peters was obliged to make almost nightly excursions in order to attend him. "The long and dreary winter of 1858-59," Peters recalled in a memoir, "was passed in one continued struggle with oppressed breathing, harassing coughs, sleepless nights, and consequent debility; with nervousness, and frequent attacks of despondency." Often it was necessary to remain at Irving's bedside for entire nights in order to help him rest. Even when he was nearly asleep, Peters noted, "his breathing would become gradually or speedily shorter and lighter, until it not only became almost imperceptible, but would absolutely stop for a space which should have been occupied by four or five ordinary respirations; then also his pulse would falter, until it seemed as if that kind heart would never beat again."[1] Happily, by February the patient appeared to be

[1] "The Illnesses of Washington Irving," *North American Journal of Homeopathy*, 9 (February 1860), 458. This article was reprinted in Peters' privately published work,

out of immediate danger. Peters' home and family were in the city, and his attentions to Irving had naturally been paid at great sacrifice to his personal comfort, not to mention his medical practice.[2] Once daily visits were no longer imperative, therefore, he made arrangements to call less frequently, deputing Pierre to keep watch over Irving and periodically to relay reports of his symptoms.[3] In this way, Pierre took up a new role as liaison between Irving and the physician[4]—and adjusted his daytime and nocturnal habits accordingly. In order to be within call in the night when the invalid might request medication or other assistance, he began to occupy a tiny "porch room" adjacent to Irving's chamber;[5] and to help regularize his performance as a medical observer, he purchased a notebook for use in part as a repository of his clinical observations.[6] Beginning on February 28, 1859, Pierre recorded in this black canvas notebook the fluctuations in Irving's health during his last months of life.

To help familiarize his lay assistant with the peculiarities of Irving's condition, Peters lent him copies of several recent articles in professional journals. Pierre transcribed from these into his journal for easy reference, and from the underlinings of some passages it appears that he studied them with care.[7] Peters expected from him a record of Irving's sleeping habits, appetite, moods, medications, and any other possibly significant developments; and as one might expect, Pierre acquitted his charge faithfully. He compiled a much more detailed medical record during the periods when Irving's health was poor than those when he was relatively robust, but he rarely neglected to write some daily observation on his uncle's condition. When business called him to New York or elsewhere he would ask Helen, Kate,

dedicated to WI, *A Review of Some of the Late Reforms in Pathology and Therapeutics* (New York, 1860).

[2] His clinic was at 19 East 15th Street (*Trow's New York City Directory for 1859-1860*, p. 290).

[3] According to a note by PMI in the 1859 Journal, p. [2], from December 18, 1858, to March 4, 1859, Peters called at SS three times per week; from March 5 to March 25 twice a week; and afterwards, "I was to report to get his instructions."

[4] Peters had high praise for PMI's care of his uncle: "... it is impossible adequately to describe the devotion of [WI's] favorite nephew, Pierre M. Irving; who scarcely had one undisturbed night for many weeks and months. He read to his illustrious uncle many hours every night . . . . When all reading matter palled upon his attention, many hours were often spent by this devoted nephew in conversation and attempts at encouragement, often without manifest relief, but without which Mr. Irving's condition might have become dreadful indeed. For many weeks he never left Mr. Irving a moment at night" ("Illnesses," pp. 458-59).

[5] A diagram of the floor plan of the cottage is in Butler, *WI's SS*, p. 29.

[6] An entry in the 1859 Journal reads: "Bought – February 1859 / No. 5."

[7] At the back of the 1859 Journal PMI headed an undated entry: "From Dr Peters' articles sent for my perusal." In the entry he wrote out excerpts from Dr. Henry Kennedy's "Cursory Remarks on the Diagnosis of Fatty Heart," in the *Edinburgh Medical Journal* for July 1859, and an article in the *British Medical Journal* for June 18, 1859, by Dr. Henry Hyde Satter, whom he designated as "now the principal authority in Europe" on asthma. In 1860 Satter published *On Asthma: Its Pathology and Treatment*.

or Sarah to "report the day," and upon his return he would copy his own deputy's observations into the record. His excursions to New York during 1859 almost invariably included a call at Dr. Peters' bustling clinic, where the two reviewed his notes from the preceding days. On the basis of these Peters would then determine the course of continuing treatment, sometimes prescribing a new restorative, depressant, or other remedy, instructing Pierre in its administration, and sending him back to Sunnyside equipped with a supply.

John C. Peters, a prominent practitioner with an elite clientele in New York, was among the leading exponents in the United States of homeopathy, the theory that disease may be cured by administering in minute doses substances which, in a healthy person, would produce symptoms resembling those of the patient himself.[8] He began treating Irving in February 1852, when he achieved striking success in relieving him from attacks of vertigo and other complaints, and he soon won his patient's unswerving loyalty. Acutely conscious of the tendency in some circles to dismiss all homeopathic treatment as quackery, and perhaps hence uncertain whether Irving placed total confidence in his care, Peters urged him to select a second physician, but without avail.[9] Irving declared himself well satisfied, especially since in practice Peters was not a doctrinaire exponent of homeopathy. Even though, as he admitted, he was "rather slow at adopting new theories," in 1854 he recommended homeopathy to John Pendleton Kennedy on the strength of his own experience.[10] When any of his friends turned up ill in New York, he did not hesitate to dispatch a note to his physician, directing him to cure them forthwith;[11] and Peters, who admired Irving and valued his friendship, sought to comply. Despite a few of their relatives' misgivings touching Peters' ideas,[12] all the Irvings at Sunnyside eventually made

[8] Peters (1819-1893) pursued his medical studies in Europe and in 1842 was licensed to practice medicine in New York. He was one of the founders of the New York Pathological Society in 1844, and he became for many years a contributor to the literature of homeopathy. From 1858 to 1861 he was editor of the *North American Journal of Homeopathy* (*DAB*, VII, 505-06).

[9] Peters, "A Letter from the Physician of WI," *The Moravian* (December 22, 1859), p. 403. See also "Illnesses," p. 460.

[10] WI to Mrs. John P. Kennedy, SS, February 21, 1854; *LLWI*, IV, 170; see also WI to Mrs. John P. Kennedy, SS, August 31, 1854; *LLWI*, IV, 179.

[11] Once, for example, he wrote Peters a note saying that his friend Mme. Cavalcante, wife of the Brazilian Minister, had just arrived in New York and was suffering from a cold, and also that one of her daughters had come down with a "severe sore throat." Would Peters kindly call on her *"in the course of the day* and make them well, as I told them you would do immediately" (WI to Peters, New York, May 6 [185?]; Scrapbook of John C. Peters—NYPL, Berg).

[12] In particular, Sarah Storrow was concerned. On January 30, 1859, Julia Grinnell, then at Naples, wrote to Helen Irving of a letter she had just received from Mrs. Storrow: "After receiving Pierre's last letter, Irving [Julia Grinnell's son] had written to Mr Storrow, giving him an extract from it, in regard to Uncle's health. I had promised Sarah that we would write to her the accounts of him whenever we received any from home. She feels quite troubled that Uncle should not have change of air and scene and be in a

him their regular attendant.[13] In emergencies he was freely to be summoned from the city,[14] and during Irving's bouts with ill health he looked forward so eagerly to the arrival of "the Doctor" that, as Pierre noticed, even the prospect of Peters' presence tended to alleviate his symptoms.

On December 20, 1858, two days after Irving returned to Sunnyside with Pierre and Helen, another physician, Oliver Wendell Holmes, paid him a social call. Holmes had accepted an engagement to give a series of lectures in New York, but he later said that his real motive for making the journey from his home in Boston was a desire to be introduced to Irving.[15] His brief visit came at an opportune time, for although Irving was hardly at his best, he had just completed *The Autocrat of the Breakfast Table* and was anxious to meet its author.[16] At the close of an animated interview—but one in which Irving's asthma was painfully evident—Holmes ventured to suggest two remedies, medicated cigarettes and "Jonas Whitcomb's Cough Remedy," which he had often prescribed with success years before, when in active practice. Irving was amenable, and so a few days later, with a note of thanks for his hospitality, Holmes enclosed a supply of both. Then, having observed him only once, and that for less than an hour, the Bostonian saw fit to write John C. Peters with a few suggestions for the treatment of Irving's maladies, particularly his cough. Peters, who by this time had attended Irving almost seven years, must have been taken aback upon receiving the unsolicited advice of this famous stranger. He was almost certainly aware of Holmes' well-known contempt for homeopathy,[17] but if not, he could have surmised as much from the distrust of his skill implied in the note he had received.

mild climate, where he could exercise daily in the open air. She enquires if his physician be a man of eminence, and it is evident to me that she has not much faith in homeopathy. She had a friend in Paris, whose nervous system was almost destroyed by it. Poor Sarah! she is truly distressed to hear of Uncle's sufferings, and not knowing Dr Peters as we do, it is very natural that she should have misgivings and doubts of his skill. I shall write to her to-night and cheer her with better news of the little doctor's patient, at the same time that I shall endeavor to do the doctor justice" (Virginia).

[13] Peters' scrapbook (NYPL, Berg) includes letters he received from Mary, Kate, and Pierre Paris Irving, besides those from WI and PMI.

[14] See, for example, Catharine Irving to John C. Peters, SS, Wednesday, 18 [April 1855]; Peters Scrapbook (NYPL, Berg). This letter refers to the occasion on which WI was thrown from his new horse, "Gentleman Dick."

[15] "Dr. Holmes' Remarks," p. 419. Holmes was accompanied on his visit by F. S. Cozzens; see Randolph, "Leaves from the Journal of F. S. Cozzens," p. 744.

[16] In a letter to Holmes WI wrote on January 4, 1859, that his "frank and cordial visit" to SS "was most opportune; for I was just then under the influence of your writings recently formed and longing to become personally acquainted with the author" (SHR).

[17] See Eleanor M. Tilton, *Amiable Autocrat. A Biography of Oliver Wendell Holmes* (New York, 1947), pp. 165-68. In February 1842 Holmes delivered three lectures collectively entitled "Scientific Mysticism" before the Society for the Diffusion of Useful Knowledge at Boston; the second and third of these were subsequently published together as an essay, "Homeopathy and Its Kindred Delusions" (1843). Over the years

On January 5, 1859, therefore, Peters launched a polite but effective counterattack in the form of a letter to Holmes setting out in detail the facts of Irving's case, the elaborate measures he had adopted thus far to control it, and a prognosis. First brushing aside Holmes' suggestions for the relief of the author's asthma (they "may serve to amuse, but cannot benefit him"), he outlined his patient's habits and general condition:

> Mr Irving is at present suffering from nervousness and sleeplessness—his cough and catarrhal troubles do not worry him now.
> Mr Irving has long been in the habit of dozing a large portion of the evening—of retiring to his bed room about 10 or 11 o'clock, of reading in bed for an hour or so; then falling asleep off & on until about 4 or 5 o'clock A.M.; after which he rarely or never gets a nap. Four hours sleep at night is his usual dosage; 6 hours sleep at night he regards as something very unusual—a thing to be remembered for a long time; but then he often gets 2, 3 or 4 hours during the afternoon & evening. You must recollect that these habits of irregular sleeping & waking have been of a score of years standing, at least, or perhaps have been the rule of a greater portion of his life—I neglected to add, that he generally wakens between 12 & 4 o'clock at night, sometimes once, sometimes twice, & reads, or even works for 1/2 or 1 hour.
> A long, sound, continuous sleep of 3, 4 or 6 hours duration is almost unknown to him—In the evening he sleeps upright in a chair, or bolstered up in a corner of the sofa; he dozes for 10, 15 or 20 minutes, then wakes for 5 or 10 minutes, joins a little in the conversation with his friends, then lapses off again into a necessarily uneasy slumber. He enjoys this gipsy and cat-like way of murdering good Christian sleep—he likes to see some one with him when he wakes—& formerly used to enjoy reading by snatches at night.
> The above may be regarded as the normal state of Mr. Irving. . . .
> Some 8 or 10 weeks ago Mr. Irving had a severe attack of fever & ague, marked by high fever during the fever paroxysms, great oppression, drowsiness . . . oppressed breathing, &c; he rapidly recovered from this, but a troublesome cough harrassed him at night. . . . This cough, catarrhal symptoms, asthmatic breathing, &c., have all subsided—But, his usual interrupted sleep has remained more feeble & short, than his wont—If he keeps awake all the day & evening he gets no sleep at night—if he sleeps a portion of the afternoon & evening, of course he cannot sleep at night —but he will get from 1 to 3 hours' slumber.—The less he sleeps during the day, the less he will sleep at night; the more sleep within reasonable limits he gets during the afternoon and evening, the more quiet he will be at night.—But the main point is, that he often gets almost frightfully uneasy, nervous, and un-

---

Holmes' distrust of homeopathy did not abate. See the preface, dated January 1861, to *Medical Essays* in his *Works* (Cambridge, Mass., 1899), IX, v.

happy while awake at night—an undefined horror & apprehension seems to possess him—he is not afraid of death, & the hereafter, but occasionally he dreads an attack of paralysis, & perhaps insanity, altho he has never hinted at the latter—still, I am confident he broods about it—

My opinion of his state, is that it is one of those cases of nervousness & sleeplessness which so often remain after an attack of fever, rendered more obstinate than they proverbially are, by the irregular habits of sleeping which is natural to your & every one's dear friend, Mr Irving—

After enumerating the remedies he had employed—including, with all "freedom from prejudice," some "reasonable homeopathic treatment"—Peters added a material clinical secret:

It is right to add that Mr Irving has enlargement of the heart—that much of his difficulty of breathing and catarrhal trouble comes from an obstructed circulation which leaves his bronchial mucous membrane more or less congested at times—[18]

Apparently this discourse more than satisfied Holmes, for upon receiving it he immediately replied, apologizing for what Peters might possibly have interpreted as his presumption. "I suppose we all do pretty much the same thing in cases like this," he wrote; "feel our way along,—heave the lead, watch the currents, throw over cargo if we must, keep the pumps going, the flag flying and trim to the wind of every day. To speak more literally we all try, as you have done, all safe means which promise better than mere inactivity seems to provide."[19]

Peters had first noticed symptoms of heart disease in Irving several years before, but he had not judged it necessary to inform him of his condition until early in 1858. For over a year after this interview Pierre was the only other person aside from Holmes who knew the secret, but according to Peters, during 1859 "the progress of the disease gradually developed it to some of the most devoted of [Irving's] family, especially to his sister-nieces."[20] Nonetheless, the heart condition was kept shrouded in such strict silence that Pierre never directly mentioned it, even in his private journal. Once during 1859 Peters seemed to him to have dismissed the malady from his mind and to regard Irving's condition as asthmatic only. Such, of

[18] John C. Peters to O. W. Holmes, New York, January 5, 1859 (Peters Scrapbook—NYPL, Berg). Peters' belief that WI brooded about the possibility of paralysis or insanity recurs in the miscellaneous notes he kept concerning WI's symptoms and the medications prescribed to relieve them (Peters Scrapbook—NYPL, Berg).

[19] O. W. Holmes to John C. Peters, Boston, January 8, 1859 (NYPL, Berg).

[20] Peters, "A Letter." According to F. S. Cozzens, upon being informed of his condition by Peters, WI immediately said: "Do not tell it to the family" (New York Ledger, 15, no. 42 [December 17, 1859], 5). PMI wrote in the LLWI that Peters had informed him "eleven months before [WI's death], that there was enlargement of the heart, but he did not then express serious apprehension from this cause" (IV, 327).

course, was not the case.[21] After Irving's death the physician explained his silence. Upon being informed of his disease, he wrote, the elderly author "at once drew the conclusion that he must sooner or later expect a sudden death" and at that time expressed the wish that Peters should not mention it to anyone. "The peculiar shrinking delicacy of Mr. Irving made him sensitive of being more an object of pity from his friends than he could avoid, and he shrank from the idea that strangers might speculate when he would fall dead."[22] To the chagrin of the physician, however, the suppression of information about the real basis of his patient's condition gave rise to misconceptions which in turn led well-meaning friends to urge "remedies" upon Irving that did him material harm. Not only Holmes—whose cigarettes, as it happened, were most helpful—but N. P. Willis, Charles A. Davis, a zealous neighbour-lady, and no doubt others all sent samples of exotic nostrums for his use.[23]

Through the spring of 1859 Irving regained his strength encouragingly—so well, indeed, that he overcame the effects even of these supposed curatives. His distressed breathing passed away, his heart became normal in action, and his nervousness subsided. Having apparently shaken off his indisposition, he seemed to many of his visitors a picture of elderly fitness. After visiting him in October, Willis confessed himself "surprised to see with how lively and firm a step he entered—removing the slouched hat . . . with as easy eloquence as ever . . . with no hindrance of debility that I could see. He is thinner somewhat . . . but the genial expression of his countenance is unchanged. . . . The reports of his illness must have been exaggerated, I thought."[24] Even Theodore Tilton, who visited Irving only two weeks before his death, described him at that time as "not so old-looking as one would expect who knew his age."[25] By coincidence, it is true, these callers tended to catch Irving on his better days, as on his irregular visits Peters often did. The journal of John Pendleton Kennedy reveals, on the other hand, that not everyone was impressed with his appearance at this time.[26] More than once the author was so tired and frustrated by his oppressed breathing that he was unable to receive callers at all.

---

[21] Peters wrote: "All this time there was an undercurrent of the disease of the heart, almost completely masked by more urgent sufferings, but still, at times, becoming terribly distinct, like the sudden glare of a concealed reptile or savage; and then so fully and completely absent that I was at times left in doubt whether it ever could have been present" ("Illnesses," p. 458).

[22] Peters, "A Letter," p. 403.

[23] The medications offered by these persons were, respectively, "Brown's Pectoral Trochees," "Jonas Whitcomb's Cough Remedy" (already suggested by Holmes), and "Goodale's Catarrh Remedy."

[24] Willis, "WI at Home," p. 2.

[25] Tilton, "Half an Hour," p. li.

[26] For a portion of Kennedy's journal entry after visiting WI on October 31, 1859, see above, p. 162.

Sustained by Pierre, Helen, and his nieces, Irving struggled to keep up his spirits. In October, when Peters was himself confined at home with a fever, he received an unexpected call from his patient, who, he later wrote, "was comparatively restored, and more anxious about me than himself. How deeply humiliated I felt, when I saw that feeble old man ... evince that complete command of mind over matter."[27] Irving was not always able to accept the discomforts of his advanced age with such philosophy, however, and to protect him from lapsing into bleak moods the members of the household sought to divert him in the evenings by parlour games, reading aloud, and dogged conversation. With similar motives they cut out potentially distressing items from the newspapers and miscellanies lying about the house. Some publications, for example, kept up a running account of Irving's health. A few of these medical reports, perhaps the ones most remarkable for their tastelessness, Pierre pasted into his journal. The supreme example of the excised notices, one from the saccharine pen of N. P. Willis, was discovered by Sarah in the Home Journal for September 15:

> Mr. Irving, by far the most honored man in our country, is, curiously enough, even less honored than loved. He is a marvel, if only by that difference from other men of genius—whose destiny it seems to have their last days sad. The setting of his sun is mellow, the clouds around and behind him rosier as he goes. There is another summer-day beauty, too, in his decline—the full moon of renown, after death, seen clearly, even before the setting of his sun.

Willis got good service from this set-piece in the funerary sublime, for he had used it to describe Irving once before, in 1857, and he was to use it once again before his death.[28] Naturally, the bland reference to "the setting of his sun" would have edified Irving less than it presumably did Willis' readership. Thus Pierre's 1859 journal became not only a medical record but also a repository of items such as this, which for his own good Irving was not permitted to see.

Most of the 36,000 words in the journal were devoted to neither of these purposes, however, but rather to an entirely separate one. Several years earlier, at a precise time to be speculated upon in the following chapter, Irving had asked Pierre to be his biographer. "Somebody will be writing my life when I am gone," Pierre quoted him in the Life and Letters as saying, "and I wish you to do it. You must promise me that you will."[29] After some demurral Pierre did promise, and presently he began to take "memoranda" of Irving's activities and conversation. By February 1859 he had already filled four notebooks

[27] Peters, "A Letter," p. 403.

[28] PMI, 1859 Journal; see also Willis, "Visit to Sleepy Hollow," p. 2; "WI at Home," p. 2.

[29] "Preface," LLWI, I, [5].

with biographical material of various kinds relating to his uncle.[30] Unfortunately, all of these are now lost; only the fifth—the one which he began on February 28—is known to exist. Yet this sole survival of Pierre's compilations is of value in itself, for as a day-to-day record of Irving's life and opinions in 1859 it is a unique resource, affording us an opportunity to view the author amongst his family.

The journal is marred by the inevitable defects of a work written for private use by a man of few words who was often hurried, and whose attention was moreover divided between his two roles as medical observer and future biographer. Pierre was not scrupulous about syntax or punctuation, and he often phrased his entries so elliptically that, unless supplemented by heavy annotation, they now seem cryptic or totally obscure. On the other hand, he possessed high qualifications for his journalizing task. During a long association with his uncle he had formed a conception of Irving's personality that enabled him to bring into immediate focus the relative significance or noteworthiness of his actions and remarks. Moreover, owing perhaps to similarities between Irving's character and his own, Pierre was not only a discerning observer but a sympathetic one as well. While not so clubbable a man as Irving, he possessed his uncle's quiet humour and his faculty for finding mirth in situations that annoyed or distressed him. He was well-read, commanded a wide store of anecdotes concerning Irving's acquaintances in England and America, and shared many of his present friendships. He had a taste for the well-turned phrases sprinkled broadcast through Irving's conversation, even though he accurately adjudged himself incapable of creating them very frequently on his own. He was intimately familiar with the materials of the *Washington,* and he shared Irving's attachment to the subject. If circumstances made him less than an ideal recorder of his uncle's daily life, therefore, nevertheless by temperament and long familiarity he was by far the best qualified observer Irving could have had.

As he appears in Pierre's journal, the Washington Irving of 1859 is an urbane bachelor uncle of wide experience and somewhat testy good nature, the developed, at times sadly weakened, yet never unrecognizably altered Irving of earlier years. Fluctuations in his health during the spring divested him on some days of his good spirits and gentle dignity, but with the return of warm weather he became his engaging self. Then he held sway at the breakfast table with brisk humour, keeping his nieces alert and atitter with comments about their coyness, their appetites, or their sewing machines; wittily mocked Ebenezer's covenanting soberness at morning prayers; or with hoarse volubility aired his prejudices concerning various individuals and vented his spleen at petty irritations. Happily, Pierre was

---

[30] Some conception of the material PMI collected in the first four journals may be formed from studying his use of them in preparing his MS Outline of *LLWI*. See below, pp. 316, 318-19.

at hand to record not only the periods of suffering but also Irving's activities and desultory conversation on these better days.[31]

Monday, February 28 (At Sunnyside). . . . He had something of a cold or influenza yesterday which is better this morning. Take to town *two* of the *four* last chapters of his *Life of Washington*.
On my return to the cottage at 5 P.M. (accompanied by the Doctor) found that he had been engaged for two or three hours in the morning on his last chapter of the *Life of Washington*. Wishes to retain the two last chapters to re-dress the concluding portion. Looks well at dinner, and seems to have had a very comfortable day. . . .

Tuesday, March 1. In his library a great part of the morning arranging papers and working some at the close of *Washington,* but was not in as good mood for writing as yesterday; not satisfied with the finishing page. . . .

[March 2]

Thursday, March 3. Not nervous during the day, but not well. I was engaged in accounts in the library in the morning, when he came in and wanted me to lay them aside, and try my hand in altering the last page of *Washington*. . . .

[March 4-7]

Tuesday, March 8. . . . Still holds on to the last chapter of *Washington,* though the printers are nearly up to it.

[31] With the exception of lengthy reports of WI's health and the medications given him, and miscellaneous matter of no apparent interest, I have included in these selections from the 1859 Journal all entries not included by PMI in *LLWI* and also those which appear in the biography significantly elaborated, condensed, or otherwise altered. I have also included a selection from PMI's medical entries so as to indicate the trends in WI's physical condition during these months. I have placed in square brackets the dates of entries excluded from this selection. Even with thorough annotation PMI's entries sometimes remain rather cryptic, and it has seemed best to provide as much information pertinent to them as is consistent with reasonable economy of space.
Although I have given PMI's journal account *verbatim,* I have made such changes in punctuation, capitalization, spelling, and format as seemed necessary to render it intelligible, self-consistent, and compact. I have regularized the erratic punctuation of the journal, whenever possible bringing its fragmentary syntax into a semblance of sentence form. However, when PMI's own punctuation has seemed especially to enhance his meaning, I have let it stand. I have altered the capitalization to conform to modern usage, and as to spelling, I have silently corrected the few obviously misspelled words in the journal and standardized the spelling of several words and proper names. I have allowed passages deleted in the manuscript to remain so when they do not add significantly to our understanding of topics being discussed in their contexts; but any material deleted in the manuscript and included here I have identified as such in the notes. I have expanded some common abbreviations of proper names, substituted *and* for the ampersand except in the case of PMI's frequent *&c.,* regularized his inconsistent dating of entries, and silently deleted a few obviously unintentional repetitions of function words or phrases. Editorial additions are enclosed in square brackets; doubtful readings are identified by question marks and are also enclosed in square brackets.

Wednesday, March 9. Ash Wednesday—W.I. went to church. I rearrange the last few pages of *Life of Washington,* not going to the city.

Thursday, March 10. I went to the city for the day with Helen. W.I. rode with her to the cars for exercise and air, and as she was replying to a letter of his niece Sarah Storrow from Florence, Italy, full of anxiety about him and wondering why he was "kept shut up at the cottage and not sent to the South,"[32] asked him if he had any message for her. "Tell her," said he, "that if she could insure for him the discovery of the Fountain of Youth by going south, he would not hesitate to start immediately; but that as he had a strong impression that Ponce de Leon who so long sought for it was at last disappointed, he was unwilling to commence the undertaking; and that at seventy-six he thought a man had better make himself contented as far as he could with the comforts of his own home."

We returned at 7 at night, walking from the station at Irvington. W.I. asleep on the sofa when we arrived. Had a tolerable night, though coughed for half an hour on first retiring. Very much in want of an amusing or entertaining book—difficult to get interested in any. Had been bothering again during the day at the last pages of *Washington,* altering and inserting new matter. Had taken a walk to the Grinnell piazza and [had] been seized with a violent spell of short breathing. The printers are up to the last chapter of *Washington;* read the proof today.

Friday, March 11. Again at last pages of *Washington,* which he showed to me. Showed by my countenance, I presume, I did not think them improved, for he gave me a rebuke, which brought out a retort.[33] I had been sorely perplexed at his continued appeal to me to dress up the Chap[ter], and had been straining my mind till my brain ached to meet the supposed necessity. I told him nature had not been overprodigal of her gifts to me, and I was not able to meet the burden he imposed; that I had taxed myself in vain to satisfy his requirements. He was sorry I felt so, undervalued my own endowments, &c. &c. That Father, Uncle Peter, and myself had been his great stand-bys in life. At night when he was asleep I went into the library and handled the closing pages anew, improving it mainly by omissions, and the insertion of a few words, and told him on retiring to his room at night I thought now it would do—was better than ever. "A single word," he said, "had sometimes great effect and was hard to hit; that I had a knack at *adapting &c.,* appropriate expressions for which I did not give myself credit," &c. . . .

Saturday, March 12. Heavy wind and rain towards morning, so that I shall not get to the city as I intended, and Eliza,[34] who came up

---

[32] Apparently Sarah Storrow's anxiety for the welfare of WI—see above, pp. 175-76, footnote 12—had not yet been dispelled by the assurances of Julia Grinnell.

[33] In the journal the words "which brought out a retort" are deleted.

[34] Eliza Dodge Irving, sister of Helen and wife of PMI's brother Oscar.

yesterday, will probably be detained also. Are invited to dine at the Hoge[s'] at 3 today. The Doctor, who came up last night, thought Uncle appeared more languid than usual. We have all thought him weaker for a few days past, though the change is not marked. He lay down on the sofa in the dining room today immediately after breakfast, for which, however, he seemed to have some appetite. It cleared up, and he walked out after a hearty lunch of oysters. Had a turn of shortness of breath after tea, for which he smoked cigarette, and burnt medicated paper;[35] but on the whole has been in better spirits today and more like himself than for some time. Slept an hour before tea and became at times drowsy, but has not slept since. It is now 5 minutes of 11 and he has retired to his room for the night. Did not go to the Hoge's.

Sunday, March 13. . . . Had not much appetite at breakfast—a beautiful day. Went to church and after church put the finishing touch to the last pages of *Washington* which I am to take down tomorrow. . . .

[March 14, 15]

Wednesday, March 16. I compare proof of last chapter of *Life of Washington* with Helen, who afterwards reads to Uncle—who seems sadly out of spirits. . . .

Thursday, March 17. . . . Asked me if last chapter of *Life of Washington* was printed last night. "Yes." "Well, I never got out a work in this style before without looking at the proof sheets." In better health could have given more effect to parts, but was afraid to look at the proofs lest he should get muddling, &c. Reminded him of his having taken them to pieces once and left out in making [them] up again notice of second term of Washington. On reaching the city I heard that Frederick Paulding had died in the night at 1 o'clock. Gave Mr. Putnam the last chapter with the corrections. On returning to the cottage at 5 P.M. found W.I. had driven up to the Bartlett's with Helen to leave for Mrs. Bartlett,[36] in compliance with her previous request, the pen with which he wrote the last words of his *Life of Washington*. . . .

[March 18, 19, 20]

Monday, March 21. . . . Today tranquil; walked out to the Grinnells', taken on his return with difficulty of breathing which continued during the greater part of the day at intervals. I brought up Tuckerman's note to me about preface[37] which I showed him; felt a

---

[35] The cigarettes had been suggested by Holmes. The "medicated paper" was probably touch paper saturated with potassium nitrate, an accepted treatment for spasmodic asthma. See George B. Wood and Franklin Bache, *The Dispensatory of the United States of America* (Philadelphia, 1868), p. 686.

[36] The wife of Edwin Bartlett, a local resident. WI had written to Mrs. Bartlett on March 14, probably to propose the visit (*Life*, II, 401, note 66).

[37] Apparently requesting that the manuscript copy of a preface to the final volume of the *Washington* be sent to Putnam so that the printing of proof sheets might be completed.

little nervous about it, and before 8 wrote a short preface to volume V; then slept on sofa.... After retiring slept at intervals until 2 o'clock, when he awoke by my crying out "Murder!" in a nightmare—dreaming that someone was attempting my life; quiet for the rest of the night, dozing a little towards morning. As I was to go to town asked me to leave the preface and Tuckerman's note; rode out Monday.

[March 22]

Wednesday, March 23.... After retiring... slept about forty minutes and awoke nervous at the idea of Irving Van Wart's family going to Europe which he had heard of for the first time... then continued most awake, reading Boaden's *Life of Kemble*,[38] the first volume of which I had brought up from the library. His watch stopped in the night and I take it down with me. Went to church to morning prayers (Lent); no fire in church, caught cold—would not catch him again at "their confounded morning prayer."

Thursday, March 24. Rather depressed at Helen's going to the city to stay till tomorrow. "It is well I'm thrown overboard sometimes and made to swim. I should otherwise be too dependent." Received yesterday [a] Lewisburg (Pa.) newspaper containing notice of a death at ninety of a Mrs. Chamberlain, formerly Miss Kimble, Ann Street, New York—a friend and correspondent of Helen's mother—which [notice] spoke of the latter's delightful letters.[39] W.I. spoke of her as full of wit, sensibility, and humor, "delightful in every mood—Helen very much like her"; "rack of bones," [she] called him as a child—very meagre.[40] ...

---

[38] James Boaden, *Memoirs of the Life of John Philip Kemble, Esq., Including A History of the Stage from the Time of Garrick to the Present Period...* , 2 vols. (London, 1825). An American edition was published at Philadelphia in 1825. WI met Kemble during his first visit to Europe, in 1805, when the latter was manager of the Covent Garden Theatre. During his second stay in Europe, WI formed a friendship with the actor. He saw Kemble again in 1832-1834, when Kemble was touring the United States accompanied by his talented daughter Fanny. For WI's impressions of Kemble in various roles, see *LLWI*, I, 156-58; IV, 241, 273.

[39] This article, from the Lewisburg *Chronicle*, March 11, 1859, is pasted onto the inside front cover of the journal. According to the obituary notice, Ann Mary Kimble Chamberlain was born in New York, November 1769. After the Revolutionary War the residence of her family "was in Ann Street, near William, where she daily saw President Washington." The passage from the obituary concerning the letters of Ann Sarah Irving (nicknamed Nancy) follows: "[WI's] sister, Miss Nancy Irving, Mrs. C. corresponded with in her earlier years, and often expressed her regret that she had not preserved her letters, which were among the most elegant compositions she ever read—fully equal, she judged, to the literary productions of the brothers."

[40] WI's affection for his sister Ann remained a tradition in his family. According to John P. Frothingham, *Genealogy*, p. 140, when WI was small Ann would say to him: "Come here, you poor little rack of bones." She would take him in her arms and sing him a song, "The moon that climbed the highest hill," that made him weep (NYPL, MS).

[March 25]

Saturday, March 26. A comfortable day, though rather depressed by the blustering weather. . . . He looks better in the face than for some time in the past. Holmes "a choice nature."[41]

Sunday, March 27. I left W.I.'s room [at] 1/4 to 6. "You leave earlier than usual," as if still loth to be left alone. Went to church; little or no coughing during the day or evening—better than he has been for some time; slept two and one-half hours after dinner. I read [*The*] *Culprit Fay* at night aloud; W.I. full of anecdote afterwards.[42] Retired at 11. Showed me preface—which is not improved.

[March 28, 29, 30, 31; April 1, 2]

Sunday, April 3. W.I.'s birthday—seventy-six this day. A dull, cheerless day, overcast at dawn, raining before 7. After breakfast showed me his Spanish chronicles in manuscript—"Don Pelayo," "Fernando el Santo," &c. Spoke of now being able to tell me anecdotes, &c. In the midst Helen brought in a bunch of flowers from Robert, the gardener—a present for his birthday.

A CARD

To the Editor of the N.Y. Tribune.

SIR: My name has recently been made use of in your advertising columns, without my knowledge or consent, as having "illustrated" an edition of the *Culprit Fay.*

I have no claims to the honor thus forced upon me, beyond having furnished one hasty pencil sketch for a vignette, which has since apparently been subjected to an equally hasty species of wood engraving; and which I considered so unworthy of the poem, that I expressly declined having my name published in connection with it.

As the advertisement in question is calculated to do my reputation material injury, both as regards professional ability and candor, I hope I may rely upon your generous sense of justice to afford me an opportunity of vindication by giving insertion to these few lines.

Very respectfully yours,   JOHN W. EHNINGER[43]

DRAKE'S CULPRIT FAY

To the Editor of the N.Y. Tribune.

SIR: An Edition of Joseph Rodman Drake's poem, "The Culprit Fay," having been recently issued by a publishing house in

[41] WI was impressed with Holmes. On January 22, 1859, he wrote to Charles A. Davis: "I was very much pleased with him and I think you would be if you knew him. I trust you have read his work, which is very much to my humor" (Virginia).

[42] *The Culprit Fay*, the poem by Joseph Rodman Drake (1795-1820), was a favourite of WI's.

[43] John W. Ehninger (1827-1899), genre-painter and illustrator.

this city, and extensively advertised for sale, I hereby announce that the edition was published without the consent of the family of the late Dr. Drake, and that the sale is peremptorily stopped.

It was the desire of the author that his poems should not be published, and to prevent it, a few copies of this and others were printed some years since for private circulation, and a copyright registered. It is, doubtless, in ignorance of these facts that these gentlemen now issue it.

Several other editions of "The Culprit Fay" have appeared at various times, which have, as in this case, been immediately suppressed.

Very respectfully,

Your most obedient servant,

JOSEPH RODMAN DRAKE DE KAY

No. 47 South street, March 30, 1859.[44]

"Did not see why," in reference to the above interdict, "the descendants of Drake should object to the publication of *The Culprit Fay* (by Rudd and Carleton?).[45] It would do more than all the Drakes (or Ducks) of the world would ever do to hand the name down to posterity," &c. There came a beautiful bouquet of flowers from Mrs. General Webb.[46] "Beautiful flowers," said he, "to a withered old man." Salad from Mrs. Hoge, Charlotte Russe from Miss Mulhollin, with a bouquet also from her. The dinner table decked with Mrs. Webb's bouquet, and the dessert improved with the additions mentioned. W.I. slept two hours in the morning, but was exceedingly depressed during dinner. We all tried to be merry, but at the close, after a spasm of coughing had driven him from the table and we felt the uncertainty of another birthday with him "on this bank and shoal of time,"[47] all rose from the table in tears; verses from Mr. Williams' children after dinner. Slept in the afternoon and dozed in his chair in the evening, and was less troubled with cough and spasms. Had a paroxysm of coughing and distressed respiration at 11 when he went to bed, but it passed off with the smoking of a cigarette. He then fell asleep for a few minutes and awoke inclined to [be] terribly depressed and nervous, as the night before. "But," said he, "Pierre, I will try to combat it." Did so—fell asleep at 12 and continued to 2; awoke in quiet

[44] New York *Tribune*, p. 1, col. 6. DeKay (1836-1886) was the son of Janet Drake, the only child of Joseph Rodman Drake. DeKay's letter was also published in the *Home Journal* for April 2, 1859.

[45] This reason is that Rudd & Carleton, the publishers, were using literary property which the Drake family considered its own. *The Culprit Fay: A Poem* was not advertised again until April 11, when a notice in the New York *Tribune*, p. 5, col. 5, announced the end of the suppression of the book: "The family of the late Joseph Rodman Drake have withdrawn their opposition to the sale of Messrs. Rudd & Carleton's edition of the Culprit Fay, the publishers paying them a copy-right."

[46] Laura Virginia Cram Webb married James Watson Webb in 1849.

[47] *Macbeth* I.vi.10.

and read and dozed through the rest of the night without cough or laboured breathing. . . .

[April 4, 5]

Wednesday, April 6. . . . W.I. hopes for a genial day to get to town, wants to see little Putnam who had asked me yesterday for the manuscript of the preface now in type. W.I. wrote yesterday to the collegian at Chapel Hill, Augustus M. Flythe.[48] Sorely annoyed at times by the want of proper selection in Ebenezer Irving's morning reading of the Bible at prayers. "Wasn't he circumcising at a great rate yesterday?" said he, in allusion [to] a chapter in which the word was constantly occurring—a glance over to me as it was reading. Returned this morning the last of the three bulky volumes of Barth's *Africa*[49] which he could not find mood to read. Told him at breakfast he was treating Barth as Sam Swartwout treated his corps of Iron Greys in the last war—"Dismissed, disgraced, and bedamned." "Poor Sam," said he. "He had great bother with his Iron Greys; first this thing was wrong, then that; at one time their guns were too light, then too *heavy*. I advised him to put two men to a gun."[50] . . .

[April 7, 8, 9, 10]

Monday, April 11. Has recourse to the Inhaler[51] at 6 while I am making the fire; a rainy day—easterly storm. Has to stem the current again with such weather. Thermometer at 6 40 degrees above zero. I shall not go to town today. Gave me yesterday the *book covers* he had used for his *Washington* manuscripts. Told also anecdote of Rudolph Bunner[52] quoting a certain article in the *Evening Post* about the time of some

[48] On April 2 PMI recorded in the journal that WI had received a letter from a student at Chapel Hill, N.C., congratulating him on his performance in the first four volumes of *Washington* and urging him, ". . . not only for his own sake, but for the sake of the country, to write an account of the Presidential career and closing days of Washington at Mount Vernon. 'Here is a request,' said he, 'that I think I will gratify at once.' The whole of the fifth volume was already printed, and waiting only the Preface, which was completed that very morning, before the receipt of the letter" (*LLWI*, IV, 278).

[49] Heinrich Barth, *Travels and Discoveries in North and Central Africa . . .* , 3 vols. (New York, 1857-1859).

[50] During the War of 1812 Samuel Swartwout (1783-1856) was a Major in the Iron Greys, a corps of volunteers to which WI's friend Henry Brevoort belonged (*LLWI*, I, 325). Swartwout later became Collector of the Port of New York and a close associate of Andrew Jackson. WI knew Swartwout during the war period, when he was serving as aide-de-camp to Governor Daniel D. Tompkins, Major-General in the New York State Militia. For an account of the Iron Greys, see James Grant Wilson, *The Life and Letters of Fitz-Greene Halleck* (New York, 1869), pp. 145-50.

[51] On April 9 Dr. Peters visited SS and began treating WI with a glass inhaling device. In his journal entry for the day PMI recorded the physician's instructions for its use: "Put a tea spoonfull of Olive tar in the Inhaler, & inhale whenever cough or difficulty of breathing or Asthma are troublesome . . . from 10 to 20 or 30 inhalations may be made at a time. If the Tar does not relieve alone, 10 drops of ether may be added to each inhalation."

[52] Bunner (1779-1837) graduated from Columbia College in 1798. He was a friend of

celebration of Jefferson's *Inauguration,* in which the Democratic procession is ridiculed;[53] allusion made [in it] to the cassiwary, Van
Zandt[54] with his prize feathers, Death on the Pale Horse and Hell
followed after;[55] quote[d] by Bunner in proof of Coleman's genius.[56]
"Oh! that is mine!" said W.I. "I'm sorry for it, you could do without
it—he needed it," said Bunner. Expressed belief last night that his
appetite was gradually reviving and that he was slowly but gradually
improving. In the library with me most of the morning, I rummaging
among my papers. Told me the account of Nat Amory,[57] of Boston,
whom he met at Palermo....

Tuesday, April 12.... Brought up today [?] *Marriage* and *Pride
and Prejudice.* Had a visit in the morning from Angelica Hamilton[58]
who inquired when the fifth volume would be out; said I had told her
on the 12th or 15th. So I had, but Putnam is printing 500 of the octavo
and 5000 of the duodecimo, and now thinks it will not be out before
the 21st.[59] Evans showed me yesterday the first of the Illustrated
Edition.[60]

Wednesday, April 13. Thermometer 47 at 6 o'clock. Has been raining
and is misty and overcast, but will probably clear—wind apparently
from the southwest. W.I. asleep after breakfast. Took a walk under the

Peter Irving, to whose daily newspaper, the New York *Morning Chronicle,* he contributed.

[53] The article in question, which appeared in the New York *Evening Post* for
May 14, 1804, ridiculed a procession celebrating the first anniversary of the Louisiana
Purchase, a *coup* for the Democratic administration of Thomas Jefferson. For an account
of the political circumstances surrounding this article, and the reprinted article itself,
see Wayne R. Kime, "WI and the 'Extension of the Empire of Freedom': An Unrecorded
Contribution to the *Evening Post,* May 14 1804," *Bulletin of the New York Public Library,*
76 (1972), 220-30.

[54] Wynant Van Zandt, Jr. (d. 1814), a prominent New York Democrat, Alderman of
the First Ward of the city, 1802-1806.

[55] A slightly garbled quotation from Revelations 6.8.

[56] William Coleman (1766-1829), born in Boston, was the law partner of Aaron Burr
in New York. He had a reputation for scholarship and literary interests, and he was
editor of the New York *Evening Post* from its inception in 1801 until his death, when
William Cullen Bryant assumed the position.

[57] WI met Nathaniel Amory at Palermo, February 23, 1805, and the two explored
the city together. See *WI: Journals and Notebooks... 1803-1806,* ed. Nathalia Wright
(Madison, Wisconsin, 1969), pp. 216-18, 223; *Notes and Journals of Travel in Europe,
1804-1805, by WI,* ed. W. P. Trent (New York, 1921), II, 78-79, 134, 136-39, 144. The
"account" of Amory mentioned by PMI is not certainly identifiable, but perhaps it was
the anecdote of an adventure at Palermo given in *LLWI,* I, 120-22.

[58] A daughter of WI's neighbour James A. Hamilton and a frequent visitor at SS.
On November 8, 1860, she married Richard M. Blatchford (1798-1875), a wealthy lawyer
living in the vicinity. She died in 1868.

[59] The octavo edition was not published until May 9, and the duodecimo until
May 11 (New York *Tribune,* May 6, p. 1, col. 2).

[60] On May 19, Putnam published an advertisement in the *Tribune,* p. 1, col. 1,
informing "the Trade" that "The Illustrated Edition of the Fifth Volume will not be
ready until July." "Evans" was Charles T. Evans, Putnam's agent.

shelter of the bank at the brook lot with him at 1/2 past 11 to 1/4 past 12, he sitting occasionally on seat—the ducks and drakes, his allusion to the demoralization of our society. A better appetite for dinner than usual; no coughing during the day. Fell asleep at 7 and continued till 1/2 past 8. While asleep Cozzens and his wife, and Darley, and Mrs. Agate[61] called—had driven up in a hack from Yonkers. I too asleep when they called. After awhile they took a walk out to the brook lot, and then Uncle awoke and I came down, and they were ushered on their return into the parlor where Uncle had been asleep at first (and the girls took them in the dining room). . . .

Thursday, April 14. An easterly wind and rain—disheartening weather, just as he seems only to need genial weather to get rid of his malady. The colored lithograph of Wilkie's painting of the crown jewels—regalia of Scotland—in dining room was given him, he told Helen this morning, by [Vallemane?].[62] I do not go to town today. W.I. confined to the house all day by the rain; reads, burns papers in the library, has quite a good appetite for dinner. . . . Retires at 1/2 past 10; a star visible, promise of a better day tomorrow.

Baron Humboldt has addressed the following note to the Berlin journals: "Overwhelmed by the number of letters sent me, and which are increasing every day, amounting to from 1,600 to 2,000 per annum—many, too, on the most futile subjects, such as demands of my autograph, and offers to cure me of all diseases—I once more make a public appeal to the persons who wish me well, and request them not to occupy themselves so much with what concerns me, in order that with the diminution of my strength, physical and intellectual, which I experience, I may be allowed a little leisure for study and composition. I trust that this step, to which I have recourse with reluctance, will not be interpreted unkindly."

This notice cut out from the *Times* of today, April 14, 1859.[63] W.I. struck with it, and if there were time half-inclined to repeat the appeal to the indulgence of correspondents made in his last volume of the *Life of Washington*.[64] Pestered to death with letters, applications for auto-

[61] Cozzens' companions were F. O. C. Darley (1822-1888), illustrator, and Elizabeth Hill Kennedy Agate, widow of Alfred T. Agate (1812-1845), also a painter and illustrator.

[62] This lithograph is no longer at SS. On February 15, 1847, WI wrote to Sarah Storrow from SS: "I wish you would send out to me by Captain Funck the album presented to me by M. Vattema[r?]e; it will be quite a resource of the cottage" (Yale). M. Vattema[r?]e may have been the person referred to in the journal, but neither PMI's hand in the journal entry nor WI's in the letter is positively decipherable.

[63] P. 3, col. 1. The letter also appeared, though translated very differently, in the New York *Tribune*, April 15, p. 6, col 4; copies of both versions are pasted into the journal.

[64] At the close of the fourth volume of the *Washington*, WI expressed his intention, should "the measure of health and good spirits . . . be still continued," to write a fifth volume covering the remainder of Washington's lifetime. He concluded his statement

graphs, presents of books for libraries, &c. &c. His impatience under the affliction: "wish there were no post office," &c. It is a terrible bore and sometimes tasks his patience to the uttermost; application for autograph this very morning from youngster who could not spell his name correctly—Erving.

Friday, April 15. . . . Told me he had found some of Amory's letters,[65] written from the Temple, and one of father, mentioning Decatur's having obtain[ed] Navy Clerkship,[66] &c.

Payne: successful in *Junius Brutus*, brought his creditors upon him who threw him in limbo;[67] in prison wrote *Teresa, or the Orphan of Geneva*, another success which got him out.[68] Then went over to Paris, where W.I. fell in with him.[69] Was once manager of Sadler's Wells.[70] Took a walk with W.I. in Pere la Chaise and sat on a tomb;[71] slim, and told of his management which W.I. incorporated in "Buckthorne."[72]

with an oblique plea for privacy: "In the mean time, having found a resting-place in our task, we stay our hands, lay by our pen, and seek that relaxation and repose which gathering years require" (IV, 478-79).

[65] PMI did not make use of these letters in *LLWI*, and their present location is unknown.

[66] The letter from William Irving, dated October 24, 1818, is published in part in *LLWI*, I, 408-09, and in fuller form in *Life*, I, 171.

[67] Under the managership of John Howard Payne, *The Tragedy of Brutus; or, The Fall of Tarquin* was first produced at Drury Lane on December 3, 1818, with Edmund Kean in the title role. The play was an immense success, being performed twenty-three consecutive times in its first season and over fifty times in its first year. *Brutus* temporarily brought Drury Lane out of a financial slump and re-established the popularity of Kean (Grace Overmyer, *America's First Hamlet* [New York, 1957], pp. 159-67).

[68] Late in 1819, almost one year after the successful production of *Brutus*, Payne lamented that his newly-achieved reputation for wealth was bringing his creditors upon him, so that "success has obliged me to keep myself out of view" (Overmyer, *America's First Hamlet*, p. 172). In the last week of 1820 he was committed to Fleet Prison for debt. By January 22 of the following year he had completed *Therese; or, the Orphan of Geneva*, which he sold to Drury Lane. The play was produced with great success on February 2. It quickly became a favourite in England, was published in legitimate and pirated editions, and by March 1 enabled Payne to write in his diary: "Liberty! delicious liberty!" (Overmyer, *America's First Hamlet*, pp. 190-200).

[69] Payne went to Paris in the spring of 1821 and met WI there. During that year WI returned to London, where he acted as Payne's literary agent, attempting to market completed works and inquiring about possible paid contributions to literary magazines.

[70] Payne assumed the management of Sadler's Wells on April 3, 1820. By November of that year, however, he had lost $7,000 of his own money and was unable to continue on credit; so he resigned.

[71] The precise date of this walk in Père la Chaise, a principal cemetery of Paris, is now known. However, unless the sequence of WI's recollections is inconsistent at this point, the walk probably occurred after August 1823, when he returned to Paris from Germany.

[72] WI was at work on the series of sketches entitled "Buckthorne and His Friends," the second of four parts in *Tales of a Traveller*, in March 1824, but he made revisions and additions through July. See *WI: Journals and Notebooks . . . 1819-1827*, ed. Walter A. Reichart (Madison, Wisconsin, 1970), pp. 304-67 *passim*; cited hereafter as *Journals*

Saturday, April 16. 6 A.M. Thermometer at 46°. Pestered with the necessity of replying to a Miss Rhoda E. White, of New York, who had written in March for his autograph to be inserted in book of autographs which she was getting up for some charitable fair, where it was to be sold; requested not only his own autograph, but the autographs of other distinguished personages with whom he had corresponded. Longfellow had sent her *ten*. He was too ill to reply to her first letter, and now the persevering saint sent him another. Her object she thought, no doubt, would excuse her officiousness. "Charity," said he, "covers a multitude of sins; but it is sins against poor authors." Drafted a reply which he meant to get one of the girls to copy, and then merely append his signature, as he did not wish to have a letter of his paraded in an autograph book.[73] "This book was to be got up in splendid style, to be bound at Paris and [to have] gold clasps," &c.

Sunday, April 17. . . . A bright day. Went to church, after it walked in brook lot, visited Maria, and after dinner took a walk in garden; remarkably well today. . . .

Tuesday, April 19. From the *Tribune* of today:

> —Washington Irving, was visited on the 3d. inst., his 76th birth-day, by his neighbors, who greeted the venerable man with honors and congratulations.[74]

Not correct: presents sent, but no visitors—too ill to receive them. A good day. Before bed time had dictated a reply to Rhoda E. White and grew nervous about it and feared he would not sleep. Slept from 11 to 2, then woke with a coughing spell. At 7 in the morning went to the library and found him preparing another reply to be dictated to Rhoda E. White—maiden, wife, or widow not known. Had a good day: walked more than usual, appetite improved, slept less after dinner and more after retiring to bed.

Wednesday, April 20. Continues to improve; walked and drove out, wrote to Charles Lanman at Washington about his brother,[75] who is still here, loafing at the tavern—but *did not send the letter*.
 From the *Evening Post* of April 19, 1859:

(Reichart). The portions which he incorporated in the work after his talk with Payne in Père la Chaise are unknown, but Payne had an intimate knowledge of the London dramatic community, the elaborate pecking-order among professional authors in that city, and poverty—all major themes of these stories. For correspondence between WI and Payne during the period 1821-1824, see Thatcher T. P. Luquer, "Correspondence of WI and John Howard Payne," *Scribner's Magazine*, 48 (October 1910), 461-82.

 [73] The letter, or a copy of it, is at SHR. In this copy, WI merely added a concluding salutation and his signature to the body of the letter, which was written in a feminine hand.

 [74] New York *Tribune*, April 18, 1859, p. 6, col. 4.

 [75] On April 1 PMI recorded in the journal: "Young Lanman and two companions call and borrow $10." On April 4, this same brother of Charles Lanman paid a second visit: "Another application from young Lanman and his companions, who had been lurking around Irvington—declined."

New York Items.—The New York Correspondent of the Boston *Transcript* says:
"Washington Irving attained his seventy-sixth year on the 3d inst. His neighbors indicated their remembrance by offerings of flowers, and by visits and greetings. Although during the past winter our beloved and pioneer American author has suffered from sleeplessness and asthma, he is, on the whole, improving in health. Happy is it that he has lived to put the finishing touch to his life of Washington, and happier still that he can look backward from a serene and honored old age, upon a literary career of more than half a century, free from all bitterness, unsullied by reproach, and followed throughout by genial associations and enduring love.[76]

In the evening at tea troubled with shortness of breath while Mr. John E. Williams was in. On retiring to his room for the night told me he thought *now* he could get along by himself, but on my assenting immediately recalled the opinion, and thought perhaps I had better remain for a night or two longer. . . .

Thursday, April 21. Drove to the station with Helen, who was going to town to stay until tomorrow. Met Williams at the station who received his intelligence of his bad night[77] with a loud laugh—ill-timed, though very probably well-intentioned; wherefore W.I. told him it might be merriment for him, but he could not join in it. "I should never go to him for sympathy," said he in relating it. The fifth volume detained by the index, which moves slower than was anticipated; will not be out before *May 1st*. . . .

April 22 (Good Friday). . . . The thermometer at 50° and the weather overcast and rainy when I left his room at 6. Helen's version of the Williams affair of yesterday: when Uncle spoke of his having a bad night, Mr. Williams was disposed to make light of it and said playfully, "I suspect your conscience of smiting you for those peaches you were eating last night that did not belong to you" (alluding to some preserves he saw them eating at tea the night before which had been sent to Mr. Grinnell, but in his absence from the country appropriated by the Holdreges, and some of which they had sent to W.I. which were on the tea table when Mr. Williams called to get Uncle's signature for a proposed engraving of Church's "Niagara"[78]— wished his name only, intending to present him with a copy of the engraving when executed—was to be done in London), and then gave a laugh. "It may be fun for you," said W.I., who was completely unstrung by his wretchedly nervous night, "but it *is* death to me." Helen then inter-

[76] New York *Evening Post*, April 19, 1859, p. 1, col. 1.

[77] On the evening of April 20 WI had been "troubled with shortness of breath," according to the journal. PMI added that WI suffered "a deplorably nervous night," with little more than two hours' sleep.

[78] Frederick E. Church (1826-1900), landscape painter, whose best-known work, "The Falls of Niagara," was being shown in Richmond, Virginia, in January 1859, and was later to be shown in New York. See also below, p. 201.

posed with a statement to Mr. Williams of Uncle's bad night—who thereupon turned to him and said in a different tone: "Did you indeed have so bad a night?" "Yes," said W.I., "I did not sleep a wink; and now you can laugh as loud as you choose." Mr. Williams was quite taken aback; had certainly intended no unseasonable levity or want of sympathy, but had not realized how thoroughly unstrung and desponding W.I. was at being thrown so unexpectedly back in his improvement. . . . On first retiring was quite disposed to talk about Captain Warman,[79] &c., which I did not much encourage, fearful of being overheard by Eliza Irving, who was sleeping in the porch room.

Saturday, April 23. Overcast and threatening to be a rainy day, but cleared up about noon. In the library looking over a bundle of old letters which he had hitherto kept apart. Took out [letters] from Leslie, Allston, Bryant, Cooper, Wilkie, Sir E. Bulwer-Lytton, Van Buren's offer of Secretaryship of Navy in 1838 and his reply,[80] and gave them to me. Spoke of his reply to Leggett's attack on him in the *Plaindealer* in 1837 for altering at Andrews' instance in "Marion's Men" [the lines] *"the British soldier* trembled, when Marion's name was heard" to "the foreign foeman trembled." His motives for it: had first applied to Murray to publish Bryant's poems. He declining, had recourse to Andrews, a fashionable bookseller, who agreed to publish at his own risk; but when in going through the press, [Andrews] found this, [he] thought it might prejudice the success of the work, and appealed to W.I., who altered it as above, from his interest both in Andrews and in Bryant. Replied to Leggett's attack in the *American,* and included to Bryant an explanation and apology for the liberty he had taken in altering, &c. [a poem] "in which you could hardly alter a word without marring a beauty."[81] . . . Bryant does not appear to have written to W.I. on the subject or to have made any complaint. In his *Letters from Spain,* published in 1859, he has this allusion to W.I., p. 204: "I am not about to describe Granada. After what Irving has written of it, I should as soon think of attempting a poem on the wrath of Achilles in competition with Homer."[82] W.I. always spoke of Bryant's poems as "perfect gems."

[79] In an obscure scandal that seems to have aroused strong feelings in WI's neighbourhood, Captain Warman was removed from his position, which was apparently with the Hudson River Rail Road. See below, pp. 205, 209, 210.

[80] PMI published portions of letters WI had received from all of these personages, except Bulwer-Lytton, in *LLWI*. See the following letters: from Charles Leslie (1794-1859), painter, *LLWI,* I, 406; II, 31, 61-62; from Washington Allston (1779-1843), painter, I, 362-64, 397-99, 401-03; from William C. Bryant, II, 472-73, 477-79; from Thomas A. Cooper (1776-1849), actor and producer, I, 197, 203-04; from William Wilkie (1785-1841), painter, II, 438; from Martin Van Buren, III, 126-27; WI's reply to Van Buren, III, 127.

[81] This incident is fully recounted in *LLWI,* III, 99-111. William Leggett (1801-1839) was from 1829-1836 Assistant Editor of the New York *Evening Post* under Bryant. In 1837 he established on his own *The Plaindealer,* in which he pursued an extremely aggressive editorial policy.

[82] Bryant, *Letters from a Traveller, Second Series* (New York, 1859).

[April 24, 25]

Tuesday, April 26. A bright mild morning. Drove to the station with Kate and Sarah who are going to town. They returned at 1/2 past 7 announcing the removal of Captain Warman. . . . He had intended to attend the meeting of the Trustees of the Astor Library today,[83] but the rain will prevent. It is now more than four months since he has been to the city. Visit of [Bruce?] and Saunders.[84]

Wednesday, April 27. Sent letter to Julia.[85] A rainy morning. I went to town, but did not call at the Astor Library. W.I. had intended to be present at the monthly meeting today, but the rain prevented. A nervous night.

Thursday, April 28. I called at Dr. Peters' to get him to come up, but he was to attend the funeral of Dr. Hull,[86] and proposed the next day. Helen and I in town. On our return found to my surprise that Uncle had been out to dine at the Hoges' with Irving and Sarah Van Wart and the boys. Seemed suddenly well again. A good night. Pierre P. Irving comes up.

Friday, April 29. Sent note to the Doctor to postpone his call, but he did not get it and came. Found Uncle much better; thinks he will get well, though he may be subject to occasional relapse. I dine at the Hoges' and find the Doctor here when I return. Walk with him to the cars. . . .

Saturday, April 30, 1859. I walk to the station with Pierre P. Irving. W.I. lies down about 1/2 past 10, and I at 11, and sleep 2 hours; a sadly harassed feeling this morning. Eliza Irving leaves today, and then—W.I. willing—I shall try the porch, as there seems little use in my remaining longer in his room at night; but we shall see. He

[83] Andrew B. Myers has noted that WI attended 107 of the 138 meetings of the Board of Trustees held during his tenure as President ("WI and the Astor Library," p. 391). In 1859 ill health obliged him to be absent from all but the May and July meetings.

[84] Frederick Saunders (1807-1902) was the author of two popular volumes, *Memoirs of the Great Metropolis, or London from the Tower to the Palace* (New York, 1852), and a miscellany, *Salad for the Solitary* (New York, 1853). He sent complimentary copies of these to WI when they appeared, and WI's letters of acknowledgment have been published by V[ictor] H. P[altsits], "WI and Frederick Saunders," *Bulletin of the New York Public Library*, 36 (April 1932), 216-17. In October 1859, Saunders was appointed Assistant Librarian and Attaché for the Astor Library, in whose service he continued until 1896. In his *Character Studies, with Some Personal Recollections* (New York, 1894), Saunders published a sketch entitled "WI," pp. 65-110, wherein he recalled a "literary party" at SS in 1859, presumably the visit referred to in the journal.

[85] Probably Julia Grinnell, absent in Europe. It is unclear whether the letter was written by WI or PMI, but the latter was certainly in regular correspondence with his sister at this time. See below, p. 256.

[86] A. Gerald Hull, M.D., one of the earliest practitioners of homeopathy in New York, died on April 25, 1859; his funeral was on April 28 at 4:00 P.M. (*Tribune*, April 28, p. 5, col. 4).

receives this morning six copies of the last volume of his *Life of Washington*, sent up yesterday by Mr. Putnam; it is advertised for delivery May 10th.[87] About 1 W.I. goes out to drive, but is too nervous yet to look at his fifth volume.

Sunday, May 1. . . . Before church reads Tuckerman's account of the Portraits of Washington in the Appendix to the fifth volume;[88] pronounces it quite an acquisition to the volume. Goes to church.

[May 2]

Tuesday, May 3. . . . All went to the city today; *i.e.*, W.I., Ebenezer I., P.M.I., and Helen. Returned at 1/4 past 7. W.I. the better for the journey. Slept alone in his room this night—I in the porch to be within call. Had a good night.

Wednesday, May 4. W.I. occupied his room alone last night for the first time in months—I sleeping in the porch to be within call. Took 10 drops of cannabis,[89] and had a comfortable night. . . .

Thursday, May 5. I took my station in the porch again last night, W.I. occupying his room alone. Alexander, coachman, ill. W.I. called at the Coffins'.[90] Better apparently today than he has yet been. Slept very little before retiring.

Friday, May 6. Had a good night. Helen and I went to the city, Helen remaining until next day. Took my station in the porch at night.

Saturday, May 7. W.I. had a good night and day. I went to the city in the morning and returned with Helen at night. On retiring W.I. observed: "Pierre, you need not mount guard tonight; I can get on without." So I slept in my own room for the first time in four months – . . . .[91]

---

[87] On May 6 the *Tribune* (p. 1, col. 2) and the *Times* (p. 6, col. 4) published identical advertisements for the fifth volume of the *Washington*, stating that "Agents and canvassers [would be] supplied with the 8vo Edition on Saturday, [May] 7th," that the octavo edition would be published May 9, and the duodecimo May 11.

[88] Henry T. Tuckerman contributed a discourse entitled "Portraits of Washington" to volume five of *Washington* which appeared as the first of the appendices to the work. The portraits described by Tuckerman were being engraved on steel for publication in Putnam's "Illustrated Edition" of the biography. Putnam combined Tuckerman's text and these engravings in another volume, *The Character and Portraits of Washington*, published in 1859.

[89] Probably an alcoholic extract of the dried tops of *Cannabis sativa*. This medication, known also as Indian hemp, was often prescribed to promote sleep, relieve pain, allay spasms, and compose unquiet nerves (Wood and Bache, *Dispensatory*, pp. 381-82).

[90] "Repose," the home of Edward Coffin, was on the Albany Post-Road about one-half mile south of SS. See Scharf, *Westchester County*, II, 241, 245.

[91] The expressive long line of periods is PMI's.

[May 8]

Monday, May 9. Had a rather disturbed night, with difficult breathing. Received a letter from Bancroft in acknowledgement of volume V of *Life of Washington*, speaking of the narrative as beautifully told, &c.[92] Angelica Hamilton also called the spoke of it, &c.

[May 10, 11, 12]

Friday, May 13. . . . Walked over with Helen to Mr. Grinnell's piazza where they sat for over an hour, he enjoying exceedingly the beauty of the day and the music of the birds. Returned home a little tired, but found a very kind and delightful letter from Professor C. C. Felton,[93] of Cambridge, who had just been reading his fifth volume of *The Life of Washington* and expressed great pleasure in the perusal. Uncle read the letter aloud. He said it was particularly gratifying to get such testimonials from such men, as he found it impossible to repress great misgivings with regard to this last volume which he had never been able to look at since it was finished. His illness came on the very next day; indeed, he was then unfit to write, and he had constantly in his mind the recollection of the Archbishop of Granada in *Gil Blas* whose homilies were thought to smell of the apoplexy.[94] His old love of fun revived with the recollection and he went to his library for the book and read the story aloud with great zest. Very nervous on retiring for the night.

[May 14]

Sunday, May 15. . . . Wanted me to draft a sort of answer to George W. Harris of Harrisburg, who had asked his authority for statement that the inauguration of Washington was delayed in consequence of question about title to be given President. Went to church and remained to dine with Mr. and Mrs. Hoge where Oscar and Eliza were on a visit. Had a fair night.

Monday, May 16. I went to town. W.I. dined again at the Hoges'; not so well—on my return noticed he looked badly. Told him I had met Jack Downing,[95] who inquired very kindly after him. "Did you tell him I was shaking in the wind?" said he. I then inform him of Cogswell's[96] delighted satisfaction with the last volume, &c.; very

[92] An excerpt from Bancroft's letter is published in *LLWI*, IV, 281-82.

[93] Cornelius Conway Felton (1807-1862) had since 1834 been Eliot Professor of Greek Literature at Harvard College. He was elected President of the College in 1860.

[94] See LeSage, *The Adventures of Gil Blas of Santillane*, Book III, Chapter IV.

[95] On his visits to New York WI often visited Charles A. Davis at his home in University Place. He appreciated Davis' letters of gossip and advice, written between visits. See WI to Charles A. Davis, SS, February 22, 1859 (Virginia); WI to Charles A. Davis, April 4, 1859 (Yale).

[96] Joseph Green Cogswell (1786-1871), teacher, librarian, and bibliographer, was in 1859 Chief Librarian of the Astor Library. During the 1850's WI saw his fellow-bachelor Cogswell regularly and looked in upon him during his recurrent bouts with ill

cheering. Cleaning house: he occupied tonight the room opposite his. . . .

Tuesday, May 17. . . . Got up and sat in his chair at daybreak, and soon after read me a very pleasant and interesting letter from William C. Preston,[97] ex-Senator, his old travelling companion in Scotland—now paralytic. Preston very eloquent then at times in conversation; his allusion in the letter to Jones of the brinn.[98] Slept altogether about three or four hours last night, and expressed his comfort at having had me at hand; saw the Doctor this morning.

[May 18]

Thursday, May 19. I accompanied Helen and Uncle Ebenezer to the city, returning with the latter to the cottage at 1/4 past 7. Found Uncle W. had had a quiet day, without *much* cough, difficulty of breathing, or nervousness. The tears came to his eyes this morning at breakfast and his utterance was choked as he attempted to speak of my *kindness*, as he termed it, in occupying the chamber with him at night. . . . The newspaper notice:

> The friends of Washington Irving will be glad to hear that his health is now becoming quite settled. He made his first appearance in New York the other day for the first time in many months. Mr. Irving's illness has been the result of long continued application and had become so serious as to cause many fears as to the final result, as he is now past 76 years of age.[99]

Friday, May 20. A dismal rainy morning—a succession of bad weather lately: first three days of *dry* storm and then three days of wet. I answer today a copy of Preston's letter received on the 17th and which I have

health; see *LLWI*, IV, 289. Cogswell was grateful for WI's interest, as appears in a letter he wrote to George Ticknor on November 25, 1858: "We were all very much distressed, at the meeting of the Trustees of the Library yesterday, to see how very ill Mr. Irving looked, and how feeble he evidently was. . . . His kindness to me in October, when I was so ill, and had no one around me but him, to sit by and comfort me, was so great and unremitted, that it has bound me to him by a new tie" (*The Life of Joseph Green Cogswell, As Sketched in Letters* [Cambridge, Mass., 1874], pp. 277-78).

[97] William C. Preston (1794-1860) went to Europe in 1817 and met WI shortly after his arrival. In September they made a pedestrian tour of Scotland in company with Peter Irving. Preston was a Senator from South Carolina, 1833-1842; in 1845 he was elected President of South Carolina College.

[98] Preston's recollections of WI are in Minnie C. Yarborough, ed., *The Reminiscences of William C. Preston* (Chapel Hill, 1933), pp. 32-49. WI's recollections of the tour through Scotland and other events are in Milledge B. Seigler, "WI to William C. Preston: An Unpublished Letter," *American Literature*, 19 (1947), 256-59. "Jones of the brinn" was a gracious Scot who came to the assistance of Preston when sore feet prohibited him from accompanying the Irvings any farther toward their destination of Llangollen. According to Preston, Jones said to him: "No sir, you shall not walk. You shall ride my cob" (*Reminiscences*, p. 39).

[99] PMI copied this unidentified notice onto a small sheet of India paper and pasted it onto a leaf of the journal.

finally deciphered for W.I. who wishes to answer it. . . . His letter is dated Charlottesville (Albemarle County), Virginia. . . .

Came into my office where I was and handed me the *Tribune* with notice of his last volume.[100] A letter from Duyckinck on the same subject and one from Tuckerman, enclosing an extract of his notice —an excellent one.[101] There was also a notice in the *Century*.

The papers announce today the death of Baron Alexander von Humboldt at the age of ninety-one.[102] . . . "Do wish I could get out of doors—this detestable weather. Don't know what to do with myself—so comfortless. So constantly in dread of going to bed and having my night's rest broken with this cough." Met Humboldt often in society in Paris:[103] "a very amiable man, a great deal of *bonhommie.*" . . .

Saturday, May 21. . . . I went to the city to look up Prescott's letters to him for which Ticknor—about to write his life—had made application,[104] and returned with Helen at 1/4 past 7. Found he had had a very quiet and comfortable day.

Sunday, May 22. Still overcast and loth to clear. . . . Became very restless and nervous, got up and tried the new chair which Mr. Ellery brought yesterday for him to use as long as he wished, but could not make himself comfortable there or anywhere; went from chair to bed and bed to chair in vain pursuit of rest. Caught a little nap in the Hoge chair after daybreak, but was very nervous on coming downstairs. To Helen's inquiry how he was: "Miserable, miserable, miserable! Ah, if I could only die at once and not live to be a burden to myself and others!" "But this nervousness that distresses you now, and shortness of breath, will soon pass off." "Yes, my dear—when I pass off." He was more quiet, however, and after breakfast came into the library where I was, and alluding to Webb's article on the fifth volume of *Washington,* said it was a cordial and acceptable article, but that he [Webb] misconceived his allusion to Hamilton[105]—as if he had done

---

[100] *Tribune,* May 20, p. 3, cols. 3-6. The review was highly favourable.

[101] An extract from Tuckerman's review is in *LLWI,* IV, 291-92.

[102] *Tribune,* May 19, 1859, p. 5, cols. 1-3; *Times,* May 19, p. 4, col. 6; p. 5, col. 1; *Herald,* May 19, p. 1, cols. 1-2. All three newspapers carried brief obituaries of the geographer.

[103] WI met Humboldt in Paris in 1823, 1824, and 1825; see *Journals* (Reichart), pp. 237, 316, 508, 512. During his first visit to Europe, WI had hoped to meet Humboldt, who from 1799 to 1804 had been traveling and residing in South America, Mexico, and the United States, but there is no record that he did see him at this time.

[104] William H. Prescott had died on January 28, 1859, and his friend George Ticknor (1791-1871), literary historian and scholar, had been delegated by the Massachusetts Historical Society to write a memoir of his life for publication in the *Proceedings* of the Society. Ticknor had written to request Prescott's letters to WI for use in that work. In his *Life of William Hickling Prescott* (Boston, 1864), pp. 166-73, 176-77, 422, 429, published as a substitute for the Memoir to the Society, Ticknor included three such letters, written in 1838 and 1839, and three from WI to Prescott, written between 1838 and 1859.

[105] James Watson Webb's review of the fifth volume of the *Washington,* in the New York *Courier and Enquirer* for May 21, 1859, p. 3, col. 3, was favourable, with a single

him injustice in representing him as *theoretically a monarchist*, p. 63, and [had] gone out of his way to impute *possible* motives to him for advocating assumption of state debts, &c., p. 57.[106] "Good heaven!" said he. "What motive could I have to do injustice to Hamilton? I have the highest admiration for him—was in his favor in early life.[107] I wish only to speak *truthfully* of him, as of all. The conjectural motives I assign to him are to his *credit*, and certainly Gouverneur Morris' letter to *Walsh*—volume III, p. 260—his own friend and correspondent, settles the point.[108] He then took a reference of that to hand to Webb whom he expected to meet at church. I intimated that possibly John C. Hamilton, in his oversensitiveness, had put a perverse interpretation of motive, and misled Webb. "Well, he had better take care. If I catch him at that business I may yet rip up his doublet for him!"

Afterwards spoke of Walsh:[109] "did not fulfill the great expectations formed of him. The Abbé Correa spoke of him as a reservoir, but no fountain."

Met Webb at church, and while alluding to his *acceptable* article, spoke to him of his misconception. Webb said that it had been suggested to him that as he had steered clear of the difficulty in other respects, he might have avoided that. "Who suggested it?" inquired

exception. After praising in particular the "great judgment and rare tact" with which WI had "presented to the public WASHINGTON only, and *his* motives in the administration of affairs," Webb continued: "But while such is our judgment of the book, and so great our appreciation of the tact displayed by the author, in confining himself solely to historical facts and the motives and purposes of WASHINGTON, without attempting to analyze the motives and purposes of others,—we cannot forbear pointing out the fact, that in the only instance in which the author has departed from the admirable rule laid down for his guidance, he has fallen into what will be held to be an error. We allude to attributing to HAMILTON theoretical opinions in favor of a Monarchy, and to his possible *motives* in advocating the assumption of State Debts and the establishment of a National Bank. Exceptions will be taken to this; and probably, with justice. Our object, however, in referring to the subject, is simply to show what caution and judgment and tact, were necessary to steer clear of rocks and shoals which beset the author on every side, in an undertaking of such magnitude and difficulty. If however, there be no error or seeming injustice in this book, except as regards HAMILTON, that can and will be overlooked and pardoned, in consideration of the justice done throughout, to his abilities and Patriotism."

[106] See *Washington*, V (8vo), 57, 62; (12mo), 53-54, 59.

[107] Late in 1804, having just learned of Alexander Hamilton's death following his duel with Aaron Burr, WI wrote from Genoa to his brother William and avowed himself "an admirer of General Hamilton, and a partisan with him in politics" (*LLWI*, I, 91).

[108] On February 5, 1811, Gouverneur Morris (1752-1816), American statesman, wrote to Robert Walsh (1784-1859), American journalist and man of letters, giving a sketch of Alexander Hamilton's character and an analysis of his opinions. The passages most pertinent to WI's interpretation of Hamilton were the first paragraphs of the letter; see Jared Sparks, *The Life of Gouverneur Morris*, 3 vols. (Boston, 1832), III, 260.

[109] After a period of travel and study in Europe, Robert Walsh returned to the United States in 1809, and became an editor of reviews and miscellanies. In 1811 he founded *The American Review of History and Politics*, the first American quarterly. He was Professor of English at the University of Pennsylvania from 1818 to 1828, and in 1837 he settled permanently in Paris, where he founded an American *salon*. From 1844 to 1851 he was the United States Consul-General at Paris (*Life*, I, 131, 412).

W.I. "He was not at liberty to tell." "I know then well enough." Told me this on return from church; said he supposed John C. Hamilton was sorry he had not been picked, mortified to find himself unnoticed;[110] "a caitiff reminded him of a certain dog who goes about with his tail between his legs, willing to do mischief, but terribly afraid of being kicked for it."

Monday, May 23. . . . Determined (the day being fine) to go to the city to see Church's painting, "The Heart of the Andes,"[111] Church having been up to see Mr. Williams and sent him a family ticket.[112] Met Webb in the cars and gave him a memorandum of Hamilton's speech in Convention from Madison's report,[113] and also a reference to Gouverneur Morris' letter [to] Walsh—volume III, p. 260 of Sparks' *Gouverneur Morris*—to show he was right about Hamilton, [that it was] necessary to mention it as a *key* to his life and to Jefferson's misgivings,[114] &c. Not done with the slightest prejudice against Washington [*sic*].[115] The room crowded to see the picture—it was the last day. Delighted with it, pronounced it glorious, magnificent: "Such grandeur of general effect with such minuteness of detail, minute without hardness; a painting to stamp the reputation of an artist at once. Did not know where he could go to look for one combining so much excellence, &c. I recalled to him the remark of [?], in allusion to some moderate *praise* I had seen of it: "It is a sign of mediocrity always to praise moderately." Said he did not recollect the remark, but it was true. . . .

[May 24]

Wednesday, May 25. . . . Goes to the city; is quiet at Irving Van Wart's until the hour of attending the meeting of the Astor Library, when he goes over. Carson Brevoort reminds him that *I* have some letters of his father—they are in W.I.'s possession. . . .

Thursday, May 26. . . . Sarah reports a disturbed night for Uncle. She was up three times; [W.I.] had one of those hallucinations.[116] Worried

---

[110] WI may have meant that John C. Hamilton, who had reason to consider himself something of an authority on the period covered in the fifth volume of the *Washington*, felt slighted at not being asked to write a review of the work. See below, pp. 321-22.

[111] Frederick E. Church's "The Heart of the Andes" won international acclaim during 1859. It was on exhibit in New York from late April until May 23, and on May 24 the *Tribune* observed that the "crowd of persons who had neglected to see Mr. Church's great picture until the last day . . . filled the exhibit room of the Studio Building yesterday" (p. 7, col. 3). The painting was next shown in London.

[112] Church had also called at SS on May 14, but WI had been indisposed.

[113] James Madison's report of Alexander Hamilton's speech in the Federal Convention at Philadelphia, 1787, is in *The Papers of James Madison . . .* , ed. H. D. Gilpin (Washington, D.C., 1840), II, 878-92.

[114] For WI's discussion of the anxiety felt by Thomas Jefferson in 1790 over the signs of encroaching aristocratic rule in the United States, see *Washington*, V, 57-59.

[115] The context indicates that PMI meant "Hamilton."

[116] WI usually slept lightly, and he often complained that his dreams were "mingling with his waking." On April 11, PMI reported that WI awoke during the night with

about copyright? Prescott's letter on the subject which he had read in a few days,[117] Ticknor having written for them. "No, it was not—but seemed under a sort of interdict against occupying the bed he was on, like an interdict about copyright." . . .

[May 27, 28]

Sunday, May 29. His answer to an inquiry [from] Allibone whether *he brought* the ivy from Abbotsford or *Melrose* Abbey[118] on the mantel piece to go to the post office. Tells him it was brought and planted by Mrs. Renwick,[119] the heroine of Burns' "Blue-Eyed Lassie," from Melrose Abbey. She put it down herself soon after the cottage was built. See an account of her in Mrs. Balmanno's *Pen and Pencil,* published in 1858.[120] Went to church. After dinner: "Pierre, I shall have to get you to mount guard again tonight. I am ashamed to ask it, but you cannot conceive what an abject coward this nervousness makes of me." I assured him of my readiness to resume my post at night in his room; he had been trying for two or three nights again to do without. Speaking of sending a box of books from his library to my office, rises: "The books are in the way of one another"—or "each other." . . .

Monday, May 30. Went to town and saw Dr. Peters. The Doctor prescribes cod liver oil, upon which he begins in the afternoon; is to take it after each meal. Walks from the Doctor's to his tailor, Cullen, between 8th and 9th Streets [on] Broadway, and thence to Irving [Van] Wart's, 33 Lafayette Place. . . . *Writes Tuesday 31st* to George Ticknor, enclosing six letters of Prescott, and to Morton on *Rosetta Stone,*[121]

the impression that he "had charge of a young man to educate & take about"; and on May 21, he noted that WI "awoke with distressing shortness of breath & a sort of hallucination about Mrs Colford Jones, as if she were by his side & he had somehow or other got to take care of her."

[117] Prescott had written to WI on December 24, 1839, urging him to write "a brief memorial" on the subject of international copyright, which would be "signed by the persons most interested in the success of the law" and would then be submitted to Congress during its debates over proposed copyright legislation. He added: "If anything can be done, there can be no doubt that you are the one who, from your literary position in the country, should take the lead in it" (Ticknor, *Life of Prescott,* p. 176). See WI's letter on the subject in the *Knickerbocker Magazine,* 15, no. 1 (January 1840), 78-79; reprinted in *LLWI,* III, 149-51.

[118] Allibone's letter of inquiry was possibly in connection with the account of WI's career he had included in *A Critical Dictionary of English Literature and British and American Authors* (Philadelphia, 1858-1871), I, 935-45, the first volume of which compilation was being reviewed favourably in 1859 (*e.g., Tribune,* April 16, p. 4, cols. 1-3).

[119] Mrs. Jean Renwick, the daughter of the Reverend Andrew Jeffrey of Lochmaben, Scotland, married William Renwick in 1791, came to New York with her husband, and spent the greater part of her life there. WI was her close friend before his journey to Europe in 1815. See *Letters from WI to Mrs. William Renwick, and to Her Son, James Renwick* (n.p., n.d.); and *LLWI,* I, 266-67.

[120] Mary Balmanno, *Pen and Pencil* (New York, 1858), pp. 172-81.

[121] Henry Morton (1836-1902) was one of the authors of the *Report of the Committee of the Philomathean Society of the University of Pennsylvania to Translate the Inscription on the Rosetta Stone,* a 160-page work lithographed in 1858 and, in a second edition, in 1859.

excusing himself from the shattered state of his health, &c. Dreadfully bored with letters of every conceivable description now that he is compelled [not] to excuse himself from the exercise of the pen. I write today to Mr. Storrow and to James Berdan.

Tuesday, May 31. See latter part of above record. Trimming and cutting away of the ivy today. A tolerable night. . . . Had been reading in Latrobe[122] about the prairies and was "in a muddle" about prairie life when he awoke. Query: "Was it then I was introduced to this prairie life?"

Wednesday, June 1. Seems and looks better at breakfast—quite face-tious and playful at breakfast which drew a remark from someone that he was better this morning. Complained or rather alluded to his throat being so parched in the morning, whether owing or not to the Doctor's medicines he could not say. Made allusion before breakfast to his being "all in a muddle about the prairies." A rainy morning. Mrs. Jaffray called for him and took him to her house to pass part of the morning. . . .

[June 2]

Friday, June 3. . . . 7 1/2 P.M.: I have just returned from the city, having received $2500 from Putnam[123] . . . .

[June 4, 5]

Monday, June 6. Thinks of going to the city with Helen and myself to escape nervous loneliness. A comfortable day. Dines at the Van Wart's and returns with me in the 1/2 past 5 train. Has a good night. . . .

Tuesday, June 7. A comfortable day. While a tea a call from Rev. Edward Everett Hale, one of the editors of the *Christian Examiner*, who brought a letter of introduction from his uncle, Edward Everett.[124]

[June 8]

Thursday, June 9. A very good night—awake, however, and coughing from 3 to 4, then fell asleep again. Went to the city and returned in the 20 minutes past 3 train. Consented to the correction about Hamilton in

In 1856 a plaster cast of the Rosetta Stone had been presented by T. K. Conrad to the Philomathean Society, of which Morton was a member. Since the inscription on the stone—in Greek and in Egyptian hieroglyphics and demotic characters—had not yet been fully translated, Morton and two other students were appointed to undertake the task. On July 13, 1859, the New York *Times* reviewed the completed project—apparently the second edition—and published a letter from Alexander von Humboldt, dated March 12, 1859, congratulating the Committee on its achievement (p. 2, col. 4).

[122] Latrobe's *The Rambler in North America*, 2 vols. (New York, 1835).

[123] Probably a payment on the balance of Putnam's indebtedness for the stereotype and electrotype plates of WI's revised works. See above, pp. 122-24.

[124] According to Hale, his letter of introduction was eighteen years old, having been written in 1841 by Alexander Everett, another uncle. Hale recorded his impressions of the visit to SS in his *Memories of a Hundred Years*, II, 74-75.

the fourth volume,[125] but thought he had treated the subject indulgently and with as much tenderness as possible. "The truth was," he said, "Hamilton was very arrogant in the matter and was too full of himself. As, however, he took his own account, did not wish to appear to make a case against him." There was to be a new edition of volume IV—of the duodecimo—and this the first opportunity that had occurred to make the alteration. . . .

[June 10]

Saturday, June 11. A visit today from Evert Duyckinck and Mr. Cooke of Richmond, author of [blank space] and brother of the Cooke who married Mary Kennedy.[126] They came at 12 and left at 1/2 past 4, staying to dinner at Uncle's solicitation, who was in excellent spirits (for him), and enjoyed the visit very much (I and Helen were in the city). . . .

[June 12]

Monday, June 13. . . . After tea in the evening receives a letter from a Mr. Van Antwerp, dated 8th June, enclosing a complimentary resolution of the Board of Visitors at West Point, proposing, if agreeable, to call on him in a body tomorrow or next day, when they should adjourn.[127] All in a flutter about it: "must stop this inundation at

---

[125] In his list of corrections ordered for the *Washington*, PMI wrote:
"June 10th, 1859. Gave Putnam the following correction for Vol IV Life of Washington –
"Octavo – p. 230 – lines 20, 21, 22 from top – for 'having in fact no object in hurrying down stairs but to deliver a letter to a fellow aide-de-camp' 78 letters put 'which, however "pressing" the letter he had to deliver, he could have spared at least a moment to do' – (78 letters)
"Octavo – p. 230 – line 22 for 'chat' put 'talk.'
"Make the same correction in the duodecimo – p. 211 – 5th & 6th lines" (NYPL, Berg). See below, pp. 321-22.

[126] John Esten Cooke was best known as the author of *Leather Stocking and Silk* (New York, 1854). He was the brother of Dr. Henry Pendleton Cooke, who married Mary Kennedy in February 1855. He wrote the life of WI for Appleton's *New American Cyclopedia* (New York, 1858-1863), ed. George Ripley and Charles A. Dana.

[127] As copied by PMI into his journal, the letter follows:

"West Point – June 8, 1859

"Washington Irving Esq
    "Sir

    "In obedience to the subjoined resolution of the Board of Visitors, now in session at the U.S. Military Academy at West Point, we have the honor to inquire of you when it will be agreeable to you to receive the Board as a *body* at your residence, that an opportunity may be there afforded of meeting you and manifesting in their collective capacity the homage due to one whose long life has been distinguished by sterling virtues & who wears with becoming gracefulness the laurels which which [*sic*] labors successfully devoted to literature have placed upon your brow–

                "With high consideration we have the honor to be
                    "Your obt Serts
                    "V. P. Van Antwerp (General V. P. Van Antwerp)
                    "John T. Heard (Colonel)"

once." Goes to the library and writes a letter to Mr. Van Antwerp, expressing his very high sense of the intended compliment, and his inability to cope with the visit from long ill health and nervousness, &c. Quite relieved when he had read it and got our approval. . . .

[June 14, 15, 16]

Friday, June 17. Quite playful and facetious today at breakfast and dinner. I in town. A good day, but his looks are not promising. Today a letter is written to Captain Warman, expressive of the sense of the neighborhood of his integrity and merits, and begging his acceptance of a sum, &c. I mentioned that this letter would be coming to him for his signature, and he said, "Did they not also address a letter to Mr. Sloan, the President,[128] expressive of their sense of his conduct, &c.? They should have done that also." Slept in the porch without being disturbed by Uncle, except that I heard him cough now and then.

Saturday, June 18. . . . Helen was going to town, but gave up when she found Uncle so nervous. "I'm a Marplot to everybody,"[129] said he. Had no idea where the passage was from: "Fair laughs the morn," &c. At breakfast was brought in a basket containing bananas, &c. &c., from Mr. Smythe, which produced a little pleasant excitement. W.I. and I drove to the station with the girls, and then to Dobbs Ferry and back, I stopping at P.O. for letters and papers while Uncle drives on. . . .

Sunday, June 19. Gentle and playful this morning—something almost childlike in his manner. I looked after breakfast in *Elegant Extracts*[130] for the passage alluded to yesterday, "Fair laughs the morn," &c. Told him I thought it in Gray's "Bard"[131] (a beautiful day). Remarked upon his having none of the American Poets in his library (Percival was just published &c.).[132] Said he did not read poetry now. I then read aloud from *Elegant Extracts* these lines of Colonel Lovelace in which occur:

> Stone walls do not a prison make
> Nor iron bars a cage.[133]

"Very pretty."

W.I. went to church. I [went] to the Presbyterian where I heard a

In 1859 the Board of Visitors consisted of sixteen persons, each representing a different state (New York *Times*, June 14, 1859, p. 5, col. 5).

[128] Samuel Sloan was President of the Hudson River Rail Road.

[129] Marplot is a well-meaning, blundering busybody in Mrs. Susanna Centlivre's *The Busybody* (1709).

[130] *Elegant Extracts; or, Useful and Entertaining Pieces of Poetry* . . . , ed. Vicesimus Knox (1752-1821). It was first published at London in 1789, and it appeared in many editions thereafter.

[131] Thomas Gray, "The Bard," II.ii.9.

[132] *The Poetical Works of James Gates Percival* . . . , 2 vols. (Boston, 1859).

[133] Richard Lovelace (1618-1658), "To Althea from Prison," stanza four.

Mr. Murray from Elizabethtown.[134] After my return [W.I.] was reading Ogilvie's "Ode to Time" in *Elegant Extracts*, p. 499, and coming to
that passage about "Old Empires,"[135] wondered whether it had not
suggested Bryant's "Lines to the Past": "Old empires sit in sullenness
and gloom."[136] He asked me if I could recollect the author of two
beautiful lines that had lingered in his memory for years, disconnec-
tedly:

> She asked of each wave as it reached the shore
> If it ever had touched the ship's tall side.

I had never met with them. . . .
Very playful and pleasant at dinner. Walk round the brook lot in
the afternoon. In the evening smoked paper in the library, and then
took his seat at the table in parlor, and opened a book to read. Had
been [for] some time at a loss for a pleasant book. "I'm reduced to my
favorite author," said he. "What is it?" asked Kate. "The fifth volume
of *Washington*. I think I'll read it now." Had not looked at it since it
was put to press. . . .

Monday, June 20. Short-breathed at breakfast, but disposed to be
facetious. Mary being cautioned by one of her sisters not to eat too
many strawberries (they being in profusion and she eating them at
each meal), replied, "They don't seem to affect me yet." "No. You
were affected enough already." "Why how smart you are this morning," said one of the girls playfully. "Yes," said Mary, "but he was
smarter still Saturday, when we rode to Mr. Bowers'," for on its being
observed that Mary had such a strong head and could not ride

[134] The regular preacher at the Irvington Presbyterian Church was the Reverend
Charles K. McHarg, its pastor since 1855 (Scharf, *Westchester County*, II, 190).

[135] John Ogilvie, D.D. (1763-1814), poet and miscellaneous writer, was the father of
James Ogilvie (d. 1820), the orator. The passage from the former's "Ode to Time"
alluded to in the journal is copied into PMI's entry for June 19. It consists of the first of
the poem's nine stanzas:

> "O thou who midst the world-enslaving gloom
> Sitst on yon solitary spire!
> Or slowly shakst the sounding doom,
> Or hear'st the wildly warbling lyre;
> Say, when thy musing soul
> Bidst distant times unrol,
> And marks the flight of each revolving year,
> Of years whose slow consuming power
> Has clad with moss yon leaning tower
> That saw the race of glory run,
> That marked Ambition's setting sun,
> That shook old Empire's towering pride,
> That swept them down the floating tide;
> Say when these long-unfolding scenes appear
> Streams down thy hoary cheek the pity-darting tear."

[136] PMI's quotation is line six of "The Past," a poem which was included in the
volume of Bryant's poetry WI had edited for publication in England in 1832. See *The
Poetical Works of William Cullen Bryant*, ed. Parke Godwin (New York, 1889), I, 121.

backwards—"Yes, but she is headstrong"---------------. This morning, a letter came by mail from Mr. Charles D. Cleveland, transmitting a new edition of his *Compendium of American Literature*,[137] with a note, dated Philadelphia, June 17, 1859, as follows:

> My dear Sir:
>
> I know that your correspondence must be very great, and I feel ashamed to add another straw to it; but if, after looking over my new edition of the *Compendium of American Literature* you feel that you can *with a clear conscience* write a few lines in its favour, I should esteem it a very great favour, and prize them more than all the "puffs" of all the Reviews and Magazines. Hoping that I have not taken too great a liberty, I remain with the warmest regard,
>
> Yours,
Charles D. Cleveland
>
> P.S. I send a copy by this mail, but the law will not let me write your name in it.

"He asks too high a price for his book," was the remark on reading the letter. . . .

Tuesday, June 22. . . . I brought up yesterday some of the first numbers of Dickens' new weekly *All the Year Round*.[138] Found him in the library reading them this morning. "Do you find anything of interest in them?" I inquired. "Yes, but how changed the feeling with which you read anything of Dickens now; he has shown himself to have such inferior qualities of heart from what you had given him credit for. He is doing now in England what he did in America: after all our extravagant homage to him which he should have been proud of, felt to be a great compliment, pouring abuse on us because we stood in the way of his own selfish interests (copyright). So he is trifling with his popularity in England," &c.[139] . . .

[137] Charles D. Cleveland (1802-1869) first published his *Compendium of American Literature* in 1858. He was also the author of Latin textbooks and the editor of a *Compendium of Grecian Antiquities* (1836), a *Compendium of English Literature* (1847), and *English Literature of the Nineteenth Century* (1853).

[138] The last number of Charles Dickens' weekly, *Household Words*, appeared on May 29, 1859. Dickens was now devoting his energies to promoting a new weekly magazine virtually identical in content, *All the Year Round*, which had begun publication in London on April 30.

[139] At this point PMI added an explanatory note: ". . . alluding to the conduct comment[ed] upon no doubt in the following extract from the New York Times of June 16, 1859." He then pasted into the journal a clipping from this issue of the *Times*, p. 4, cols. 4-5, consisting of an editorial entitled "Dickens upon Dickens." The article had been prompted by the concluding number of *Household Words*, in which, according to its author, Dickens "felicitate[d] himself on the final triumph of his plans" to "extinguish" the periodical. See "A Last Household Word," *Household Words*, 19 (May 29, 1859), 620. The *Times* editorialist noted, however, "that this triumph was only secured by a wanton sacrifice of property on his own part, in order to injure the property of others; thus affording him nothing more than the very questionable victory which any man may earn who will set fire to his own palace in order to destroy his neighbor's

1/2 past 10 A.M.: the mail is brought in. Opens a package: "Here's a book I've got to *pay for*"; but was quite relieved when he found it to be Cozzens' *Acadia, or A Month Among the Blue Noses* recently published—with a note from him. Then opens another note which he reads and throws down with, "Writing, writing, writing—eternally writing notes about things you don't care about."

A young gentleman from Albany calls; sends word he is about to visit Spain and would like to see Mr. Irving. Mr. Irving excuses himself through me on account of illness. Afterwards Mrs. Hamilton and Mrs. Schuyler call—and he sees them. Mrs. S. had just been reading *Salmagundi* for the first time with her mother by to explain the allusions. "Kissing Bridge," she said—her mother said, "was the bridge over Canal Street." "Oh no!" said Mr. I. "She was kissed in the wrong place. It was beyond Jones' Woods on the road to Harlaem, near Hellgate."[140] Mrs. Schuyler expressed herself to Helen very much pleased with the fifth volume of *Washington*. A storm of rain after dinner. In the evening came—forw[ard]ed by Mr. Wilbur—a pamphlet on Dr. Morton's Etherization,[141] and a letter from James [Brown?], [?], applying for subscription on his behalf. Did not see with what propriety they send it to him. Dr. M. a resident of Boston, &c....

Thursday, June 23.... I walked to the station and returned with the *Herald.* On the carriage's return from taking [Kate, Mary, and Ebenezer] to the station drove out with Uncle toward Dobbs Ferry and got the papers on our return, and a letter to me from Tuckerman, with this:

> Please give my respects to your uncle and thank him for his kind note which I found on my arrival. I trust his health is improving.

hut." The writer proceeded to set forth the tangled facts of the controversy between Dickens and his publishers, Bradbury and Evans, which had brought about the present state of affairs. For a review of the incident, see Edgar Johnson, *Charles Dickens: His Tragedy and Triumph* (London, 1953), II, 943-45.

[140] In *Salmagundi,* No. 1 (January 24, 1804), "Anthony Evergreen," arbiter of "the fashionable world," was described as an ancient bachelor who "can recount the amours and courtships of the fathers, mothers, uncles, and aunts, and even the grandames, of all the belles of the present day.... and can relate a thousand pleasant stories about Kissing-Bridge" (*Salmagundi,* pp. 34-35). In the second number, Evergreen alludes to "a worthy old gentleman of his acquaintance, who had been somewhat a beau in his day, whose eyes brightened at the bare mention of Kissing-Bridge. It recalled to his recollection several of his youthful exploits at that celebrated pass" (p. 51). WI's account of the location of the bridge agrees with James Grant Wilson's in *The Memorial History of the City of New-York . . .* (New York, 1893), II, 162.

[141] This pamphlet may have been Nathan P. Rice, *Trials of a Public Benefactor, As Illustrated in the Discovery of Etherization . . .* (New York, 1859). William T. G. Morton (1819-1868), a Boston dentist, was the discoverer of the surgical use of sulphuric ether. He first used ether on a human patient in 1846, and letters patent for its use were granted him and a chemist, Charles T. Jackson, in November of that year. Morton insisted that the discovery was solely his own, however, and other practitioners contested his assertion. Congressional committees were formed to render a decision on the matter, and their hearings, drawn out over nearly two decades, brought Morton honour but no wealth (*DAB,* VII, 270).

When he is again at Putnam's, be so good as to ask him to write his name on the flyleaf of the first volume of a set of the Washington Biography. I want the copy thus endeared to add to my autograph collection of volumes; I would not give him any inconvenience, but hope, when in the city and at his publishers, he can spare a moment for the purpose. I am rejoiced at the cordial reception the completed work meets from the press and the public.

Read the extract to him in the carriage, which elicits a kind remark about Tuckerman, of whose biographical essays he entertains a high opinion.[142] . . .

Friday, June 24.[143] Had a tolerable night. I in town during the day. Brought up a letter for him, marked "Private," and postmarked Charleston, S.C. Had a restless, sleepless night. I kept awake all night, *in his room*, but fortunately had slept three or four hours before retiring. After daybreak he opened the Charleston letter, without adverting to the postmark, and found it to contain only a newspaper slip, from the Charleston *Mercury* of June 21, 1859.[144] . . . And after I had read it: "Did you ever read," said he, "such an unmeaning thing?" He supposed at first it was from a northern paper, and that some extreme antislavery man had meant to impute suppression or concealment of Washington's full opinions, when he thought his extracts covered the whole ground. But on a more careful perusal than I gave it at first, I perceived it was from a Southern source, and that the writer intended to immolate Washington on the altar of the cherished institution—to cling to slavery and sacrifice the Father of his country, and that the object was to show, not that Washington was entitled to *more* credit than Mr. I. had given him, but open to a graver stigma for his opinions against slavery, &c. "As if," said Mr. I. when I showed him it was from a Southerner, "the greatest reproach you could make against a man [would be] that he was opposed to slavery. Did you ever know such fools, willing to incur the opprobrium of the whole world for their accursed slavery?" This last was at breakfast, June 25. . . .

Saturday, June 25. . . . Mr. Smythe called—a director in the Hudson River Rail Road. Spoke to him about Captain Warman's removal. Great earnestness about it. I found Smythe in the parlor when I came up from train (1/2 past 5) with Kate. Uncle then out taking a drive, but returned before Smythe left.

---

[142] Tuckerman was the author of several biographical works including *Mental Portraits* (1853) and *Essays, Biographical and Critical* (1857). He also wrote travel accounts, art criticism, and literary criticism.

[143] At this point PMI wrote in pencil the following phrases, which he incorporated into the regular entries for June 24 and June 25: "all unstrung – fearfully dismantled – unmeaning – willing to incur the opprobrium of the whole world."

[144] Immediately beneath this passage in the journal a newspaper clipping pasted onto the sheet has been ripped away. It was probably the article referred to by PMI and later reprinted in *LLWI*, IV, 297-99.

I brought up Vanderlyn's crayon likeness of W.I. taken in Paris when he was 22,[145] and asked the girls who it was, &c. He had requested me to ask Irving Van Wart to send for it; and Irving, I found, had written before at his request, and now had it. . . .

Sunday, June 26. Quiet and composed this morning. Drives to church. Very much like himself at dinner with great tendency to playfulness and fun. After dinner sitting on the piazza and looking up the river. Helen observed, "What a beautiful afternoon." "Yes," said he, "It is a beautiful afternoon and a beautiful place whoever it belongs to." "Isn't it in Shakespeare the expression," asked Helen, " 'A poor thing but mine own'?"[146] "Yes," said he. "Shakespeare has a phrase for every thing." . . .

Monday, June 27. I went to town and sent up Dr. Peters in the 11 o'clock train to Tarrytown where the carriage met him. He remained at the house until it was time to leave for the afternoon train of 4:33. I met him at the station on my return. He has given some new directions about the treatment; thinks Uncle looks very bad, though he seemed very glad to see him and was more quiet when he left—had slept some in the morning before he arrived. Playful and pleasant at dinner. Went out to drive at 1/2 past 5. On his return received a basket of fruit from Mr. Smythe, with a note stating that Captain Warman would have been re-instated but for the threatening language of the *Irvingites*, and that he hoped yet that it might be brought about. . . .

Tuesday, June 28. A quiet comfortable day—things very warm. I returned from town in the afternoon at 5. Angelica Hamilton, a Miss *Gyle*? of Boston, a Mr. Ware of [blank space] and Rossiter, the artist, called towards 1/2 past 6, and saw him in the piazza. Angelica thought he looked very feeble and very much changed. Afterwards Cozzens and his wife and little daughter of four years old (Lucy, I believe) called and remained until 1/2 past 9. We were most of the time on the piazza, but Uncle went in after awhile, leaving Cozzens and myself to take a smoke on the piazza. Something said by Cozzens about his sitting for a likeness to Mr. Hicks, the artist,[147] to accompany a representation of the literary class in some contemplated grand painting, in which the commercial class, &c. were to be represented—did not gather what. Only his reply, that he was dwindling away so fast that he would soon make an excellent subject for a miniature for Mr. Hicks—if he took miniatures. . . . Retired at about 11. . . . He would fall asleep while I was reading, then wake and fall asleep again under the lulling sound. When he [fell] asleep the last time (the room being

---

[145] John Vanderlyn (1776-1852) painted WI's portrait in 1805. An engraving after the painting is in *LLWI*, I, opposite title page; a photograph of the engraving is in *Life*, I, 68.

[146] A misquotation of *As You Like It*, V.iv.36: "An ill-favored thing, sir, but mine own."

[147] Thomas Hicks (1823-1890), American painter, was a first cousin of Edward Hicks, the famous American "primitive" painter.

excessively hot and the light attracting insects through the open windows), I put out my lamp; in a few minutes he started up with one of his spasms of nervousness and continued awake and nervous the whole night, with exclamations of "misery, misery, misery," "Will this never end," &c., from time to time begging me to go to my own room; that there was a forlorn comfort in having someone by to groan to, but that I could not help him (alluding to the story of the sot who said to a brother sot in the gutter, that he could not help him up, but would lie down in the gutter with him). A little playfulness or fun would thus blend at times with his extremest distress. . . .

Wednesday, June 29. Seemed tranquil at and after breakfast for awhile, and disposed to converse in a pleasant way; then Helen —before 10—tries to read him asleep. Walked out in the shade—a very hot day—alone, while I was taking a bath. On his return to the house Helen asked him where he had been. "Had been taking a walk to the brook lot to look after his ducklings;[148] counted thirty; had lost some. Robert said the frogs seized them—he was surprised at that—and there was a black snake at the end of the pond which carried off some and which he had tried in vain to catch." I was reading Mrs. Stowe's *Minister's Wooing* and asked him his impression of Burr, whom she had introduced in the June number of the *Atlantic Monthly* and was now continuing in the July number.[149] "Burr full of petty mystery —made a mystery of every thing; when he called on him at Baltimore in the morning, must come again in the evening; five or six in the room—he would take one in one corner and say a word or two, another in another, and so on. Met him again at Fredricksburg and rode with him in the stage to Richmond. Could not well make out what he was sent for."[150] . . .

[June 30]

Friday, July 1. A quiet, comfortable day and night—the best he has had in a long while. Slept *alone* again. Seems to be rallying. "A muffled day"—his singular expression for a chill, sombre day about this time, a day shut in with haze, &c.; an instance of *curiosa felicitas* of expression of frequent occurrence in his conversation.

---

[148] A small brook ran southwesterly toward the Hudson River from a pond atop a knoll to the east of WI's cottage.

[149] PMI wrote "Mrs. Snow's" for "Mrs. Stowe's." *The Minister's Wooing,* Harriet Beecher Stowe's historical novel of post-Revolutionary Massachusetts, was published in book form in October 1859, after having been serialized in the *Atlantic Monthly.* Aaron Burr was introduced as a character in the June issue of that magazine (vol. 3, p. 740).

[150] In an undated entry at the end of the 1859 Journal, PMI added a few other phrases about Burr, probably gleanings from a conversation with WI: "Burr – this ill-fated man, who had hitherto shone like a comet to dazzle & bewilder – a man of shabby infamy." WI's relations with Burr are summarized in *LLWI,* I, 190-203.

[July 2, 3, 4, 5]

Wednesday, July 6. Goes down to the city, not intending to cross to Jersey City to see Irving Van Wart and family off in the *Persia,* but changes his mind when he finds Helen and myself going. In exacerbation about Uncle Ebenezer who came down in cars. Walks from the cars to the foot of Cortlandt Street, then crosses on boat and walks to the steamboat dock at Jersey City. The little steamer crowded. The large steamer [*i.e.* the *Persia*] out in the stream. W.I. very restive, proposes return; I and Helen demur. Irving and family on board of the tug, or small steamer, but do not see him till it is pushing off; he hails me and says he will return in boat, but sends a message back by Mr. Hoge that he could not. We then return to the ferry, cross, and take omnibus at the other side. Uncle and I alight, go to Putnam's, Helen proceeds to Stewart's.[151] I leave Uncle at Putnam's for my office where I had appointed to meet Uncle Ebenezer who also came down, and am soon joined by Uncle W., and afterwards by Uncle E. Uncle W. is evidently at a loss what to do with himself. . . .

Thursday, July 7. Just before sitting down to breakfast, Catharine —the waitress—informs Uncle of a stranger at door, who wishes to see him. She informed him he was ill; but he had come from a great distance and begged to see him if but for a few moments. Uncle, who was excessively troubled at the time with shortness of breath, begged me to see him. I went to the door and found a very ordinary looking personage with a carpet bag at which I cast a very suspicious glance. Asked if I was Mr. I. *Not* Mr. W.I., I told him; he is ill and unable to see anyone. "It would be a great gratification to see him if but for a few moments; had come a great distance; had called four years before, but was not at home; trusted he might not be disappointed." I returned to Uncle, [who was] struggling for breath, and told him he would have to see him for a moment. W.I. went to the door and invited him into the library (the rest of the house I presume in confusion at that early hour—only 1/2 past 7). The stranger took a chair and was going in for a long. Mr. I's difficulty of breathing prevented conversation, and he had to excuse himself. The stranger then asked for his autograph. W.I. nervous, &c.; said he could not write it then, but would send it to his address, which the stranger then gave as follows on an envelope ready stamped: "C. W. Van Vleck—Clockville, Madison County, New York."[152] Then asked Mr. I. his charge, saying, "It is a principle with me always to pay for such things." "It is a principle with me," replied Mr. I. indignantly, "never to take pay"; and the gentleman left. As Uncle detailed these things at breakfast, Helen is reminded of an anecdote told her of Longfellow last summer at Nahant. A person wrote him, wishing him to send him an acrostic, the first letters of

151 Alexander Turney Stewart (1803-1876) was the owner of "Stewart's," the largest dry-goods store in the city, which did a trade among wealthy and fashionable folk.
152 Clockville was a village about fifteen miles east of Syracuse, New York.

which should spell "my sweet girl." "Write it as if it were some beautiful girl with whom you were in love, just as if it were for yourself"; and at the foot of the letter were these words: "Send bill."

I went to town after breakfast; stopped in at Scribner's to inquire for some book, where I met E. Duyckinck, who had lately been up to the cottage with Mr. Cooke, of Richmond. Told me Cooke was delighted with his visit—pronounced W.I. "a finished gentleman."[153] Showed me Sharpe's *Recollections of Samuel Rogers*, by Longman, &c.,[154] which I bought and brought up to W.I. Uncle turned at once to some passages which he remembered Rogers had read to him, such as [blank space].[155]

A good deal troubled with shortness of breath before going to bed; had recourse to the fumigation of paper to expel the phlegm which caused it. Had a good night, without attendance of any kind. His nervousness seems to be leaving him and his general health seems to be improving; looks better. . . . *Has slept alone since June 29th*. Edgar and Amanda up (7th), so that Ebenezer Irving could not read papers or get his usual nap. Gathered together some eight or ten papers when he went off to bed at night. W.I.: "Ah! give him all," &c.[156]

Friday, July 8. Kate and Sarah go to town after breakfast. Uncle seems to relish the *Spring chicken* for breakfast. Just before 9 (Alexander[157] having gone to the city to consult the Doctor) I started for the post office to get the papers and letters. Uncle accompanied me about two hundred yards up the lane—a fine day—sun. "How beautiful—how beautiful!" exclaimed he, as he glanced at the trees and the &c.; "and yet most of the trees have sprung up of their own free will." Brought back a letter from Sarah Storrow. [W.I.] asked if I could imagine where Uncle Ebenezer went when he accompanied us to the city the other day and gave me the slip to avoid surveillance. Edgar told him yesterday: "It was to see the Central Park;[158] had been once before, and did

---

[153] WI also enjoyed the visit. On June 24 he wrote to Cooke, acknowledging receipt of a copy of *Leather Stocking and Silk* which Cooke had sent him: "I look back with great pleasure to the visit of yourself and Mr. Duyckinck as giving me a day of most agreeable social chat, which is quite a god send to an invalid in the country" (Library of Congress).

[154] *Recollections. By Samuel Rogers*, ed. William Sharpe (London and New York, 1859). The edition published by Longman, *et al.*, was the London edition.

[155] WI met Samuel Rogers (1763-1855), English poet and banker, in 1820. In 1824 he planned to write a brief biography of Rogers commissioned by Galignani, the Paris publisher, but he never did so. Rogers' well-known breakfasts were vivacious affairs in which the poet displayed his gifts as a *raconteur*. For WI's recollections of Rogers' table talk, see *LLWI*, II, 195-98; for his description of the poet's social manner, see III, 309.

[156] By 1859 Ebenezer was totally deaf, and he ordinarily occupied himself days by combing the New York newspapers. In 1856 WI spoke to a visitor of his diminishing ability to communicate with his elder brother: "Alas! [Ebenezer] can not now hear what I say to him; but, thank God, we can yet *see* each other!" (Richards, "SS," p. 13).

[157] The coachman.

[158] Plans for Central Park were proposed as early as 1850, but work did not begin on it until land was purchased in 1856. Early in June, 1859, the Park Commissioners gave notice that a portion called "The Ramble" had been completed: ". . . a year ago it was a

not find it; failed also this time." [W.I. was] afraid he might be robbed, or come to injury of some kind; if he would only let him know would get a carriage and go with him—make a party; but he keeps his lips sealed.

[July 9]

Sunday, July 10. A good night without nervousness—though some shortness of breath. Is going to church. Bishop Smith,[159] of Kentucky, preached. Relished his ale (Bass's) at dinner; a fair appetite and very playful. "What a pity, Kate, we had [not] known Louis Napoleon was such a warrior when here, had breakfast with us, and turned conversation on military matters. He should be at no loss for a topic now."[160] Slavery: "I shouldn't mind about the 'Niggers' if they had only brought them over before they had drilled off their tails." "But Uncle," said Helen, "I really don't believe you would engage in the slave trade, though Uncle Ebenezer might." "Ah, my dear, you do me too much honor; but why your Uncle Ebenezer?" "Because he thinks the Almighty permits slavery, and therefore it must be right—sanctioned by the Bible." "And what did you say to that?" "I said the Bible tells us to do unto others as we would that others should do unto us; and I asked him how *he* would like to be a slave." "And that stumped him. Well, I shouldn't mind about the Niggers if they had only brought them over before they had drilled off their tails" (comes in here I think). . . .

[July 11]

Tuesday, July 12. Am writing in the library in the morning at 1/2 past 10. Calls me out to the piazza to see "what a picture there was on the river"; no wind no tide, vessels motionless in front, clouds moving so lazily that "Even in their very motion there was rest"; the sounds of the hammer from workman on a house at the opposite side of the river borne *distinctly* across the water; not quite so pictorial, however, as "The wolf['s] long howl from Oonalacka's shore."[161] "That's the way," pointing to one of the lazy vessels baking in the sun, with its boom creaking to and fro, "that['s] the way we used to travel to Albany in former days—baking in the sun and trying to keep within the shade of the sail. We thought it the order of things then to roast in summer and freeze in winter." (A Christmas off Sunnyside and Tappan Sea).

hopeless mass of rocky prominences . . . now it is more beautiful than any garden which we know of. Let the public go and see it" (*Tribune*, June 3, 1859, p. 7, col. 4). Throughout the summer admiring citizens toured the Ramble. On August 22 the *Tribune* reported that on the day before over 20,000 persons visited the site, "not a single intoxicated person was seen, and there was no disorder" (p. 7, col. 3).

[159] Benjamin Bosworth Smith (1794-1884). He was the Presiding Bishop of the Protestant Episcopal Church from 1868 until his death.

[160] In the summer of 1859 France, under Louis Napoleon, now Napoleon III, was engaged in the Franco-Austrian War.

[161] *The Pleasures of Hope*, Part I, in *The Poetical Works of Thomas Campbell*, ed. W. E. Aytoun (New York, 1870), p. 21.

Remarks today at noon that he feels he is getting on—getting well; he has expressed occasional confidence before, but never so strongly. Is more encouraged than ever. Drive out to the Schuylers' with him and Helen. A hot afternoon; find them reclining, taking a siesta. Call afterwards at the Hamilton[s']; Mrs. Hamilton only at home. Return at 1/2 past 7. Spend the evening on the Piazza; sturgeons leaping every few moments—surprised to find them so far down the Hudson; remark about it in a note to Drake's *Culprit Fay*.[162] Retires at 11.

[July 13]

Thursday, July 14. Had a good night, and has a comfortable day. I returned in the cars with Samuel Ruggles[163] beside me; wished he could stop and see W.I. He then spoke of Uncle's pressing invitation to visit him: "Come and see me, and I will give you a book and a tree." Brought up a fresh bottle of "Protoxite of Iron, or Peruvian Syrup" and a vial of coffea from Mr. Snelling—Dr. Peters being out of town.[164] Also brought up the *Evening Post*, in which there is an allusion to *Knickerbocker's New York* from the Boston *Courier*.[165] "Am pretty much

[162] The note, which appears at the conclusion of *The Culprit Fay*, refers to no particular line: "The reader will find some of the inhabitants of the salt water a little farther up the Hudson than they usually travel, but not too far for the purposes of poetry" (Frank L. Pleadwell, *The Life and Works of Joseph Rodman Drake [1795-1820]* [Boston, 1935], p. 174). The note did not appear in Drake's manuscript version of the poem or in the first published edition of the poem (1836).

[163] Samuel Bulkley Ruggles (1800-1881), public servant. He was former President of the New York Canal Commission, a trustee of Columbia College, and a promoter of the New York and Erie Railroad.

[164] Andrew Snelling was Dr. John C. Peters' father-in-law. The "Protoxite of Iron" was a general conditioner. WI had begun taking it on June 30. The "coffea," or the "seed of Caffea Arabica . . . has acquired much reputation as a palliative in the paroxysms of spasmodic asthma" (Wood and Bache, *Dispensatory*, p. 180).

[165] The article in the *Evening Post*, July 14, p. 2, col. 2, was entitled "Bonner, the Editor of the Ledger." It was devoted to exemplifying the violent differences of opinion over Robert Bonner, the editor of that popular weekly. Since assuming the editorship of the *Ledger* in 1851, Bonner had spent lavishly to attract famous contributors, such as Bryant, Edward Everett, and Mrs. E. D. E. N. Southworth, who produced literary fare suitable for family reading. The *Evening Post* cited one favourable published opinion of Bonner and one unfavourable. The latter, from the Boston *Courier*, denounced the publisher's very name as "synonymous with braggart." According to the Bostonian writer, those who praise the *Ledger* for its moral tone have "loose notions of morality." The writer was particularly unhappy with a work which had recently been appearing in the magazine. PMI pasted the continuation of this vituperative attack into his journal: "But there is something worse than all this. The reading world has been afflicted for sometime with a series of papers of measureless stupidity, entitled a 'True History of the Colony of New Plymouth.' The writer is fool enough to fancy that he has wit: that his coarse travesty of the early Puritan history is funny: that he may perhaps rival Knickerbocker's celebrated History of New York. Even if he succeeded as far as his vanity leads him to suppose, his success would not be worth having. Knickerbocker is good of its kind; but the kind is poor. Burlesque travesty will do in small portions, taken with large admixtures of honest sound reading. But even the graceful genius of Irving failed to make a long-continued work anything but a heavy affliction of the human race, and we cannot doubt that at this moment he would give a good round sum to call in and burn every copy in existence. Who can read it? Who ever did read it through, except

of his opinion," said he, after reading it. Showed him a poetic piece of Bryant in the *Ledger* of July 23d^{166} which I brought up—dated in advance. "A very fine piece—great deal of tenderness and feeling. Who would have thought the old man had so much blood in him?"

Friday, July 15. A good night. Very comfortable in the morning. The new sewing machine (cost $55) introduced and set in operation. W.I. very facetious at dinner about it: did not think much of it, thought you could put a piece of cloth in the drawer and it would come out a dress coat, &c. A broom standing at the front door after dinner, forgotten by the chambermaid: "I suppose," to me, "that is stood there as the sceptre of dominion." Looks better, seems better, but rather nervous on going to bed....

Saturday, July 16.... Pointed out some openings he wished to have made this spring on the bank, if well; too much shut in at present, darkens the rooms, &c.^{167} Rainy morning; gets letter from Charles Augustus Davis; rain all day. Proposes backgammon after tea with Helen. Gets a bad throw, and gives up to the great amusement of all present who had predicted such a result. "Well, I don't care to be bothered for amusement."

[July 17]

Monday, July 18.... Drove out in the afternoon.—Inquired in the evening whether Henry, a mulatto coachman recently engaged to take the place of Alexander who was ill, ate with the other white servants. Sarah said she had letten them manage it among themselves, and that they gave him his dinner &c. afterwards. Thought it a pity. Then adverted to the anecdote of the black in the omnibus with him, &c.—of which I have a record.^{168} I had brought up Poe's *Poems*.^{169} Read over "The Raven." "What a capital hit that was. Such a strange, weird interest in it." Helen proposed that I should read it aloud to the girls. "No—too dismal to go to bed upon." (Next day he read it aloud to them while I was in town, but not in an effective manner—his voice too thick, &c.) Saw little of Poe, thought him an unsafe character. Got one or two letters from him, one asking permission to use certain materials of his for a story; gave him permission.^{170}

from a sense of duty because Irving wrote it? His other charming works have protracted the agony of this jest, and kept it from sinking into oblivion...."

^{166} Bryant's "The Sick-Bed" appeared in the *Ledger*, 15, no. 20 (July 23, 1859), p. 1, col. 1. See *Poetical Works*, II, 58-60.

^{167} WI is referring to the "bank" of foliage around the front parts of the cottage.

^{168} PMI's record of the anecdote is lost.

^{169} A new edition of Poe's *Poems* had recently been published by the firm of Blakeman & Mason (*Tribune*, June 18, p. 1, col. 3).

^{170} Three letters from Poe to WI are extant: on June 7, 1836, Poe wrote soliciting a contribution to the *Southern Literary Messenger*, which he was then editing (J. W. Ostrom, ed., *The Letters of Edgar Allan Poe, with New Foreword and Supplementary Chapter* [New York, 1966], II, 676-77); on October 12, 1839, he wrote enclosing a copy of

Thursday, July 19. Had a good night. At breakfast got talking of Miss O'Neil—exquisite actress, lost herself so completely in her characters.[171] Declined at Birmingham an offer of introduction—did not want to have the illusion broken. "Well," said Scott, when he told him this, "that was very complimentary to her as an *actress*, but I cannot say it was so complimentary to her as a *woman*."[172] Brought up in the afternoon Madame D'Arblay's *Diary*,[173] about which he had been speaking at breakfast—two thick, closely printed octavos; rather dismayed when I brought them, though he had been inclined to think he would like to look them over at breakfast. Difficulty in finding books to suit him. A Mr. Hugh Erwin, of Nashville, called—a stranger—knew the Williams[es]; talked about Clay. Uncle expressed warm admiration of Clay; his seeing him at Washington in earlier life; his going out to take leave of him, Clay mounted on his horse. "If I can do anything for you let me know." "Does he think," thought I, "That I have been courting him all this time for a selfish object?" Pierre P. Irving came up at tea time; had been nearly three months since he was up before.

[July 20]

Thursday, July 21. A good night. A fine cool day. Oscar takes Uncle Ebenezer to West Point and Uncle drives out with Mr. Morgan to General Webb's, Dr. Creighton's, and so through Sleepy Hollow home; a very pleasant day. Mary Hamilton calls in the evening.

[July 22]

Saturday, July 23. A good night and good day. Helen and I dine at Mr. Williams' expecting to meet Mr. Bellows,[174] who did not come. Showed Uncle in the morning Mr. Putnam's account of sales, &c., from May, 1858 to 15th July 1859—fourteen and one-half months, showing an increase of sa[le]s, $14,000 in stock, and in stock and cash of himself and Evans $22,000.

Sunday, July 24. Had a pretty fair night and looks well. Got speaking at breakfast of his visit to Louis Philippe at St. Cloud with our ministers,

"William Wilson," a tale he wrote after requesting permission to make fictional use of "An Unwritten Drama of Lord Byron," WI's contribution to *The Gift . . . for 1836* (Philadelphia, 1835), pp. 166-71 (*Letters*, II, 688-90); and on June 21, 1841, he wrote to solicit a contribution to *Graham's Magazine* (Virginia).

[171] See WI to Henry Brevoort, Birmingham, December 28, 1815; *LLWI*, I, 342-43.

[172] This anecdote is related in fuller detail in *LLWI*, I, 345.

[173] Mme. Frances (Burney) D'Arblay, *Diary and Letters of Madame D'Arblay . . .* , 2 vols. (Philadelphia, 1842). WI had made use of the *Diary and Letters* in his *Life of Goldsmith*.

[174] Henry Whitney Bellows (1814-1883), Unitarian clergyman, was a brilliant conversationalist and was prominent in the civic, social, and religious life of New York. A controversial theological and social thinker, he published in 1859 his best-known volume, *The Treatment of Social Diseases*.

Mr. King and Mr. Wheaton.[175] Made a second visit to the royal family at [blank space] near Paris [blank space]. At dinner: used to read all the details of a painful nature in wars (speaking of some of Raymond's details of the Battle of Solferino[176] which he avoided), but [now] skipped them—"his stomach had lost its tone, could not digest horrors any longer." Walked over to the Holdreges' alone after dinner. . . .

Monday, July 25. A good night. Looks well. Gave an imitation of Deacon Walker at Johnstown after breakfast. I go to P.O. and bring back papers with the news of peace between France and Austria.

[July 26]

Wednesday, July 27. Goes to town to attend the monthly meeting at the Astor Library. Stops at Cozzens' in alighting from the cars. At 11 comes to my office. Talk about destroying his journals, &c., and letters to him, &c. Said he had few letters of distinguished persons; could not encourage any correspondence with them. All his time in this way had to be given to "the bores of this world" who were constantly demanding replies to theirs, &c. Returned in the Express[177] to Tarrytown.

Thursday, July 28. Great dismay at Uncle Ebenezer's sudden determination to go to the city to enjoy the cool day. Would not say where he was going—his perverse refusal to have any one accompany. Uncle W's annoyance in consequence of his deafness—could not communicate, &c.

Friday, July 29. Itinerant musician and wife playing before the door of cottage. Annoyance—the wife goes in kitchen to get breakfast; orders *man* off.

---

[175] This visit to the King of France was late in the summer of 1844; see *LLWI*, III, 362-63. William Rufus Devane King (1786-1853) had recently been appointed United States Minister to France. He was elected Vice-President of the United States in 1852. Henry Wheaton (1785-1848) was in 1844 the United States Minister to Prussia. WI had reviewed Wheaton's *History of the Northmen* in the *North American Review*, 35 (October 1832), 342-71.

[176] Preliminary reports of the Battle of Solferino between the forces of France and Austria began to appear in the *Times* on July 11, 1859, and the first account of the battle by Henry Jarvis Raymond, the *Times'* correspondent, appeared on the following day, p. 1, col. 6; p. 8, cols. 1-2. Raymond (1820-1869), who in 1851 had collaborated in founding the New York *Daily Times*, the lineal ancestor of the modern *Times*, won acclaim for the superiority of his detailed dispatches in reporting the Battle of Solferino. His further accounts of the battle appeared in the *Times* of July 14, p. 4, col. 1, and July 22, p. 2, col. 3. Since the latter article probably inspired WI's comment on "Raymond's details," a short illustrative passage from it is given here: "At one point by the side of the road ten or fifteen peasants were burying the dead. They gathered them from the field upon hand-barrows, from which they were rolled into the hollow places on the roadside, from which gravel had been taken to repair the track; – and after five or six, or as many as the space would hold, a foot or two of dirt was shoveled over them. No attempt was made to remove any of their clothing, or to lay them side by side or in any particular position. They were tumbled in just as it happened, – and were covered up just as they chanced to fall. In many cases they were laid lengthwise in single file, and then covered over, – and a second row being next put in, – then a third, a fourth, &c. In this way over 200 had been buried in a single place."

[177] The Express train of the Hudson River Rail Road left New York at 2:45 P.M.

Saturday, July [30]. Letter from Jack Downing from the Springs,[178] urging his coming; dislike to leave home. Continued shortness of breath. Davis's opinion of Louis Napoleon's abrupt termination of the war.[179] Excellent appetite of W.I.; great improvement in this respect, but shortness of breath continues, with at times "barking" coughs at night.

[July 31; August 1, 2, 3]

Thursday, August 4.... Thinks of going to hear the music at McVickar's church,[180] but gives it up. (Spoke of irksomeness of attending family prayers this morning, with Ebenezer Irving's strange selections, mumbling voice, &c.—had to school himself to it.) Music not good; a sermon fifty minutes in length. "Tediousness," said W.I., "seems a necessary element in all religious services."...

Friday, August 5.... Seemed to have a craving for news when I came up—anything probably to take his thoughts from himself and his distress. "What news?" to me. Told him I had been collecting dividends. "Pleasant business," said he. In the evening Mr. Holdrege and Susan [called].... The conversation turned on Mrs. Stowe's *Minister's Wooing*, in which Burr was introduced, and thence on Burr. Mr. Holdrege asked him if he had ever met Burr. "Yes, breakfasted tête à tête before going to Europe; forgets conversation; talked to him about his intended travels.[181] Then mentioned duel's taking place in his absence, of his changed opinion of Burr when he came to see more of him at Richmond, of the lawyers entangling themselves and Burr in a few brief remarks disengaging, &c.; of his petty mysteries, of his being a man of *large views* and paltry means—arts—to accomplish them, &c."

Saturday, August 6.... Get a letter from Mr. Storrow from Brattleboro. Answer it. Call from George W. Greene, Mrs. Schuyler and Miss Mary Hamilton, Dr. Phillips and wife and daughter, Mrs. Taber—all in at once.... Proposed after tea I should read aloud Tennyson's *Idyls of the King*, which I had recently bought.[182] Soon fell asleep. Took it to bed with him at night, but did not relish him; too artificial. I remarked to him that he did not appear to write from impulse. "No, he writes from the head; too intent on fabricating his verse to write from the heart; too busy in this writing down to the conceptions of the vulgar." Read

[178] Saratoga Springs, New York.

[179] Louis Napoleon and the Emperor of Austria had signed the Peace of Villafranca on July 11.

[180] The Reverend John McVickar (1787-1868) was pastor of St. Barnabus Church, which served the Protestant Episcopal parish of Irvington.

[181] For WI's acquaintance with Burr prior to his first visit to Europe, see *Life*, I, 24-26, 35, 36.

[182] Tennyson's *Idyls of the King* was first advertised for sale in New York on July 27 (*Tribune*, p. 1, col. 2). By August 13, the eleventh thousand of the work was being advertised (*Times*, p. 1, col. 5).

this line after breakfast the next day (Sunday): "At this he snatched his great limbs from the bed."[183] "That is," said he, "he pulled himself out by the leg." I mentioned another homely expression: I'd "abolish him."[184] "Not half so strong," said he, "as the threat your father used to tell of his hearing from someone: 'I'd bury de *name* of you in a fortnight'—make way with the whole family."

Helen drove out with him today. Her allusion about leaving and making room for others:[185] "Never—what would I do without you," &c.

Sunday, August 7. Seems better this morning—has had a *good night*, for him. Discussed Tennyson after breakfast (see before of yesterday). "His *In Memoriam* about which they say so much—very artificial. His *head* at work to see how many ways he could turn the same thought." Going to church; sacrament. Called me into library before church and read aloud these lines from Tennyson:

> At last it chanced that on a summer morn
> (They sleeping each by other) the new sun
> Beat through the blindless casement of the room,
> And heated the strong warrior in his dreams;
> Who, moving, cast the coverlet aside,
> And bared the knotted column of his throat,
> The massive square of his heroic breast,
> And arms in which the standing muscle sloped,
> As slopes a wild brook o'er a little stone,
> Running too vehemently to break upon it.
> And Enid awoke and sat beside the couch,
> Admiring him, and thought within herself,
> Was ever man so grandly made as he?[186]

"Now all this to me is beastly, a perfectly animal picture. It may be pretty, but it is very offensive to me. Means to be so truthful—now poetry is *not* truthful, it colors truth, enriches it." "Very stiff, artificial." Continued reading Tennyson's First Idyl until the carriage drove to the door for church, then closed the book, and putting a paper in to mark the place where he had left off, said: "Well, I shan't go mad with this poetry, though I dare say I shall learn to esteem it." At dinner, quoting some fine passages from Shakespeare, "Ah!" said he, "when one thinks of Shakespeare and one or two others, it is idle for any one else to pride himself upon authorship." Quoted afterward:

---

[183] Tennyson, *Idyls of the King* (Boston, 1859), "Enid," p. 7.

[184] Geraint, husband of Enid, is insulted by a dwarf attendant of King Arthur. The dwarf "Struck at him with his whip, and cut his cheek," at which Geraint's "quick, instinctive hand / Caught at the hilt, as to abolish him" ("Enid," *Idyls of the King*, p. 17).

[185] The "others" who might have taken up the custodial duties being performed by PMI and Helen, or who might have wished to do so, included Oscar and Eliza Irving, Edgar and Amanda Irving, and Sanders and Julia Irving.

[186] "Enid," *Idyls of the King*, pp. 4-5.

We are such stuff
As dreams are made of, and *all* our life
Is rounded with a sleep.

"And *our little life,*" said I, correcting him. "No," said Helen, "'all our life,' I think." I referred to the text. For awhile none of us could recall the drama in which it was. I hunted first through *Macbeth,* thinking it there. W.I. thought it in *Midsummer Night's Dream;* at last I bethought me it was in *Tempest,* and verified the truth of my correction.[187]—he went afterwards to pay his usual Sunday visit to Robert, the Gardener's. Amusement with the children: "No trouble, nothing but an amusement to him," to Maria. . . .

[August 8, 9, 10, 11, 12]

Saturday, August 13. Had a fair night and was comparatively well. Had a talk about the Biography. Did not want it to be spread [?], did not care about it—suggested it because for the set it might be a saleable work, &c. &c. &c.[188] (rain)

Sunday, August 14. Had been reading some *Household Pictures of the Revolution* dedicated to him,[189] which I brought up some days [a]go. Quite touching, some parts of it. I remarked I had heard little from father about their residence at Rahway. He recollected to have heard his mother say the Hessians quartered in the house were very kind. Went to church; Dr. Seabury[190] of New York preached. I said at dinner, "I believe he is considered very High Church." "Yes," said he, "high as game that has been overkept."

[August 15, 16, 17, 18, 19]

Saturday, August 20. W.I. free from shortness of breath. Drive up with him. Helen and Sarah to the Rev. Mr. Mead's, and to G. W. Greene's, who occupies the house just north of him. Greene shows likeness of his grandfather, Washington's present, &c.

Sunday, August 21. . . . A good deal distressed with labouring breath after dinner. Gave Helen a letter to read which he had received the day before from Mr. R. S. Oakley, Cashier, proposing to come up some morning with Mr. Forrest, mathematician, to spend an hour or so.[191]

---

[187] *The Tempest,* IV.i.146-48. PMI did not notice that the proper quotation is "dreams are made *on,*" not *of.*

[188] The preceding sentence is carefully deleted in ink in the journal. By "the set" WI probably meant the edition of his revised works.

[189] *Personal Recollections of the American Revolution. A Private Journal . . . ,* ed. Sidney Barclay [pseud. of Lydia Minturn Post] (New York, 1859). See *LLWI,* IV, 277-78.

[190] Samuel Seabury (1801-1872), rector of the prosperous Church of the Annunciation in New York, was a leading voice in the Protestant Episcopal Church.

[191] In his response to Oakley, WI wrote on August 22: "Since I had the pleasure of seeing you I have suffered greatly from asthma; and am still troubled by sleepless nights and shortness of breathing which at times render me nervous and good for nothing. You must take your chance for finding me worth visiting, but hoping your visit may happen

The letter was long and occupied some time. "Ah! if he could only give me his long wind, he should be most welcome." . . .

[August 22, 23, 24]

Thursday, August 25. W.I. has had a quiet night, free from nervousness or much shortness of breath. Got speaking at breakfast table of John B. Church[192] cutting the Prince Regent.[193] Was it so? "Yes; they belonged to the Jockey Club. Prince a royal scamp—the scorn that broke out at his death." I instance[d] the lines of Moore on the death of Sheridan: "And there too is whose life, a sick epicure's dream,"[194] &c. I alluded to his [the Prince Regent's] being styled "the first gentleman in Europe."[195] "Yes, so some one exclaimed of Thurtell, the murderer,[196] when he came out in small clothes, &c., dressed for execution: 'What a gentleman!" Alluded to the common practice of swearing in the earlier days of New York: "Could not utter a sentence without sending a *damn* with it to give it force." Received yesterday a letter from J. J. Flourney, dated New Athens, Georgia, August 18, 1859, which—suspecting from the first line or two it would be disagreeable—he handed over to me without reading. The writer describes himself as "a poor deaf and semi-mute wight"; he aspired to be an author and had written to W.I. to usher his work, and complains that W.I., "under plea of ill-health (expressed by an amanuensis) turned the cold shoulder on a suffering author!" "And this *great*

on one of my good mornings when I am *in tune*, I remain . . ." (Virginia). After WI's death Oakley published a florid verse tribute to him in the *Evening Post,* April 4, 1860, p. 5, col. 4.

[192] John Barker Church, brother-in-law of Alexander Hamilton, was an Englishman who, having come to the United States during the Revolutionary War, in 1779 married a daughter of General Philip Schuyler and proceeded to acquire large sums of money by supplying the American armies. Church invested much of his capital in the United States during the early years of the nation. Several of these years he spent in London and Paris (John C. Miller, *Alexander Hamilton: Portrait in Paradox* [New York, 1959], pp. 129, 464-65; Nathan Schachner, *Alexander Hamilton* [New York, 1946], pp. 104, 370, 389).

[193] George IV (1762-1830), who was appointed Prince Regent when his father was declared insane in 1811, had in 1785 contracted an illegal marriage; on April 8, 1795, he married another woman, his cousin Caroline Amelia Elizabeth of Brunswick. The Prince's notoriety at this time may have prompted John B. Church to "cut" him.

[194] In his tribute to Richard Brinsley Sheridan written at the death of the dramatist in 1816, Thomas Moore addressed three stanzas (lines 17-28) to the Prince Regent, the first stanza of which follows:

"And Thou, too, whose life, a sick epicure's dream,
Incoherent and gross, even grosser had pass'd,
Were it not for that cordial and soul-giving beam,
Which his friendship and wit o'er thy nothingness cast:—"

(*The Poetical Works of Thomas Moore,* ed. A. D. Godley [London, 1929], p. 454).

[195] See Lewis Melville, *The First Gentleman of Europe* (London, 1906).

[196] Born in Norwich, England, John Thurtell (1794-1824), having failed as a bombazine manufacturer, took up prizefighting and gambling, in the latter of which pursuits he lost large sums of money. In 1823 he slew a creditor, William Weare, and despite a powerful speech in his own defense while on trial, was hanged.

Irving has written a voluminous *History of Washington*, omitting his greatest trait—his piety!" &c. . . .

[August 26, 27, 28, 29]

Tuesday, August 30. Helen had packed yesterday to go to Mr. Ames['s][197] with W.I., but he is not in the mood for the visit today. A cloud upon his spirits; very much disheartened. A cold day, fire in the office. Resolve to drive over to White Plains. Drove over to White Plains with Helen and W.I. . . . After out return W.I. was sitting in the library reading the newspapers when some strangers were visiting the grounds; some *lady?* in black came close up to the east window and peered in. W.I. in a fit of indignant impatience thrust the paper he was reading against the glass, and the lady decamped in quick order. "Such a sheer piece of impertinence I never saw." "Under a murky cloud today." One of the annoyances of visitors—underbred. Talk of going to Mr. Ames['s] in Orange County tomorrow to make a long promised visit. . . .

Wednesday, August 31. . . . Rather out of sorts this morning, but still disposed to go to Mr. Ames's and to stop at the Kents'[198] in Fishkill for a call.[199]

To Fishkill—W.I., Sarah, Helen, and myself. Dined at Kent's; the Judge not at home. Crossed to depot at 5 P.M. Arrive at depot at Craigville. No conveyance to be procured to Mr. Ames['s]. The ladies start for Mr. Ames['s] on foot, to send carriage from the house, leaving me with Uncle. A sudden storm of wind and rain before they got one-fourth of the way. Put in at a Mrs. Stead's and send boy to notify Mr. Ames of our arrival with a bribe of a half dollar. Boy a long time gone (was not to return); the rain ceasing, Helen borrows shoes and they start for the house and meet the carriage. Get in and drive to the station for us. Our patience by this time exhausted. A new coachman—Frenchman—did not know the road; had to send the gardener with him. Arrive at the house at 1/2 past 7, and send back for our baggage—three trunks and a travelling bag—which we had been obliged to leave without protection at the station. . . .

Thursday, September 1. Took a drive to Chester. The coachman very slow, W.I. out of all patience. "This man must have been accustomed to drive a hearse." The sun was troublesome, and he was impatient to

[197] Barrett Ames, a wealthy cotton merchant, had a country residence near Craigville, New York (Scoville, *Old Merchants*, I, 137). Ames was the father of Hector Ames, one of WI's attachés at Madrid, and of Sarah Craig Ames Van Wart, Irving Van Wart's second wife.

[198] William Kent (1802-1861), son of the distinguished jurist James Kent, was a judge in New York, but he made his home in Fishkill.

[199] The journey to Barrett Ames' residence entailed riding about twenty miles north along the east bank of the Hudson River to Fishkill, crossing the river, riding about fifteen miles southwesterly from Newburgh, opposite Fishkill, and finally riding (or in this instance, walking) from Craigville to the Ames estate.

get back. Brilliant Aurora Borealis that night. Helen and I got out of our bed at 1, dressed and walked the piazza, admiring it. So light you might have read.[200] None of the rest saw it but Mrs. Winton, the housekeeper.

Friday, September 2. W.I. not so well this morning. Aurora Borealis again at night, but not so brilliant by any means as the previous night.

Saturday, September 3. Found in the *American Monthly Register?* (as to the title) the account from the *Tribune* of [blank] June, 1850, of Cooper, Bryant, Tuckerman, &c. visiting the Foxes at Rufus Griswold's rooms (in the University),[201] and adverted to the enigma of the manifestations. "Ah! the only way to get at the truth is to bring the mediums to the stake—that was the good old way."

Afterwards alluded to a party of the previous year Helen and I had attended at Mrs. Haight's at Goshen; on the green, with lights, &c., and the little negroes, like mud turtles, thrusting their heads up from under the ropes to look on. Said it reminded him of the dance of the royal family at Dresden, with benches raised for the outside spectators to look on, and see royalty amuse itself (King led the dance—he in it).[202] . . .

Sunday, September 4. Still at Mrs. Ames's. Helen, Mary Peet and myself go to the Methodist meeting, and in the afternoon drive to a camp meeting near Oxford[203]—that is, Barrett and myself in one-

[200] This occurred early on the morning of September 2. According to the New York newspapers, it was "superior to anything of the kind that has been seen in this latitude for many years" (*Tribune*, September 3, p. 5, col. 3).

[201] On June 8, 1850, the New York *Tribune* published an article entitled "An Evening with 'The Spirits,'" p. 4, cols. 3-4, describing a seance conducted by the Misses Margaret (1833-1893) and Catharine (b. 1839) Fox, then at the beginning of their spiritualistic fame. The sisters had arrived in New York from their home in Rochester in May 1850, and the *Tribune* was the only newspaper in the city which took their reputed powers seriously. "An Evening with 'The Spirits,'" the second of its lengthy articles on the Foxes, recounted a gathering at the chambers of the Reverend Dr. Rufus W. Griswold on Broadway. The party consisted of "persons whose general character for intelligence and probity, was a guarantee against their being deluded by hasty impressions, and who, probably without exception, had no prepossession in favor of the principal actors in the movement." Among the company were James Fenimore Cooper, George Bancroft, John W. Francis, N. P. Willis, William Cullen Bryant, and Henry T. Tuckerman. The spirits communicated to the visitors by means of rappings on the table around which they sat. In order to ascertain whether the Fox sisters were genuine mediums, each of the visitors fixed his mind upon a certain individual and then asked the spirits to describe him according to a code supplied by the Misses Fox. In order to assist the spirits, each person would ask such questions as, "Was he a physician?"; a knock meant "yes." John W. Francis thought of Robert Burns; Cooper thought of a sister who had died upon being thrown from a horse fifty years before. The spirits gave correct answers to every question asked them.

[202] For WI's description of the royal balls at Dresden in 1823, see *LLWI*, II, 136-37; see also *Journals* (Reichart), pp. 103-05.

[203] Oxford was about two miles south of Craigville. Miss Mary Peet and her mother were visiting Barrett Ames at the same time as the Irvings.

horse wagon, W.I., Mr. Ames, Helen, and Sarah in the barouche. W.I. in the morning tells them of his going to a camp meeting not far from Tarrytown with a young lady; sees an old negro seated on a stump rocking to and fro with his hands clasping his knees. Looks up at them with a curious glance and supposes they had come to look and laugh. Gives them a passing shot: "Jesus will carry de day"; then, "If God Almighty were not too strong for de devil, der'd be no living in dis world." Two black nymphs behind fanning themselves: "Let old Scip(io) alone, I'll warrant he'll give dem der own." Afterward told story of the Captain of one sloop meeting Gabriel Requa,[204] the Captain of another, as they were beating to and fro. Requa cried out to the other not to swear, &c. "Ah, Gabriel," said he, "is that you? How are they all in Tarrytown? I understand you are all going to heaven like hell." They had lately held a camp meeting and there were many converts. Spoke in the evening of Talma;[205] of his having seen him several times, of his going to the Theatre at Paris with Vanderlyn to see some piece in ridicule of the English. The Englishman in the piece is made to exclaim, "God damn it! God damn it! God *damn* it!" three times with increasing emphasis on the last. They sat behind some ladies, one of whom appeared troubled at the fun made of the English, lest they might be sensitive, &c. Turning to W.I.: "*Vous etes Anglais, Monsieur?*" "*Oui, Madame.*" "Ha, ha—God damn," said [s]he.[206] Great shortness of breath after his return from camp meeting.

Monday, September 5. . . . Return to Sunnyside before 2. W.I. pleasant at dinner, sleeps heavily in his chair in the evening, and awakes about 10 with shortness of breath and great nervousness. . . . Learn that a Mr. R. S. Oakley and Mr. Forrest came up the day we left; also Leslie[207] and wife and child in our absence.

[September 6]

Wednesday, September 7. . . . I go to the city and return to Mr. *Hugh Erwin* the number of *Harper's Monthly* which he had left, containing the article about W.I.[208] Brought up in the 1/4 to 2 train Goodrich's *Recollections,* &c.,[209] [blank space] third and fourth volumes of

[204] Gabriel Requa (1760-1809), one of a family of Huguenot origin which settled in Tarrytown (Scharf, *Westchester County*, I, 443). See also *The Old Dutch Burying Ground of Sleepy Hollow* (Boston, 1953), p. 16.

[205] WI was introduced by John Howard Payne to Francois Joseph Talma (1763-1826), the French tragedian, in April 1821 (Luquer, "Correspondence of WI and John Howard Payne," p. 467). He saw Talma often at Paris in 1823, and on November 28, 1823, he recorded a long conversation with the actor; see *Journals* (Reichart), pp. 247-48. WI's "Conversations with Talma" was published in *The Knickerbocker Gallery* (New York, 1855), pp. 15-22.

[206] This was in 1805. See *Life*, I, 69.

[207] Pierre Leslie Irving, PMI's former assistant.

[208] Probably Richards, "SS, the Home of WI."

[209] Samuel Griswold Goodrich, *Recollections of a Lifetime, or Men and Things I Have Seen . . .* , 2 vols. (New York, 1856).

Knight's *Half Hours with the Best Authors,*[210] and the last *Eclectic,* several numbers of *All the Year Round,* and four last numbers of *Littell's Living Age.*

Thursday, September 8. Wedding of Theodore's Leazie to Rev. Mr. Reese;[211] Kate, Sarah, and Mary go down. W.I. has had a good night and is much better this morning. I walk to the station and bring back the *Herald.* Finding him reading with great pleasure Milburn's *Ten Years* [blank space],[212] which had been sent to him before. Read some negro anecdotes to me with which he had been amused or touched; his eyes filled as he read one of them. Milburn had visited the cottage and they had had a talk about Burr. Wanted letters of introduction to persons in Europe, but W.I. knew of none [to] whom he felt authorized to give letters. Told anecdote of Thomas Winton sending some work about *Fox* to Murray, and demanding a thousand guineas. Murray wrote a letter declining, then going out meets acquaintance. "Only think—here's a Thomas Winton offering me his work and demanding 1000 guineas. Now who the devil is Thomas Winton?" "Thomas Winton? Why, he's the Bishop of Winchester."[213] "My God! You don't say so!" Then hurries back to the shop: "Have you sent that letter?" "No." Sits down, and writes an acceptance—greatest pleasure, &c.[214] An instance of Murray's subserviency to the aristocacy.

First met Eugenie Montijo at Granada. Her father then Count of Teba—afterward, by the death of his elder brother, Count Montijo.[215]

Friday, September 9. Went to the city with W.I. to see about exchange of wagon, the one purchased for $225 proving too small.[216] Selected

[210] Charles Knight, ed., *Half-Hours with the Best Authors...* , 4 vols. (London, 1847-1848).

[211] The Reverend Theodore Irving officiated at the wedding of his second daughter, Elizabeth, to the Reverend George B. Reese, his assistant at St. Andrew's Church, Staten Island, where the ceremony was held. The Reverend Pierre Paris Irving gave the bride away. "Among the relatives and friends, the Hon. Washington Irving was prevented from being present, being detailed by illness at his residence at 'Sunnyside'" (*Tribune,* September 10, p. 7, col. 2).

[212] The Reverend William Henry Milburn, *Ten Years of Preacher Life...* (New York, 1859). In the fall of 1859, Milburn (1823-1890), who was blind, was lecturing in New York on the topic: "What a Blind Man Saw in England." He was advertised in the newspapers as "The Poor Blind Boy of the Prairies" (*Tribune,* September 15, p. 1, col. 2).

[213] Thomas Winton was the episcopal name of George Tomline (1750-1827), Bishop of Winchester from 1820 to his death.

[214] Murray published Tomline's work, *Memoirs of the Life of the Right Hon. William Pitt,* in two volumes in 1821. The *Memoirs* described the life of Pitt to 1793, severely attacking Charles James Fox along the way.

[215] WI met the Count de Teba near Granada on March 27, 1828, and found him "a most agreeable man. Sadly cut up in the wars—lost one eye—maimed of a leg—a hand wounded by bursting of a gun" (*Journal of WI, 1828...* , ed. Stanley T. Williams [New York, 1937], p. 27). Years later he recalled that he also met the Count's little daughter, Eugenie Montijo; see *LLWI,* IV, 133-34). In 1853 Eugenie Montijo married Napoleon III of France, and in 1859, while Napoleon III was taking part in the war in Italy, she was proclaimed Regent of France.

[216] On August 11 Kate, Sarah, and PMI had inspected a "light waggon" at J. M. Quinby & Co., a carriage dealer at 620 Broadway, New York.

one at Quinby's for $275. After leaving Quinby's went to Astor Library to see the new division just opened (containing American and European History and General Literature),[217] and thence he went to Jack Downing's (Charles Augustus Davis'), who drove him afterwards to the station at Chamber Street for the 3:20 train. Spent two or three hours with Davis. Has been much better since his return from Orange County—good nights.

Saturday, September 10. . . . (Yesterday morning: "Did not wish to see new faces and did not care to have new faces see him—of old could not see too much." Gouverneur Kemble had called when he was in town.) Helen, I, and Sarah went in the evening to the Hamiltons'; met there Sam B. Ruggles, George Sumner, and Mrs. Carson, of Charleston, daughter of Mr. [Pettigrew?] and sister-in-law of Mrs. Brevoort. Charades; W.I. at home playing backgammon with Kate.

Sunday, September 11. . . . About 5 in the afternoon Mr. George Sumner, a guest of the Hamiltons, calls over and remains to tea. W.I. scarcely able to hold any conversation; Helen and I do the talking. Mr. Sumner had been at Madrid with W.I.; reminded him of a remark of his then that the best things of an author were spontaneous, the first pressure of the grape, the squeezings after not so rich. W.I. said of Lamartine: "Had he been Lamartine he never would have given such a savage picture of the French, his own nation; and had he done so, he would have killed himself"[218]—or something to that effect. He left about 9, Helen and I walking to the head of the lane with him. . . .

[September 12]

Tuesday, September 13. Had a better night. Drove out with Helen in the new carriage. After dinner took up a volume of Percival's *Poems* which I had just bought, and read aloud, "She has no heart," &c.[219] "That's very beautiful," said he, "flows so easily and naturally; there's no hammer in that." Speaking of Leigh Hunt, whose death was

[217] During August 1859, the Astor Library was closed for alterations. Joseph Green Cogswell and four assistants dusted and re-arranged 100,000 volumes in the Library's collection, moving many into a newly-completed wing, a duplicate of the original building. The library was re-opened on August 31, with the collections for "history and belles-lettres" in the north wing and "science and the arts" in the south (*Tribune,* August 31, p. 7, col. 2; *Times,* August 31, p. 4, col. 4).

[218] Alphonse de Lamartine (1790-1869), French man of letters and politician. In 1842 WI had expressed an unfavourable view of Lamartine as a travel writer; see *Journals,* III, 214. Lamartine wrote no volumes of explicit social criticism, but WI may have been referring to his autobiographical works, *Les Confidences* (1849) and *Nouvelles Confidences* (1851), written in the aftermath of his disappointment in the French Revolution of 1848.

[219] The poem begins:
"She has no heart, but she is fair,—
    The rose, the lily can't outvie her;
She smiles so sweetly, that the air
    Seems full of light and beauty nigh her."
(Percival, *Poetical Works,* I, 200-01).

mentioned in today's paper:[220] "Never met him, and never liked him. A dash of vulgar flippancy about his writings; belonged to a Cockney clique for whom he had no relish (Hazlitt among them—a low fellow); their vulgar junkettings for which Mrs. Holloway had to pay."[221] Played whist at night.

[September 14, 15]

Friday, September 16. . . . Whist in the evening. Had two packs—thick and thin. "These cards are so thick I cannot get along with them." "But Uncle, those you have are the *thin* ones." "Well, then, it is because they are *not thick*," &c. A burst of laughter. Retires at 11, and has a good night.

Saturday, September 17. A rainy day. The Quarto *Washington* and the Sunnyside edition of twenty-one volumes[222] sent up yesterday by Putnam, and opened by me this morning. Margaret and Catharine[223] leave in the 11 o'clock train—in tears. W.I. finishes *Quits*, a novel by the authoress of *The Initials*:[224] "very much pleased with it." Has now *Cecil, or the Adventures of a Coxcomb*,[225] borrowed by me from Irving Paris. Wants works of a continuous interest in his present condition. Whist in the evening.

[September 18, 19]

Tuesday, September 20. . . . Retiring from the dinner table before the rest, his new shawl thrown over his shoulders drags behind him. "I look," says he, "I look like a bird of paradise with my long tail"—the first expression of playfulness during the day. Dozes during the evening, retires at 11. . . .

Wednesday, September 21. . . . Dr. Peters comes up with me in 3:20 train. Dinner, as yesterday, after his arrival. Dr. Peters at dinner tells an anecdote of a drunkard's applying to him for *six pence*—knowing he was drunk. Apropos to which W.I. tells anecdote of his walking the streets of London, smiling at the recollection of some joke of his about [Gill's?] applying for a long extension—18 months or so—for payment

---

[220] Leigh Hunt (b. 1784) died at London on August 28, 1859.

[221] WI saw Hazlitt (1778-1834) many times during his years in London and was not always so critical of the essayist; see Luquer, "Correspondence of John Howard Payne," p. 466. He did think Hazlitt "low," however; see *Journals* (Reichart), p. 252. Hazlitt published a slighting notice of WI in *The Spirit of the Age* (London, 1825), pp. 409-10, 420-22, misspelling his surname as "Irvine."

[222] The Sunnyside Edition was first advertised for sale on August 30 (*Tribune*, p. 1, col. 2).

[223] Housekeepers.

[224] Mrs. E. D. E. N. Southworth, *The Initials: A Love Story* (Philadelphia, 1856). I have been unable to identify *Quits* as a work of Mrs. Southworth or to find a copy. Her best-known work, *The Hidden Hand*, was being serialized in the New York *Ledger* in 1859.

[225] Mrs. Catharine Grace Frances (Moody) Gore, *Cecil . . .* (London, 1841).

of his notes ("Well, I've heard of men asking for time; but [Gill?] asks for eternity"), when he is accosted by a woman: "Ah, God bless your merry face; surely you're not the man that will refuse a poor woman a *six pence*." He put his hand in his pocket and gave her—the smallest he had—a *Six* [?   ], guinea. "So much had I to pay," said he, "for laughing at my own joke—and it served me right."...

Thursday, September 22.... At dinner could not repress a slight facetiousness: "The people up here so busy in making a fortune or preparing to break that they had no time to give to the care of the roads"; highways and encroachments on [them] had been the subject of conversation....

[September 23]

Saturday, September 24.... I brought up *Bohn's Hand-book of Games*[226] for the whist, &c. W.I. did not play, but watched us that he might amuse himself by looking on. Soon, however, became very drowsy. Retired at 1/2 past 10. At dinner no appetite; conversation turned upon Dr. Parmly doing nothing, &c. for Rossiter and his children.[227] "Well, I don't know him but I take the liberty of despising him."

[September 25, 26, 27]

Wednesday, September 28. The Doctor was with him at 1 and then again from 3 to 4 during the night, as he was very nervous. Helen went in to the Doctor who slept in the porch room to rouse him. Was tormented with an idea that he had a big book to write (so the Doctor said) before he could sleep. Drove out in the morning with Helen and Julia. After his return a call from Mrs. Richard Dodge,[228] nurse and baby, and Miss Williams, daughter of John Williams. Great demonstrations about the baby. Uncle came in the room, but looked quite nervous and left to lie down upstairs. Then a call from Mr. Harrod (father of Mrs. Bartlett), a Dr. R----, wife and daughter. Mr. Harrod had brought a letter from the venerable Dr. Nichols (of Portland) who died last January at 76, thanking him for an autograph of W.I. which he had sent him in the September previous, and as he seem[ed] very desirous to show it to Mr. I., I copied it, with the assurance that Dr.

---

[226] *The Hand-book of Games*, ed. H. G. Bohn (London, 1850).

[227] Eleazer Parmly (1797-1874), a prominent New York dentist, was the father-in-law of Thomas P. Rossiter, the artist. On September 24 the *Tribune* reported (p. 11, col. 2): "Mr. Rossiter has a collection of his pictures at his gallery, No. 17 West 38th-St., which will be thrown open to the public, gratuitously, on Friday of each week...." Dr. Parmly's niggardliness may have been in refusing to hire a hall for Rossiter's exhibit. It was customary for artists of note, as Rossiter was, to rent rooms for their showings and to defray at least some of the expense by collecting a 25¢ admission fee.

[228] Richard Irving Dodge, nephew of Helen Irving, was married on April 3, 1858, to Julia Paulding, the only daughter of Frederick Paulding (1810-1859). They were married at Christ Church, Tarrytown. Ebenezer Irving to Katrina Irving, SS, March 4, 1858 (SHR).

Nichols never said what he did not think. It was as follows: "Accept my thanks for the autograph you have sent me of the American Addison, who in delicacy and exquisiteness of wit and humor equals his illustrious original, while in force and compass he is so much his superior." W.I. pronounced it a very flattering opinion. I assured him it was very sincere, told him who Dr. Nichols was as well as I knew, &c. Visitors abounded today—eighteen or nineteen, Sarah said. W.I. denied to all, but once or twice he was caught in the parlor and excused himself and left. Dr. Peters came up in the 7 o'clock train.

Thursday, September 29. . . . I had tried in vain to find a book at the library. Must try again today, though in his present state it is hard for him to find entertainment in anything, and to get a book of the right sort and [in] large enough type for easy reading is equally hard. I fear the deplorable nervous distress of which he was so long the victim a few months back is re-establishing itself, while he has not the strength he then had to contend with it—for he is much weaker than he was. . . .

[September 30]

Saturday, October 1. Has had a comfortable night, and has an appetite for his breakfast. (Helen and I, Sanders and Julia go to the city, they to visit Pierre P. Irving and Theodore and return to the cottage on Tuesday.) On our return at 1/2 past 7 find Doctor there, who had come up in the 3:20 train and was about returning. Uncle had been much better during the day, and the moment we entered began to tell us of his having walked across the bridge to Mr. Grinnell's road and so along that to the lane and down home with a firm, brisk, erect tread without fatigue or the least oppression of breath. *Seems to have got rid of the asthma.*

Sunday, October 2. Has had a tolerable night, though not his quantum of sleep. Showed him a letter of father to his mother written at Caughnawaga in October 1787, when he was just twenty-one, giving pictures of his life on the Mohawk. Quite amused with it; then launched into eulogium of his brother William: "Ah, how I did love that man!" and the tears started to his eyes. "There was a natural richness of mind about him that made him the most delightful of companions. How I used to delight to set him going with his world of anecdote. I knew just what key to touch." Then went on to recount some of his anecdotes, "William Welsh," &c. Then reverted to their sports at home, a little busy world of their own in which they mimicked the big world without—the siege of Valenciennes.[229] Had to make their own toys, coin their own amusements, playthings—made them probably more inventive; now everything came to hand. Spoke of old Dr. Rodgers,[230]

[229] In July 1793, after being bombarded by the allied forces of Austria and England, the French garrison at Valenciennes, a town in northern France, surrendered and ended the siege.

[230] The Reverend John Rodgers (1727-1811) was the pastor of the church attended by WI's father. He was a leader of American Presbyterianism, the first Moderator of the

"with his buzz-wig, silver mounted cane, well-polished shoes, and silver shoebuckles." . . .

[October 3, 4]

Wednesday, October 5. Had a comfortable night—coughed a little about 3 o'clock. Told anecdote of his feeding sparrows at Madrid; of an old crow coming at the time and seizing the crumbs; of his tying a big piece of crust to a string as a bait; of his coming next day, seizing it and flying off in triumph, when suddenly—jerk—he is brought up by the string and tumbled over (the conversation had been on sparrows and rooks).[231] Is reading *Walter Thornley, or a Peep at the Past,* by Mrs. Sedgwick,[232] lent him by the Hamiltons. Some good picturing in it [of] the river, he says, but an absurd story. Took a drive in the valley of the Neperan[233] with Julia Sanders and Sarah. Asked him at dinner if he returned by the blacksmith's. "No, that road was not fit to travel; took great pains in having it laid out, but the neighborhood had done nothing to keep it in repair—the men all so busy going to the city to make fortunes or get ruined that they cared nothing to keep the beautiful drives that were opened to them." After dinner Sanders asked him why it was in these misty mornings that, when the mist cleared off, a film was left on top of the grass like cobweb. "It must be the spiders putting out their clothes to bleach," was the whimsical reply. Has been uncommonly well today. Speaking of Leatherstocking: "No one would care to meddle with that class of character after Cooper. He has made it so completely his own."[234] W.I. played one game of whist in the evening. The Doctor came up and spent the night.

Thursday, October 6. Had a good night. Seems much better. Has taken no opium for two or three days.[235] Julia and Sanders went to the city to return Saturday afternoon. Received in the evening a telegraphic dispatch from Charlotte at Cayuga Bridge,[236] saying she would be at the Astor House next morning.

Friday, October 7. . . . At dinner in the afternoon got speaking of Cooper (started by an article on Cooper written by Tuckerman in the

Presbyterian General Assembly (1789), and an active preacher in New York from 1765 to 1810.

[231] The characteristics of rooks and their "cousins-german," crows, form part of the subject-matter of "The Rookery" in WI's *Bracebridge Hall.*

[232] Mrs. Susan Anne Livingstone (Ridley) Sedgwick, *Walter Thornley* . . . (New York, 1859). The setting of the novel was Massachusetts in 1780.

[233] A small river in the vicinity of SS, running southward.

[234] For a similar testimonial to Cooper's making the subject-matter of the Leatherstocking Tales "his own," written immediately after Cooper's death in 1851, see *Life,* II, 392, note 80.

[235] Peters had begun administering opium in small doses to WI on his visit to SS of September 30.

[236] Cayuga Bridge was at the northern tip of Cayuga Lake, a few miles north of Charlotte's home in Levanna, New York.

October number of the *North American*).[237] Thought it a very fair, discriminating article. Tuckerman a good critic—admirable, a magnanimity, gentlemanlike. Thought Cooper's Leatherstocking Tales, &c. would never be meddled with—a creation. "In life they judge a writer by his last production, after death by what he has done best. Look at Shakespeare. You do not think of [blank space] but of *Macbeth*, &c. So it will be with Cooper. His Leatherstocking; his Mabel[238] a beautiful character. He has done what cannot be taken from. His delineation of those scenes, and that class of character," &c.

Of the *Century*:[239] no attraction to him, no life or vivacity; wearied of its "eternal good sense"; got all the news in the daily papers, no interest therefore on that score. . . .

[October 8, 9]

Monday, October 10. Did not sleep much after 2 o'clock. Drives up to Tarrytown to see Julia and Sanders start for Canandigua. I walk to the station with Sanders, and remain with him and Julia until the train arrives at 12:16, the others—Uncle, Helen, and Sarah—returning before. The Doctor comes up to see Mrs. Holdrege ill of dysentery, and stops in at dinner to get an account of Uncle. Whist in the evening —Kate, Uncle, Helen, I. W.I. in the course of the game: "I do not like to be guilty of pretension, but I must say I'm the very worst player that ever was. I think if I had Mrs. Sidesbottom[240] here, I'd almost borrow her spectacles." Retires very much at a loss for something to read. He is hard to suit just now, and many books that I bring from the library go back unread.

[October 11]

Wednesday, October 12. A so-so night. I go to town and return to dinner. Has had a very good day and seems quite like himself. Give him an account of amount of sales under the last agreement with Putnam of April, 1858: from May 1, 1858 to October 10, 1859, about $48,000 exclusive of Evans' account, &c. Seemed surprised at the amount. Told me he had received a note from Mr. Balch, enclosing a circular against Bishop Onderdonk's restoration just now agitated.[241]

---

237 "James Fenimore Cooper," *North American Review*, 89 (October 1859), 289-316. The article was prompted by the re-issue of six of Cooper's novels by W. A. Townsend & Co., New York, with illustrations by F. O. C. Darley.

238 Mabel Dunham, the heroine of Cooper's *The Pathfinder* (1840).

239 A New York weekly which began publication on December 25, 1858, and ceased publication on March 13, 1860.

240 Mrs. Sidesbottom "was an inveterate card player of Liverpool, whose partner at whist he once was, and who pettishly offered to lend him her spectacles when he mistook the card" (*LLWI*, IV, 313-14).

241 The circular was sent by L. P. W. Balch, a layman active in the Protestant Episcopal Church of New York. Benjamin Tredwell Onderdonk (1791-1861), Protestant Episcopal Bishop of New York, was elevated to the episcopacy in 1830. He was a successful leader until 1844, when he was impeached and brought to ecclesiastical trial. The charges of "immorality and impurity" brought against him were somewhat vague,

A Private Journal, 1859 / 233

Thought it very much to be deplored that the subject had been agitated, but would not meddle with it. Whist in the evening—Helen and I, Uncle and Kate. Goes to bed in good spirits and rejoiced he has *Doctor Thorne*[242] to read; has got quite interested in its pictures, &c.

[October 13]

Friday, October 14. Helen and I return unexpectedly this afternoon. W.I. looking well. Showed me a letter from Mrs. E. J. Ellet,[243] dated 13th, stating that "Mrs. Chase, the lady who saved Tampico in the late Mexican War,[244] is very desirous of paying her respects to you during her brief visit to the United States, and begs me to ask if you will receive a call from her, and on what day next week. x x x [punctuation Pierre's] She speaks Spanish perfectly and is anxious to converse with you about some of her Spanish acquaintances whom you probably know. If you will be so kind as to appoint a day, she will go to Irvington and call upon you. I hope your health will permit of your receiving a visit. Perhaps one of your household will be so kind as to answer this letter at your earliest convenience, addressing Mrs. Ellet, care of William M. Lummis, New York." No whist tonight.

[October 15, 16, 17, 18, 19]

Thursday, October 20. Uncle had no sleep, having taken cold from his Monday trip, but was quiet during the night and free from nervousness. Kate and Charlotte came down to Edgar's (to remain a few days and then go to Staten Island) and bring this report. I return in the afternoon, leaving Helen at Eliza's to come up next day. Uncle very glad to see me; says he is better and stronger, notwithstanding his cold. . . .

but Philip Hone specified them in his diary as habitual intemperance, "lightness of deportment," and overzealous "laying on of hands" among the ladies under his spiritual care (Allan Nevins, ed., *The Diary of Philip Hone, 1828-1851* [New York, 1936], p. 723). In judicial proceedings which were much criticized, Onderdonk was suspended indefinitely from his duties. His conduct during the suspension was unexceptionable, and in 1859 a resolution was offered to the New York diocesan convention requesting the House of Bishops to terminate his sentence. Many esteemed men spoke in favour of the resolution, and it was passed (*Tribune*, September 30, p. 4, col. 3; p. 7, cols. 1-2; p. 8, cols. 1-2; October 1, p. 5, cols. 4-5; p. 6, cols. 5-6). The case was not yet closed, however, for the General Convention of the church, meeting in Richmond, failed to act on the resolution from the diocese of New York. Onderdonk was never reinstated; he died before the next General Convention was convened. See William Perry, *The History of the American Episcopal Church, 1587-1883* (Boston, 1885), II, 279-80.

[242] A novel by Anthony Trollope, published in 1858.

[243] Mrs. Elizabeth Ellet (1818-1877), prolific authoress and former enemy of Edgar Allan Poe. She was the sister of William M. Lummis, at whose home she had been living since the death of her husband in January 1859. Her chief literary production of that year was *Women Artists in All Ages and Countries*, which was published in November.

[244] This was Mrs. Franklin Chase, wife of the United States Consul at Tampico in 1846. Mrs. Ellet's claim that Mrs. Chase had "saved Tampico" was a gross exaggeration; see Justin H. Smith, *The War with Mexico* (New York, 1919), I, 276-81.

Friday, October 21. A very good night; troubled a little with cough in the morning before rising, cold better. After breakfast showed me in the *Home Journal* of October 22 he had been reading "Gelyna, a Tale of Albany and Ticonderoga Seventy Years Ago," published in the *Talisman* and written by Gulian C. Verplanck.[245] Afterwards got speaking of Verplanck: "Just, upright, honorable; never allowed his prejudices or antipathies to sway his judgment of men or things; but without manner, uncouth from a boy; without fluency—abrupt, cold, not companionable. 'Too much of a frog, Sir, too much of a frog,' as Ogilvie,[246] the orator, said of him." (The quotation in the piece about Albany—Sturgeon—claimed by F.H. *his*, written for the *Chronicle*.)[247] Knew Verplanck before he went to Europe slightly.[248]

[October 22, 23, 24]

Tuesday, October 25.... Whist in the evening. On retiring I said to him playfully: "Well, Uncle, you must not keep awake tonight to take your medicine"—intending a sportive allusion to his struggle of the night previous to keep awake to take a pill at 1/4 to 11, and thus breaking his rest for the night.[249] A sudden reply: "Wherefore I retire with my unimportant feelings...."[250]

Wednesday, October 26. Grinnells and Irving Van Wart return from Europe. I remain in town in consequence overnight. Next day (27th)

---

[245] "Gelyna" first appeared in *The Talisman* for *MDCCCXXX* (New York, [1830]), pp. 302-35. This volume was published under the pseudonym "Francis Herbert." Verplanck (1786-1870), a New York lawyer, politician, and author, wrote about one-half of its miscellaneous contents. See Robert W. July, *The Essential New Yorker: Gulian Crommelin Verplanck* (Durham, N.C., 1951), pp. 105-19.

[246] James Ogilvie; see footnote 135. WI had met Ogilvie in the United States and saw him again at London in 1817. In "James Ogilvie and WI," *Americana*, 35 (July 1941), 435-58, Richard B. Davis expresses the belief that the character of Glencoe in WI's "Mountjoy," published in the *Knickerbocker*, 14 (November and December 1839), 402-12, 522-38, was a sympathetic portrayal of Ogilvie. See also *LLWI*, IV, 188-89.

[247] In "Gelyna" the pseudonymous author "Francis Herbert" begins his narrative by debunking certain erroneous legends current, "even among the fashionable classes," concerning Albany. He continues: "Another set of good folks, especially in New-York and Philadelphia, have no notions about it, but those derived from the old traditionary jokes upon its ancient Schepens and Schoutens, its burly Burgomasters, its seventeen-petticoated beauties, 'its lofty spires glittering with tin, and its hospitable boards smoking with sturgeon.'*" In a note to the starred passage, "Francis Herbert" adds: "I quote from an anonymous jeu d'esprit of my own, written when I was very young. It had great currency in its day, but now sleeps undisturbed, as it deserves to do..." (*The Talisman*, p. 302). For an account of WI's contributions to the New York *Morning Chronicle*, and the reprinted articles themselves, see Wayne R. Kime, "An Actor Among the Albanians: Two Rediscovered Sketches of Albany by Washington Irving in 1803," *New York History*, 56 (October 1975), 409-25.

[248] Verplanck had contributed to the *Analectic Magazine* during WI's editorship in 1813-1814; see *LLWI*, I, 299. He visited London in 1817, and WI acted as his unofficial guide (July, *Essential New Yorker*, p. 53).

[249] WI had had no sleep whatever the night before.

[250] The preceding passage, beginning "On retiring...," is carefully deleted in the journal.

return in the afternoon with Irving Grinnell, and Irving Van Wart comes up in the evening. Find Uncle had had no return of fever and was doing well. A little inclined to be nervous on retiring at night (27th). A bed made for Irving Van Wart in library; Irving Grinnell slept in porch room.

Friday, October 28. A very good night. Sarah, Kate, and I went to town and returned in the 3:20 train. Julia Grinnell (daughter) came up in the same train and spent the evening at the cottage. William Grinnell arrived from Ingleside at 9 in the evening, to return with Charlotte on Monday.

Saturday, October 29. W.I. troubled considerably with cough. Not much appetite for breakfast. Whist in the evening. Laurence and Frederick Grinnell call.

Sunday, October 30. A good night. A cold, sombre day. Confirmation at church; does not go. After church a call from Mrs. Stanard,[251] Mary and Angelica Hamilton. They announce Mr. Kennedy's intention to call tomorrow at 12 on his way down from Idlewild.[252] Visit of the Gardener's children in the afternoon to see Charlotte. Laurence and Frederick Grinnell call in the evening.

Monday, October 31. Mr. Kennedy and N. P. Willis and Mr. Wise, author of *Los Gringos,*[253] call on W.I. between 2 and 3. Had taken the cars from Idlewild to Sing Sing and thence by carriage to Sunnyside. W.I. had given up expectation of seeing Mr. Kennedy and was out driving when he arrived. Got up a hasty lunch for them. Kennedy took the 4 o'clock train to New York, and Willis and Wise returned to Idlewild on the up train soon after. I met Willis at the station as I was alighting from the 3:20 train with Helen, who returned to Sunnyside after a week's absence in attendance on Eliza.[254] Whist in the evening.

[November 1, 2]

Thursday, November 3, to Tuesday, November 8. I went to the city and staid at the Oriental until Tuesday, November 8, when I returned. Uncle better, though somewhat troubled with his cough. Had been in the city once in my absence; called at my office and found it locked —the last time he visited New York. It was Saturday, November 5; lunched at Charles A. Davis's.

---

[251] Mrs. Robert C. Stanard, whose home in Richmond, Virginia, was the resort of many visiting dignitaries.

[252] The home of N. P. Willis.

[253] Kennedy and Willis both left records of this visit; see above, pp. 162, 179. Their companion was Henry Augustus Wise (1819-1868), whose *Los Gringos*, an account of experiences in the war with Mexico, had been published in 1849.

[254] Eliza Irving was taken ill with dysentery on October 24, and Helen had been with her since.

Wednesday, November 9. Went to town, and on returning in the evening Helen called my attention to the following slip from the *Tribune* of the day:

> —The Paris correspondent of *The Times* writes, Oct. 28: "Hume, the well-known American rapping medium, has just passed through Paris with his wife on his way to America. He not only has not lost his power of evoking spirits, but has acquired new and more terrible power. Instead of confining his miracles to conversation and communion between the living and the dead, he now places living but widely separated friends in connection, and enables them to hold converse together.[255]

Lossing[256] called today.

Thursday, November 10. The conversation turned on some personal experiences with Hume in the evening. W.I. alluded to the new power—communion with the living—and I cited Judge Edmonds' explanation of it in his "Intercourse with the Spirits of the Living."[257] W.I. fell asleep. His cough not so troublesome as the night before. Is evidently stronger than he was.

[November 11, 12]

Monday, November 14. Going to town for a few days with Helen. The wedding of Susan Minturn tomorrow.[258]

Returned Wednesday, November 16. Found W.I. had been suffering from a renewal of his asthma. A Mrs. Storms called just at twilight to pester him for an autograph in her book; he asleep. Kate tried to fight her off with offer of a loose one, but she was pertinacious, and Kate had to seize a moment of partial wakefulness to get him to write one. She did not, however, see W.I. Showed me a letter from [blank space] containing an application for a subscription to the Plymouth monument.[259] Would not answer it—"self-worshippers."

[255] *Times* [not *Tribune*], p. 2, col. 5. Daniel Dunglas Hume (1833-1886) was on a European tour in 1859, and the New York newspapers reported his progress faithfully.

[256] Benson J. Lossing (1813-1891), the prolific author, sketcher, editor, and wood-engraver. In his *The Hudson, from the Wilderness to the Sea*, Lossing described a visit to SS in 1850 (pp. 341-43), the visit of November 9, 1859 (pp. 343-45), and a third visit in 1860 (pp. 345-49).

[257] John Worth Edmonds (1799-1874), a New York lawyer, published in 1853 a work, *Spiritualism*, which went through nine editions in two years. Although his views damaged his legal career, he maintained them with courage and persistence. See Vivian C. Hopkins, "The Spirits and the Honorable John Worth Edmonds," *Bulletin of the New York Public Library*, 62 (October 1959), 479-506. In 1859 he addressed a series of ten letters on various aspects of spiritualism (*e.g.*, "Healing Mediums," "Speaking in Many Tongues") to the New York *Tribune*. I have found no record of a work by Edmonds having the title quoted by PMI.

[258] Susan Minturn, daughter of Robert Bowne Minturn (1805-1866), Moses H. Grinnells' business partner and a resident of Irvington, married Thomas Baring on November 15. WI had paid a visit to the Minturns on June 18.

[259] On July 21, the *Tribune* announced the plans of the people of Plymouth, Massachusetts, for a "grand celebration" on August 2, "at the laying of the corner-stone of the National Monument to the Forefathers" (p. 6, col. 6). On July 27 the *Tribune* published a rather wry editorial on the forthcoming celebration, noticing that three commemorative monuments had already been placed "on, or, rather, near that rock which

Brought up *Leaves from an Actor's Notebook,* by Vandenhoff, which he thought might be amusing. Bewildered between Vandenhoff father and Vandenhoff son at night in his dreams.[260]

Thursday, November 17. Called to see Dr. Peters for prescription for his asthma, which was distressing him for the last few days. Helen spoke of our taking rooms in the city which we were anxious to do. Would not entertain the idea at present; mentioned it in presence of the girls. His bad whist playing: "A bad hand yourself, your partner comes to your relief 'with a wet sail.'"

Friday, November 18. Ebenezer Irving went down; freight train off the track; W.I.'s worry about his going down. Brought up *Ellen Middleton;*[261] looked at it, found it very painful, did not want to read it. Next day brought up *Deerslayer,* which he had never read.

Sunday, November 20. At breakfast Helen mentioned dream of seeing a spirit—the nightmare consequent therefrom, her dread. I mentioned if *I* had seen a spirit I would have questioned it. She did not want to have anything to do with spirits in this life, and appealed to W.I., who thought we were better adapted for communion in the flesh. I then said to her in an undertone, so that W.I. (who is now a little hard of hearing) might not know, "He forgets his 'St Mark's Eve.'"[262] He asked what was said. I told him. He then related anecdote of Hall and himself, and their compact.[263] The conversation then turned on spiritualism, Helen speaking rather contemptuously of it and asserting the spirits only told you what you knew already, &c. I asserted that it was an interesting subject for inquiry; the mass of educated minds were sceptical on the subject of a future life; that even Paley in his *Evidence*[s] said he never met a person who thought there was too much evidence of a future life, &c.[264] What evidence–[265]

Wednesday, November 23. Returned from the Clarendon Hotel, where we had spent the two last days. Found W.I. had been tolerable during our absence. The asthma still troublesome. Whist in the evening. Mr. Grinnell came in from the Holdrege's. Dix[266] called on Tuesday, [November] 22.

an envious foreigner who had no Pilgrims among his Ancestors called the 'Blarney-stone of New England'" (p. 4, cols. 2-3).

[260] John M. Vandenhoff (1790-1861) and his son George Vandenhoff (1820-1884), the author of *Leaves from an Actor's Note-Book . . .* (New York, 1860 [1859]), were both actors.

[261] Lady Georgina Charlotte Fullerton, *Ellen Middleton: A Tale* (New York, 1854).

[262] A sketch recounting superstitions and tales of departed spirits, published in *Bracebridge Hall.*

[263] See above, p. 166.

[264] "I deem it unnecessary to prove that mankind stood in need of a revelation, because I have met with no serious person who thinks that, even under the Christian revelation, we have too much light, or any degree of assurance which is superfluous" (*Evidences of Christianity* in *The Works of William Paley, D.D.* [London, 1830], I, 1; see also *Works,* II, 196-204).

[265] The last unpunctuated question is added in pencil to PMI's regular entry in ink.

[266] William G. Dix (d. 1898), minor author. Dix was visiting WI for the first time. He brought a note of introduction from the Reverend James Selden Spencer. Dix recounted

Thursday (Thanksgiving), November 24. Edgar and Irving Paris come up. Uncle finishes *The Deerslayer*; character of Natty Bumppo (Deerslayer) rather overwritten; some interest in the story, but an immense deal of twaddle in the conversations—long, droning, &c. Governor Morgan[267] called to pay his respects. Edgar visited *cemetery*, mistaken after for W.I., who had not visited it in more than a year. . . .

Sunday, November 27. Went to church. Asthma apparently abating. In the evening "we ought to contrive some religious game" to keep him awake. Sunday evening before he had remarked, "I must get a dispensation from Dr. Creighton to allow me to play whist on Sunday evening." Had had recourse to this two months or more to keep awake. "Now, Uncle," said Helen, "we are not going to let you go to sleep"; and she and I both tasked our powers of conversation (she especially) to keep him awake. He kept up till 9 when sleep overtook him—though he still tried to struggle against it.

Monday, November 28. I, Kate, and Sarah went to town in the 8:39 train, leaving Helen and Mary with Uncle. Helen remarked that he appeared rather more depressed. Walked out to the brook lot about 11, but returned with shortness of breath. Mrs. Hoge and Irving Van Wart (who had come up to her house on Saturday to spend a few days) called. W.I. has a playful conversation with her; his remarks when she told him not to rise on her leaving, about her father Dr. Heren[268] having some good jokes to swallow. Did not drive out, as he feared it might produce difficulty of breathing. On coming up in the 3:20 train, had been admiring the brilliant sunset in the cars. On returning found them just finishing dinner with Rev. Pierre P. Irving there. Asked W.I. if he had noticed the brilliant sunset. "Yes," had been admiring it from his seat at the table which looked south upon the brilliant bank of clouds lit up, &c. It was the last he was ever to look upon. Had been rather depressed during the day, but could not repress a playful anecdote at dinner. Asked Pierre P. Irving to take wine with him, and as usual filled his wine glass with ale, which he took instead, as usual. "You pledge me in ale," said P.P.I. "That reminds me of a story I have. Old Captain [Roach?]—alluding probably to an anecdote current with my father—to some one who tasted a wine he had been cracking up, and affected to disparage it. After sipping: 'I don't think so much of this wine.' 'Sir, you may be a good judge of small beer, but by God! you're no judge of wine!'" This reminded W.[I.] of another anecdote of the old Captain. "Had a captain of a ship dining with him, and after awhile brought out some crack Madeira that had passed from garret to

the visit in a letter to Spencer which the latter read before a public meeting of the officers of Tarrytown in tribute to WI, December 1, 1859 (New York *Herald*, December 2, p. 5, col. 2).

[267] Edwin D. Morgan (1811-1883), Governor of the State of New York from 1858 to 1862.

[268] The Reverend Francis Herron (1774-1860) was President of the Western Theological Seminary at Allegheny, Pennsylvania.

cellar. 'There, Sir, taste that.' The Captain bolted it without tasting it: 'A very good glass of wine,' said the Captain. 'Sharp,' said the Captain to his black servant whom I recollect, 'bring out a bottle of Teneriffe. There Sir, take that. By God!' [and] tasted the other wine." Told the anecdote with his usual spirit. Between dinner and ten slept; after ten proposed we should take our usual game of whist—"never cared for the game." We played five games—"no player, and only to keep him awake." Anecdote of the lady: "Sir, I'll lend you my spectacles." Did not see the card—had tried to excuse himself. Had been troubled a good deal with difficulty of breathing throughout the day, but not in so severe a form as he had had it. In the evening was cheerful, though still a little troubled with difficulty of breathing. On retiring for the night at 1/2 past 10, Sarah, who always took charge of his medicines, went into his room to arrange them as usual. "I must arrange my pillows for another weary night." He said to her, "I feel so dreadfully depressed" (or downhearted), and then exclaimed, "If this could only end" or "When will this end"—she scarcely recollects which, for almost at the same moment he gave a slight exclamation, as if in pain—placing his hand on his left side—repeated the exclamation and the pressure of the hand, caught at the footboards of the bed, and fell backwards, striking on the hip and falling over on the head. I was in the parlor, heard the sound, and cries of Sarah which immediately followed brought me in an instant to his side. I raised his head in my arms; he was to all appearance unconscious, and he gave but a few slight gasps (or breaths) and expired. Though continued to administer brandy in a spoon, and Kate and Helen to bathe his arms and feet, &c., but it was evident to me it was in vain. We went at once on the alarm for Dr. Carruthers,[269] and when he came—more than an hour—he pronounced life extinct. . . .

Tuesday, November 29. Offers of services, &c. from all quarters. Dr. Peters, Mr. Grinnell, Julia and Irving came up in the noon train. Dr. Peters went into the library, followed by Mr. Grinnell, who called in Irving. His wig off displayed his head, &c. (would not have known him). Just after dinner, when I had had no sleep for hours, and [was] disturbed and distressed by the heavy blow, the reporters of the *Times* and *Tribune* called for particulars, &c.—a sad intrusion which I had to meet (the *Times* [reporter's] name *was* Snow). Then retired, and slept till morning.

Wednesday, November 30. A beautiful bright day yesterday and today; trust it may be so tomorrow for the funeral. He is to be buried tomorrow from Christ Church, Tarrytown, at 1 o'clock; the procession of relatives and pallbearers to leave the house at 12. He had purchased a lot of ground in the new cemetery above the old Dutch Church, to which he had had the remains of his father, mother, his brothers William and Peter removed, &c., and all who were in the vault at New

[269] Dr. Horace Carruthers, a Tarrytown physician.

York.[270] The only wish he had ever expressed in regard to his funeral was to lie by the side [of] his mother. Sanders arrives about 12 from Canandaigua. The *Express* of yesterday evening says: "The death of W.I. is more than a national loss," &c. "The flags upon the City Hall and many public and private buildings and vessels are set at half mast today, in honor of his memory. The mayor has called a special meeting of the Common Council for 3 o'clock on Wednesday afternoon to take appropriate action on the occasion."[271] The *Times* of today says: "Immediately upon receipt of the intelligence at City Hall the flags were displayed at half mast. The Mayor of . . . . The Historical and other Societies of the city will, it is anticipated, hold special meetings and take action in honor of the venerable deceased."[272]

[270] This was in 1853; see *LLWI*, IV, 160-61.

[271] New York *Daily Express*, November 29, p. 1, col. 1.

[272] New York *Times*, November 30, p. 1, col. 3. The *Times* write "venerated," not "venerable."

Part III

The Continuing Collaboration

Chapter Seven

The Genesis of the *Life and Letters*

The news of Irving's death prompted widespread demonstrations of regret in New York, and on November 30 the Hudson River Rail Road announced a special train to carry passengers from the city to the funeral the following day.[1] On December 1, all shops in Tarrytown were closed by 11 A.M., private homes were wreathed in black crepe, and the streets were hung, according to the New York *Herald*, with "festoons of black and white cambric, and occasional mourning rosettes."[2] Carriages and farm wagons from surrounding communities glutted the streets, and by 12:30 P.M., when the train arrived from New York, the assembled crowd already numbered over two thousand.[3] The press of humanity was so great that it prevented

[1] New York *Times,* November 30, 1859, p. 1, col. 3.

[2] New York *Herald,* December 2, 1859, p. 5, col. 3. The *Times* reported: "Every store was as fully closed as on a Sunday, while the white and black drapery of mourning was everywhere displayed. It hung in festoons from nearly every house.... It hung in front of the churches of most denominations. Even the railroad depot had its sign of grief" (December 2, p. 4, col. 6).

[3] New York *Herald,* December 2, 1859, p. 5, col. 3.

several of the Irving family who were on the train from making the three-mile journey from the station to Sunnyside in time to attend the brief private service conducted there prior to the public observances at Christ Church. At the close of the family ceremony, a hearse, followed by carriages containing Irving's immediate relatives and close friends, formed a funeral cortege which, as it passed slowly northward along the post road, was swelled by the carriages of neighbours and other mourners until it became almost a mile long. Schools in the vicinity had been closed for the day, and children stood along the road, dressed in their best clothes, silently watching the procession as it passed. At the church, the majority of the persons gathered for the public service had been obliged to remain outside. Even so, the sanctuary was so densely packed that several ladies fainted from the heat, and fears were expressed that the upper gallery might collapse. After the funeral service, mourners filed past the open coffin for over an hour,[4] and then the long procession re-formed and moved toward Sleepy Hollow Cemetery, where Irving was to be buried. By this time it was growing late in the afternoon; and just as the coffin was being lowered into the grave, the sun set with an especially colourful effect.[5] "Dear, blessed Uncle!" wrote Helen to a niece a few days afterward. "What a beautiful memory he has left behind him; and how kindly every thing seemed ordered to the last. That exquisite day of his funeral—just such an one as he loved on earth. As if winter itself had waited that there might not be a discordant element."[6]

During the next few days lengthy accounts of the funeral, some of them profusely illustrated, were published in the daily and weekly press, and editors hastily assembled a variety of articles to satisfy the demand for details about the late author—accounts of his last moments, reports of recent visitors to Sunnyside, and such old chestnuts as anecdotes of his inability to speak in public or his unwillingness to

[4] The New York *Times* reported that "at the least estimation over five thousand persons" filed past the coffin (December 2, 1859, p. 4, col. 6). John C. Peters estimated the viewing period as "several hours" ("Illnesses," p. 471).

[5] Virtually no one who wrote an account of the funeral failed to associate this sunset with the close of WI's life. Charles A. Davis' notice in the New York *Commercial Advertiser* was typical: "The day too was a truly *Irving day,* such as he has so often sketched and painted—a mild, bland, soft sleepy Autumn day, bright above, and that brightness softened down to earth, through a hazy horizon. It was the first day of Winter, but Autumn seemed to have solicited this *one more day for itself,* and winter yielded it for the sake of Irving, and those who fondly cherished delightful recollections of him. Every feature of the scene breathed in touching harmony with the occasion" (December 2, p. 4, col. 1). On December 19, 1859, Fitz-Greene Halleck wrote to Davis: "It is highly gratifying to know that . . . the perfect sincerity of feeling & of language characterizing your description of the closing scenes at Sunnyside has influenced, in greater or less degree, all similar publications that have, thus far, met my eye, and that your happy expression of a graceful thought, blending, as it does, the summer beauty of the day of burial with the beauty of Irving's character, has already become inseparable from his fame" (NYPL, MS).

[6] Helen Irving to [Catharine Frothingham Dennis], [SS, December 1859] (Virginia).

sit for portraits. George Putnam allowed the New York *Evening Post* to publish excerpts from an essay on Irving in G. W. Greene's *Biographical Studies*, then in press,[7] John C. Peters wrote a narrative of his experiences as Irving's physician,[8] and Charles A. Davis and G. W. Curtis published florid eulogies of his character.[9] Irving's good friends the Reverends John A. Todd, William Creighton, and James Selden Spencer all preached sermons on the occasion of his death, and their respective congregations promptly arranged for publication of the discourses in pamphlet form.[10] Tuckerman indited "Sunnyside," a laudatory poem describing with filial reverence *"His* life, that gladden'd all the land";[11] and a lesser versifier, swept up into this chorus of praise, compared Irving to Homer, Shakespeare, and Milton.[12] Presently the Massachusetts Historical Society convened to hear tributes from Longfellow, Edward Everett, Holmes, Charles Sumner, and Colonel Thomas Aspinwall, Irving's long-suffering former agent in London.[13] Other dignitaries spoke before the New-York Historical Society, and that organization delegated William Cullen Bryant to prepare a discourse on Irving's life and writings for presentation the following April 3.[14]

Within only a few days of Irving's death, the volume of obituary comment and reminiscence had grown so great as to impel two enterprising persons to advertise forthcoming collections of Irving "memorials." James O. Noyes, the editor of the *Knickerbocker Magazine*, was busy arranging such a compilation, but he encountered difficulty tempering the enthusiasm of his contributors. For example, John W. Francis sent him a lengthy reminiscence of Irving as a schoolboy, which, on the plea that his "space [was] small," he returned for

[7] "Irving and his Writings," New York *Evening Post*, November 30, p. 1, col. 2. *Biographical Studies*, published in December, included two essays on WI: "Irving's Works," pp. 155-76, from which the excerpt in the *Evening Post* was taken, and "Irving's Washington," pp. 177-222.

[8] Actually Peters wrote two such accounts, "A Letter from the Physician of WI" and "The Illnesses of WI," the latter of which was an expanded version of the former. "The Illnesses" appeared as an article in the *North American Journal of Homeopathy*, as a pendant to Peters' *A Review . . .* (see p. 173, footnote 1), and as a pamphlet in itself. At its outset Peters wrote that he had prepared it "because I have not only been frequently requested so to do, but it has been hinted to me, almost imperatively, that I ought to satisfy the wishes of his distant admirers in this respect" ("Illnesses," p. 451).

[9] Davis, "WI," New York *Commercial Advertiser*, December 2, 1859, p. 4, col. 1; Curtis, "WI," *Harper's Weekly Magazine*, 3 (December 17, 1859), 803.

[10] Todd, *The Death of WI: A Discourse . . . December 11, 1859* (New York, 1859); Creighton and Spencer, *Sermons on the Occasion of the Death of WI . . .* (New York, 1859).

[11] New York *Evening Post*, December 6, 1859, p. 1, col. 4.

[12] Edward J. O'Reilly, "On WI," in the Peters Scrapbook (NYPL, Berg). The newspaper in which the poem was printed is designated by Peters as the New York *Express*.

[13] *Proceedings of the Massachusetts Historical Society, 1858-1860*, pp. 383-420. A special meeting in tribute to WI was held on December 15, 1859.

[14] See *Irvingiana*, pp. xxix-xxxvi. The speakers were George Bancroft, John W. Francis, Luther Bradish, and Charles King.

condensation. A "few anecdotes" to "make the matter of half a page" would suffice, he pleaded.[15] But while Noyes was assembling testimony for a single article in the *Knickerbocker*, C. B. Richardson, a New York publisher, was more ambitiously engaged in getting out a souvenir volume, *Irvingiana*, which he managed to publish before the end of the year.[16] Edited with an introductory biographical sketch by Evert Duyckinck, *Irvingiana* brought together a miscellany of material published about Irving both after his death and long before. As a source of information about him, therefore, the work was redundant; as discriminating criticism of his character or his writings it was rendered useless by its tone of sentimental eulogy. Nonetheless, it was eagerly awaited, sold well, and was praised for its contents. The reviewer for the Boston *Transcript* thought it "valuable and interesting" in itself, although he recognized that its lasting importance would be for the popular sentiment it encapsulated: "As a spontaneous offering on the part of [Irving's] countrymen, his younger brothers in the field of authorship and his contemporaries and companions, the book is a charming evidence of genuine feeling."[17]

Concurrently with the printed "Memorials," this "feeling" for Irving was demonstrated, or exploited, by "offerings" of various other kinds. Apparently without irony, the Boston *Transcript* reported that by "a singular coincidence" plaster copies of a "cabinet bust" of Irving were being offered for sale beginning on December 30, the identical day when *Irvingiana* became available in Boston bookshops.[18] The New York *Tribune* announced that Thomas Hicks, Irving's recent guest at Sunnyside, was at work on a full-length portrait of the author in his study which would be completed and reproduced for sale beginning on April 3.[19] According to an unidentified New York newspaper, the famous photographer Matthew Brady had just "recovered" a supposedly destroyed daguerreotype of Irving from which he was producing a colour portrait "of most remarkable excellence."[20] Memorial statuary was proposed for New York's Central Park;[21] or, by one correspondent of the *Evening Post*, for Sunnyside, where "it

[15] James O. Noyes to John W. Francis, New York ("Knickerbocker Office"), December 9, 1859 (SHR). Francis may have sent Noyes a copy of the remarks he had prepared for presentation before the New-York Historical Society; these covered over four pages in the closely printed *Irvingiana*, pp. xxxii-xxxvi.

[16] The work was advertised in the New York *Evening Post* of December 18 as to be published in a few days (p. 3, col. 3).

[17] Boston *Evening Transcript*, December 30, 1859, p. 2, col. 4. George Bancroft was only one of many obituary orators who emphasized this national feeling toward WI. In his address before the New-York Historical Society, he commented: "No American since Washington has taken with him to the grave the undivided affection of the American people like Irving" (*Irvingiana*, p. xxx).

[18] Boston *Evening Transcript*, December 30, 1859, p. 2, col. 4. The sculptor was John Adams Jackson (1825-1879).

[19] New York *Tribune*, March 20, 1860, p. 5, col. 2.

[20] Peters Scrapbook (NYPL, Berg).

[21] New York *Times*, December 19, 1859, p. 4, col. 1.

would be seen from the decks of vessels which glide along the river."[22] Further poems in praise of the late author were forthcoming, and on December 31 a short-lived *Irving Magazine* published its first issue.[23]

The proliferation of testimonial Irvingiana did not abate until after the commemoration of the late author's birthday on April 3, 1860. Not surprisingly, all this material provided a fair field for collectors and begat many scrapbooks. During February, John C. Peters received a note from a collector requesting a copy of his pamphlet on Irving for an "album";[24] a few weeks later he received a note from C. B. Richardson offering to pay him for a dozen copies of the same work, since "[s]everal collectors have applied here for it."[25] Peters was himself an industrious aggregator of memorabilia. He pasted into his ornately leatherbound scrapbook a variety of keepsakes—published articles relating to Irving, short notes from various members of the Irving family relating to his professional attendance on them, and many other curiosities. For example, when he came to visit the family on November 29, the morning after Irving's death, he made a hurried list of "Books on WI's Drawing [Room] Table," and from one of these, a copy of *Pilgrim's Progress*, he tore an illustration to include in his collection![26] Yet, rapacious as it was, Peters perhaps justified his pilferage on the basis of his sincere regard for Irving—a sentiment he shared with the great majority of collectors who had known the author less well than he. Like the unrestrained and even fulsome obituary praise in the newspapers, the indiscriminate quest for Irvingiana by Peters and other compilers of scrapbooks was a symptom of the adulation the late author had inspired in his American public.

The norm among the posthumous written and spoken tributes to Irving was of lavish praise for every aspect of his life and character. This pattern was adhered to so consistently, in fact, that for one to declare himself publicly in less fervid terms must have seemed almost to invite suspicion as to the depth and genuineness of one's affection. Longfellow sensed the difficulty, and in enclosing to Pierre a copy of his resolutions before the Massachusetts Historical Society he expressed concern that their calm tone should not be taken as evidence of tepid feelings. He need not have worried, for in reply Pierre assured him of the whole family's "entire and unmixed gratification" at the remarks and went on to set forth his own attitude toward the recent saturnalia of praise. "For me," he said, "highly as I estimate the genius and character of my lamented relative, and profoundly thank-

---

[22] New York *Evening Post,* December 1, 1859, p. 2, col. 3.

[23] *The Irving Magazine. A Weekly Journal of Information and Literature,* survived through nineteen numbers of its second volume, ceasing publication with the issue of November 3, 1860.

[24] J. V. Fredrickson to John C. Peters, New York, February 21, 1860 (Peters Scrapbook—NYPL, Berg).

[25] C. B. Richardson to John C. Peters, New York, March 12, 1860 (Peters Scrapbook—NYPL, Berg).

[26] Peters Scrapbook (NYPL, Berg).

ful as I am for the many testimonies to his hold on the American heart, my taste shrinks instinctively from the language of unrestrained eulogy."[27]

Within a few days of Irving's death it was common knowledge that Duyckinck and Bryant were at work on biographical memoirs; but even amidst the first outpourings of posthumous praise, speculation began as to which person would assume the authorship of a full-length biography. The newspaper publication of excerpts from G. W. Greene's *Biographical Studies* immediately gave rise to a suggestion in the *Evening Post* that he planned to undertake the task.[28] Greene hastened to correct this error, however. On December 3 he issued a disclaimer in the same newspaper, adding that persons "of taste and ability in the family"[29] were well qualified for the work and would doubtless write it. Two days later, the *Evening Post* offered a new candidate, advancing the claim that F. S. Cozzens was about to publish a long "Author's Reminiscence of Washington Irving" in the New York *Ledger*.[30] Cozzens quickly and indignantly quashed the rumour. "I cannot conceive of anything that would be more intrusive and indelicate at the time," he wrote in a letter published December 6, "nor more repugnant to the feelings of any respectable writer, than the intention attributed to me."[31] (Apparently he based his statement on a nice distinction between a *reminiscence* and a *biography*, for, in fact, he was about to publish an essay on Irving in the *Ledger*.)[32] The suggestion that Irving's nephew, Pierre M. Irving, was to be his biographer did not appear in newspapers until December 9, when an anonymous report to that effect was published in the Albany *Evening Journal*.[33] This report went unchallenged. On December 24, Willis and Morris' *Home Journal*, which was never far behindhand in retailing literary gossip, confided that the individual alluded to in G. W.

[27] PMI to Henry W. Longfellow, SS, December 23, 1859 (Harvard). In a letter to John C. Peters written on an unspecified date shortly after WI's death, PMI expressed somewhat more fully his feelings at the loss of his uncle: "From the moment you told me there was enlargement of the heart, I could not help, from time to time, making special inquiry in that menacing quarter; but I knew that Mr. Irving was prepared to die, and that a sudden death had no terror to him—all he dreaded was a lingering decline of body and mind, a condition of helpless infirmity from which he was spared by that blow which came so suddenly at the last. It did much to reconcile us to the shock" ("Illnesses," p. 462).

[28] New York *Evening Post*, p. 1, col. 2.

[29] P. 1, col. 3.

[30] New York *Evening Post*, December 5, 1859, p. 4, col. 2.

[31] New York *Evening Post*, December 6, 1859, p. 1, col. 2.

[32] Cozzens, "WI," New York *Ledger*, 15, no. 42 (December 24, 1859), 4.

[33] *Irvingiana*, p. lxix. The anonymous author of this notice had knowledge of WI's private affairs, for he knew that "his entire manuscripts and correspondence were left in the hands of Pierre M. Irving, who is admirably adapted to the task" of writing a biography. He also recalled the day in 1858 when WI made his will, recounted in general terms some of WI's conversation at that time, and added that the "main provisions" of the will referred to "the establishment of Sunnyside as a permanent abode for the name and house of Irving."

Greene's letter of three weeks before, "we presume, is PIERRE MUNRO IRVING, Esq. . . . He is Mr. Irving's literary executor, and there is reason to suppose that he was looked upon by his uncle as his future biographer."[34] The *Home Journal* failed to specify its "reason," but to anyone familiar with the close relationship between Pierre and Irving the information that the former was his uncle's delegated biographer would have come as no surprise. Characteristically, Pierre made no public announcement of his own, but he must at least have corroborated the original rumour in the Albany *Evening Journal* before it was reprinted as the concluding item in *Irvingiana*.

Several weeks were to pass between the time when his role as future biographer came to public attention and that when he was able to begin focusing his concerted attention on the task before him. He and Ebenezer had been designated co-executors of the will, and in practice, of course, this meant that all the duties of the office would be performed by himself alone. Accordingly, on December 7 he wrote out and verified a memorandum listing the heirs to the estate,[35] and at about the same time he compiled a full list of Irving's assets at the time of his death and began keeping an exact and thorough record of the estate's income and disbursements.[36] Assisted by Helen, he probably did manage during December to extract and tentatively to identify some of the personal papers his uncle had left secreted in the Byzantine crannies of the Putnam desk; but he had not yet completed that task by mid-January when, having set the estate in order, he returned with Helen to their comfortable quarters at the Clarendon Hotel.[37]

No doubt it was understood as a matter of course that Pierre's biography would appear under the imprint of George Putnam. However, an installment of the work would clearly not be forthcoming within a few weeks or months, and meanwhile Putnam, whose sales of *Washington* and the uniform sets of the revised works were soaring,[38] was painfully conscious of the possibilities for a well-timed addition to his list of Irving titles. Since the funeral speculation had circulated that additions to the canon of the author's works in print might be anticipated,[39] but as yet nothing definite was afoot. Probably within a few days of Pierre's return to the city, therefore, Putnam proposed to him that he authorize a new edition of *Salmagundi* for publication in the near future. Both men were aware, of course, that during his lifetime Irving had not permitted the reprinting of *Salmagundi* under his own name; yet Pierre knew that in private his

---

[34] No. 724 (December 24, 1859), p. 2, col. 1.

[35] "Memorandum as to the Heirs of WI . . . which was verified December 7, 1859, by PMI" (SHR). The list included Ebenezer and twenty-four nephews and nieces.

[36] For a discussion of a possible use to which the Account Book had previously been put, see above, p. 124, footnote 81.

[37] PMI to C. C. Felton, New York, January 18, 1860 (Harvard).

[38] Putnam, *A Memoir of Putnam*, II, 31-32.

[39] "WI and His Books," an unidentified newspaper clipping in the Peters Scrapbook (NYPL, Berg).

uncle was not really hostile to the book—that his youthful folly in the
History of New York had mortified him far more than the miscellaneous raillery of the earlier production. In 1842, he also knew, Irving had
actually included *Salmagundi* among the works he unsuccessfully offered to Lea and Blanchard for republication.[40]

Personally, Pierre thought his uncle's mature deprecation of the
work "rigorous and over-sensitive."[41] He agreed with Duyckinck,
whom Putnam proposed as editor of the new edition,[42] that "we
cannot suppose [Irving] insensible to the many excellences which the
work undoubtedly possesses."[43] As his uncle's executor and eventual
biographer he acknowledged a certain obligation to respect his wishes
and preserve his good name; but as we have repeatedly seen, he was
of too independent a temperament to permit himself to become a mere
extension of Irving's will. A new edition of *Salmagundi* could do
Irving's reputation no real harm, he may have reasoned; on the contrary, it would serve to keep his name fresh in the popular mind.
Pierre decided to break the precedent of his uncle's policy and authorize Putnam to republish the work.

Before his undertaking came to fruition, however, it was interrupted by a complication which neither Putnam nor Pierre appears to
have foreseen. An advertisement of the forthcoming new edition in
the March 31 issue of *The Albion*, a weekly miscellany, met the eye of
William Paulding, a son of Irving's primary collaborator in writing
Salmagundi; and on April 3 the younger Paulding addressed to his
cousin Pierre an inquiry concerning the work. His father, he wrote,
was "unable to make the enquiry for himself or to take any interest in
the question,"[44] but for his own part he wished to learn "whether this
is a publication authorized by you (as part of your late Uncle's works),
or a speculation of Mr. Putnam's—the terms of the advertisement
seeming to imply the latter."[45] William Paulding's note was cordial in

---

[40] WI to Messrs. Lea & Blanchard, New York, March 10, 1842 (Harvard).

[41] *LLWI*, I, 211.

[42] At first, apparently, it was planned that Duyckinck would *only* edit the edition,
and not write the introductory essay which he eventually did provide for the published
work. On April 7, 1860, Putnam advertised in the New York *Times* as follows: "Mr.
Bryant's address on Washington Irving [delivered before the New-York Historical
Society on April 3] will be handsomely printed on tinted paper, and will be prefixed to
the new and beautiful edition of *Salmagundi* . . . . The address will also be issued
separately in a few days" (p. 6, col. 4). The incongruous conjoining of Bryant and
Salmagundi was not mentioned again, however. Bryant's *Discourse on the Life, Character,
and Genius of WI* was published on May 7 and *Salmagundi* on May 12. PMI paid
Duyckinck $100 for his part in preparing the latter volume (Account Book, p. 40).

[43] "Editor's Preface," *Salmagundi; or, the Whim-Whams and Opinions of Launcelot
Langstaff, Esq., and Others* (New York, 1860), p. [vii]. In his *Discourse*, Bryant observed
of *Salmagundi* that "Irving never seemed to place much value on the part he contributed
to this work, yet I doubt whether he ever excelled some of those papers" (pp. 15-16).

[44] According to Amos L. Herold, *James Kirke Paulding, Versatile American* (New
York, 1926), p. 141, Paulding's "mental powers declined appreciably" in his last years.

[45] William I. Paulding to PMI, Coldspring, Putnam County, New York, April 3,
1860 (Yale). Paulding pasted to his letter the advertisement in question:

tone and was probably not intended to call into question Pierre's right unilaterally to authorize publication of the book. In 1835 James Kirke Paulding had himself published a new edition of *Salmagundi*, apparently without sharing royalties with Irving,[46] and there was no natural reason why, between friends and relations, the reverse procedure should not be acceptable. Nevertheless, it is true that the copyright to the 1835 edition had not yet expired, and from the tone of William Paulding's letter it seems possible that, had he learned that Putnam was publishing the book without due authorization, he might have interfered on his father's behalf.

Subsequent correspondence between Pierre and William Paulding, if indeed there was any, has not survived, and thus the reasons why they took the step they did must remain conjectural. James Kirke Paulding died on April 6, and it is possible they came to an oral agreement on the matter when they met during the next few days. In any case, William Paulding, as his father's executor, agreed with Pierre to divide the royalties equally between the estates of the two late authors. Perhaps his duty as an executor obliged Paulding to protect all the lawful property of the estate, including the copyright on this work, and hence to require some accommodation from Pierre.[47] If so, the compromise was certainly reached without rancour on either side. Pierre had not driven a hard bargain with Putnam,[48] and over so small a matter he was not likely to fall out with a cousin with whom he was on terms of close friendship. Three years later, reckoning his accounts with Putnam to that date, Pierre noted that the sales of *Salmagundi* had totalled only 2,717, and that Paulding's share of the royalties amounted to $32.41.[49] In this instance, at least, Putnam had overestimated his possibilities for profit.

Now in Press

(Uniform with the National Edition of Irving)

SALMAGUNDI

An Entirely New Edition

Edited, with Notes, by E. A. Duyckinck, Esq. Beautifully printed on tinted paper.

Price $1.50

[46] This was as part of a fourteen-volume collection of his *Works*, published by Harper and Brothers, New York.

[47] James Kirke Paulding bequeathed to William I. Paulding his copyrights and manuscripts (Herold, *Paulding*, p. 141). It is thus possible that the latter was in fact looking out for his own interests in writing to PMI. On the other hand, the copyright to *Salmagundi* was not especially valuable, and the Paulding family was prosperous. It seems more likely that other motives prompted William I. Paulding to come to the agreement with PMI he did.

[48] PMI agreed to pay the cost of engraving stereotype plates, illustrations, and the services of Duyckinck in return for a royalty of 25 per cent on the purchase price of each copy sold (Account Book, p. 40).

[49] *Ibid.* During the period May 1863 to January 1866, *Salmagundi* was a more profitable item for the estate of WI, since outlays for the production of the work had already been made. The amount of royalty payments accrued during that period was $437.50; as before, PMI split this amount with William Paulding (Account Book, p. 101).

Even though Pierre was unable to give concentrated attention to the embryonic *Life and Letters of Washington Irving* until early in 1860, he was undisturbed at the delay, for he had already devoted a substantial amount of time and thought to the project. The exact date when he began to do so is impossible to specify, since in the tantalizingly brief and general preface to the biography—his only explicit statement on the matter—he merely wrote that when Irving first proposed the task to him, "some years before his death," he did not immediately accept it. "Though deeply sensible of the confidence implied in such a request," he continued, "my first impulse was to decline an office so responsible, and for which I felt myself so little qualified." Only after Irving had repeated the request "with an earnestness which showed the subject had seriously engaged his thoughts,"[50] he said, did he accept the office. Fortunately, on the basis of certain other evidence from the hand of Pierre, it is possible to fix at least hypothetically the approximate dates on which some of these interchanges occurred.

The first request for Pierre to write the biography may have come as early as the fall of 1847 and was probably not made after July 1850, but a narrower estimate cannot be substantiated.[51] The probable dates of the later conversation which resulted in Pierre's decision to write the biography may be inferred, however, from three interrelated facts. The first, from an extant topic outline of the *Life and Letters* compiled by Pierre, is that between some time in 1852 and October 5, 1854, a period of nearly two years at the least, he kept no memoranda of his uncle's talk, habits, and activities—but that on the latter date he resumed doing so.[52] The second, also from Pierre's manuscript outline, is that in March and April 1856 he was keeping a running account

---

[50] "Preface," *LLWI,* I, [5].

[51] The earliest date at which PMI certainly kept a record of WI's activities and remarks is January 1848. In his MS Outline of the topics to be covered in his account of WI's life in 1847 and 1848, he wrote: "In the beginning of 1848 Mr Irving on a visit to John Jacob Astor – My memorandum of a dinner January 9, 1848 – Conversation about ghosts" (Chapter XXIV). The published passage written on the basis of this memorandum is in *LLWI,* IV, 35-36. The MS Outline includes another brief item—one not included in the biography—which suggests that PMI may have been recording WI's conversation as early as October 1847: "Hard at work on his Life of Washington in October – Remark upon the wonderful achievements of our troops in Mexico" (Chapter XXIV). There is no indication in the MS Outline or elsewhere of activity of PMI's prior to this date which might be interpreted as tentative preparation for the role of biographer. What is probably the latest date at which WI could have made his first request for PMI's biographical cooperation, July 1850, is supplied by the terms of WI's will dated July 28 of that year. In this document he bequeathed to PMI, besides $5,000 and the manuscript of the *Washington,* "all my letters, correspondence and private memoranda which may aid him in preparing a memoir of me, should he be inclined to write one" (NYPL, MS). This provision indicates that PMI had not yet decided to write the biography, but it suggests that WI had by this time broached the subject to his nephew.

[52] "Resume my memoranda Oct 5 . . . after an interval of nearly two years" (MS Outline, Chapter XXXIII [1854]).

of his uncle's activities in his now-lost notebooks.[53] The third detail is that in the published *Life and Letters* he adopted the narrative format of a journal, with notations of Irving's occupations and remarks on specific days, beginning September 27, 1855, and continuing to his death.[54] Taken together, Pierre's resumption of his journalizing in October 1854 and his evident continuation of it in 1855, 1856, and without significant interruption to the end of Irving's life suggest that beginning at that earliest date he regarded the procedure as a regular duty. This inference suggests in turn that October 5, 1854 was not far from the time when he finally acceded to Irving's wishes. The close conjunction between October 5, 1854, and August 4 of the same year—the date on which Irving deeded to Pierre the plot of land adjacent to Sunnyside—would seem to lend plausibility to this theory insofar as it suggests that Irving may have been earnestly repeating his request that Pierre write the biography at about that time.[55] As we have seen, in August 1854 Pierre had recently retired from his position as Pension Agent and was about to relinquish his Notaryship. It was a period during which he might well have been considering which new projects to take on in the future and thus have been disposed to think seriously about his uncle's proposal. In short, the coincidence between the dates of Pierre's approaching retirement from his professional career, Irving's gift of a plot of land where he hoped Pierre and Helen would live, and Pierre's resumption of his biographical memoranda suggests that he may have made his decision to write the *Life and Letters* between August and October, 1854, when the five years of his closest companionship with his uncle were still before him.

As Pierre wrote in his preface to the *Life and Letters*, he accepted the charge only after Irving had given him "the assurance that he would be able to place in my keeping materials which he would only confide to a relative, and which would of themselves go far to furnish a picture of his life from his first launch in the world." Once he had enlisted his nephew's cooperation, Irving made good his promise. Not long afterward, Pierre wrote, "he placed in my possession a mass of material, consisting of journals, note-books, diaries at scattered intervals, and a large collection of family letters with files of others from various correspondents, which, as he said, he had neither time nor spirit to examine or arrange."[56] Later developments were to reveal that Irving had not yet emptied his desk drawers, but what he did turn over to Pierre was a rich collection of source material which kept him occupied at intervals over many months while the *Washington* was in preparation. He transported this unique research collection to this

[53] MS Outline, Chapter XXXV (1856). See below, p. 319.

[54] *LLWI,* IV, 196 *et seq.*

[55] As well as seeking to secure PMI's continuous assistance as a collaborator on the *Washington;* see above, pp. 132-33.

[56] "Preface," *LLWI,* I, [5]-6.

private office in William Street,[57] and in the intervals of freedom from other duties and avocations he sorted, arranged, and classified his material, occasionally burrowing in the Astor Library to throw needed light on problems raised by his readings in Irving's life history.[58] No doubt during his visits to the office Irving interrupted his monologues on the *Washington* to answer such questions about his lifetime as had recently occurred to Pierre. He might have been uncooperative to gossip-mongers of the N. P. Willis stripe, but he placed no barriers before his nephew. Indeed, he took an active interest in furthering the project. On his own initiative he secured the loan of his letters to Henry Brevoort, Jr., his close friend in youth, and turned them over to Pierre for reading and copying.[59] From time to time he located further correspondence in the recesses of his desk, and he either suggested to Pierre that he seek to borrow letters written to other friends, including Paulding, Gouverneur Kemble, and members of the Hoffman family, or—what is equally likely—he borrowed them himself.[60]

With his research efforts thus simplified through the assistance of his uncle, by February 1859 Pierre had already completed a topic outline of Irving's life to 1820, arranged by chapters.[61] As we have

[57] *Trow's New York City Directory* for 1854-1855, p. 374.

[58] A few traces of this library research appear in PMI's MS Outline. To find details about Judge Egbert Benson, President of the New-York Historical Society to which WI had dedicated his *History of New York* in 1809, he consulted John W. Francis' *Old New York* (New York, 1858), pp. 63-65; for information about WI's dedication of Bryant's *Poems* (1832) to Samuel Rogers, he checked the back files of the *Athenaeum* and the *New York Mirror*; and in order to prepare an account of WI's reply in 1837 to a published attack by Joseph Seawell Jones, he copied the published letter from WI in the New York *American* for January 7, 1837 (MS Outline, Chapters 21, 60, 67). Egbert Benson went unmentioned in the biography, but the two other topics are discussed, respectively, in *LLWI*, II, 475, 477, and III, 104-09; III, 99-100.

[59] "Preface," *LLWI*, I, 6.

[60] PMI had in hand letters from WI to all these persons before February 1859; see footnote 61.

[61] This date has been established through analysis, first, of the latest possible dates at which PMI could have received information which he included both in the MS Outline and in *LLWI*, I; and second, of the earliest possible dates at which he could have received certain material *not* included in the MS Outline but included in the biography.
Information included in the MS Outline and also in *LLWI*, I:
1. MS Outline, Chapter 1; *LLWI*, I, 14-18—ancestry of the Irving family. The outline includes a reference to "William de Irwyn." PMI learned of this ancestor through Colonel Jonathan Forbes at some time after Irving Van Wart met Forbes in the summer of 1857 (Irving Genealogy, pp. 20-22). He had no substantial information about William de Irwyn to outline before the late summer of 1857.
2. MS Outline, Chapter 17 (1809); *LLWI*, I, 175-76—information concerning the authorship of various parts of *Salmagundi*. A notation in the MS Outline, Chapter 17, compared with similar notations in outlined chapters 28, 35, and 58, reveals that PMI entered this material in his "Notebook 3" in March or April, 1856.
3. MS Outline, Chapter 18 (1808) *et seq.*; *LLWI*, I, 215 *et seq.*—WI's letters to Henry Brevoort. From an incident in May 1859 wherein Carson Brevoort requested of PMI, through WI, the return of his father's letters—see above, p. 201—it appears that they had already been in the possession of PMI for some time. From PMI's reference in the biography to WI's assistance in securing these letters (*LLWI*, I, 6), and from other data, it appears that PMI may have had the Brevoort letters in hand as early as 1854.

seen from the 1859 journal, until the end of his life Irving willingly expatiated to Pierre on topics of biographical curiosity. Moreover, as Pierre wrote in the *Life and Letters*, shortly before his death he suggested other persons in Europe and America from whom letters might be secured "which, if still in existence, might be of interest."⁶² Probably these persons included Emily Foster, the English girl with whose family he had often visited while at Dresden in 1822-1823, and Prince Dmitri Ivanovich Dolgorouki and Mlle. Antoinette Bolviller, both of whom he had known during his first years in Spain. Thus, although in a depressed mood in August 1859 he told Pierre that "he did not care about" his biography, Irving had already long and industriously belied himself by contributing to its genesis. He might continue to dismiss the petitions that he write his own memoirs, but even as he shunned the labour and the immodesty of an autobiographical work, by his collaboration with Pierre he was placing a distinct personal stamp on the *Life and Letters*.

Information not included in the MS Outline but included in *LLWI*, I:
1. *LLWI*, I, 211-12—quotations from Duyckinck's introduction to *Salmagundi* and from Bryant's *Discourse*. PMI could not have seen either of these works many weeks prior to their publication in May 1860.
2. *LLWI*, I, 223—PMI's account of the discovery of an autobiographical manuscript by WI relating to his love of Matilda Hoffman—see below, pp. 257, 262-63. PMI could not have had this information before WI's death on November 28, 1859.
3. *LLWI*, I, 266—a reference to Mrs. Balmanno's sketch of Jean Renwick. On May 29, 1859, PMI cited Mrs. Balmanno's *Pen and Pencil* (1858) as including a sketch of this lady; see above, p. 202. PMI seems to have made the journal entry for his own reference. If so, the entry suggests that the MS Outline, which includes no reference to Mrs. Balmanno, was completed to 1811 before May 29, 1859.
4. *LLWI*, I, 116-22. WI's recollections of Palermo, 1805, "gathered from the lips of Mr. Irving." The 1859 journal, PMI's sole known repository of information about WI in that year, includes a single brief reference to Palermo, dated April 11, 1859; see above, p. 189. Unless PMI kept another record of WI's comments and habits during 1859—and there is no reason to suppose he did so—he "gathered" the material in the quotation from WI at a time prior to beginning the journal in February of that year.
    The information included in both the MS Outline and *LLWI* indicates that PMI probably began writing the outline after the late summer of 1857, when information concerning William de Irwyn could first have come into his hands. The information included in *LLWI*, I, but not found in the MS Outline shows that PMI could certainly not have outlined WI's life to 1809—the year in which Matilda Hoffman died—before November 28, 1859; it suggests further that he had not outlined the biography to 1811 (under which year the reference to Mrs. Balmanno appears) before May 29, 1859; and it suggests further that he had not outlined the work to 1805 (under which year the quoted passage relating to Palermo appears) before February 28, 1859. Although the two latter inferences are only hypotheses, the facts that throughout the 1859 journal PMI made no mention of outlining the *LLWI*, that the bulk of his research recorded in the journal pertained to WI's life *after* 1820—the last year of WI's life recounted in the first volume of *LLWI*, and that in May 1859 PMI was searching for WI's letters written between 1828 and 1830 (see below, pp. 256, 269) suggest strongly that by February 1859 he had completed his preliminary gathering and organization of material pertaining to WI's life to 1820. This possibility is further strengthened by the evidence that he had been gathering information concerning WI's early years—specifically, the Brevoort letters and the Paulding information—three or more years before.

⁶² "Preface," *LLWI*, I, 6.

Once Pierre's role as his uncle's delegated biographer became known within the family, several relatives contributed material or assisted in gathering still more. Ebenezer supplemented the file of Irving's letters to his brothers William and Peter by turning over those to himself. Irving Van Wart, probably during his visit to England in 1857, secured the letters of Irving to his sister Sarah.[63] Irving Paris supplied the correspondence with another sister, Catharine, and Sarah Storrow sent her extensive file of letters across the Atlantic.[64] Julia Grinnell was especially helpful, exerting herself while on her European excursion as a literary detective on her brother's behalf. During April and May of 1859, she was dogging the footsteps of the elusive Mlle. Antoinette de Bolviller from Florence to Rome and back again. On May 17 she reported in a letter to Pierre the discouraging news that the lady was about to enter a convent and could not be reached directly. Julia had located an intermediary, however, through whom she had written "to ask for the letters – or if she were unwilling to part with them, to have them copied." She added that she had asked the intermediary, an Italian physician, "to inquire . . . for tidings of Dolgorouki."[65] The path of the latter proved quite difficult to trace, but presently Julia's persevering efforts to secure the Bolviller letters met with success, and within a few weeks after her return from Europe in August 1859, Pierre had them in hand.[66]

[63] PMI certainly had the letters of WI to Mrs. Van Wart in his possession by 1860 but had probably received them earlier (Irving Genealogy, p. 19; MS Outline, Chapter 40 [1823]).

[64] These letters were in the possession of PMI by 1862 and were probably received by him several years before.

[65] On the first page of the 1859 Journal, PMI summarized the information he had received from Julia Grinnell: "Mademoiselle Antoinette de Bolviller left Rome 17th July, 1858, soon after the death of her mother – was in Florence, in April 1859, detained by the illness of a maid-servant, but had again taken apartments in Rome at No. 32 Via Bocca di Leone – had left Florence early in May, 1859 – Julia then wrote to Dr. Valery at Rome – a physician in extensive practice – to ask for the letters – or if she were unwilling to part with them, to have them copied. Miss B. was never a [Cha-----ine?] – but used to dress in black like a Nun – is an amateur painter and frequents the galleries for the purpose of study & copying the old masters – Julia asked the Doctor to inquire of her for tidings of Dolgorouki.
Her letter dated May 17, 1859"

[66] See LLWI, II, 273, and MS Outline, Chapter 49 (1828). Julia Grinnell also gave assistance to PMI by copying extracts of letters from WI for use in the biography. The Beinecke Library, Yale University, owns two fragmentary letters, WI to Mrs. Catharine Paris, Madrid, July 25, 1842, and WI to the same, Madrid, January 12, 1843, copied by Julia. PMI's most valuable copyist, however, was probably Helen. The Beinecke Library owns a letter from WI to Henry Brevoort, Jr., New York, May 15, 1811, copied in her hand, and also copies made by her of two letters from WI to John Furman, a friend in youth, dated July 26, 1802, and October 24, 1804. Some insight into PMI's methods as a biographer is afforded by these copied documents. First having deputed Helen to copy the Brevoort letter in full, he then proceeded to make extracts from her transcription for quotation in the biography. Following a similar procedure with the two letters to John Furman, he first had Helen make full copies and then collated these against their originals, making the necessary corrections and additions. An extract from the earlier of the letters to Furman appeared in LLWI, I, 46, but the other letter and the Brevoort extract were not included.

By far the most significant assistance given Pierre in his preliminary research had come, of course, from Irving himself. Indeed, Irving
even managed to exert a profound posthumous influence over his
nephew's conception of his lifetime, for by leaving certain information to be discovered after his death, he lent a special biographical
significance to that previously unmentioned material by the mere fact
of his apparent reticence to divulge it while alive. In particular, despite his utter openness in regard to other episodes of his life history,
he never once spoke to Pierre of his early love for Matilda Hoffman,
daughter of the New York jurist Josiah Ogden Hoffman, and of his
deep grief at her death in 1809. This silence is the more noteworthy in
light of his unquestionable awareness that Pierre was acquainted with
at least the general outlines of the tragic romance, for during his
lifetime it had already taken on semi-public status as a sentimental
tale accounting for his bachelorhood.[67] In any case, perhaps in part
because of Irving's apparent aversion to discussing the matter, but
more pertinently because he had very little reliable information at
hand bearing upon his affection for Matilda Hoffman, Pierre did not
originally plan to devote much space in the biography to this crisis in
his uncle's emotional life. Compiling the topic outline of his account
of Irving's life to 1820, he gave no special prominence to the incident.
He planned for his discussion of it to share a single chapter with a
notice of Irving's portrait by John Wesley Jarvis, a denial that the
"original" of Ichabod Crane was one Jesse Merwin, and quotations
from Irving's miscellaneous letters to Henry Brevoort, Jr.[68] The romance was to be simply one of several topics taken up in the course of
recounting Irving's activities during 1809.

Shortly after his uncle's death, however, Pierre discovered new
evidence which resulted in a radical alteration of these plans. Sorting
through Irving's desk, he opened a drawer to which his uncle had
always kept the key, and found, together with a miniature portraying
Matilda Hoffman, and a braid of hair marked as hers, a package
labelled on the outside "Private Mems." Opening it, he discovered a
manuscript, written in Irving's hand, and giving a minute and moving account of his love for Matilda. In this statement Irving explained
that his attachment to the girl had developed while he was a law
student in the office of her father, Judge Hoffman. His most resolute
attempts to interest himself in the uncongenial legal studies were
useless, he wrote, but Hoffman persisted in liking him, professing a

---

The manuscript of the published *LLWI* has not survived. The only extant manuscripts associated with the book are, as in these instances, research notes and rejected,
unused, or recopied material, the 1859 Journal, and the MS Outline. One item in the
Beinecke Library, a copied letter from WI to William H. Prescott, n.p., December 24,
1839, reveals that PMI did at least some of his own transcribing. The two sheets of this
copy are numbered in his hand "201" and "202," suggesting that at some point he
intended to include them in the biography.

[67] See *Irvingiana,* p. xliii; Bryant, *Discourse,* p. 20; Putnam, "Recollections,"
pp. 604-05. See also *Life,* I, 103, and 405-06, notes 178 and 179.

[68] MS Outline, Chapter 20 (1809).

high opinion of his abilities, and favouring his suit to his daughter. He urged Irving to complete his preparation for the law and promised, once this was done, to give him Matilda and take him into the firm. Animated by Hoffman's generous encouragement, and considering himself thereby bound in honour to carry his suit to Matilda no further until he should have provided himself with better prospects, he renewed his dedication to legal studies. Irving's narrative continued with a portrayal of himself during Matilda's decline:

> In the midst of this struggle and anxiety she was taken ill with a cold. Nothing was thought of it at first, but she grew rapidly worse, and fell into a consumption. I cannot tell you what I suffered. The ills that I have undergone in this life have been dealt out to me drop by drop, and I have tasted all their bitterness. I saw her fade rapidly away beautiful and more beautiful and more angelical to the very last. I was often by her bed side and in her wandering state of mind she would talk to me with a sweet natural and affecting eloquence that was overpowering. I saw more of the beauty of her mind in that delirious state than I had ever known before. Her malady was rapid in its career, and hurried her off in two months. Her dying struggles were painful & protracted. For three day[s] & nights I did not leave the house & scarcely slept. I was by her when she died—all the family were assembled round her, some praying others weeping, for she was adored by them all. I was the last one she looked upon—I have told you as briefly as I could what if I were to tell with all the incidents & feelings that accompanied it would fill volumes. She was but about seventeen years old when she died.—
>
> I cannot tell you what a horrid state of mind I was in for a long time—I seemed to care for nothing—the world was a blank to me—I abandoned all thoughts of the Law—I went into the country, but could not bear solitude yet could not enjoy society—There was a dismal horror continually in my mind that made me fear to be alone—I had often to get up in the night & seek the bedroom of my brother, as if the having a human being by me would relieve me from the frightful gloom of my own thoughts.
>
> Months elapsed before my mind resumed any tone; but the despondency I had suffered for a long time in the course of this attachment, and the anguish that attended its catastrophe seemed to give a turn to my whole character, and threw some clouds into my disposition which have ever since hung about it. When I became more calm & collected I applied myself, by way of occupation, to the finishing of my work [the *History of New York*]. I brought it to a close, as well as I could, and published it but the time & circumstances in which it was produced rendered me always unable to look upon it with satisfaction. Still it took with the public & gave me celebrity, as an original work was something remarkable & uncommon in America. I was noticed caressed & for a time elated by the popularity I gained. I found myself uncomfortable in my feelings in NYork & travelled about a little. Wherever I went I was overwhelmed with attentions; I was full of youth and animation, far different from the being I now am, and I was

quite flushed with this early taste of public favour. Still however the career of gaiety & notoriety soon palled upon me. I seemed to drift about without aim or object, at the mercy of every breeze; my heart wanted anchorage. I was naturally susceptible and tried to form other attachments, but my heart would not hold on; it would continually recur to what it had lost; and whenever there was a pause in the hurry of novelty & excitement I would sink into dismal dejection. For years I could not talk on the subject of this hopeless regret; I could not even mention her name; but her image was continually before me, and I dreamt of her incessantly.[69]

Having read the manuscript of which this extraordinary confession formed a part, Pierre could have no doubt that the loss of Matilda Hoffman had been a major turning-point in Irving's emotional life-history—at least as he himself had at one time conceived of it. He could not help being extremely curious, moreover, as to the circumstances under which his uncle had unburdened himself on a topic so painful as this. The sixteen-page manuscript was fragmentary and devoid of place and date; but his preliminary research in Irvingiana served him well in identifying its addressee, and from references in it to "Dresden" and "Emily and Flora"[70] he accurately surmised that it was part of a letter originally written to Mrs. Amelia Foster, the mother of the two girls and Irving's frequent companion in 1822-1823.[71]

Even with its origin in place and time thus hypothetically ascertained, the manuscript raised vexing questions. What could explain Irving's unusual openness toward this woman whom he had only recently met? From his reading of the journals Irving had kept at Dresden, Pierre knew how thoroughly he had enjoyed this English family, but he could not have guessed from the journals that the relationship between them was so close as the fragmentary manuscript before him seemed to imply. "You wonder why I am not married,"[72] Irving had written to Mrs. Foster, evidently without resentment at her frank curiosity. His mood and his motives in confessing to her what, before and after, he kept in silence were an intriguing mystery. The journals revealed that Mrs. Foster was an intelligent and charming woman living away from her husband at that time; had Irving perhaps felt a romantic interest in her? The journals also indicated that of the two Foster daughters Irving had shown more attention to the elder, Emily, than to Flora; and Pierre knew of his uncle's fond memories of this vivacious girl years afterward.[73] Was Emily at

---

[69] *Life*, II, 255, 257-58.

[70] *Life*, II, 262.

[71] Mrs. Amelia Morgan Foster was the third wife of John Foster (1765-1831). Her daughters Mary Amelia ("Emily") Foster (1804?-1885) and Flora Foster (1806-1876) were her eighth and ninth children. See *Life*, I, 448, note 143.

[72] *Life*, II, 261.

[73] See *Journals* (Reichart), pp. 97-154 *passim*. WI's papers included a letter addressed to him from Emily Foster, now Mrs. Emily Fuller, on May 25, 1856, to which WI had sent a cordial reply. See *LLWI*, IV, 218-20.

the root of the emotional excitement that had precipitated the letter to her mother? On the face of the evidence at hand, either interpretation seemed possible.

Whatever the answers to the puzzle confronting him might be, Pierre was interested in learning what he could. In February 1860, therefore, at the very outset of his renewed biographical research, he wrote a letter to Mrs. Emily Foster Fuller, the elder daughter of the fragment's supposed addressee,[74] soliciting the use of the correspondence between Irving and the family—and no doubt hoping privately that in compliance with his request she would shed some light on the mysterious manuscript. Mrs. Fuller replied as follows:

> Thornhaugh Rectory, Wansford,
> Northamptonshire, March 10, 1860
>
> Dear Sir:
>
> I have sent a few extracts from Mr. Irving's letters that I thought were characteristic, or might be generally interesting, but only a few, for he expressed so strong a desire that his correspondence should be strictly private, that I have only chosen those that I think he would not have disliked being made public, or I should feel as if I had violated the sacred confidence of a friendship so valued. The passages I have sent give an idea of his life in Dresden. Sought after by all in the best society, and mingling much in the gay life of a foreign city, and a court where the royal family were themselves sufficiently intellectual to appreciate genius; but really intimate with ourselves only, and to such a degree that it gives me a right to judge of some points in his character. He was thoroughly a gentleman, not merely externally in manners and look, but to the innermost fibres and core of his heart. Sweet-tempered, gentle, fastidious, sensitive, and gifted with the warmest affections, the most delightful and invariably interesting companion, gay and full of humor, even in spite of occasional fits of melancholy, which he was however seldom subject to when with those he liked—a gift of conversation that flowed like a full river in sunshine, bright, easy, and abundant. He stayed at Dresden till we left, and then accompanied us on our return home, even into the packet-boat, and left us in the channel. That was not happily our last parting; he visited us in England, and I saw a good deal of him in London afterwards; but the farewell in that open boat, with the looks of regret on all sides, seemed the real farewell, and left the deepest impression. The picture he received in Paris was the little miniature you mention.[75]

---

[74] The most probable reason why PMI addressed his request to Mrs. Fuller rather than to Mrs. Flora Foster Dawson, her younger sister, is that he knew the address of the former as of 1856 from the letter she had written to WI in that year; see footnote 73. WI had had no correspondence with Mrs. Flora Dawson since February 5, 1846, when he wrote her a letter from London declining an invitation to visit her home (Brown University). It is in any case uncertain whether the letter to Mrs. Dawson was in the possession of PMI.

[75] The "miniature," a head of Herodias given WI by Emily Foster, was hung at SS; see *LLWI*, II, 129; IV, 219.

I am, dear Sir,

Yours very truly,

Emily Fuller

You are quite welcome to make any use of my letter that you please. It is a very faint testimony of a real friendship.[76]

Mrs. Fuller enclosed a collection of transcribed extracts from Irving's letters written at this period, but informative and vivid as they were, they were of little value for furthering Pierre's unspoken purpose. They only confirmed what he already knew: that Irving had enjoyed the Fosters, and also that, while absent from them during his tour from Dresden to the Riesengebirge in May and June, 1823, he had been emotionally upset. From Mrs. Fuller's firm avowal that she felt a sense of delicacy concerning the relations between her family and Irving, Pierre must have understood that no further assistance would be forthcoming from this compliant-yet-guarded source. Thus, unless he chose to begin sleuthwork in new directions, he must use Irving's autobiographical manuscript in the *Life and Letters* without an adequate understanding of the circumstances under which the author had written it.

The transcriptions sent by Mrs. Fuller did include a few new bits of information, however, and before passing on to other subjects he decided to test whether, used in conjunction with passages from Irving's journals for 1822-1823, these fragmentary letters might at least enable him to determine the date on which the manuscript had been written. With this purpose in mind, he wrote out a digest of Irving's activities and whereabouts during part of his acquaintance with the Fosters. It began: "In the evening of November 28, 1822 W. I. enters Dresden & puts up at Hotel de Saxe. April 17. 1823 determines to quit Dresden *soon.*"[77] The journal showed, and Pierre noted in his digest, that Irving left Dresden on May 20 and was absent on his tour to the Riesengebirge until June 26.[78] Pierre also carefully noted that during this period Irving mailed letters to Mrs. Foster on May 24, May 28, June 2, June 13, and June 19. Comparison of an incident mentioned in Irving's journal entry for June 20 and also referred to in an undated fragment written to Emily Foster and now sent by her for his own use as biographer, revealed that Irving had mailed one further letter, to Emily, probably on June 23.[79] From the dates given on the other transcribed letters sent him by Mrs. Fuller, Pierre was able to ascertain that he now possessed substantial fragments of all the letters Irving had recorded in his journal as having been mailed, excepting those of May 28 and June 19.[80] Pierre's digested entry from the journal for

[76] *LLWI*, II, 128-29.

[77] PMI, Misc. Notebook.

[78] See *Journals* (Reichart), pp. 158-77.

[79] See *Journals* (Reichart), p. 174; and *LLWI*, IV, 387.

[80] The extracts PMI received from Mrs. Fuller appear, arranged chronologically, in *LLWI*, II, 153-60.

May 28 indicates that he assumed the letter mailed that day to be rather routine in content ("[May] 28. Got a letter from Mrs. F. at post office – x send reply"), but his summary of the entries from June 15 to June 19 reveals that he believed the letter Irving mailed on the latter date to be more significant:

> (15) Receive long letter from Mrs. F. (17) Write to Mrs. F. but did not send it yet (18.) Remain at home all day – letter from Mrs. F – continued my letter giving anecdotes of self. 19. Letter from Mrs. F. giving account of her children & asking hints – finish my letter & as weather partly holds up put it in post office–[81]

The coincidence that between June 15 and 19 Irving was at work on a long, single letter to Mrs. Foster "giving anecdotes of self," while during the same period he received three letters from that productive lady, one of them "asking hints," clearly suggested to Pierre that the fragmentary manuscript now in his own possession was either part of the letter of June 15-19 or else a transcription thereof.

As to Irving's motives for writing the letter, he was of course still unsatisfied; the journals had told him only that it was written over several days, that it formed part of an exchange of confidences between his uncle and Mrs. Foster, and that the lady was interested in eliciting whatever "hints" he might offer. Perhaps he formed a surmise on the basis of the conjunction in Mrs. Foster's letter between the "account of her children" and her wish for "hints" from Irving, but if so, the evidence at hand was much too scanty to justify entertaining it very seriously. The one point on which he did feel confident was that Irving's letter of June 15-19, 1823, was the one which he possessed in fragmentary form. He decided that the manuscript was a transcript of the original,[82] probably because he assumed that all the original correspondence from Irving to the Fosters was in the hands of Mrs. Fuller. The absence of a new transcription of this revealing letter from the packet she had enclosed for his use tallied with her avowed reluctance to break silence over Irving's close relations with the family.

Despite the only partial success of his attempt to discover the circumstances of its origin, the fragment did intensify Pierre's sense of the importance Irving had himself attached to the loss of Matilda Hoffman as a determining event in his lifetime. His uncle had dramatized himself rather conventionally, it was true—as a sentimental hero despondent and inconsolable after sitting beside the deathbed of one he "idolized." Yet from the various subsequent incidents which seemed to corroborate the sentiments it expressed, Pierre could

---

[81] PMI, Misc. Notebook. The digest follows PMI's notes on the dates at which WI acquired and sold various portions of his SS acreage.

[82] PMI wrote in *LLWI*: "From an entry in Mr. Irving's diary, while at Prague, in June, 1823, mentioning the writing and sending to Mrs. Foster, from that city, a letter 'giving anecdotes of self,' I had surmised that the faded manuscript, so long preserved, was a transcript from that letter" (IV, 213-14).

not doubt Irving's sincerity in writing it. While he still wondered what had impelled his uncle to write the fragment, the manner in which he had himself recently discovered it showed that its primary biographical importance was for its account of Matilda. Thus, dismissing the problem of Irving's relations with the Fosters as insoluble and in any case ancillary to the major pattern of his life history, Pierre turned his attention again to preparation of the *Life and Letters*.

The published biography reveals how radically his discovery of the manuscript fragment prompted him to revise his earlier plans for recounting Irving's life in 1809. In the *Life and Letters* he devoted an entire chapter to the Matilda Hoffman episode alone; and quoting freely from Irving's statement to Mrs. Foster, he portrayed the incident in precisely the same sentimental and legendary light that his uncle's living reticence and posthumous confidence had directed him to do. Using the fragment as the nucleus of his account, he added a selection of anecdotes exemplifying the persistence in later life of Irving's regard for the memory of Matilda. He mentioned that her Bible and Prayer-Book were "in all changes of climate and country, [Irving's] inseparable companions"; he told of an incident nearly thirty years after her death when, being shown a piece of her embroidery in the course of a visit with her family, he suddenly sank from vivacity "into utter silence, and in a few moments got up and left the house." He told of a conversation a few years before Irving's death wherein, shortly after remarking to a niece that he "was never intended for a bachelor," he handed her in silence a faded sheet with Thomas Campbell's love poem, "What's hallowed ground?" transcribed onto it in his own handwriting. And as a concluding instance of what he called Irving's "sacred recollection" of Matilda, Pierre quoted a passage from a notebook of 1822: "She died in the beauty of her youth, and in my memory she will ever be young and beautiful."[83]

More than fifty years after the publication of the *Life and Letters*, another biographer of Irving, George S. Hellman, cast doubt on Pierre's portrayal of his uncle's unhappy romance, claiming that he had fabricated a "misleading legend." According to Hellman, "the legend that Irving remained a lifelong bachelor because of Matilda Hoffman's death half a century before his own, is due solely to the sentimental desire of his nephew and first biographer, Pierre M. Irving."[84] Clearly, on the basis of all the available evidence, this

---

[83] *LLWI*, I, 222-31.

[84] *WI, Esquire: Ambassador from the New World to the Old* (London, 1925), p. 48. Hellman added: "In his attempt to perpetuate this gentle myth, Pierre M. Irving had recourse to comments, suppressions, and to elisions" (p. 49). Stanley T. Williams also found fault with PMI's portrayal of the Matilda Hoffman episode. According to Williams, PMI "sanctioned and encouraged the story, popular throughout the nineteenth century, that Irving never married because of his loyalty to the memory of Matilda Hoffman." Williams praised Hellman's "valuable biography" for having succeeded in "qualifying P. M. Irving's attitude" and correcting "P. M. Irving's exaggeration" of the importance of the episode to WI (*Life*, I, 407, note 185). For further discussion of the attitudes of Hellman and Williams to the work of PMI, see below, pp. 310-12.

serious charge is false. If anyone perpetuated a myth that the loss of Matilda Hoffman was a determining factor in Irving's lifelong bachelorhood, it was not so much Pierre as Irving himself. It was he who was moved years after her death at the mere mention of her name; he who kept silence about a rumour which he knew was abroad—and which, if it were false, he could easily enough have denied; and he, after all, who left his autobiographical account for Pierre to publish.[85] Irving's fond memory of his early love—sentimental, affected, and "fabricated" as it may appear to some[86]—was a genuine facet of his mind and character, and by his own avowal it exerted a powerful force upon him. The accusation of Hellman that the love affair between Irving and Matilda Hoffman was inflated into a "gentle myth" by his mendacious nephew is thus not only unjust to Pierre, but it also reveals a gross impercipience of Irving's emotional makeup. Pierre announced at the outset of the *Life and Letters* that his primary aim in writing the work was "to make the author, in every stage of his career, as far as possible, his own biographer";[87] and in his account of this dramatic passage in Irving's lifetime, he succeeded in doing so.

Irving's collaboration with his delegated biographer during his lifetime and, indirectly, after his death thus determined to a significant degree the contents of the *Life and Letters*. Yet the most pervasive influence which he exerted over the work in its final firm was probably owing not so much to his specific acts of assistance and direction as to the sheer volume of the unpublished material he placed at Pierre's disposal. He fulfilled his promise of turning over to Pierre personal papers "which would of themselves go far to furnish a picture of his life" so literally that, excepting the period of his childhood from which no written records survived, the story of his career was patent virtually from his own writings alone. To some degree, this ampleness of data supplied by Irving, his relatives, and his acquaintances dictated by itself the format of the *Life and Letters* as a work dominated by quoted material. Pierre recognized that by judicious selection from his wealth of resources he could hope to achieve the desirable effect of immediacy in portraying the events of the author's life. Perhaps, too, he was relieved that this surplusage of material afforded him an opportunity to prepare a satisfyingly thorough account of Irving's career without being obliged to narrate the preponderance of it in his own diffident and self-distrustful person.

In proposing to write a "life and letters"—essentially a collection of correspondence, journals, recorded conversations, and other ma-

[85] Moreover, contrary to the suggestion of Hellman (*WI, Esquire*, p. 49), PMI did not write in *LLWI* that the lifelong bachelorhood of WI was solely the result of this catastrophe. Rather, he quoted from WI's own explanation in the confessional letter to Mrs. Foster, in which WI had enumerated financial, ethical, and temporal reasons. See below, pp. 304-05.

[86] For example, Stanley T. Williams remarks that the "tenderness of this courtship may amuse a modern mind" (*Life*, I, 102).

[87] *LLWI*, I, 6; see also II, 364.

terial arranged in roughly chronological order, interlinked by brief narrative passages and interrupted by only a minimum of interpretive discussion—Pierre conceived of his work as similar in format to John Gibson Lockhart's *Memoirs of the Life of Sir Walter Scott* (7 vols., 1838), a biography which Irving had admired.[88] He first planned that the *Life and Letters* would fill three volumes, and in the end papers of the first volume George Putnam announced that the work would "probably" be completed in two further installments.[89] However, as Pierre must have anticipated from the outset of his composition in 1860, he was constantly to be plagued by limitations of space. The abundance of information at hand implied the necessity for stern selectiveness, and to keep the total length of the work within his scheme he would need to formulate a rigid set of criteria for usable material. Complex and at times vexing, this problem of procedure was to bedevil him throughout the writing of the work. As he presciently wrote in his preface to the first volume, the role of a delegated biographer was in fact a "delicate office."[90]

Should he, for example, divulge information which he either knew or supposed that Irving would prefer for him to suppress? There is of course no reason to believe that Irving had ever asked Pierre to refrain from mentioning any incident in his career. (After all, if he was really determined to suppress information he would presumably not have allowed his nephew to learn it in the first place.) Within the limits imposed by his restricted space and his firm but rather vaguely defined sense of duty to his late uncle, Pierre had an absolutely free hand; his difficulties arose in arriving at a set of principles to guide it. As he looked over a slightly overlong draft of the initial volume, he probably found it easy enough to delete some passages, such as one from a letter Irving had written expatiating on the advantages of travel in Europe. The young American's lofty scorn for his former "errors and prejudices" and his avowed new awareness of "the peculiar blessings"[91] of the United States gave an appealing insight into his cheeky habit of mind and his unabashed nationality; but the letter could safely be omitted, since the same traits would be fully enough treated elsewhere in the volume. Just as certainly, an anecdote dating from 1816 and dealing in some way with the "nether garments of Mrs.

[88] Allibone, "A Visit to WI, June 12, 1855" (Huntington).

[89] In his list of publications included in the end papers of Bryant's *Discourse*, Putnam announced:

In preparation, uniform with these "Works" [the National Edition]
THE LIFE AND LETTERS OF WASHINGTON IRVING
Probably filling 3 vols. 12mo. (p. [7])

See also PMI to John P. Kennedy, New York, February 19, 1863 (Peabody).

[90] *LLWI*, I, 6.

[91] PMI, Holograph Notes (NYPL, Berg).

Bradish"[92] fell by the wayside, presumably on grounds of propriety. The more difficult cases were ones which raised issues less clear-cut than these.

Upon reviewing his draft account of what he had designated was Irving's "second essay into print,"[93] Pierre came up against such a case. It was known within the family that Irving had participated in a bitter public war of words on the eve of the New York state elections in March and April, 1804. Peter Irving, who was espousing the gubernatorial aspirations of Aaron Burr in the New York *Morning Chronicle*, a daily newspaper he edited, had found himself being so viciously abused by a rival editor that, determining at last to retaliate while at the same time preserving the good name of the *Morning Chronicle*, he founded another newspaper, the *Corrector*, whose announced aim was to chasten the intemperance of the enemy.[94] Though a mild-spoken man himself, Peter was seconded in this new design by his brother Washington, then twenty-one and much less given than he to inoffensiveness of speech. Throughout the ten issues of the *Corrector*, pseudonymously edited by one "Toby Tickler," the younger Irving ingeniously assaulted the opposition with scurrilous ridicule.[95] He was so effective that, even though the *Corrector* failed to win the governorship for Burr, he actually did succeed in partially muzzling Peter's journalistic foe. Now, almost sixty years after Irving's adolescent escapade, Pierre knew that it had been forgotten by the public. Nevertheless, after examining the files of newspapers involved in the skirmish[96] he had written out an account of it for the biography. With pardonable partiality—pardonable because what he

[92] MS Outline, Chapter 27 (1816). One other rejected anecdote, of which only faint traces remain in the extant papers of PMI, dealt with the "strictures" of WI's "brother," probably Peter, against certain passages in his biographical sketch of Thomas Campbell, written in 1810 as an introduction to *The Poetical Works of Thomas Campbell* (Baltimore, *et al.*, 1810). (Holograph Notes—NYPL, Berg).

[93] PMI, Holograph Notes (NYPL, Berg).

[94] The historical circumstances of this incident, with selections from PMI's draft account of it, are set forth by Wayne R. Kime in "Peter Irving, WI, and the *Corrector*," *American Literature*, 43, no. 1 (March 1971), 108-14.

[95] All contributions to the *Corrector* were anonymous, but on the basis of linguistic and other evidence articles from each of the newspaper's ten issues have been selected and edited by Martin Roth as *Washington Irving's Contributions to 'The Corrector'* (Minneapolis, 1968).

[96] PMI did examine the files of at least one New York newspaper of 1804, as is indicated by the parallelism of phraseology between a statement published in the *Corrector* on April 4, 1804 (no. 3, p. 10, col. 2) and reprinted in the New York *Evening Post* the following day (p. 2, col. 5). In this passage "Toby Tickler," the pseudonymous editor of the *Corrector*, explains his motives and intentions: ". . . I hope my correspondents will direct their attention more particularly to anecdotes of a political nature. Nothing but dreadful necessity, the most flagitious conduct on the part of my enemies, will ever induce me to enter the recesses of private life, and detail circumstances with which the public have no legitimate concern." In his account of the *Corrector* incident, PMI wrote that prior to the publication of the *Corrector* Peter Irving's opponents "grew bolder from the consciousness of immunity, and from traducing the public character of his friends carried their assaults into the recesses of private life, outraging the feelings of

wrote was true to the ascertainable facts—he presented both Peter and Washington Irving with sympathy and condemned their adversary, James Cheetham, as "an editor governed by no sentiment of delicacy or honor." Emphasizing Peter's moderation and reluctance to engage in "bandying abusive epithets," he pointed out that fraternal loyalty, not political persuasion, had actuated Washington's acid pen:

> ... he was keenly alive to the ungenerous treatment extended to one [Peter] proverbial from a child for refraining from the abuse of others, and was by no means lenient when he undertook to apply the lash. Some of the severest sarcasms in the Corrector came from his pen, and more than one of the epithets stuck to the parties through life. "They would tell me what to write," said he, "and then I'd dash away." But there was ever more of wit than malice in his effusions.[97]

In short, while he placed his uncle in the favourable light he believed him to deserve, Pierre did not shrink from setting forth the details of this pungent incident in Irving's politico-literary history.

On second thought, however, he decided to omit the entire incident from the biography. Limitations of space may have played some part in enforcing his decision, but it is likely that other considerations played a larger role. Irving had not concealed his early political scribblings from Pierre, and in fact during 1859 he had taken obvious pleasure in telling the whole Sunnyside circle an anecdote of one of these exercises in abuse.[98] Pierre also knew, however, that he told no one else. The problem arose: to what degree should he follow his uncle's practice of maintaining public silence regarding incidents of equivocal savour such as this of the *Corrector*? After all, justify it and explain it away as he might, the episode had been characterized not only by unseemly behaviour on the part of Cheetham, the villain of the piece, but by harsh retaliatory tactics on that of the Irvings. Was it really necessary to draw attention to an obscure episode wherein his uncle's conduct had perhaps been ambiguous and was in any case now forgotten? The last thing Pierre wished to do in the *Life and Letters* was to alienate Irving from the public regard. On balance, in the present instance the considerations of economy and propriety outweighed the already compromised one of thoroughness. A narrative of Irving's unsettled youth might well prove to be controversial enough, Pierre may have concluded, without mentioning the *Corrector*.

Once he had ruled to himself on nice questions of editorial policy such as this one, Pierre encountered no other serious difficulties. The task of authorship was demanding, however, and the period during

families, and with flagitious license invading the weakness of female frailty" (Kime, "PMI's Account," p. 110).

[97] Kime, "PMI's Account," p. 108.

[98] See above, pp. 188-89.

which he wrote the first volume was outwardly uneventful for him and Helen. Vacationing at Saratoga each summer, they alternated their regular residence between Sunnyside and the Clarendon Hotel, near which Pierre maintained an office-study at the Bible House. They remained on familiar terms with Oscar and Eliza Irving, Irving and Sarah Van Wart, and Helen's sister Jane Ann Dodge Frothingham, to whose children they felt especially close.[99] Pierre faithfully collected and dispensed funds for Irving's estate, waging a campaign of sales and re-investments, chiefly in bonds. On occasion he amused himself with genealogical research,[100] but he spent the greater portion of his working time on the biography. Inevitably, he was often distracted by the events which led to the outbreak of the Civil War in the spring of 1861, and in the succeeding months by the disastrous series of Union defeats. Yet he made headway, and in April 1862, "with the most unfeigned diffidence,"[101] he published the first volume of the serial biography.

At this point, he suspended his exertions and reconsidered the organization of the *Life and Letters* thus far. He had already completed a topic outline covering almost the entire period he had intended to cover in the next volume,[102] but he was doubtful whether he should limit the work to the three-volume format he had first conceived for it. As the topic outline eloquently testified, Irving's life during the period 1820-1846 had been eventful in the extreme, and only the most rigorous selectiveness would enable him to cover these years in the space he had allotted himself. Looking ahead, he saw that the body of small but flavourful details which he planned to select from his manuscript notebooks for the account of the author's last years would further exacerbate the problem of space. He was disturbed at what already appeared to be the cramping insufficiency of his projection for the total length of the work. From the first he had intended to assemble a generous, circumstantial picture of Irving's travels and acquaintances; but to omit from the succeeding volumes too much of the autobiographic material he had collected would surely frustrate this aim. Perhaps he would do best to relax his rigour somewhat and write a leisurely fourth volume. He was considering this possibility when he received in the mail an unexpected parcel consisting of eighteen long, informative letters, dated between 1828 and 1830, and addressed by Washington Irving to Prince Dmitri Ivanovich Dolgorouki.

[99] Frothingham, Genealogy, pp. 90, 141 (NYPL, MS).

[100] In 1860 PMI was still in correspondence with Colonel Jonathan Forbes, one of his informants in the Orkneys (Misc. Notebook).

[101] *LLWI*, I, [5]. The work was published in the United States on April 15 (New York *Tribune*, p. 8, col. 1).

[102] In fact, he seems already to have completed the composition of much of the volume. On May 10, 1862, less than four weeks after the first volume was published, he wrote to Henry W. Longfellow that he hoped "in a short time to begin with the printing of the second volume, which has been a little delayed by the receipt of additional matter since the appearance of the first" (Harvard).

The efforts of Julia Grinnell in 1859 to discover the whereabouts of Dolgorouki had not been successful, but early in the following year Count Adam Gurowski, the Polish writer and patriot then living in New York,[103] had undertaken to assist Pierre in his search for the retired Russian diplomat. Gurowski was ignorant of Dolgorouki's precise address, but he offered to enclose Pierre's letter of application in a packet of diplomatic mail, so that it would be forwarded from St. Petersburg to its proper destination. Accordingly, on March 5, 1860, Pierre addressed to Dolgorouki a request for the "very great favor" of his sending to New York the letters in his possession addressed to him by Irving. Apologizing for making the application as a stranger, he explained the gesture on the basis of his uncle's interest in the matter. "Mr Irving often spoke to me," he wrote, "of his intercourse and correspondence with you, and signified to me not long before his death that his letters to you would be of value in a Memoir of his life."[104] Many months passed without a reply from Dolgorouki, and by the time Pierre had completed his manuscript of the first volume he had evidently concluded that his application of two years before had either been misdirected or silently refused. In planning his account of Irving's first stay in Spain as part of the second volume, therefore, he was unable for want of information to give any prominence whatever to Dolgorouki.[105]

The Irving-Dolgorouki letters were a valuable acquisition to Pierre's biographical archives, and they quickly enforced a decision to abandon the attempt to squeeze the *Life and Letters* into three volumes. The letters would probably have been more welcome, of course, had they arrived a bit sooner than they did, for the expanse of Irving's long lifetime still to be outlined must have seemed to Pierre a sufficient editorial challenge without this new collection of material to be scanned, shaven, and fitted into place. What was more, the headlong progress of the Civil War made it difficult for him to take his own gentle labours very seriously just at this time. In the summer of 1862, Confederate forces under General Robert E. Lee were pushing northward amidst bloody battles toward the Union capital, and Pierre was following the campaign with anxious concern. "Our poor reeling nation will yet steady itself in the midst of the breakers," he wrote in July to his old friend Daniel Roberts. "A rebellion of such measureless iniquity, so flagrantly inexcusable, cannot succeed."[106] Nevertheless,

[103] Count Adam Gurowski (1805-1866) fled from Poland after the suppression in 1830 of the revolution he had helped organize. After several years spent traveling and writing in Europe, he came to the United States in 1849, where he continued his literary pursuits. From 1861-1863 he served as a translator for the State Department.

[104] PMI to Prince Dolgorouki, New York, March 5, 1860 (Yale). What appears to be a draft of a similar letter from PMI to Mrs. Robert Tyler, also dated March 5, 1860, is at the Library of Congress.

[105] In the MS Outline for the years 1828-1830, numbered as Chapters 49 through 57, Dolgorouki went unmentioned. However, PMI left large blank spaces on the sheets containing these summarized chapters, as if anticipating the possible arrival of material to fill them.

[106] PMI to Daniel Roberts, New York, July 21, 1862 (Huntington).

confident as he might be of an ultimate Union victory, he could not help wondering about the contemporary usefulness of his work. The torn nation could hardly be expected to sustain its interest in the life and writings of the amiable author whom only a few years ago it had admired so lavishly, and the gradually decreasing size of Putnam's royalty payments on the revised works suggested that in fact it was not doing so.[107] Pierre's labour on the biography sometimes seemed to him grotesquely unsuited to the times. "[W]ere it not that I am committed to the task," he told Roberts, "I should feel like dropping the pen."[108]

Happily, a favourable response to the first volume, both in the journals and in letters from friends, helped dispel these gloomy thoughts and instill in him new energy and confidence. Upon receiving a note from the attentive Longfellow, he responded on May 10 with sincere thanks:

> I will not say that I have been gratified – I have been more than gratified – I have been extremely touched by the receipt of your very kind note of congratulation. Absorbed and oppressed as your mind must have been of late,[109] I greet your assurance of the "extreme interest and satisfaction" you have taken in the first volume of the Life and Letters with a deeper welcome than ordinary compliment, & I thank you for breaking silence with these words of sympathy and cheer. I have been something of a self-tormentor as to the reception the biography was likely to meet with, and it is a great relief to me to find that I have thus far executed my delicate & difficult task in a way to find favor with such as yourself. It will be a great encouragement in the labor that still lies before me.[110]

[107] For example, the following are the amounts recorded in PMI's Account Book, pp. 20-30, as payments received monthly from Putnam during the year beginning June 1861:

June 1861	$334.00	
July	333.50	
August	232.50	
September	313.00	(Less $75.00 repairs to stereotype plates)
October	308.70	
November	295.14	
December	200.65	
January 1862	203.00	
February	137.75	
March	166.50	
April	188.50	
May	120.00	
June	121.00	

[108] PMI to Daniel Roberts, New York, July 21, 1862 (Huntington).

[109] Longfellow was severely depressed after a tragic accident the previous year in which he had lost his wife Fanny. See Newton Arvin, *Longfellow. His Life and Work* (Boston and Toronto, 1963), pp. 138-39.

[110] PMI to Henry W. Longfellow, New York, May 10, 1862 (Harvard).

A congratulatory letter from Roberts a few weeks afterward prompted a similarly frank reply. By now, he wrote, the biography was again his "sole employment," and he predicted that with luck he would publish a second volume "about the first of September."[111] Pierre was seldom far wrong in prognostications of this sort, and here he was almost as good as his word: the volume appeared on September 25,[112] carrying the biography up to Irving's return to America in 1832. Even after Pierre's drastic alteration of his earlier plans for coverage, from a period of twenty-six years to one of twelve, this volume was somewhat longer than its predecessor. As matters stood, it appeared that even a four-volume format would afford him little enough space.

His concern that the martial character of the times would detract from the popular success of the *Life and Letters* had been a reasonable one, but it proved to be unfounded; for while George Putnam may have been a lax accountant, he was a shrewd salesman. Before the outbreak of the war he had emphasized the contemporaneity of Irving's conciliatory *Washington*, advertising it as "a good book for the times and a noble present."[113] In 1860 he had begun to offer for sale volumes of a new, significantly entitled "National Edition" of the revised works.[114] Now, amidst the fighting, he continued to insist that Putnam publications were the works of the hour. To the bellicose he offered serial complications of instant history and biography, such as Frank Moore's multi-volume *Rebellion Record*, with engraved illustrations, or *The Book of Heroes and Martyrs*; and to the pacific he offered—a biography of Washington Irving. In his newspaper advertisements he gave the *Life and Letters* top billing, characterizing it as "pleasant reading and an agreeable relief from the depressions and excitements of the time."[115] In one advertisement, for the completed biography, he quoted a review from the Boston *Courier* which characterized the reading of the work as "like turning from the dusty high road, with its vulgar clatter of carts and carriages, into a quiet green lane. . . . Amid the fevers and tumult of the times . . . a book like this is a blessing past utterance. . . . For an hour or so we forget the distracting questions of the day, and in the solitude of our chamber we enjoy a truce from care and troublous thoughts, and bless the book that brings it."[116] On the day the first volume appeared, Putnam unilaterally proclaimed it "The Book of the Year."[117] He had accurately divined

[111] PMI to Daniel Roberts, New York, July 21, 1862 (Huntington). PMI told Roberts, from whom he had not heard for ten years and thought it twenty, that he was "not a fixture in New York, but generally divide[d] the year between town & country." Probably he pursued his work on *LLWI* at SS as well as at the Bible House.

[112] New York *Tribune*, p. 6, col. 1.

[113] From an unidentified newspaper clipping in the Peters Scrapbook (NYPL, Berg).

[114] New York *Tribune*, April 7, 1860, p. 6, col. 4. Publication of the edition continued through 1861. See *The New Englander and Yale Review*, 21 (January 1862), 168.

[115] New York *Tribune*, March 11, 1862, p. 1, col. 3; September 20, 1862, p. 8, col. 1.

[116] New York *Tribune*, December 18, 1863, p. 6, col. 4.

[117] New York *Tribune*, April 15, 1862, p. 8, col. 1.

the mood of the bookbuying public, for continuing popular affection for Irving and distasteful repletion with what the Boston *Courier* called "the dreary record of slaughter" combined to make the first two volumes a distinct sales success. With slight exaggeration no doubt, the Boston *Transcript* announced that by "universal consent, the literary incident of the trade this season, is the publication of the life of Irving."[118]

Had Irving been able to witness the popularity of these first two volumes, he would have been pleased to know that reading the biography was to the American public what he once claimed that reading the courtly legends of early Spain was to him—a "mental tonic" and a welcome escape from "the sordid collisions of the world."[119] Pierre was satisfied, too, although the precise terms of Putnam's sales gambit and the puffery of the newspapers gave him less satisfaction than the reception of the work by serious critics, which was almost unanimously favourable. The negative reaction was limited to a brief notice in the *North American Review* objecting to the first volume on the ground that the Irving portrayed there did not fit the anonymous reviewer's conception of what the mature author must have been like as a young man. "We have read this volume with profound interest," this person wrote, "but we are sorry it has appeared. . . . We doubt whether the publication does justice to Irving's early career. There must have been in one whose old age had so much of majesty and beauty a higher style and stronger staple of manhood, than this volume attributes to the first half of his life."[120] In itself, of course, an objection based on an *a posteriori* formulation of Irving's youthful nature need not be taken seriously.[121] Nevertheless, Pierre felt sufficient respect for a strict conception of biographical propriety that he would have been disturbed to encounter criticism of his quoting materials which, according to the reviewer, "could never have [been] designed for the press."[122] It was true that Irving had explicitly authorized him to publish the letters, journals, and other papers. It was also clear that to write his uncle's early life solely in light of his character in maturity, as the *North American* counselled, was to misrepresent by grossly suppressing the evidence—to erect a kind of lifeless statue. Yet on the other hand, the question rose up again: what

[118] Quoted in Putnam's advertisement in the New York *Tribune*, September 20, 1862, p. 8, col. 1. Both these comments referred to the first volume.

[119] "Spanish Romance," in *Spanish Papers and Other Miscellanies, Hitherto Unpublished or Uncollected*, ed. PMI, 2 vols. (New York, 1865), I, 455. WI wrote that he kept "a shelf or two of parchment-bound tomes" by him as "mental tonics, in the same way that a provident housewife has her cupboard of cordials."

[120] 95 (July 1862), 284.

[121] The complaint of the *North American Review* notwithstanding, at several points in the first volume PMI actually had drawn upon his knowledge of WI as an older man to point out the early manifestation of traits which characterized him in maturity. See, for example, *LLWI*, I, 227-28.

[122] *North American Review*, 95 (July 1862), 284.

good *could* be served by emphasizing Irving's faults and foibles at the expense of his better qualities? Pierre must have recognized that a major difficulty as he continued the biography would be to steer a course between those who would suppress every detail unsuited to their preconceived notions of Irving's character and those on the other hand who would leave no weakness, enmity, or error unrecorded. Perhaps after the second volume had appeared he took ironic notice of the *North American*'s brief and grudging comment on it, expressing gratification at "the late and slow, yet unremitted development of Irving's mental capacity."[123]

The objection of the *North American* was a lone voice in the wilderness, for other publications expressed precisely the opposite view, lavishing praise on the ample selections in the *Life and Letters* from Irving's journals and correspondence.[124] As was customary in contemporary magazines, extended reviews of the biography tended not to be minutely analytical. Ordinarily they consisted of a single introductory paragraph of impressionistic comment on the work as a whole, or as a volume, followed by a synopsis of its contents, interspersed with quotations. Only one review of the first two volumes broke the pattern, and this one, a thoughtful essay by Henry T. Tuckerman, was actually more an estimate of Irving prompted by the publication of Pierre's work than a review of the biography itself. Nevertheless, Tuckerman revealed an intelligent and sympathetic sense of Pierre's aims and methods thus far, and his evaluation, which appears below, is easily the most judicious commentary on the first two volumes yet published:

> The rare good fortune which attended Washington Irving as an author, and which it was his still more rare privilege to enjoy unenvied, has smiled upon his posthumous fame, so far as that is affected by the most authentic tribute to his memory. In confiding to his favorite nephew the task, or rather we should say, the labor of love, involved in editing his correspondence and writing his life, the same good taste that guided his pen and his conduct throughout life are apparent. Intent only upon a candid presentation of the facts of his relative's career and a just exhibition of his character, the biographer has, with remarkable consistency, kept his own individuality, opinions, and even natural partiality, in abeyance. He rarely comments on an incident, or expatiates on a trait; there is scarcely an irrelevant or superfluous observation in the volume[s]. He states carefully, and with sufficient details, the circumstances of Irving's childhood, youth, and manhood; and he

[123] *North American Review*, 96 (October 1862), 574.

[124] See *Littell's Living Age*, 74 (September 1862), 579, and the *Atlantic Monthly*, 10 (November 1862), 648. Other reviews of *LLWI*, volumes one and two, appeared in the *Athenaeum*, no. 1800 (April 26, 1862), pp. 560-61 (vol. I), and no. 1820 (September 13, 1862), pp. 331, 333 (vol. II); *Colburn's New Monthly Magazine*, 127 (February 1863), 165-76 (vols. I and II); the *Continental Monthly*, 1 (July 1862), 389-400 (vol. I); the *Cornhill Magazine*, 6 (August 1862), 274-75 (vol. I); see also footnote 125.

gives a few significant anecdotes of the boy and the youth; sketches the family life, the social environment, and the public events, so far as they influence the fortunes, impress the mind, or enlist the feelings of his eminent kinsman; he indulges in no speculations of his own, and with a refinement akin to that of his subject, avoids all rhetorical artifice. . . . His self-abnegation as a biographer is exceptional, for we can recall no instance where a judicious writer in this difficult and delicate branch of literature has more completely succeeded in making the reader oblivious of his own personality. It is not until we reflect on the work, that we appreciate its merit; it is not until we ponder the result, that we are aware of our obligation to his reticence not less than to his revelations. We seem, for the most part, to listen to the story of his experience from the lips of Washington Irving himself; for his letters are like his talk to those who knew and loved him. . . . Only those who have tried the experiment of collating and arranging in an harmonious whole a mass of letters, notes, and other personal memoranda, can justly estimate the patient skill thus exhibited; only those who enjoyed the personal intimacy of Washington Irving can perceive the intrepid discrimination herein manifest, or thoroughly realize how fortunate the endeared man and the successful author has been in his biographer.[125]

No doubt the claim that Pierre "conceals no weakness while exaggerating no virtue" was overgenerous. After all, he was writing what Tuckerman referred to as "a tribute to [Irving's] memory." Yet it was true that by the sparseness of his commentary he had managed to evoke an air of scrupulous detachment which in turn lent the *Life and Letters* an air of faithfulness and objectivity. The anonymous reviewer for the *Atlantic Monthly*[126] singled out this feature of the first two volumes for particular mention: "To borrow a happy illustration which we found in a newspaper a few days since, [Pierre's] own portion of the book is like a crystal of a watch, through which we see the hands upon the face as through transparent air. . . . It is very evident that it is a truthful biography, and that the hand of faithful affection has found nothing to suppress or conceal."[127] The fact was, of course, that in preference to influencing the reader's responses by

[125] Tuckerman, "Irving's Life and Letters," *Christian Examiner*, 73 (September 1862), 271-72.

[126] The reviewer was quite possibly Evert A. Duyckinck. On April 21, 1862, George Putnam sent him an advance copy of the first volume of *LLWI*, with a request that he write a notice of it for the May issue of the *Atlantic Monthly* (NYPL, MS—Duyckinck Collection); see also Putnam to Duyckinck, April 15, 1862 (NYPL, MS—Duyckinck Collection). On May 31, however, Putnam wrote again to Duyckinck, apologizing that the review, which the latter "had taken so much pains to do," had not yet been published. James T. Fields, the editor of the *Atlantic*, had written to him that "the newspapers had so exhausted nearly all the extracts [from *LLWI*] & they had been copied here and there so extensively that he [Fields] thought the Atlantic would be accused of being behind-hand & so left [the review] after all; waiting till the other volumes appear so that a general article could be given" (NYPL, MS—Duyckinck Collection).

[127] *Atlantic Monthly*, 10 (November 1862), 648.

exhortation Pierre had sought to achieve the same effect silently, by his selection and arrangement of material.

In his account of Irving's life to 1832 Pierre drew avowedly and quite freely upon a variety of sources, including not only his uncle's letters and journals but also notes from private conversations with him and information about him received from friends and relatives —such as the "intelligent female" who passed along the story of an English lady in Italy who, when asked by her daughter to identify "Washington," replied in astonishment: "Why, my dear, don't you know?... [H]e wrote the Sketch Book."[128] On the other hand, he did elect to omit certain mildly unsavoury details, as we have seen; and from the vantage point of more than a century afterward he appears at times to have been needlessly cautious. Certainly one might question whether he might not properly have included such harmless items originally intended for publication as Irving's opinion of Lord Byron's unpublished diary.[129] One unfamiliar with his chronic problems of space or unsympathetic to his concern to preserve propriety and his family's privacy might also find fault with his practice of publishing only selected passages from Irving's letters and journals. However, it is important to bear in mind that in influential contemporary quarters he was thought too bold in just this regard. Within his self-imposed limits of space and varieties of material, Pierre had realized his biographical aims admirably thus far. Washington Irving does speak through volumes one and two of the *Life and Letters* in his own engaging voice, and Pierre's success in allowing him to do so was a triumph of creative editing. In light of Irving's substantial role in giving shape and substance to the work, the egregious puff of the Buffalo *Advertiser* that it was in "every way worthy of a place beside the other works of the great author"—that is, of Irving himself—possessed an ironic dimension of literal truth; but it was Pierre who deserved the credit for composing what another newspaper, the Sacramento *Daily Union,* denoted "a full-length, flesh-and-blood portrait."[130]

As we have seen, when the Dolgorouki letters arrived late in the spring of 1862, Pierre, who was then still anticipating that the second volume would carry Irving's life up to his return from Spain in 1846, had already outlined almost the entire contents of that proposed installment. Thus, having revised his plans and published in September a second volume bringing the record up to 1832, he now had only a few additional chapters to outline in order to complete its successor, which would cover the period 1832-1846.[131] With assurance

[128] *LLWI,* I, 134.

[129] He thought it "skimble-skamble stuff" (MS Outline, Chapter 43 [1824]).

[130] Quoted in Putnam's advertisement in the New York *Tribune,* September 20, 1862, p. 8, col. 1.

[131] The numbering of chapters in PMI's MS Outline is not consistent with the chapter-numbering in the first and second volumes of *LLWI*. Chapters in each volume of the published work are numbered as separate series beginning with chapter one,

born of repeated success he set about his now-routine labours. The third volume of the *Life and Letters* was published on May 30, 1863,[132] and the journals received it with as favourable expressions as those given its predecessors, although with appreciably less fanfare. Their main topic for comment was not the work itself but the inconsequential one of its author's failure to make good his original estimate of its length when complete.[133] The *North American Review* relented still further from its displeasure with the first volume, and in a brief notice postponing extended discussion of the biography until it should be concluded, growled that "Irving's noble nature grows rapidly upon the reader, and we are now almost content to have had such weary details of a somewhat vapid youth."[134]

By far the most significant feature of the third volume of the *Life and Letters* as distinct from the first two went totally unmentioned by the reviewers, but to one interested in Pierre and the development of his relationship with his uncle it is immediately evident. This feature was the degree to which the biographer resisted the natural temptation to give prominence to precisely these topics, and thereby to acknowledge and trace the growing importance to Irving of the interconnection between himself and his nephew. In his account of Irving's life during the period 1832-1846, Pierre is scarcely visible at all as a character; and even though he does at some points discuss himself in relation to Irving's affairs, he omits a great many pertinent details. We never read of his marriage to Helen, for example, although that event might have deserved mention in light of Irving's particular

while in the MS Outline PMI numbered his chapters consecutively throughout. The MS Outline chapter corresponding to the final chapter of the second volume of *LLWI* was numbered 60, and PMI continued that sequence through chapter 77, which dealt with events in 1844. He had completed the MS Outline through chapter 77 prior to the arrival of the Dolgorouki letters in the spring of 1862. When he resumed work on the outline, he adopted a new numbering system: beneath the heading for chapter 78 he wrote "Chap. XIX"; beneath the heading for Chapter 79, "Chapter XX"—and thereafter he dropped the original sequence, continuing to use Roman numerals. The first Roman numeral in the MS Outline, XIX, conformed to the chapter number in the third volume of *LLWI*—see III, 342, beginning Chapter XIX in May 1844—and in this single instance the outlined chapter and the published chapter began and ended with the identical material. Thereafter PMI returned to his practice of numbering chapters in the MS Outline without regard to any external reference. The fact that the first Roman-numbered chapter in the MS Outline is numbered identically with the corresponding chapter in *LLWI* indicates that PMI did not outline this chapter until he knew that eighteen chapters of the third volume preceded it. This in turn indicates that he did not resume work on the MS Outline until he had fitted the Dolgorouki materials into the second volume.

[132] New York *Tribune*, p. 6, col. 4. The third volume was advertised as "in press" in the *Tribune* of March 31 (p. 6, col. 1).

[133] See *Colburn's New Monthly Magazine,* 129 (September 1863), 49-63, and the *Quarterly Review,* 114 (July 1863), 151-79; for further discussion of these reviews, see below, pp. 291-93. Selections from a review of the third volume of *LLWI* in the Boston *Transcript* were published in Putnam's advertisement in the New York *Tribune,* May 30, 1863, p. 6, col. 4.

[134] 97 (July 1863), 287-88.

affection for them both. The critical assistance Irving had given Pierre early in 1839, during his campaign for the Notaryship of the Bank of Commerce, also goes unmentioned, even though it was an act motivated by the author's strong desire to fix his nephew and niece in his own vicinity. At one time Pierre did plan to mention his appointment in 1841 as United States Pension Agent[135]—an event which fixed him even more firmly in New York; but he thought better of it. He did publish Irving's 1843 letter to Julia Grinnell praising himself and Helen, but in a cut version, with the names modestly deleted.[136]

Unfortunately, Pierre's reluctance to portray himself as a character in Irving's biography was not so useful a trait as the "self-abnegation" as a narrator which Tuckerman and others had praised in the first two volumes; for once he began to recount the years when his relationship with Irving became a significant feature in the life of the author, his modesty as an individual threatened to interfere with his responsibility as a biographer. So far as he failed to give due emphasis

---

[135] PMI, Holograph Notes (NYPL, Berg). The sheet which includes a notation of PMI's intention to include this detail consists of extracts from letters written by WI in 1841 and notations of other affairs occurring in that year. It was scissored from a leaf in the volume containing the MS Outline—Chapter 68, part 3 (1841).

[136] The manuscript text and the published passage appear together below. PMI's alterations of the manuscript version are indicated by italics at the pertinent points in that text:

Manuscript (Yale)	LLWI, III, 313
I perfectly agree with *your idea of Pierre and Helen. Never was there a better suited union.* I feel deeply my separation from them; they both seemed to take the place of others dear to my heart, whom I had lost and deplored. *Pierre* came to my side when I was grieving over the loss of my dear brother Peter, who had so long been the companion of my thoughts; and I found in him many of the qualities which made that *dear* brother so invaluable to me as a bosom friend. *The same delicacy of feeling and rectitude of thought; the same generous disinterestedness; and the same scrupulous faith in all confidential matters*: while *Helen* in the delightful variety of her character, so affectionate, so tender; so playful at times, and at other times so serious and elevated; and always so intelligent and sensitive continually brought to mind her mother; who was one of the tenderest friends of my childhood, and the delight of my youthful years. God bless and prosper them both! *and it gives me joy to think that they are prospering; and that Pierre is effectively taking root and thriving in his native city.*	I perfectly agree with you in your idea of and -----. I feel deeply my separation from them; they both seemed to take the place of others dear to my heart, whom I had lost and deplored. ----- came to my side, when I was grieving over the loss of my dear brother Peter, who had so long been the companion of my thoughts, and I found in him many of the qualities which made that brother so invaluable to me as a bosom friend; * * * while -----, in the delightful variety of her character, so affectionate, so tender, so playful at times, and at other times so serious and elevated, and always so intelligent and sensitive, continually brought to mind her mother, who was one of the tenderest friends of my childhood, and the delight of my youthful years. God bless and prosper them both! * * *

to his own affairs as they interacted with Irving's, that is, he failed to trace out a prominent trend in Irving's mature life—his growing dependency on the advice, companionship, and other assistance of his nephew.

Lest Pierre's diffidence be overemphasized, it should be said that his allusions to himself, Helen, or anyone else besides his subject were firmly governed throughout the *Life and Letters* by a single sensible principle: that Irving was to occupy centre stage. Thus, when an interchange between himself and his uncle aptly revealed some feature of the latter's personality or of his concerns at a certain time —as, for example, the unfortunate exchange of letters in 1847 wherein Irving refused to be bullied into a conception of literature as hack work—Pierre was quite forthright in presenting it. Nor, indeed, in narrating this incident did he hesitate to present himself in an unfavourable light or to confess his mortification at the time.[137] Everyone has his limits, of course, and in recounting Irving's sharp reaction in 1844 to "a correspondent's suggestion that he should rent the cottage," Pierre reached his. He judged it expedient to adopt Boswell's face-saving device of referring to oneself as an anonymous "gentleman"—or in this case, a "correspondent."[138]

At one time Pierre had intended to include in the third volume of the *Life and Letters* a considerably larger number of illustrative anecdotes than he finally did. Probably he was deterred from doing so not only by unwillingness to flaunt his own role in his uncle's life but also by other considerations such as solicitude to avoid giving offense to living persons, a desire to protect the privacy of family members, and the consciousness of limited space. Whatever the reasons in particular instances, the third volume was deficient as a whole in the small, piquant details which might have varied and enlivened its portrayal of Irving.[139] Pierre knew this, regretted it, and planned to make up for it in the fourth volume by drawing heavily upon the memoranda in his five notebooks compiled between 1848 and 1859. In February 1863, he wrote to John Pendleton Kennedy that he had amassed a supply of "interesting and autobiographic material"[140] to present in this final installment. Once the third volume was complete. he even set about augmenting his stores by getting in touch with some of his uncle's

---

[137] See *LLWI*, IV, [13]-19.

[138] See *LLWI*, III, 394; MS Outline, Chapter 79/XX (1844).

[139] One of these, listed in the MS Outline under 1842, dealt with the relations between WI and Charles Dickens. The outlined passage follows: "Feb. 10 1842 – Appointed Minister to Spain –... Struggle about accepting – Lionized at Washington – He & Boz [Dickens] were there at same time – Incident at the Dickens party at Mrs. C. Jones" (Chapter 68, part 4). No other record of the "incident" survives.

[140] PMI to John P. Kennedy, New York, February 19, 1863 (Peabody). With his letter PMI enclosed thirty-six letters addressed by WI to Kennedy and lent to PMI by Kennedy for use in preparing the biography—"I am ashamed to think how long ago." PMI continued: "In entrusting them to me it was with the assurance that I need be in no hurry to return them, but I did not mean to abuse this license—yet it was only yesterday that I finished the extracts I think of using."

cronies in the 1850's, including Cogswell, Davis, and Professor Francis Lieber.[141] He looked forward to writing an account of the period in which he had himself known Irving most intimately; and now, with what he anticipated would be the easiest of the four volumes to write before him, he was eager to complete his biographical task. Sixty years of age, he was ready to throw off the harness and put himself out to pasture. He intended for the final volume to afford an unprecedented degree of insight into the elderly Irving's private life; he even planned to relax his procedure of cautiously censoring his own appearances as a character in the book. With luck, he thought, the *Life and Letters* would easily be ready as a completed work in time for the Christmas trade.

[141] See *LLWI,* IV, 114-17, 247-48, 289.

Chapter Eight

An International Episode

At the outbreak of the Civil War in America, the prominent English publisher Richard Bentley was so violently hostile to the Union states that he entertained with satisfaction the possibility of strong British intervention on behalf of the Confederacy, to which England was already extending both sympathy and practical aid. "This at least these bragging bullies will learn," he wrote truculently of the Union leaders in his diary for January 1, 1862, "that there *is* a limit beyond which they dare not venture to offer insult to Old England."[1] However, despite his animus toward the North, on February 27 of the new year Bentley recorded in his firm's account-book his agreement, negotiated through an associate,[2] to

[1] Richard Bentley, Diary No. 5 (Illinois). A general discussion of Bentley's business career, based on the extensive collection of his papers in the University of Illinois Library, is by Royal Gettman, *A Victorian Publisher* (Cambridge, England, 1960). Gettmann refers to WI only once in passing and does not mention PMI.

[2] This person, whom Bentley referred to in his diary as "my good friend Mr. Kimball," was Richard Burleigh Kimball (1816-1892), a resident of New York and an author. For another instance of Kimball's assistance to Bentley, see Jay Leyda, ed., *The Melville Log: A Documentary Life of Herman Melville*, 2 vols. (New York, 1951), II, 467.

do business with a Yankee publisher, George Putnam: he would pay
Putnam £50 per volume for advance sheets of Pierre M. Irving's forthcoming *Life and Letters of Washington Irving*.[3] One consideration
which may have led the publisher thus to except the elder Irving from
his resentment and include a work about him in his select list of titles
was that of prior personal connection. On three occasions during the
lifetime of the author, Bentley had published the English editions of
his works; and on the whole their relations had been friendly and
honourable.[4] A more powerful argument in favour of publishing the
Life and Letters, however, was simple economic prudence. Bentley
knew that in spite of Irving's regrettable nationality he had long been
set down by many as essentially English in his sympathies, and he
must have surmised that even in the present angry atmosphere the
biography would give little offense to a British audience. Moreover,
even though he had not seen the work as yet, he was being offered it at
a pleasantly diminutive sum. In all, the publication of an English
edition from advance sheets seemed a promising speculation. On
March 26, Bentley received a letter from Putnam informing him that a
portion of the proof for the first volume of the *Life and Letters* was
being forwarded, but adding that he need not feel obliged to publish
unless still disposed to do so. "Of course I have much pleasure in
confirming the arrangement," he confided to his diary, "& shall write
to that effect. I shall try to induce Mr Pierre Irving to come to England
to render the book copyright."[5]

The attempt to lure Pierre away from New York, made by Bentley
for the transparent purpose of protecting his modest investment,[6] was
of course unsuccessful, as he must have suspected it would be. Pierre
had virtually nothing to gain, but much to lose in time and expense
from the journey. He was busy writing his book, and even if Putnam's
arrangements with Bentley would imply an additional remuneration
to himself, the amount involved was so small as to be scarcely worth
his notice.[7] Faced with his author's intention of remaining in New

[3] "*Life and Letters of Washington Irving*. published in advance of American
publication £50 per vol. for early sheets to republish from" (Richard Bentley, Account
Book, 1861-1871, pp. 23-24—Illinois).

[4] The three English editions published by Bentley were of *The Alhambra, Astoria,*
and *The Adventures of Captain Bonneville*. For details of the relations between author and
publisher, see Gordon N. Ray, "The Bentley Papers," *The Library*, 7 (September 1952),
185; *LLWI*, IV, 87-89.

[5] Bentley, Diary No. 5, March 26, 1862 (Illinois). In case Bentley was no longer
interested in *LLWI*, Putnam had requested that he forward the sheets to Smith, Elder &
Co. of London.

[6] A foreigner who was resident in or came to England was permitted to claim
English copyright over his works first published while he was on British soil. In other
cases, such as that of *LLWI*, although "an author might enter into a contract with a
foreign publisher, he could not sell the foreign rights in his book for he had none"
(Simon Nowell-Smith, *International Copyright Laws and the Publisher in the Reign of
Queen Victoria* [Oxford, 1968], pp. 33, 52).

[7] The financial arrangements between PMI and Putnam for the publication of
LLWI are unknown. However, Richard Bentley wrote explicitly in his diary that his own
agreement was with Putnam rather than with the author.

York, therefore, Bentley was obliged to attempt the difficult feat of protecting the *Life and Letters* against piracy by other English booksellers,[8] to whom the work of a foreign author not rendered copyright by the author's presence in England at the time of publication was fair game for reprinting without payment of royalties. According to the agreement with Putnam, the advance sheets of the first volume arrived in good time to ensure that the English and American editions of the work would appear almost simultaneously—on April 16 and April 15, respectively.[9] However, within a few days after the Bentley edition was offered for sale, a second one, at less than one-third the price, appeared at London under the imprint of Henry G. Bohn, the publisher of inexpensive volumes for the masses.[10] The Bohn edition came as no real surprise to Bentley, who for years had been seeking with varying degrees of unsuccess to protect his interests against the incursions of this opportunistic competitor. It irritated him, however, for Bohn was effectually siphoning away the profits from what gave promise of becoming a relatively popular work. Yet so long as Pierre M. Irving insisted on remaining in the United States, Bentley could hope for no fundamental change in the situation. Until some other idea presented itself, his only recourse—almost ineffectual—was to advertise his publication as the sole "Authorized" one and to "caution" the public "to ask for Bentley's edition."[11] The advance sheets for the second volume arrived in good time, and the English and American editions were again published almost simultaneously;[12] but Bentley knew well that within a few days he could expect a cheap reprint of his own text, for which he was paying good money, to emerge from the press of Bohn. As he anticipated, Bohn's edition of the second volume made its appearance in the bookshops; and as he also expected, his "cautions" and appeals to the good faith of potential customers came to very little.

[8] This was a difficult task. Defining "piracy," Simon Nowell-Smith has explained that prior to international copyright agreements, "as long as the work of a foreign author was not legally protected it was common property; it was no more piratical for a publisher to print it than for a peasant to graze his pigs on common land" (*International Copyright*, p. 15).

[9] London *Times*, April 16, 1862, p. 13, col. 2; New York *Tribune*, April 15, 1862, p. 8, col. 1. The advertisement for the English edition included the following statement: "Mr. Bentley has purchased the English interest in this work, which will be published in England in advance." This implied *caveat* to prospective pirates was consistent with Bentley's assurance to WI in 1851 that prior publication in England was absolutely necessary in order for the work of an American to secure English copyright; see *LLWI*, IV, 89, 193.

[10] The Bentley edition was priced at a substantial 7s. 6d; Bohn's, at 2s. (*The English Catalogue of Books Published from January, 1835 to January, 1863* [London, 1864], p. 398).

[11] London *Times*, September 17, 1862, p. 12, col. 7. The term "authorized" was legally almost meaningless in this case. It signified only that Bentley had entered into an agreement to publish the work in England. See Nowell-Smith, *International Copyright*, p. 45.

[12] In England on September 17 (London *Times*, p. 12, col. 7); in the United States on September 25 (New York *Tribune*, p. 6, col. 1).

Having twice been victimized in this exasperating ritual, Bentley conceived a plan to secure unquestioned English copyright over the third, and as he then supposed, concluding volume of the *Life and Letters*. He would solicit a contribution to the work from a *bona fide* British subject, publish it as a pendant to the American text, and then claim the protection of English copyright law over the entire volume. It might seem dubious whether an appended section such as Bentley had in mind could be interpreted as extending its copyright privilege over the whole of the work with which it was incorporated; indeed, the law was unclear on the point.[13] Yet the added material would certainly lend new force to his claims of exclusive publishing rights, and perhaps it would discourage Bohn from braving the threat of legal proceedings by publishing a third volume of his own. Much was uncertain, but Bentley decided to pursue his scheme. In some way he managed to make contact with Mrs. Flora Foster Dawson, the younger of the two daughters of Mrs. Amelia Foster, Irving's former friend at Dresden,[14] and inquired whether she would be willing to assist him in his distressing situation. As we have seen, Mrs. Dawson had not been consulted by Pierre in the course of his own research over two years before, and she was evidently pleased to receive this belated attention from the publisher. She responded that she would be glad to cooperate in any way she could, adding that Mr. Pierre Irving had already committed one error about the Foster family which required correction.

Sensing the lady's eagerness to serve him, Bentley encouraged her adroitly in a second letter, expressing gratitude for her helpfulness and asking her advice as to the best way of correcting Mr. Pierre Irving's error. He hoped she would understand that financial pressures, such as the one now being forced upon him by Bohn, made it impossible for him to offer more than token payment for her kind assistance, but he assured her that he would be glad to receive her contribution at her earliest convenience. Mrs. Dawson's guileless and garrulous reply to Bentley's blandishments, probably written in March 1863, exists in only fragmentary form; but it vividly reveals how accurately the publisher had taken her measure and how fully he had enlisted her as a partisan. The extant fragment begins in mid-sentence, apparently after Mrs. Dawson had summarized the memoir she proposed to write and added some remarks complimentary to Bentley:

[13] All that was clear was that a British subject was entitled to copyright privilege over his works published in England and that a national of a country not subscribing to a copyright convention with England—such as the United States—could only, and even then shakily, obtain British copyright by residence and first publication in British territory; see footnote 8. Simon Nowell-Smith does not refer to the approach envisioned by Bentley in the case of *LLWI*, and I have not encountered a reference to such a case elsewhere.

[14] Mrs. Dawson was the wife of the Rev. Alfred Dawson, Rector of Flitwick, Bedfordshire; see above, p. 260, footnote 74. An entry by WI in his cash memorandum book for 1836-1837 suggests that this may have been her address at that time (NYPL, MS).

a tribute of praise from me who am so little known to you can afford I am aware but little satisfaction – still it is the truth and as such I speak it and do not feel satisfied till I have spoken it – Persons are eager & uneasy till they have delivered themselves of angry and unpleasant feelings – I feel the reverse – *those*, I like to suppress and extinguish; but to goodness and worth I feel I *must* bring my offering of praise and throw my mite into the scale.

I have done – and if I have wearied *you*, with your kind heartedness you will not grumble, for it has been a great relief to me – Now let me assure you that what you have offer'd me, with such considerate regrets, I will accept with infinitely more pleasure than double the sum offer'd in a differing manner –

And as you have again stimulated me to proceed with writing the Reminiscences I will find the courage and zeal to do so at once – Let me conclude this long note with withing you every success in disposing of the work, the just remuneration for which it has been attempted to draw from your hands –

Believe me to be

Your's most truly,

Flora Dawson

My eldest Son has just received a most honorable appointment as Chief Engineer to a New Railroad at Alexandria – he is but 24 – and we are most gratified at such a high proof of his steadiness & ability I know I shall have your congratulations –[15]

On April 6, 1863, Mrs. Dawson wrote again to Bentley, apologizing that "Easter, with its visits in and out of town, has rather delayed me."[16] In the meantime, she continued,

... I write to say, that as it was your desire the mistake about my mother being "the daughter of Lord Carhampton" should be rectified, it has occurred to me, that our American cousins, for whom no doubt in some measure Mr Pierre Irving writes, are very fond of a sounding title, and I think I see through the whole work a desire to show how Washington Irving was intimate with the great and noble of all lands – It might therefore suffice to change the words into "whose sister was Countess of Carhampton."

This would probably please his American readers better, than what we should think a greater distinction, that the family of Foster came in with William the Conqueror and that my father could count thirteen unbroken descents and that the Fosters were well known in the history of the county both before and after the time of the Gallant Sir *John* Foster of Bamborough Castle Northumberland where many a goodly monument in the old church tells of their prowess – or that my father in more modern days could move England from one end to the other by his splendid eloquence and political interest – I conceive all this or much more

[15] Flora Dawson to Richard Bentley, n.p., [March 1863] (Illinois).

[16] In 1863 Easter fell on April 5; thus Mrs. Dawson was in error when she dated her letter "March 6." At the head of this letter, she wrote: "My present address is 10 Leighton Grove, Tuffnell Park, Kentish Town N.W."

would come very tame to an American ear compared with some recent connexion with an Earl, or Nobleman of any sort, English or Irish –[17]

From Mrs. Dawson's discourse on her family's origins, honours, and "unbroken descents" it appears not only that she shared Bentley's jaundiced view of "our American cousins" but also that, in her own way, she felt all the reverence for sounding titles that she discerned so contemptuously in them.

After dismissing the problem of the correction as "a mere trifle . . . much best left to you to do as you think best," Mrs. Dawson recurred to a topic of deeper significance to herself. Apparently she had held a conversation with her elder sister, Mrs. Fuller, in which that lady had attempted to dissuade her from writing the sort of memoir she planned. But as she informed Bentley, she had no intention of abandoning the project:

I have however once again to allude to Washington Irving's attachment to my sister Emily Foster now Mrs. Fuller –[18]

She seems to have some objection (which seems to me quite unnecessary) to the fact being mentioned   But I still maintain that the history of Washington Irving's life is imperfect without it – It was not a private matter between ourselves. *Every one* who knew him at the time was aware of it – and this was brought forcibly before me the other day – for my daughter Mrs. Wilson, who has had the pleasure of waiting on you twice,[19] was engaged in conversation with Sir Richard Airey (Major General Sir Richard Airey KCM, Quarter Master General of our forces) and they were speaking on the subject of Pierre Irving's Life of W. Irving –

He had not yet read it but meant to, having been intimately acquainted with him – he seemed *amazed* that the attachment to my sister had not been mentioned –

"Why" he said ["]*We* all thought he was going to marry her"[20]----The *WE* included many other friends moving like himself, in the highest circles of London – Indeed Sir R. Airey was called from my daughter to the duke of Cambridge, who was [letter breaks off][21]

[17] The incorrect statement of Mrs. Foster's relation to Lord Carhampton is in *LLWI*, II, 127.

[18] Emily Foster Fuller was the wife of the Rev. Henry Fuller, Rector of Thornhaugh, Northamptonshire (*Life*, I, 448, note 143).

[19] Since the purpose of Mrs. Wilson's "waiting on" Bentley is unspecified, it is natural to speculate that Bentley may have made his first contact with Mrs. Dawson through this intermediary. Mrs. Dawson might have sent her daughter to Bentley to discuss a book she thought of publishing—see below, pp. 308-09—or to inform him that she possessed information which might be useful for a memoir of WI.

[20] Airey had himself been one of Emily Foster's beaux at Dresden and had been piqued when he was displaced as a favourite by WI. See *The Journal of Emily Foster*, ed. Stanley T. Williams and Leonard B. Beach (New York, *et al.*, 1938), pp. 114-17; Walter A. Reichart, *WI and Germany* (Ann Arbor, 1957), pp. 93-94.

[21] Flora Dawson to Richard Bentley, Kentish Town, [April] 6, 1863 (Illinois). A natural time for an interview between Mrs. Dawson and Mrs. Fuller would have been at

Mrs. Dawson was determined to make public this "attachment." Very probably when Bentley had suggested to her that she write a "Reminiscence" of Irving he did not anticipate any revelation quite so heady as what she proposed; and it may be that he was somewhat disquieted by the almost scandalous flavour of the promised contribution. If so, any reservations he felt were outweighed by his overriding determination to foil the cupidity of Bohn. Perhaps he even took comfort in the thought that Mrs. Dawson's remarks would embarrass Pierre M. Irving, and indirectly through him the United States. Certainly as the Civil War progressed he did not relent in his hatred for the Union. On July 7, 1863, he wrote gloatingly in his diary: "The Confederate Army under Gen Lee advancing in force in the invasion of the North, threatening Washington, Baltimore, Pittsburgh, & Philadelphia. May they succeed! & thus put an end to this wicked war. By this time New York must be sweating at the thought, that the North will now have to pay *in kind*."[22]

Thus Mrs. Dawson wrote away on her account of Irving at Dresden, even though she was faced with the necessity of writing without the cooperation of her disapproving sister. Mrs. Fuller had control of the letters from Irving to Mrs. Amelia Foster and herself and did not permit her the slightest access to them. It is in fact doubtful whether Flora Dawson even asked, for the scanty evidence available indicates that after the hypothetical interview wherein Mrs. Fuller expressed her "objection" to her sister's plan, the two held no substantial communication whatever about the matter.[23] Nevertheless, at the eleventh hour Mrs. Fuller did learn in some way that Mrs. Dawson was completing a memoir, and that alarming news impelled her to compile a contribution of her own. Hurriedly she assembled excerpts from several of Irving's letters to the family—the majority already published in the *Life and Letters*, rewrote a passage from a journal she had kept in the summer of 1823 while Irving was accompanying the Fosters from Dresden to Rotterdam, and dispatched this miscellany to the publisher. She had been obliged to prepare her memoir in such haste that instead of copying out the passages from Irving's letters she simply wielded her editorial scissors at a few points and sent along the originals to Bentley.[24] No doubt the publisher was pleased to receive

Easter. Mrs. Dawson's home at Flitwick was about thirty miles southeast of Cambridge; Mrs. Fuller's, at Wansford, was about twenty-five miles northeast of the same city. An Easter interview between the two women was thus feasible since they lived only a short day's journey apart.

[22] Richard Bentley, Diary No. 5, July 7, 1863 (Illinois).

[23] The overlapping coverage and disagreement over details between the two ladies' published discussions of WI suggest strongly that they did not consult each other concerning the memoirs. See below, pp. 295-98, 306.

[24] I discovered the manuscripts of most of the WI letters published in Mrs. Fuller's interpolated memoir, filed in a manilla folder marked "unidentified," among the extensive Bentley Papers at the University of Illinois. The extant manuscripts include excerpts from the following WI letters written in 1823: May 21-24, May 28, June 1, June 13, and June 23. Passages have been cut away from the manuscripts of two of these

this apparently unsolicited offering.[25] When the English edition of the third volume appeared, on May 26, 1863,[26] Mrs. Fuller's contribution and her sister's appeared, ironically, together, following the text of the American edition.[27]

Now, having brought forth his Britannically enriched work, Bentley sought to protect his market for it. Designating himself by his sounding official title, "Publisher in Ordinary to Her Majesty," he disingenuously advertised the volume in the London *Times* as the "concluding" installment of the *Life and Letters* and boldly warned all prospective pirates: "This work is copyright, and booksellers are hereby cautioned against any infringement of such copyright."[28] He had thus almost brought his ingenious plan to fruition. Too soon, however, he learned that all his efforts had been wasted, since he had failed to interfere with Bohn's determination to pirate the work. Very sensibly, Bohn simply reprinted the American text, ignored the English interpolations, and hurried to the bookstalls with a product whose low price of 2s., the same as for each of his first two volumes, was no doubt just as devastating to his competitor's sales as ever.[29]

letters, both addressed to Mrs. Foster: the first was from a letter dated at Prague, May 28, 1823; the second, in which the top five-eighths of a sheet is cut away and text on both sides is lost, was from the letter of June 1. The length of the passages cut away from the second letter renders it impossible to speculate intelligently about their probable content, but the tiny deletion in the passage from the letter of May 28, which can have included no more than, perhaps, an allusion to "Emily," corroborates the view of Stanley T. Williams that Mrs. Fuller's deletions of manuscript material pertained to matters of "trivial" significance (*Life*, I, 451, note 227). The published texts of the two letters from which the deletions were made are in *LLWI*, IV, 395, 398. Letters or extracts published in Mrs. Fuller's memoir but not extant in manuscript form among the Bentley Papers were two undated extracts, probably from the letter of June 8 (*LLWI*, IV, 388-90), and a letter from WI to Mrs. Foster, Bordeaux, January 9, 1826 (LLWI, IV, 403-05).

[25] Several small details suggest, however, that Mrs. Fuller's contribution arrived barely in time, and that it occasioned delay in the volume's being offered for sale. That Mrs. Dawson's contribution had arrived earlier in the printing process is suggested by the fact that Bentley was able to incorporate part of it—a letter of WI to Mrs. Dawson, written in 1846—in the text of the volume, pp. 314-16, and that her memoir preceded Mrs. Fuller's in the appended chapters. The possibility that Mrs. Fuller's contribution was rather hastily added to the work is suggested by the unusual number of proofreading errors which mar the text of her memoir, while the preceding pages are almost free of them. The probability that publication of the volume was delayed, either by the necessity of setting Mrs. Fuller's memoir in type or by some other complication, is suggested by Bentley's taking the for him unusual step of advertising the work prior to its publication. In this advertisement he announced the third volume as to appear "immediately" (London *Times*, May 22, 1863, p. 13, col. 5).

[26] London *Times*, May 26, 1863, p. 15, col. 2.

[27] *LLWI* (Bentley), III, 334-413. Because the Bentley edition is scarce, and also because the Putnam edition has been reprinted by the Gale Research Company (Detroit, 1967), the interpolations in the Bentley edition of the third volume of *LLWI* are cited hereafter as they were reprinted in the fourth volume of the American edition (pp. [337]-409). Unless otherwise indicated, subsequent citations of *LLWI* refer to the American edition.

[28] London *Times*, May 26, 1863, p. 15, col. 2. Bentley had used these exact words in his pre-publication announcement of May 22; see footnote 25.

[29] To this point, the only other textual difference between the edition of Bohn and those of Putnam and Bentley was that, unlike them, Bohn numbered his pages and

Yet those who did purchase Bentley's third volume of the *Life and Letters* received a generous dose of racy material in its eighty-one additional pages in return for their extra outlay of funds. Under the mysterious initials "E. P."—which have never yet been traced to any editor or author in Bentley's employ—the contributions of Flora Dawson and Mrs. Emily Fuller were introduced by a writer who claimed that they "were received too late to be incorporated in their proper place in this work, but have been considered too interesting to be omitted. There has not been time to communicate with Mr. Pierre Irving, that he might insert them."[30] Prefaced in this way by two misleading implications—that the "letters and anecdotes" were spontaneous offerings, and that Bentley, or "E. P.," actually would have contacted Pierre had there only been time—the interpolated passages followed.

Early in her memoir, which appeared first, Mrs. Dawson announced its central theme.

> [Irving's] first attachment was known to us, in all the details that since have been given to the world. An eminent writer [Pierre] has stated that "it was his only love," but this is an error. The author of his "Life and Letters" makes no direct mention of it, possibly because the object of this second attachment still lives, and has herself thrown a veil over those *warmer* sentiments on the part of Mr. Irving which she appreciated but could not return. But as his first attachment has been given to the world, it seems but fair that those who wish to study the character of one of the most amiable of men, as well as one of the most celebrated of our writers, should not be misled by the idea that he passed in cold, bachelor serenity through the years of his prime.

Mrs. Dawson's introduction moves toward a palpitant evocation of the passion stirred in Irving's breast by his proximity to the young Emily Foster; but then, in a coy manner characteristic of her narrative style throughout the memoir, it breaks off:

> His was not a nature to remain cold and insensible, to shut itself up in bachelor security. A thousand long-dormant hopes and visions arose. Every hope was not, could not be, buried in the tomb. His very love for Matilda H------, related with trembling and subdued voice in the dark shadows of twilight, and reawakening with all its force the visions of domestic bliss, all stirred within him hopes and aspirations which were—never to be realized!
> Enough of this at present. I will recur to it at some future page.

After a detailed account, dated December 23, 1822, of the first meeting between Irving and the Fosters, the memoir proceeds through several anecdotes, interspersed with quotations which Mrs. Dawson pre-

chapters consecutively throughout the work rather than beginning new series with each volume. However, see footnote 77.

[30]*LLWI*, IV, 338.

sented as "being word for word what Irving said." In one undated passage, switching from the past tense to the more dramatic present, she recounted a critical incident which occurred during one of Irving's regular visits to the Foster residence:

> Evening after evening is spent in happy converse. Why is it that, at times, a deep shade gathers on his brow? Yesterday, a large party were here . . . all good, kind-hearted people Irving has learned to like, to some extent at least. He was languid, pale, depressed beyond measure, and hardly spoke; yet he did not leave us till all the world was gone, nor, indeed, till long after. He said he would write in the morning.
>
> He has written. He has confessed to my mother, as to a true and dear friend, his love for E----, and his conviction of its utter hopelessness. He feels himself unable to combat it. He thinks he must try, by absence, to bring more peace to his mind. Yet he cannot bear to give up our friendship—an intercourse become so dear to him, and so necessary to his daily happiness. Poor Irving!
>
> Irving has sent lovely verses to "Emily," on her birthday.
>
> He has almost resolved to make a tour in Silesia, which will keep him absent for a few weeks.
>
> My mother encourages him to do so, and leads him to hope that, on his return, he will feel more cheerful and contented. He sometimes thinks he had better *never* return.
>
> That would be too sad.

According to Mrs. Dawson, one morning a few days after the crisis just summarized in her narrative, Irving arrived at the Foster home carrying a manuscript in which he had written "the history of his first love." He left it, she wrote, "under a sacred promise that it should be returned to him," should be shown to no one else, and should not be copied. "The promise," she added, "was faithfully kept. . . . Every word seems still before me, though years have passed since I last saw those pages. Were it not a breach of confidence, of that compact made between those, of whom two [Irving and Mrs. Amelia Foster] have been called away into a better and brighter world, I could even now recall the whole, in nearly his own words." Presently, Mrs. Dawson claimed, Irving took the advice of Mrs. Foster and set out on a journey which would necessitate his absence for several weeks. The letters he wrote to the family while on this expedition—those from which, as we have seen, Mrs. Fuller had sent excerpts to Pierre for publication—"point out the truth," according to Mrs. Dawson, that Irving's depression of spirits was caused by his love for Emily, who returned his affection "by the *warmest friendship* only."

In the final extended segment of her account, Mrs. Dawson detailed incidents which occurred after Irving's return to Dresden. She drew the memoir toward its close by recalling his visits with the family in later years, including one in 1846, when he was at London to assist in the negotiations over the Oregon boundary question. (At this period, she observed, he had "smoothed the lion's ruffled mane without debasing the stripes and stars.") Her concluding comment was an insinuating profession of hope that as an elderly man Irving's "gentle heart was satisfied" with his "dear, domestic circle," and of trust that at death his soul had passed "into the regions of eternal bliss."[31]

Mrs. Fuller, in the bland contribution which followed her sister's flamboyant dose of gossip, made no mention of an emotional involvement in 1823 between Irving and herself, emphasizing instead his affectionate relations with the whole family. Recounting from her own journal Irving's farewell to them at Rotterdam, she wrote that the sight of him "so pale and melancholy . . . was a very painful moment to us all. We have not often felt so grieved at parting with a dear friend."[32] Like Flora Dawson, she briefly noticed Irving's subsequent meetings with the family, although at one point she remarked candidly that a visit he made to their home in Bedfordshire was "not so cheerful . . . as we could have wished."[33] She gave no indication that she was even aware of her sister's memoir—and indeed, at the time of writing she was no doubt uncertain of the precise terms of Flora's claims. Perhaps she hoped that her silence regarding whatever her sister may have written, and her own portrayal of Irving as no more than a close family acquaintance, would serve together as implicit signals to the reader that her own story was the prosaic truth and that Flora's confection was beneath her notice. If such was her intention, however, she badly miscalculated. Rather than casting doubt on Flora Dawson, by her silence as to the merits of her sister's claims she lent credibility to Flora's characterization of herself as one whose "delicacy" of sentiment impelled her to guard "carefully" the letters from Irving "calculated to lay bare his true feelings."[34] Mrs. Fuller's sense of propriety forbade any public airing of her private affairs, and she took no opportunity now or afterward to discuss in print the allegation made against her will by her sister. The result was that she failed by her disapproving silence to give clear reasons why her sister's account should not be taken seriously.

The English response to the interpolated passages by the two ladies was somewhat varied, but surprisingly it was never once characterized by incredulity. The virulently anti-Union *Quarterly Review*, which had disposed of the first two volumes of the *Life and Letters* with a single brief slur against Irving for certain "insults" he had supposedly "cast upon England,"[35] seized joyously upon Flora Dawson's revelation as a stroke for the English people. On the ground that with the close of the third volume "as much of the career of

[31] *LLWI*, IV, 338-78.

[32] *LLWI*, IV, 386. Mrs. Fuller had commented in similar terms on this parting with WI in her 1860 letter to PMI. See above, p. 260.

[33] *LLWI*, IV, 387.

[34] *LLWI*, IV, 363.

[35] "The Confederate Struggle and Recognition," *Quarterly Review*, 112 (October 1862), 535-70; the quotation is from p. 540. This article purported to be a review of several recent works, including the first and second volumes of *LLWI*, but as its title indicates, it was a propaganda piece in support of the Confederacy.

Washington Irving as is likely to have any special interest for English readers terminates," the *Quarterly* announced its decision to review the *Life and Letters* immediately. With evident zest, the anonymous reviewer quoted a lengthy passage from Pierre's account of Irving's love for Matilda Hoffman, and then continued:

> Thus speaks the editor in his first volume; but there is considerable danger incurred in this publishing biography by instalments. Before the third volume was through the press, a little correspondence has been brought to light which shows that the hero's heart did not remain so absolutely true to its first impression as had been supposed—that, in point of prosaic fact, he did fall in love some fifteen years later with a fair English girl into whose society he had been thrown in Germany, quite seriously enough to be made uneasy by Miss Emily Foster's friendly, but decided, rejection of his addresses. Still, this early attachment, if not quite so exclusive as romance would fain have pictured, exercised, no doubt, a lifelong influence on his character.

If this report of Irving's infatuation with a "fair English girl" extrapolated somewhat from the statements of Flora Dawson, who had never written in so many words that Emily had refused him, it was certainly true to her strong implications. The reviewer concluded with a bit of condescending praise for Irving, who had always felt an "intense fondness for . . . our little England," and who merited "a modest place in that great Parthenon of literary renown" inhabited by "the great British race."[36] In short, the *Quarterly Review* had used the Flora Dawson account as ammunition for a propaganda attack against the Union states, one of whose most esteemed authors it presented as unsuitable for the hand of an English maiden and ranked as a "modest" figure in the *English* literary tradition.

W. H. Ainsworth, the outspoken editor of *Colburn's New Monthly Magazine*, viewed the interpolated material secured by Bentley in quite a different light. Before publishing his review of the third volume, he wrote a blunt letter to the publisher expressing distaste, apparently, both for the matter divulged by Flora Dawson and for Bentley's underhanded manner of rendering it public.[37] In the review, Ainsworth praised the character of Washington Irving as "beautiful" but was much less generous to most of those involved in the production of the *Life and Letters*. Showing some of the fashionable malice toward the Union, he pointed out the "unexplained delay" in publishing this volume—eight months had elapsed since publication of its predecessor—and then dryly remarked that he supposed "Mr. Pierre M. Irving, like many others, must have been with the army." Turning then to the former Misses Foster—or rather, oddly, to Mrs.

[36] *Quarterly Review*, 114 (July 1863), 151-79; the quotations are from pp. 151, 160-61, 179.

[37] This letter is lost, and its contents may be inferred only from Richard Bentley's comments on it and from Ainsworth's later comments on *LLWI*. See footnotes 38 and 39 below.

Fuller—Ainsworth became more directly critical. After summarizing the English additions to the volume, he confessed that "they are not much to our taste ... we cannot think it well that the object of an unrequited affection should herself—even vicariously—put it on the record for publication."[38] Although Bentley, as the English publisher of the *Life and Letters*, was naturally implicated in Ainsworth's criticism of the work as a whole, for some reason he escaped mention in the review. Nevertheless, he had been deeply offended by the comments addressed him privately by the editor. Fortunately Flora Dawson, who seems to have taken criticism with equanimity, was at hand to smooth his ruffled mane. On July 10, 1863, he recorded in his diary having received "a kind letter from Mrs Dawson to make amends for the Ainsworth insolent letter."[39] At this point, until an easily predictable reaction should be received from Pierre M. Irving in New York, Bentley's collusion with Flora Dawson had run its course.

Thus far Bentley's activities had gone entirely unsuspected by Pierre. Since his brief correspondence with Mrs. Fuller in 1860, he had turned his mind to the myriad other problems of writing the biography. In deference to her expressed desire for her family's relations with Irving to remain private—which he very naturally took as touching in some way upon the revealing autobiographical memoir—when he introduced Irving's account of Matilda Hoffman in the first volume of the *Life and Letters* he gave no indication that he was aware of its being addressed to Mrs. Foster. Describing the manuscript, he wrote only that "it bore the impress of being a transcript, which he had retained from a letter written as far back as the publication of Bracebridge Hall [1822]. The ink was faded, and it was without address, but it carried internal evidence of having been written to a married lady, with whose family he was on the most intimate terms, and who had wondered at his celibacy, and invited a disclosure of his early history."[40] With equal tact, in recounting Irving's Dresden period in the second volume Pierre made no reference to the autobiographical letter; but at that point he did make acknowledgement to Mrs. Fuller for her "kindness" in providing him with samples of Irving's

[38] *Colburn's New Monthly Magazine*, 129 (September 1863), 49, 61.
[39] Richard Bentley, Diary No. 5, July 10, 1863 (Illinois). Ainsworth did eventually publish remarks more directly critical of Bentley. In a review of the fourth volume of *LLWI* he took occasion to set forth "the manner in which [the work] came before the world through the hands of [its] London publisher": "It will be remembered that between the first two volumes and third there was a considerable interval. The latter was repeatedly announced, and announced as the 'concluding volume.' ... and when Mr. Bentley at last sent it forth, there were appended two chapters, upon which we made some remarks at the time of their appearance. We have now the biographer's own account of them." After summarizing PMI's account—see pp. 303-06 below —Ainsworth passed on "to the more agreeable subject of Irving himself" ("Irving at SS," *Colburn's New Monthly Magazine*, 131 [July 1864], 297-98). Ainsworth had not explicitly censured Bentley, but by repeating his earlier criticism of the third volume and by providing a sympathetic forum for PMI, he had done what amounted to the same thing.
[40] *LLWI*, I, 223.

correspondence.[41] His manuscript outline of the fourth volume reveals that he planned to publish in it a pleasantly reminiscent letter from Irving to Mrs. Fuller written in 1856,[42] but since the Fosters ceased to play a significant role in Irving's life after his farewell to them in July 1823, his interest in the family for serious biographical purposes was now, he assumed, essentially over.

By July 1863 he was well advanced in writing the final volume of the *Life and Letters*. In his usual fashion he had prepared an outline of the volume—through December 1857—and he was at work on the text when his labours were interrupted by his discovery of the transatlantic activities. He first got wind of Bentley's additions to his work upon reading the gleeful article in the *Quarterly Review*.[43] Amazed and incensed, not only at Bentley's obvious bad faith but also by what appeared from the report of the *Quarterly* to be Mrs. Fuller's reneging on her scrupulous refusal to divulge private information, he impatiently awaited a copy of the English edition of the third volume. Once it arrived,[44] he of course quickly realized that of the two ladies his ire was more properly to be directed at Mrs. Dawson than at Mrs. Fuller, who was not clearly a party to the divulging of her sister's unseemly story. And yet, unfamiliar as he was with the officious spirit of Flora Dawson, he must have wondered why, if Mrs. Fuller was really so determined to keep silence, she had been unable or unwilling to impose the same reserve on her sister. After he had been to such trouble to honour Mrs. Fuller's *published* wish to protect her family's privacy, Pierre could hardly contain his resentment against both the Englishwomen.

He immediately dispatched a letter to Bentley demanding to know his justification for such an underhanded piece of impertinence; but Bentley, who could feel no special wish to conciliate a stranger and a Yankee, particularly after his own plans had aborted so disastrously, gave him no satisfaction. He merely replied that publishing the interpolations had been a necessary device for him to protect his interests, adding that he had duly paid the ladies for their cooperation.[45] Such an explanation could hardly mollify Pierre; in-

[41] *LLWI*, II, 153.

[42] MS Outline, Chapter XXXV (1856).

[43] *LLWI*, IV, 215.

[44] PMI's copies of volumes three and four of the Bentley edition are in the general collection of the New York Public Library. Opposite the title-page of the third volume he wrote in pencil:

Interpolations –   p. 314 – &
Chapters XXIII & XXIV – from p
334 to the end – p 413 –
81 pages in all

He pencilled brackets at the beginning and end of the interpolated passages. For his other marginal notations, see footnotes 52 and 70 below.

[45] PMI to Fitz-Greene Halleck, New York, February 29, 1864 (Boston Public Library). Other than the report of PMI, no evidence exists that Bentley paid Mrs. Fuller. In light of the circumstances under which she seems to have prepared her memoir, it does not seem likely that she would have solicited payment from him.

deed, it is impossible to imagine a plausible one that could. No matter how much anger he felt toward the publisher, however, few avenues of retaliation were open to him. In these antagonistic times any exposure of Bentley's false dealings might well elicit from the English public a reaction pricisely the opposite to what it properly should. The most Pierre could do with any dignity would be to include in the final volume of the American edition a suitable denunciation of Bentley and his machinations—which that personage might delete in his own edition if he pleased—and to cease cooperating with him in his efforts to ward off the depradations of Bohn. These two reprisals, unpleasant enough but in his opinion more than merited, Pierre resolved to make.

Deciding how to repay Bentley in kind was a simple, even trivial problem in comparison to the dilemma facing him now that the Dawson-Fuller interpolations had appeared. Should he ignore this material, which had already been heralded in England as an embarrassing and veracious revelation, would he not tacitly be granting the accuracy of the memoirs while at the same time discountenancing his own reputation as a trustworthy biographer? On the other hand, should he merely reproach the ladies his purpose would be no better served, for his words would be interpreted as mere spite, and the allegations of Mrs. Dawson would go unchallenged. As Pierre viewed the matter, the only way to preserve his image as a reliable narrator of his uncle's life history was to place the whole of the Dawson-Fuller interpolations before the American audience and to discuss that material according to its merits. Adopting this course would necessitate the sudden intrusion of more than eighty unrelated pages into the fourth volume and a corresponding abridgement of his account, much of it already outlined, of Irving's last years. To be imposed upon to this extent was a bitter pill to swallow, but Pierre believed that he had no choice. Whatever the degree of truth in Mrs. Dawson's claims might be—and determining that would require a bit of analysis—he had been placed on the defensive. Having occupied himself with the biography at intervals over several years, in his eyes he had suddenly been challenged to vindicate himself as its author.

Thus, setting aside his occupations immediately prior to the disruption, Pierre gathered about him Irving's letters and journals from the Dresden period once again in order to aid him in analyzing the two ladies' statements. A comparison of the Irving manuscripts to the published accounts by Mrs. Dawson and Mrs. Fuller quickly uncovered convincing evidence that the women had not consulted each other in preparing their separate memoirs. For example, each had described an incident recounted to her by Irving at Alexisbad in July 1823, where while on a solitary walk he had been frightened by what he had referred to in his journal as "the movement of two ill looking fellows";[46] but in their accounts of the incident they were at

---

[46] WI, *Journals* (Reichart), p. 194.

variance in many details. According to Mrs. Fuller, while taking a stroll Irving "caught sight of the shadowy figures of two men closely following him." Hastening his pace and apparently leaving them behind, he fell for a few moments into a reverie, looking into the darkness ahead:

> But what was that? A shadow of a different nature crossed his path; and, as he looked up, he again, and now distinctly, saw those unpleasant, inquisitive persons, who were still closely following him, evidently with no good design, and who were now so near upon him that he heard the crush of the leaves under their feet. What would have been the end of this adventure there is no knowing, had he not at that moment espied an opening among the trees, and the welcome sight of the lights of the town, for which he made in all haste.[47]

Mrs. Dawson's version bristled with particulars and was far more dramatic than that of her sister. According to her, while out seeking a view of Alexisbad Irving had discovered himself lost on a dark mountain, when suddenly to his relief he saw the "red glare" of a fire:

> He made at once toward it, not doubting that where there was a fire there were men; but he had no sooner come in front of it, than he repented of his haste. Four men lay around it, with swarthy faces and outlandish garments; and their countenances, lit up by the fitful blaze of the fire, looked ominously bad. They started forward at his approach; and one wild-looking, brawny fellow, fixed his eyes with a covetous stare on Mr. Irving's gold chain which dangled from his watch pocket. Irving was certainly not pleased with the company he had fallen into; but his self-possession did not desert him even for a moment, and, if he did not feel pleasure, he still thought it best to affect it.
>
> "Good evening to you, my friends," said he, using the few words of German he could command. "I saw your fire from below, and am come to ask one of you to show me the way to Alexis Bad." With that he came still more forward, and stood familiarly by them.
>
> The men turned round and consulted for a moment together; then the oldest, apparently, among them, spoke:
>
> "We cannot go with you to Alexis Bad, but thither lies your way."
>
> They pointed to the intricacies of the forest, and Mr. Irving gave a nod. "It is well," he said; but, having given one look to the stars, the friendly stars above him, one thought to the direction in which he had been walking, he was sure the men had directed him wrong—purposely wrong, since no inhabitant of those forests could be ignorant of the situation of Alexis Bad. However, with admirable coolness, he stood to warm himself a few minutes by the fire, then wished them all again "Gute nacht"; then, following the route they had pointed out, which led diametrically opposite to the right one, he commenced quietly walking onward. No

sooner, however, did he find himself beyond the ruddy glare of the fire, than he threw himself down into a small hollow of the rock where the grass grew thick and high, and lying perdue and motionless, though with ear and eye stretched to the utmost, he beheld exactly what he expected—the four ruffians stealing on after him in the track they supposed he had followed at their instigation. Indeed, he heard a muttered oath of the fellow who had eyed his watch chain, at the folly which had let him pass on. They had barely cleared the spot where he lay, passing, indeed, within a few yards of him, when, with a stealthy movement, as of one who had before then seen an Indian creep through the bushes in the hunting fields of his own America, he crept from tree to tree till he was convinced he had the right point of the compass before him.

This extravagant tale, to which Mrs. Dawson prefixed the title "Washington Irving, his Ramble and his Robbers," continued with a description of his pursuit by the "dark denizens" of the forest, who catching sight of him as he attempted to escape, were "hot on his track" until, after a terrifying run, he found himself "directly opposite the open door of a little hut, where a woodsman's wife, her eldest son, and several other workmen stood chatting together,"[48] and where he was safe at last.

After reading this, Pierre perhaps turned again to Irving's laconic entry in his journal: "Walked at dusk find myself far from home in lonely part of the forest – my alarm from the movement of two ill looking fellows by lonely house in forest." Mrs. Fuller's dramatization of the incident seemed a plausible fleshing-out of the tale Irving had related to her; but Mrs. Dawson's gothico-Falstaffian creation was evidently done not only without consultation with her sister, but with a much greater concern for stirring effect than for adherence to fact. The dialogue, the interpretation of Irving's thoughts at successive moments, and the general showiness of the anecdote all revealed the luxuriance of that lady's imagination.

However, Pierre's closer examination of Mrs. Fuller's testimony cast some doubt over her own trustworthiness as well. Her narrative of the events on the journey to Rotterdam harmonized with the record in Irving's journal, but the collection of letters received from Irving raised questions. In 1860, Mrs. Fuller had included among the transcribed excerpts she sent Pierre a portion of a letter addressed by Irving to Mrs. Foster on June 13, 1823. As it was published in the *Life and Letters*, this letter began:

> I have just got your letter, my dear Mrs. Foster. I thank you a thousand and a thousand times for the very kind solicitude you express about me, you who have so many dear, delighted things at home to occupy heart and soul, to trouble yourself about a wanderer like me.[49]

48 *LLWI*, IV, 373-75.
49 *LLWI*, II, 158.

In the unauthorized addition to the third volume, an entire paragraph intervened between the first and second sentences of this passage.[50] Other excerpts in the later publication varied in small ways from what were purportedly the same texts in the earlier one. For example, a sentence which Pierre had quoted in the second volume, from a transcribed letter dated at Prague, June 8, 1823, read: "Thank you, my dear Miss Foster, for you[r] kind attention in sending me the plan of my route . . ."; in the interpolated version the *Miss* Foster had become *Mrs.*[51] In themselves, perhaps, these inconsistencies were not of major importance; but compounded with Mrs. Fuller's eccentric arrangement of material in the newly published selections—some of which simply duplicated the earlier text, while others melded into a single "letter" passages which had before been published separately, and still others omitted text originally included, to substitute something else[52]—they suggested either incompetence on Mrs. Fuller's part or a deliberate attempt by her to confuse the reader. On the whole, the several gratuitous inconsistencies between the two collections of excerpts supplied by her suggested to Pierre what was in fact the case—that the latter was a hurried performance.

Nevertheless, set beside her sister's account, the flawed one of Mrs. Fuller was discretion and accuracy itself. True, some of the items in Mrs. Dawson's assemblage of anecdote and commentary were authentic and sound. For example, her recollection of Irving relating an anecdote of himself being accosted at a Methodist revival by an old negro bore the stamp of truth, for Pierre had heard him tell this same tale in 1859.[53] Similarly, her extended commentary on the author as "an admirable *relater* . . . [whose] countenance varies with his mood"[54] was corroborated by Pierre's own experience. Yet with great regularity, quite aside from what he could infer from her penchant for

---

[50] *LLWI,* IV, 401-02.

[51] *LLWI,* II, 158; IV, 388.

[52] The Fuller interpolations included selections from all the letters sent by her to PMI in 1860 and published by him in *LLWI,* II, except one to Mrs. Foster dated May 4, 1823, and including WI's verses "To Miss Emily Foster on her Birth-Day" (II, 151-53). Two letters from which PMI had published no excerpts in the second volume, one dated May 28, 1823, and the other undated, were also included in the interpolations (IV, 387-88, 392-96). The later collection included a larger portion of each letter than had been published in the earlier one, but the task of collating the two groups of excerpts was complicated by Mrs. Fuller's having supplied different selections from certain letters. See, for example, *LLWI,* II, 153-54, and IV, 399-400. (The confusion in this instance was worse compounded by the originally published date of one letter being changed in the interpolated version.) Similarly, as published in the interpolation (IV, 401-03), the text of WI's letter of June 13, 1823 is radically different from the excerpts given in the second volume (II, 158-60).

That PMI made some effort to unscramble these selections is indicated by a marginal notation he made in his copy of the Bentley edition beside the undated, previously unpublished letter: "Prague, June 22 or 23d" (III, 395). He made no further notations beside the excerpted letters, however; probably he abandoned the attempt to analyze Mrs. Fuller's procedures in detail as an enterprise not worth his trouble.

[53] *LLWI,* IV, 345; see above, p. 225.

[54] *LLWI,* IV, 353.

chiaroscuro, sentiment, and striking scenes, Pierre encountered evidence of Mrs. Dawson's untrustworthiness. Much of her account purported to be based on a journal kept at Dresden, but she tended to become somewhat vague at crucial points. For example, she presented in journal form the incident when, in her words, Irving "confessed to my mother, as to a true and dear friend, his love for E----," but she failed to specify the date on which this interview had occurred.[55] Elsewhere Mrs. Dawson quoted freely from the excerpts of Irving's correspondence already published by Pierre, but she presented them as if they had originated with her.[56] Finding himself referred to as an "eminent writer" who had supposedly written that Irving's affection for Matilda Hoffman "was his only love,"[57] Pierre saw too that she was not above putting words in one's mouth in order to further her purpose.

Scanning these equivocal procedures, he found it impossible to guess whether Mrs. Dawson was deliberately misrepresenting him or whether, loose-tongued gossip that she obviously was, she was so bent on telling her tale that she simply paid no heed to his exact words. Her confident tone in discussing the manuscript of Irving's confessional letter suggested that she had no suspicion of her fatuity in making some of the statements she did. With calm assurance, she had declared it "evident" that "subsequently" to showing this "memorial of the past" to the family, Irving had "destroyed" it: "His faithful biographer puzzles himself to find for whom it was written, and when; only finding the first and last sheet, which enabled him to judge it was written to a lady, and that she was married."[58] Yet surely the extended passages from the manuscript published in the *Life and Letters* should have shown Mrs. Dawson that the "memorial" was still extant in some form; and by reading more carefully Pierre's account of the letter, she would have learned that only the first and last sheets were *missing* from his copy.[59] Interestingly, Mrs. Dawson's fond memory of the confessional letter ("so beautiful, so touching") in-

[55] *LLWI*, IV, 358.
[56] For example, see *LLWI*, IV, 341, and II, 159; IV, 342, and II, 158; IV, 342-43, and II, 155.
[57] *LLWI*, IV, 342.
[58] *LLWI*, IV, 362.
[59] *LLWI*, I, 223. Mrs. Dawson was not the only person who misinterpreted PMI's account of the manuscript. Correcting her error, he wrote: "A more careful reference to the first volume of the biography, will show her that *only the first and last sheets were missing*, and that there remained sixteen consecutive pages." Elsewhere in the fourth volume, in a note to Mrs. Dawson's reprinted account, he explained the matter again: "The fragment is numbered from page 3 to page 18, the first and second pages and the last being missing" (*LLWI*, IV, 216, 362). Walter A. Reichart seems to have taken these statements to mean that the manuscript included only one page following the extant fragment. He wrote: "The missing final page of this manuscript might have given the answer to much of our speculation, but it is irretrievably lost" (*WI and Germany*, p. 96). However, it is clear that having been confronted with a fragmentary manuscript PMI had no real way of telling how many pages it had included when complete. For a statement by him showing his ignorance of how many "last" pages there were, see below, p. 335.

cluded no information about it whatever that Pierre had not already made public in the first volume.[60] Had she seen the manuscript?

Pierre's suspicion that Mrs. Dawson's account was unreliable was heightened by manuscript evidence he had at hand which flatly contradicted some of her statements. In the Dresden journals Irving had repeatedly referred to two of his acquaintances as "Cockburn"—his traveling companion on the tour to the Riesengebirge—and "Col. Barham Livius"—an intimate at Dresden; in Mrs. Dawson's version these names metamorphosed into, respectively, "young Colbourne (son of General Colbourne)" and "Barham Surás."[61] According to Irving's journal, Mrs. Foster urged him to remain close to the family rather than making a journey to the Riesengebirge; in Mrs. Dawson's account, when Irving spoke of making the tour Mrs. Foster "encourage[d] him to do so."[62] Pierre had ample reason to believe that Irving had mailed his autobiographical letter to Mrs. Foster from Prague on June 19, 1823; but according to Mrs. Dawson, he brought it himself to the entire family.[63] In light of conflicts regarding basic matters of fact such as these, Pierre could hardly accept without question Mrs. Dawson's further statement that Irving had "related with trembling and subdued voice in the dark shadows of twilight" his "love for Matilda H------." Recalling Irving's fixed silence about Matilda prior to 1823 and in later years, it was difficult to imagine him discoursing on the subject, no matter how feelingly, before the entire Foster family. Yet here was Mrs. Dawson claiming that before the day when Irving supposedly brought them his manuscript, he had "long wished us to know every detail of his first affection."[64] How could she know that? Why, moreover, should Irving have "related" his love for Matilda orally? At one point Mrs. Dawson claimed that he did so, but at another she wrote that he lay the facts of his first love before the Fosters by delivering them a letter.[65] Did he do both? If so, why? Surely the manuscript now in Pierre's hands, wherein Irving had replied to the lady's query as to the reasons why he was not married,[66]

---

[60] Mrs. Dawson wrote: "There were from sixteen to twenty pages, touching on many incidents of his youth, which led him into that deep and intense attachment which was returned to his heart's desire by that sweet girl. Their first, their last interview, all was there; even some faint description of his broken-hearted loneliness when that sweet dream was over" (*LLWI*, IV, 361). Compare this with PMI's statements in *LLWI*, I, 223, and the quoted excerpts in I, 225-27.

[61] *Journals* (Reichart), pp. 125-78; *LLWI*, IV, 343, 362. In his article, "WI's Friend and Collaborator: Barham John Livius, Esq.," *PMLA*, 56 (June 1941), Walter A. Reichart explained one of Mrs. Dawson's errors as "the result of inaccurate transcription of poor handwriting." He added: "While glancing at my own notes one day, I discovered that the word Livius could look like Surás" (p. 513, note 4).

[62] *Journals* (Reichart), p. 148; *LLWI*, IV, 358.

[63] For a discussion of the analysis which led PMI to his conclusion concerning the dates when the letter was written and mailed, see above, pp. 261-62. Mrs. Dawson's statement is in *LLWI*, IV, 361.

[64] *LLWI*, IV, 343, 361.

[65] *LLWI*, IV, 343 (oral); 358, 361 (written).

[66] "You wonder why I am not married. I have shewn you why I was not long since –" (*Life*, II, 261).

showed that he had not yet at that writing held the alleged conversation with her. In short, Mrs. Dawson's account was riddled with exaggerations, apparent self-contradictions, and outright errors which, taken together, seriously weakened the credibility of her primary claim.

Yet, as we have seen, Pierre had discovered for himself more than three years before that Irving's Dresden journals did point to an unusual degree of intimacy with this family. After occupying himself agreeably for several months with private theatricals, dancing, lessons in German and Italian, walks through the lush parks, and carriage rides to the outskirts of the Bavarian capital—in many of which pastimes Miss Emily Foster had evidently added to his enjoyment —he had abruptly decided on April 17 to "quit Dresden soon."[67] Two weeks later, on April 30, he seemed, just as abruptly, to have changed his plans again; for after spending a "Very pleasant Evening" at the home of his attractive friend Madame de Bergh, he had "returned home in very good spirits determind to see society & gather myself up."[68] Four days later, he had written the lines "To Miss Emily Foster on Her Birth-day," a copy of which Pierre had received from Mrs. Fuller; but from then until his departure from Dresden on May 20, the journal showed no sign to suggest that he might have been suffering the depression of a rejected lover. Now, noting that Mrs. Dawson's sometimes-dated account evidently placed Irving's "confession" to Mrs. Foster a few days previous to Emily's birthday, on the morning after an evening at the Fosters' when he had been "languid, pale, depressed," Pierre re-examined his uncle's journal to ascertain how fully it corroborated the particulars of the Dawson story. The only entry which supported Mrs. Dawson in any degree, he saw, was the one for April 28, two days before Irving had expressed determination to "pick himself up." The summary of that day ended uncharacteristically, and perhaps with a suggestion of something unutterable:

> ... read french in the Evg.–
> call at Lowensterns–⟨sit⟩ then at Livius–&c &c &c &c &c

[69]

[67] *Journals* (Reichart), p. 140.
[68] *Journals* (Reichart), p. 146.
[69] *Journals* (Reichart), p. 144.

Could this be the evening when Flora Foster had noticed Irving's depression? It seemed possible. On the basis of the evidence at hand it was certainly not possible to refute all Mrs. Dawson's claims. Pierre's scrutiny of the manuscript evidence relating to Irving's tour from May 20 to June 26, 1823, yielded conclusions no more definitive than those he had arrived at concerning the stay at Dresden.[70] Thus, having made a careful study of Mrs. Dawson's account, he was sure that as a whole it was utterly untrustworthy; and yet on the crucial question whether Irving had been deeply in love with Emily Foster, as this tasteless lady averred, he was unable to form a definite opinion. One general point was certain, however, and it would be useful in his published comments on Mrs. Dawson's memoir: had she really been able to recall "every word" of the autobiographical letter, as she wrote she could, she would not have made some of the statements about it which she did.

Upon completing his manuscript of the fourth volume, Pierre proceeded with the cooperation of Putnam to return his favours to Richard Bentley. In the United States the work was published with appropriate fanfare early in December,[71] in good time for the Christmas trade; in England, proof sheets failed to reach Bentley until December 17[72]—making it impossible for him to publish the work during that profitable season. Moreover, when the proofs did arrive, they were wanting the voluminous index to the entire work which had been prepared as a labour of love by S. Austin Allibone and published in the American edition.[73] The "authorized" English edition of the fourth volume thus failed to appear until January 14, 1864, and even then it was *sans* index.[74] Meanwhile, the reliable H. G. Bohn bustled into print with a hastily and inadequately *indexed* version which,

[70] That he analyzed the two interpolated accounts in relation to the evidence of WI's journals is indicated by his marginal comments at the outset of Mrs. Fuller's re-written narrative from her journal. Beside her first sentences ("Mr. Irving dined with us. We walked to the Grossen Garten"—*LLWI* [Bentley] III, 384; corresponding to the American edition, IV, 378), he wrote the date "May 16," which he had ascertained from the journal. See *Journals* (Reichart), pp. 151-52. At the bottom of the same page in his copy of the English edition, he wrote: "May 20 – Leaves D."

[71] "The Publisher has the satisfaction of announcing that the 4th volume of this delightful and attractive work is completed, and will be published Wednesday, December 9" (New York *Tribune*, December 8, 1863, p. 6, col. 1). The biography was offered for sale in two editions—the Sunnyside and the National— and in formats priced from $6.00 to $32.00 for the four volumes (*Tribune*, December 17, p. 6, col. 4). Three days after the fourth volume was published, Putnam advertised in the *Tribune* as follows: "Booksellers awaiting supplies are urged to exercise their well known patience for a few days, when he [Putnam] expects to have a sufficient quantity to fill the orders received" (December 12, p. 8, col. 5).

[72] Richard Bentley, Account Book, 1861-1871, p. 47 (Illinois).

[73] See the acknowledgement to Allibone for performing this helpful service: *LLWI*, IV, [5].

[74] London *Times*, January 14, 1864, p. 12, col. 6. Following the numbered pages of his edition (vii + 305 pp.), Bentley added a "Notice": "A copious INDEX to this work is in course of preparation, and will be ready in February, price One Shilling."

naturally, must have outsold Bentley's.[75] In light of these events alone, it is unlikely that Putnam ever received the agreed-upon £50 for "advance" sheets to the fourth volume.

In the work itself Pierre took opportunity to revenge himself further upon Bentley. Turning his attention to the recent affair immediately prior to introducing Irving's correspondence with Mrs. Fuller in 1856, he wrote that since "the London publisher of the biography"—temporarily withholding the name of this individual—"has taken the surprising liberty of introducing two whole chapters . . . at the end of the third volume, without my knowledge or consent, giving some further particulars of the author's life at Dresden, I feel it necessary again to recur to the subject." Then, having concluded his discussion of the additions themselves, he stated his intention to publish as an Appendix to the volume "the new matter so unwarrantably obtruded . . . by Mr. Richard Bentley." In the Appendix he roundly denounced Bentley's " 'double editing' " as "a proceeding, I imagine, without precedent in the annals of literature."[76] Not surprisingly, Bentley saw fit to delete from his edition almost all traces of this scathing denunciation.[77]

[75] It is impossible to specify the exact date on which Bohn published his edition of the fourth volume, since he did not advertise the publication of his new titles in the newspapers. However, according to W. H. Ainsworth, "Mr. Bohn had already published both volume and Index" before Bentley managed to prepare his own index to *LLWI* ("Irving at SS," p. 297). Bohn's edition was priced, like its predecessors, at 2s., but Bentley raised the price of his from 7s. 6d., that of the first three volumes, to 10s 6d. Subsequently, he raised the price of each volume of *LLWI* to that level (*The English Catalogue of Books . . . January 1863 to January 1872* [London, 1873], p. 199). During 1864 both publishers offered four-volume-in-two editions for sale, Bohn's at 7s. and Bentley's at an unknown price.

[76] *LLWI*, IV, 214, 220, [337].

[77] Bentley's edition of the fourth volume includes none of PMI's references to him by name. For PMI's explanation that "as the London publisher of the biography . . . has taken the surprising liberty of introducing two whole chapters . . . without my knowledge or consent . . . I feel it necessary again to recur to the subject. This new matter, to which the bookseller has resorted as a device to obtain a copyright . . ." (*LLWI*, IV, 214-15), Bentley substituted a statement that "as the London publisher of the biography . . . has introduced two chapters . . . without my knowledge . . . I feel it necessary to recur to the subject. This new matter, to which the publisher has resorted . . ." (IV, 189). The text of Bohn's edition (IV, 908) duplicated the passage as revised in Bentley's.

Except for chapter-numbering and pagination—see footnote 29 above—the only textual differences between Bohn's edition and Bentley's were, first, that whereas Bohn published an independently compiled index, Bentley published a shortened version of the Allibone Index to the Putnam edition; and second, that Bohn published one explanatory footnote included in neither of the other two editions. This footnote, signed by himself, was in reference to a passage in WI's autobiographical manuscript which PMI had quoted in his discussion of Mrs. Dawson's claims. Commenting on WI's reference to himself as having been "involved in ruin," he wrote: "This doubtless alludes to his bankruptcy in 1818, while resident in Liverpool, and carrying on business in partnership with his brother. The firm was gazetted on January 1, 1818, as Washington Irving, of Liverpool, carrying on trade with Ebenezer Irving, of New York, merchant, and obtained a certificate May 26, 1818. His failure appears to have been caused by the loss of a large cargo of guns, consigned by the firm and their brother-in-law, Mr.

In deep contrast to the scorn he heaped upon Bentley, Pierre treated the two ladies with polite, if strained, forbearance.[78] For example, summarizing a passage from Mrs. Dawson's account of the Irving manuscript he wrote:

> ... the written sheets were brought to the family by Mr. Irving himself, at Dresden, and left for their perusal, under a sacred promise that the manuscript should be returned to him; that no copy should be taken, and that no eyes but theirs should ever rest upon it—a promise, adds the same authority, faithfully kept.[79]

In light of Mrs. Dawson's having divulged information about Irving and her sister which, by her own avowal, they both wished to keep secret, the irony of the concluding phrases in this passage can hardly be overlooked; but Pierre gave no sign that he was aware of it. He introduced his response to her statements with circumspection, and even, given the circumstances, with magnanimity. There "are some things in the journal of Mrs. Dawson a little calculated, though no doubt unintentionally," he urbanely observed, "to mislead, or rather to be misunderstood."[80]

Mrs. Dawson claimed that Irving had felt "a hopeless and consuming attachment" to Emily Foster, adding that it "was fortunate, perhaps, that this affection was returned *by the warmest friendship only* ... since it was destined that the accomplishment of his wishes was impossible, for many obstacles which lay in his way." The clear suggestion of these assertions—that Irving had wished to marry Emily Foster—was Pierre's primary point for rebuttal. After quoting her words, he wrote:

> While I am not disposed to question, for a moment, the warmth or sincerity of his admiration for the lady, that he ever thought of matrimony at this time is utterly disproved by a passage of the very manuscript to which the sister refers. . . . In that manuscript, after recounting the progress and catastrophe of his early love, forever hallowed to his memory, and glancing at other particulars of his life . . . all given with the frankness and unreserve of perfect confidence, he closes, by saying:

Van Wart, of Birmingham, as a joint speculation, to the United States, in 1815, during the short war. After the peace, Mr. Irving instituted a suit in America, claiming indemnification on the plea that the guns were American, not English property, and were shipped for American purposes (shooting the English?), but Mr. Irving lost his suit; and the Birmingham gunmakers their money. The only dividend which the firm appears ever to have paid was fivepence in the pound, April 18, 1828" (IV, 909). Bohn's motives for including his footnote are unknown. The two most obvious explanations seem to be either that he wished—perhaps for legal protection—to publish a volume which differed in a substantial way from Bentley's, or else that he wanted to take a fashionable swipe at American bellicoseness and hostility to England.

[78] To Mrs. Fuller he was even gracious, praising once again her "beautiful testimonial to [WI's] character" published in the second volume of *LLWI* (IV, 218).

[79] *LLWI*, IV, 214.

[80] *LLWI*, IV, 215.

You wonder why I am not married. I have shown you why I was not long since. When I had sufficiently recovered from that loss, I became involved in ruin. It was not for a man broken down in the world, to drag down any woman to his paltry circumstances. I was too proud to tolerate the idea of ever mending my circumstances by matrimony. My time has now gone by; and I have growing claims upon my thoughts and upon my means, slender and precarious as they are. I feel as if I had already a family to think and provide for.

The reader will perceive from this passage, addressed to Mrs. Foster, at Dresden, after months of intimate friendship, what color there is for the assertion that Mr. Irving ever made advances for the *hand* of Miss Emily Foster, however great or undisguised may have been his admiration for her.[81]

Pierre was willing to grant that Irving had "admired" Miss Foster —even with "warmth"—but on the strength of Irving's own testimony he refused to accept the implication that his uncle had sought the girl in marriage. Of course, the autobiographical letter was not really in itself the ironclad proof of Irving's sentiments that Pierre suggested it was. After all, Irving may have had thoughts which he thought it best not to divulge even to Mrs. Foster. Still, the quotation Pierre published was satisfactory for practical purposes, for it *was* a point-blank refutation of Mrs. Dawson's suggestion. There was no denying that the evidence against her virtual assertion of Irving's desire to marry Emily easily outweighed the published evidence in favour of it.

A concern to conserve his remaining space in the fourth volume, and perhaps also a prudent wish to avoid seeming overly contentious toward Mrs. Dawson, led Pierre to forebear from challenging her on many other points. Probably for the same reasons he made no reference to the inconsistencies between Mrs. Fuller's bland account and the transcribed letters he had received from her three years before; he did not even point out the redundancy of the later contribution. In the Appendix to the volume he did include a few remarks on the two memoirs reprinted there, but only one of these constituted a significant challenge to either lady. In her reference to Irving's depression on the trip to the Riesengebirge, Mrs. Dawson had claimed that the author of the *Life and Letters* "apparently does not know or does not reveal the real cause" of it—namely, disappointment as a lover. In a note to the passage Pierre quietly professed himself "too familiar with [Irving's] occasional fits of depression to have drawn from their recurrence . . . any such inference as that to which the lady alludes." He might have written much more to the purpose, for he knew that his uncle had been oppressed during the spring of 1823 by several concerns aside from Emily Foster: he was regretful at having lost money

[81] *LLWI*, IV, 215-17.

through speculation; he was frustrated at having been unable to write creatively; he was saddened to hear that his late brother William's wife had suffered a mental collapse; and he was lonely for his family. However, rather than enumerating these other circumstances—most of which he had already set forth in the second volume for those who cared to read of them—Pierre merely observed that Irving's " 'memorandum book' and letters show him to have had, at this time, sources of anxiety of quite a different nature."[82] Restraint and economy were the rule throughout his reply to Mrs. Dawson. Without special pleading, he met her partway but firmly rejected her claim of Irving's matrimonial ambitions.

But if he acquitted himself with exemplary reserve in public, in private Pierre made no attempt to conceal his opinion of the two Englishwomen, particularly Mrs. Dawson. What incensed him still was not so much her allegations themselves as her clandestine manner of making them. On February 29, 1864, he aired his views on the whole affair in a letter to Fitz-Greene Halleck, his acquaintance of Astorian days. Acknowledging the poet's recent information that a sonnet, "Echo and Silence," published in Mrs. Fuller's memoir and apparently assumed by her to be of Irving's composition, was in fact written by Sir Egerton Brydges,[83] he continued:

> It is by no means the only blunder that she & her sister have made. Mrs. Dawson in particular is remarkable for the careless inaccuracy of many of her statements – If you compare the two accounts you will see that she is at variance with her sister in the night adventure at Alexisbad—The two sisters must have rushed into print without comparing notes to be confronted with such a discrepancy.... I have dealt with the ladies as tenderly as possible, but I have nevertheless been exceedingly incensed at their most indelicate, unseemly & impertinent irruption into the English edition.

He could not resist a private fling at the ladies on the basis of their nationality. "Mr. Bentley writes me," he continued, "that he paid them for their contributions, and I am sometimes half-inclined to suspect that they were encouraged by their husbands (clergymen of the Church of England) whose poverty may have consented to such a compromise of decency on the part of their wives."[84] Ludicrous as it is, this savage rake at the Church of England as the indirect cause of the want of "decency" in English women is a just measure of the rage which the Foster incident had kindled in Pierre.

It is possible that Pierre's privately expressed view of the matter was relayed to the American public through Donald Grant Mitchell,

---

[82] LLWI, IV, 363 and note.

[83] See LLWI, IV, 405-06. A discussion of this misattribution and of PMI's attitude toward Mrs. Fuller and Mrs. Dawson is in Francis P. Smith, "WI, the Fosters, and Some Poetry," American Literature, 9 (1937), 228-32.

[84] PMI to Fitz-Greene Halleck, New York, February 29, 1864 (Boston Public Library).

who reviewed the completed *Life and Letters* in the *Atlantic Monthly.*[85] While it seems unlikely that he would have requested of Mitchell that he discuss this unpleasant episode, we do know that the two men were in contact not many months before the review appeared. As late as January 19, 1864, Pierre wrote to Mitchell acknowledging the author's gift of a new edition of his *Dream-Life*—one which included as its preface an insightful reminiscence of Irving.[86] No evidence exists to prove that at some time afterward he expressed to Mitchell his opinions of Bentley and Mrs. Dawson, but similarities of sentiment, phraseology, and subject-matter between his letter to Halleck and Mitchell's published review suggest that the biographer did convey his views to the reviewer either directly or indirectly. For example, by some means Mitchell knew—what he could not have learned from the *Life and Letters*—that the two former "Misses Foster . . . are now wives of clergymen of the Church of England"[87]—Pierre's exact phrase in his letter to Halleck. He also knew that "Echo and Silence," the sonnet written by Irving in the scrapbook of Emily Foster and published by her as his own, was by Sir Egerton Brydges.[88] He agreed with Pierre's private estimate of all three apparent *collaborateurs* in the interpolated English edition, and like him, he reserved his most acidic remarks for Bentley. Using an epithet Pierre had employed in the letter to Halleck, Mitchell first surveyed the "unseemly interpolations" by the ladies and then turned his attention to the publisher:

> Mrs. Fuller, the elder of the sisters, and the special favorite of the author, gives upon the whole a modest and pleasant account of their association with Irving. . . . The contribution of the younger sister, Mrs. Flora Dawson, is in a somewhat exaggerated and melodramatic vein, in the course of which she takes occasion to expend a great deal of pity upon "poor Irving," who is made to appear in the character of a rejected suitor for the hand of her sister. It is true that the testimony of Mr. Irving's biographer, and of his private papers, is largely against this absurdly romantic construction; but, although it had been perfectly authentic, it is almost incredible that a lady of delicacy should make such blazon of the affair, for the sake of securing a copyright to "Her Majesty's Publisher in Ordinary." We are sorry that Mrs. Dawson has not made a better *début* in literature. As for Mr. Bentley, we can characterize his conduct in the matter only by the word —disgraceful. In the whole history of griping literary piracies (of which Americans must bear their share) we can recall no one which shows so bad a taste, and so bad a faith, as this of Mr. Bentley, the "Publisher in Ordinary to Her Majesty."[89]

[85] "WI," *Atlantic Monthly*, 13 (June 1864), 694-701.

[86] PMI to Donald G. Mitchell, New York, January 19, 1864 (Yale). See "A New Preface" in *Dream-Life: A Fable of the Seasons* (New York, 1863), pp. [iii]-xiv.

[87] Mitchell, "WI," p. 698.

[88] Mitchell wrote that "the well-known lines entitled 'Echo and Silence' " in Mrs. Fuller's memoir "certainly do not prove very much for the writing-mood of Mr. Irving,—whatever they may prove for Sir Egerton Brydges" (p. 698).

[89] Mitchell, "WI," p. 698.

Whether or not his influence lay behind this attack,[90] Pierre must have felt warm at heart as he read how Mitchell was ruffling the mane of the English lion. Naturally, the Foster affair had loomed much larger in his mind than in those of his readers. The topic never inspired general discussion either in England or in America, and even in the months before he had published his reply to Mrs. Dawson there is no evidence that her surprising claims had coloured the common reader's opinion of his work in the unflattering tones he feared it might. Once the fourth volume of the *Life and Letters* had been published and a few reviews written, the episode was quietly forgotten. Mrs. Dawson had been sufficiently answered, Bentley had been rebuked twice over, the *Life and Letters* had won discriminating praise, and England's hopes for the survival of the Confederacy were on the wane. After all the frustration this incident has caused him, Pierre must have been delighted to bid it farewell on such favourable terms.

Flora Dawson was not quite finished, however, for the exchange with Pierre had failed either to alter her views about her sister's love life or to curb her penchant for gossip. In fact, her contribution to the *Life and Letters* only solidified her comradeship with Bentley, for in 1864 he published *Princes, Public Men, and Pretty Women*, a collection of ephemerae by her hand. In this work she further exercised her talent for self-dramatization and indulged her love of titles, wealth, and notoriety. In the preface to *Princes, Public Men, and Pretty Women*, dated August 1864, she explained the reasons why she felt competent to write such a book:

> Having passed many years at foreign courts, and mingled with men whose 'names are famous in story'—and being connected by ties of friendship and consanguinity with several who were themselves leaders and actors in the stirring events which convulsed Europe for more than fifty years—I have been enabled to gather, from eye-witnesses, a number of curious and interesting incidents. From among these I have at present taken only a few slight sketches—such as might best suit the tone and character of this work.[91]

Two of Mrs. Dawson's "slight sketches" were devoted to Washington Irving, the first of which dealt with his religious views, and the second with his "political influence"—that is, his residence in London during the treaty negotiations concerning the northern boundary of the United States.[92] In both pieces she was at pains to point out, as of old, Irving's English sympathies, and to set him apart from the common

---

[90] The relationship between Mitchell and WI is one of the primary themes of Waldo H. Dunn in *The Life of Donald Grant Mitchell* (New York, 1922). Although he does mention Mitchell's review of *LLWI*, Dunn gives no indication of the way in which he may have gathered his information in preparing the article.

[91] *Princes, Public Men, and Pretty Women: Episodes in Real Life*, 2 vols. (London, 1864), I, iii.

[92] "The Author and the Divine; or, WI and the Rev. Charles Simeon," II, 131-42; "WI's Political Influence," II, 143-53.

run of "American demagogues";[93] but only in the first sketch did she take an opportunity to allude delicately to her recent rehearsal of Irving's tragic passion. Setting the scene of a visit he had paid the Fosters a few years after the Dresden period, she summarized his intervening career in this way: "Some pleasures were past; some hopes had been crushed; some anticipations had faded away since then; but poetry, music, converse sweet on many themes, still made those days a faint reflection of former happiness."[94] No matter what Irving's biographer might have done to gainsay her claims, that Irving had suffered crushed "hopes" was in Mrs. Dawson's mind an unassailable fact.

From the outset of her campaign to publish this theory, Flora Dawson's only ally had been Bentley. Faced with her sister's refusal to cooperate, and aware that Mrs. Fuller had corresponded with Pierre desiring that he respect a wish for privacy, she felt almost alone in her crusade. Her reference in the interpolated *Life and Letters* account to Pierre, who "either does not know or does not reveal the real cause" of Irving's depression in May and June 1823, suggests that she may even have suspected Pierre and Mrs. Fuller of collaborating in some way. Whether or not she did, at least by her coy allusion to Irving's blasted "hopes" in *Princes, Public Men, and Pretty Women*, she managed to have the last insinuating word; for neither Pierre nor Mrs. Fuller were to be drawn into further controversy. Five years later, in his three-volume revision and condensation of the *Life and Letters*, Pierre merely reiterated his position.[95] His reasoned conclusions and her own beliefs, however, she had arrived at them, were as irreconcilable as sense and sensibility.

Over a century has passed since Pierre published his final opinion of Flora Dawson's claims, but in that time further analysis of her statements has revealed very little more about the relationship between Emily Foster and Irving than his delegated biographer was willing to grant. In an edition of Irving's journals published in 1919, George S. Hellman and W. P. Trent advanced a theory that Irving made a proposal to Emily Foster on March 31, 1823, but the evidence they produced to justify the view was very weak.[96] The discovery and subsequent publication in 1938 of Emily Foster's private journal during the Dresden period revealed that she had been aware of Irving's esteem for her but that she did not return it ardently. "[G]ood dear

---

[93] *Princes*, II, 148. Elsewhere Mrs. Dawson wrote: "He [WI] stands, indeed, alone, an honorable exception. Who among his countrymen has dared to act like him? Who has had the courage and the independence to give a faithful picture of England?—to describe as she is, this gem of the ocean? Where shall we now find the American, who, nourishing a fervent affection for his own country, still *loves old England?*" (II, 144).

[94] *Princes*, II, 136-37. In a footnote to the passage preceding this, referring to the "deeply prized intimacy of the Dresden days," she wrote: "See Life of Washington Irving."

[95] *LLWI*, "Revised and Condensed, in Three Volumes" (New York, 1869), III, 314-15.

[96] *Journals*, I, 173, note 1; 174, note 1.

nice," she thought him.[97] The journal also confirmed Flora Dawson's claim to Bentley that a rumour had been abroad in Dresden to the effect that Irving and the elder Miss Foster were to be married. On April 28, 1823—the same day for which Irving had concluded his own journal entry with a cryptic string of ampersands above an inverted pyramid of parallel horizontal lines—Emily Foster had written in hers: "Party at Friesen's—that report that I am to marry 'certo signore autore'—begins to annoy me—Kleist joking about it—got up when ----- appeared to leave me tete a tete with him I was quite angry—"[98] Emily Foster's journal does not show, however, that Irving ever proposed to her or that he wished to marry her. Her anger at the party on April 28 was undoubtedly upsetting to Irving and probably did account for the unusual marks in his journal; but her record of the incident gives no indication that she was disturbed or offended at *Irving's* behaviour to her. In short, while her journal lights up our knowledge of her mind at this period, it fails to corroborate the claims later made by her sister.

Surely the most extraordinary phenomenon in the lengthy and inconclusive discussions of the relationship between Irving and Emily Foster already in print has been that, while the account of Flora Dawson has sustained a reputation for credibility far exceeding its merits,[99] both the tone and the substance of Pierre's response to her statements have consistently been misrepresented and censured. In spite of his readiness to grant virtually everything known at present about Irving and Emily Foster—and that on the basis of less information than we now have—his acumen has been overlooked and he has been falsely miscast as the villain of the piece. George S. Hellman, who in his capacity as co-editor of Irving's journals breathed new life into the Foster controversy,[100] claimed in his subsequent biography that as part of a design to perpetuate "the tradition of Irving's exclusive devotion to his early romance" Pierre "sought to suppress"

[97] *Journal of Emily Foster*, p. 130 (May 4, 1823).

[98] *Journal of Emily Foster*, pp. 128-29.

[99] In his brief reference to Mrs. Dawson's account, George S. Hellman was without the slightest reserve as to her credibility (*WI, Esquire*, p. 49). Stanley T. Williams recognized that Mrs. Dawson's "love of the sentimental is obvious" (*Life*, I, 249), but in his narrative of WI's early relations with the Fosters he nevertheless drew upon her account for anecdotes unmentioned elsewhere (I, 239, 240). He also treated her journal-like but undated account of WI's confession to Mrs. Foster, "as to a true and dear friend, [of] his love for E----," as a *bona fide* journal entry; and, exaggerating a valid point, he remarked in her favour that many "details" in her narrative "agree with those in Irving's journal" (I, 449, note 151). Walter A. Reichart was still more generous to Mrs. Dawson. While he did not gainsay her "volubility" (*WI and Germany*, p. 94), he accepted her as a "creditable witness" (p. 97) and took several of her otherwise unsubstantiated statements at face value (see pp. 98-99).

[100] Hellman had not made up his mind about PMI by the time the journals were published in 1919, six years before his biography of WI. Nevertheless, in the introduction to the journals he and W. P. Trent looked askance at PMI's use of these documents in *LLWI* as having been aimed at perpetuating "sentimentalized legend and sophisticated record" (*Journals*, I, xx).

evidence of his uncle's affection for Emily Foster. According to Hellman, this suppression took the form of deleting certain passages in the journals—in particular, that for March 31, 1823:

> On that day, after dining at the Fosters, Irving returns from an evening party, from which, on scrutinizing the diary, we are able to make out he goes "home very much   ." "Very much" *what*? Oh Mr. Nephew and Biographer, we surmise that the adjective you so provokingly rubbed out was "depressed," and that it was during these last moments of March that Washington Irving unsuccessfully asked Emily Foster to be his bride.[101]

One may inquire how Hellman knew that this erasure was by Pierre? Surely if Pierre had been determined to deny Irving's affection for Emily—which from his own words he obviously was not—he could have concealed this "evidence" by, say, destroying the entire notebook. As to Hellman's wild "surmise" that the missing word must have been "depressed" and that the word's absence shows that on March 31 Irving had asked Emily Foster to marry him, such a leap of blind faith requires no comment. To put the case charitably, Hellman's notion that Pierre was an unscrupulous fabricator of a romantic myth about Irving's love life betrays his unfamiliarity with Pierre's actual practice as a biographer.

Stanley T. Williams, who has expended more energy than any other modern scholar in an attempt to arrive at the facts of Irving's relationship with Emily Foster, was much more interested in the original association between these two persons than in the way the rumour of their romance surfaced in 1863. Accordingly, in his biography of Irving he virtually ignored Pierre's role in the controversy at the time the *Life and Letters* was published. However, he judged it "probable" that Pierre "withheld" sensitive information about Irving and Emily Foster,[102] and his casual references to Pierre as a "protective" biographer[103] lend tacit credit to Hellman's notion that he was a rigid if not an unprincipled censor of material facts concerning this passage in his uncle's life. Williams regarded Pierre as having been not only secretive, but also spiteful. In his sole reference to the circumstances under which the Dawson-Fuller additions were reprinted in America, he wrote that Pierre "included the letters, though with bitter reproaches and denials of the truth of Mrs. Dawson's assertions, as an appendix to his concluding volume."[104] Clearly, this statement is in important respects incorrect and misleading. The record shows that Pierre took pains to deny only one of Flora Dawson's claims—that Irving had wished to marry Emily Foster. The record also shows that Pierre's "bitter reproaches" were not directed, as Williams' syntax

---

[101] *WI, Esquire*, pp. 55-56. For an accurate transcription of the journal entry, see *Journals* (Reichart), p. 133.

[102] *Life*, I, 407, note 185.

[103] *Life*, I, 252; II, 475.

[104] *Life*, I, 449, note 150.

invites us to believe, at Mrs. Dawson, whom he handled with great tact, but at Bentley. Furthermore, a familiarity with Bentley's motives and methods, which Williams did not possess, would have shown him that Pierre's expressions of reproach were hardly the overboilings of a splenetic cynic caught in his foul play. Pierre had been double-crossed and treated inexcusably by Bentley, and the "Publisher in Ordinary to Her Majesty" deserved all he got. With his plans for the concluding volume of the *Life and Letters* sadly deranged, and with his good faith as a biographer called into question as a result of collusion between Bentley and members of a family he had thought honourable and treated as such, Pierre's bitterness was wholly understandable. It is to his credit that he comported himself in public with the restraint he did.

Ironically, after a long and finally unsuccessful quest for definitive answers about Irving's affection for Emily Foster, Stanley T. Williams concluded in 1935 on a note which Pierre had sounded more than seventy years before him. That is, seen in the perspective of Irving's long and eventful lifetime, his months at Dresden with the Fosters were really not very crucial, for they left no deep or lasting impression on his character and they in no way constituted a turning point in his lifetime.[105] True, he passed through an emotional period there, compounded of many strands, but he soon outlived it; and as his letter of 1856 to Emily Fuller reveals, his memories of Dresden were happy. The loss of Matilda Hoffman affected the course of his lifetime; his friendship with Emily Foster did not. The miniature of Matilda he kept hidden, with an account of his love for her, in a secret compartment of his desk; "The Head of Herodias," a gift from Emily, he hung in the sitting room of Sunnyside, in plain view.

Regarded not as an incident in Irving's lifetime but as an episode in the composition of the *Life and Letters*, however, the Emily Foster affair takes on a new significance as an instructive case study showing Pierre at work as his uncle's biographer. It reveals that his methods and judgments in attempting to identify Irving's manuscript fragment and assess its significance were thorough and sound. It shows that the position he took in the *Life and Letters* after evaluating Flora Dawson's claims was cogent and justified. It validates his denunciation of Bentley, and it points up his notable reserve in responding to Flora Dawson. With these conclusions before us, we may now dismiss some of the false views of Pierre as a biographer and personality which have spring up in the fertile soil of inadequate study and easy surmise. The Foster affair was a troublesome, unpleasant experience brought on by forces entirely outside Pierre's control; and not the least of its direct effects, as we shall presently see, was to render the final volume of the *Life and Letters* a far less satisfying work than it would have been had he been able to complete it according to plan. The episode ended tolerably to himself, but once it was over Pierre would very likely have

---

[105] *Life*, I, 251-52, 254; see *LLWI*, IV, 216, and 363, note.

agreed with a comment to be made by Charles Dudley Warner in his brief biography of Irving (1881). After quoting from Flora Dawson's perfervid record of the supposed "confession" to Mrs. Foster, Warner observed: "It is well for our peace of mind that we do not know what is going down concerning us in 'journals.' "[106]

[106] Warner, *Washington Irving* (Boston and New York, 1881), p. 134.

Chapter Nine

The Completed Collaboration

In his own words, Pierre had decided to publish the Dawson-Fuller interpolations in the American edition of the *Life and Letters* "not as a matter of choice, but of necessity."[1] This decision was of course a severe disruption to his plans, for it entailed the sacrifice from the fourth volume of more than eighty pages of space which he had earmarked for other purposes. The consideration of cramped space is insufficient of itself, however, to explain certain characteristics of the work as Pierre finally published it. For example, in recounting Irving's life during the years 1853-1854, where he had planned to include a generous selection of his uncle's letters to members of the Kennedy family, he made no attempt to condense his material.[2] His entire account of the years 1848-1854 was in fact done substantially according to the scheme he had set down in his manuscript outline before he learned of Bentley's additions to the third volume. Only the chapters covering the years 1855-1859 were appreciably thinner in their por-

[1] *LLWI*, IV, [337].
[2] See MS Outline, Chapters XXX-XXXIII (1853-1854); PMI's extracts from WI's letters to the Kennedys during this period are in *LLWI*, IV, 135-211 *passim*.

trayal of Irving than what the outline, Pierre's 1859 journal, and his later remarks reveal that he had intended to write. It seems possible, therefore, that having already written out a manuscript of the volume through 1854 by the time Bentley's escapade came to light, he decided simply to leave that portion of the work unaltered and condense his account of Irving's last five years.[3] Yet even if this supposition is accurate, it still fails to explain the *type* of coverage he gave his uncle in his survey of the later period—the kind, not the amount, of material. Questions of brevity or expansiveness aside, the subject-matter he selected for use in the concluding pages of the *Life and Letters* reveals that, between the time when he outlined these chapters and the time when he prepared the published text, Pierre radically altered his conception of his aims as biographer of the elderly Irving.

While he did omit much material from his account of the years 1855-1859 which at one time he had planned to use, his chief motive for doing so was not a desire to achieve economy of space but rather a rigourous conception of biographical propriety. Exactly why this sentiment took so sudden and firm a hold over him during the summer of

[3] PMI did not outline the work beyond 1857. He wrote a heading, "Chap. XXXVII / 1858," on the page following that for 1857, but no entries beneath it. Although the reason or reasons why he did not outline the biography for 1858 and 1859 cannot be stated authoritatively, one explanation seems plausible: PMI may actually have intended to complete the outline but have been distracted when he was about to begin doing so by some interruption, such as the receipt of news concerning the Dawson-Fuller interpolations. This theory is supported by the fact that in his outline of the year 1852 he had included a reference to the memoir of WI by Charles A. Davis, which was dated "June 1863." Since PMI was thus writing his outline of events in 1852 sometime not earlier than June, he would have been at work outlining the chapters for subsequent years at some time afterward. As we have seen—see p. 294 above—he learned of the Dawson-Fuller interpolations from reading the July issue of the *Quarterly Review*.

Even if he was temporarily distracted from completing the topic outline, however, it remains to account for his not completing it once he had an opportunity to do so. The facts that his published account of the years 1848-1854 agrees generally with his topic outline of it, and that his published account of the years 1855-1857 notably does not, suggest together that at the time he changed his plans for the remainder of the volume he had completed a manuscript text of the former passage but had not completed, or perhaps even begun, the latter. The primary logistical reason for this change of plans was of course the cramped space remaining to him, owing to the interpolations. The fact that his account of the years 1855-1857 is substantially briefer than what the MS Outline reveals he once intended suggests that he wrote the chapters recounting these years after receiving the news of the interpolations.

If, as thus seems clear, PMI wrote his account of WI's life from 1855 to 1859 at some time after discovering the interpolations and realizing their implication for his prior plans, then in writing these final chapters he knew they would necessarily be shorter and organizationally simpler than their predecessors. He also knew that in his five manuscript journals he had at hand a ready-made thread of narrative, a chronological outline of WI's activities. The "journal" format of LLWI, which begins at September 27, 1855, suggests that in preparing a manuscript of the final chapters PMI used his journals as a basic outlining tool in lieu of the more formalized one he had previously compiled. Various reference marks in the 1859 Journal which correspond to passages included in the biography lend strength to this suggestion. The reason why PMI failed to complete his topic outline of LLWI, therefore, was probably that he decided his journal entries between1855 and 1859 would serve his organizational purposes adequately.

1863 is impossible to state with certainty, but it is natural to speculate that the Foster affair—easily the most exasperating incident that had occurred in the whole checkered course of his labours on the *Life and Letters*—affected his views. Certainly the "tribute" of Mrs. Dawson was perfectly designed to serve as a vulgar case in point warning him against divulging further details of Irving's personal life. Indeed, if he was able to regard it objectively at all, the entire Dawson-Fuller incident stood as sterling proof that public discussion of Irving's private life was folly. This vexing episode may well have taught Pierre the practical wisdom of playing the censor with a heavy hand, and other concerns may also have impelled him in the same direction. For example, in July 1863, just at the time he learned of the interpolations, the vicious New York Draft Riots broke out and raged for three days and nights.[4] During this particularly tense period of the Civil War, it must have been no simple task for so concerned a bystander as he to weigh points of editorial procedure with so nice a care as he had in writing the previous volumes. Besides, by now he was probably impatient to complete the biography. If the final chapters did not measure up to his more ambitious plans of a few months before, he perhaps thought to himself, at least they would be finished.

Whatever may have been the proportionate influence upon him of these or other considerations, Pierre resolved to discuss Irving's last years according to a set of principles actually more characteristic of his own personality and predilections than what he had written into the manuscript outline. Since youth he had been essentially a private man, affectionate and dear to his family and close friends but appreciably more restrained toward others, and seldom clamourously gregarious. He had respected the privacy of other persons, always keeping confidences scrupulously, but for the most part had kept his deepest thoughts to himself. These habits, deeply ingrained in his nature, were inconsistent with his plan of divulging to the general reader facts of Irving's character and experiences which he had learned only through an intimacy with his uncle over many years. Perhaps until he saw Flora Dawson's betrayal of what she called a "sacred trust" he failed to realize that he could not be comfortable in setting aside what he must have come to interpret as an implicit obligation to respect Irving's privacy. If this was indeed the case, once he realized what he was about to do he quickly changed his ways. He shared Irving's contempt for the prying habits of the journalists who wrote to please a "private public." He was no professional journalist—the small financial reward he would receive from the *Life and Letters* would be in no proportion to the labour he was expending in preparing it; why then should he emulate the N. P. Willises? The public revered Irving, after all, and it was anticipating an "official" biography to justify and confirm its sentiments. Pierre's own regard

---

[4] The Draft Riots occurred July 14-16, 1863. See Lee, *Discontent in New York City, 1861-1865*, pp. 121, 142.

for his uncle was rooted in a thorough knowledge of both his strengths and his weaknesses, but the intelligent affection he felt was impossible to impart through a book. Why should he jeopardize the public's admiration of Irving—who richly merited it—by including in the *Life and Letters* material which might only confuse some readers and detract from their appreciation of his character? What right had they to know items of that sort anyway? Pierre seems to have decided that the general reader was neither entitled to know overmuch about Irving's private life nor prepared to interpret such information correctly; and accordingly, he wrote with new circumspection.

In the manuscript outline of the fourth volume he had expressed an intention to emphasize his own relationship with the elderly Irving to a degree more befitting its real importance in Irving's life history than he had done in its predecessor; but in the published work he did not do so. He made no attempt to deny the closeness of the relationship, of course, nor to gainsay Irving's dependence on him. At intervals he offered valuable insights into kinds of assistance he had lent Irving in preparing the *Washington*,[5] and in recounting the events of 1859 it was simply impossible to discuss the author at home without acknowledging his own presence there. Yet he did give much less prominence to himself as an influence in Irving's later lifetime than he had intended and the facts required. For example, in his outline of topics to be covered under the year 1855, after referring to the publication of the first volume of *Washington*, he had written this entry: *"Determines now with my assistance in preparing roughly Hist: of the Administration &c. to complete the work to close of Washington's Life. Urges me to relinquish business & give him my undivided time."*[6] Yet in the published *Life and Letters* there is no indication that Pierre played any part in Irving's decision to complete the *Washington*, that Irving ever urged him to quit his business, or that Irving wished, or indeed ever received, his full-time assistance. These were material omissions from a biography that purported to be reasonably thorough and definitive.[7] Other items of lesser import but of value for a proper understanding of Irving's relationship with Pierre were also excluded. The outline reveals, for example, that Pierre had intended to publish excerpts from letters exchanged between himself and Irving concerning what he labelled "the Griswold and Mercer affair." He had discovered evidence that Rufus W. Griswold, his correspondent in 1842 on the topic

---

[5] That these scattered details were thoughtfully selected and, taken together, afforded a suggestive body of material for a sketch of the collaboration between the two men is demonstrated by the fact that the summary of their cooperation in preparing volumes two through four of the *Washington*, pp. 135-37 above, is assembled primarily from references in *LLWI*.

[6] MS Outline, Chapter XXXIV (1855).

[7] Concluding the work, PMI wrote: "My task is finished. I have traced the career of the author from its commencement to its close, as far as possible, through his own letters and words; and if the reader has not imbibed a correct idea of his personal and literary character in this way, it would be idle to attempt a more formal delineation of his virtues as a man, or his genius as a writer" (*LLWI*, IV, 331).

of Irving's literary ethics, had borrowed from the *Washington* an error concerning Hugh Mercer, a colleague of Washington, and had reproduced it in the serial biography of the first President which he himself had begun publishing in 1856.[8] We read nothing of this incident in the *Life and Letters*, however, and thus we are deprived not only of the amusement which a recital of its details would probably have afforded, but also of a useful insight into Pierre's continuing role as guardian of his uncle's literary interests. Similarly, although by 1856 Irving and he were collaborating in the collection of material for the *Life and Letters* itself, we read nothing of the manner in which the former promoted the progress of that undertaking.

Pierre was not only reticent to appear as a character but was no longer willing to play the role of a reportorial intruder into Irving's private habitat. A brief passage from his topic outline for the year 1856 will afford us an indication of the rich selection of observations he had at one time intended to present. For the passages immediately prior to introducing Irving's letter to Mrs. Fuller, written in July of that year, he had planned to rely almost solely on his own notebooks: "Attends Everett's Oration on The Character of Washington March 3. Anecdote. See Note Book March 31. 1856. Letter to H. T. Tuckerman. (Take in from Note book to April 9. 1856) and then a few pages in Note Book 4."[9] Unfortunately, all of this is absent from the *Life and Letters*, and what Pierre substituted for it was of much lower lasting value. To flesh out his account he drew upon a variety of innocuous material, including reviews of Irving's writings, published accounts of visits and interviews at Sunnyside, and selections from Irving's correspondence. Besides factual introductions to passages quoted from his journals or from other sources, in these chapters he wrote only about four hundred words of authorial commentary on his uncle.[10] The predominating journal format in the final chapters of the *Life and Letters*[11] only suggested an intimate observation of Irving's doings and sayings. It was a form largely devoid of the content it implied.

Pierre's use of the material he had at hand to portray the elderly Irving reveals clearly some of the main considerations that shaped the lineaments of his portrait. He took pains, first of all, to ensure that the account would be inoffensive. How actively he sought to keep this section of the work uncontroversial is suggested by his cautious use of the entire 1859 journal, eighty-one of whose dated entries he used in recounting that year's events, and fully seventy-six of which appeared

[8] "Letter from P. M. I. Dec. 12 about the Griswold & Mercer affair – The Doctor had published two numbers of The Illustrated Life of Washington – & had copied the *Mercer* error" (MS Outline, Chapter XXXV [1856]). See p. 168, footnote 102 above; see also Jacob Blanck, *Bibliography of American Literature*, III (New Haven and London, 1959), 229.

[9] MS Outline, Chapter XXXV (1856).

[10] See *LLWI*, IV, 280, 285, 299-300, 310, 312.

[11] See *LLWI*, IV, 196 *et seq.*

in judiciously trimmed versions.[12] For example, whereas in his journal for September 13, 1859, he had recorded Irving's vitriolic opinion of the recently deceased Leigh Hunt, in the biography he was more discreet:

1859 Journal	*Life and Letters*
Speaking of Leigh Hunt, whose death was mentioned in today's paper: "Never met him, and never liked him. A dash of vulgar flippancy about his writings; belonged to a Cockney clique for whom he had no relish (Hazlitt among them—a low fellow); their vulgar junkettings for which Mrs. Holloway had to pay."	Speaking of an English writer whose death had been announced in the papers, he remarked: "I never met him, and never liked him. He belonged to a Cockney clique for whom I had no relish. They used to hold junkettings at the house of my landlady, Mrs. H-------, with whom I lodged soon after I went up to London... and they sometimes forgot to pay for them."[13]

Even on a topic of such importance to Irving as negro slavery—a topic which, considering the times in which he was writing, he might have felt called upon to present his uncle as discussing with some vehemence—he was cautious. In June 1859, when Irving learned of a South Carolinian's criticism of him for presenting George Washington as being opposed to slavery, he had bristled: "Did you ever know such fools, willing to incur the opprobrium of the whole world for their accursed slavery?" In the biography, Pierre cut short the outburst: "Did you ever know such fools?"[14] In order to avoid overly frequent references to the present sectional conflict, Pierre even altered the text of a memoir of Irving which Charles A. Davis had written for his use. Describing the author at Saratoga Springs in 1852, Davis had written that "altho' he was at once surrounded by a very gay and brilliant circle assembled there, from near and distant parts of our *then* 'Union,' he was sure to *secede* at once from any circle that attempted to make a *Lion* of him." In the *Life and Letters* Davis' harmless and, indeed, rather lame witticism had vanished: "Although he was at once surrounded ... by a very gay and brilliant circle assembled there from near and distant parts of our Union, he was sure to withdraw at once from any circle that attempted to make a lion of him."[15] As these revisions suggest, Pierre's surgery on his usable material was almost invariably extractive.

[12] The five exceptions were the entries for March 18, September 18, September 30, October 11, and November 27.

[13] See above, pp. 227-28; *LLWI*, IV, 308-09. Of course, any reader of *LLWI* familiar with contemporary literary affairs would have recognized Hunt as the subject of WI's comments.

[14] See above, p. 209; *LLWI*, IV, 299.

[15] Davis to PMI, New York, June 1863 (NYPL, Berg); *LLWI*, IV, 114.

Originally he had intended to skewer certain individuals of whom Irving had disapproved; but in order to preserve the dignity of the book he refrained from doing so, or if he did insult someone he managed to do the job obliquely.[16] The primary instance of his earlier plans in this regard was the treatment he had proposed to give to a heated controversy, referred to in the manuscript outline as "*The Hamilton affair*,"[17] in which Irving had been directly involved. The ill feelings arose in 1857 when Irving's neighbour, John C. Hamilton, discovered that in the recently published fourth volume of the *Washington* he had criticized the conduct of Alexander Hamilton in a temporary falling-out the young military aide had had with Washington in 1781.[18] John C. Hamilton was an industrious celebrant of his father's achievements, having published a two-volume *Life* of the statesman (1834, 1840) and edited a seven-volume edition of his *Works* (1850-51). At this time, in fact, he was about to begin publishing another multi-volume work, one with the revealing title *The History of the Republic of the United States of America . . . as Traced in the Writings of Alexander Hamilton and his Cotemporaries.*[19] Angered at the remarks in the *Washington*, Hamilton addressed a strongly worded letter to the Washington, D.C. *Daily National Intelligencer* criticizing Irving's interpretation of the Hamilton-Washington incident as "not quite reconcilable with the candor of his character" and accusing him of "an unwise zeal in Washington's behalf."[20] Many details of the ensuing events remain unknown, but an entry in Pierre's 1859 journal reveals that Hamilton was still so sensitive about Irving's view of his father that he incited James Watson Webb to refer unfavourably to the interpretation in the latter's review of the fifth volume of *Washington.*[21] It was John C. Hamilton whose persistent enmity prompted Irving in 1859 to make a trifling "correction" in the offending passage,[22] even though in private he insisted that Alexander Hamilton had been "too full of himself." We may recall, too, that

[16] For example, see *LLWI*, IV, 309-10 (N. P. Willis).

[17] MS Outline, Chapter XXXVI (1857).

[18] See *Washington*, IV, 211.

[19] See above, p. 168, footnote 101. John C. Hamilton's elder brother, James A. Hamilton, who also lived at the family estate in Irvington, was likewise an advocate of his father. In 1869 he published *Reminiscences of James A. Hamilton; or, Men and Events at Home and Abroad, During Three Quarters of a Century*, explaining in the preface that he had been "induced to undertake this work by a desire to do justice to his father against the aspersions of Mr. Jefferson and more recently of Martin Van Buren in his *Inquiry into the Origin of Political Parties in the United States* [New York, 1867]" (p. iii).

[20] *Intelligencer*, June 20, 1857, p. 3, cols. 1-2. The letter was reprinted under the title "Washington and Hamilton" in *Littell's Living Age*, 54 (July 1857), 250-53.

[21] See above, pp. 199-201.

[22] WI had written: "In considering this occurrence, as stated by Hamilton himself, we think he was in the wrong. His hurrying past the general [Washington] on the stairs without pausing, although the latter expressed a wish to speak with him; his giving no reason for his haste, having, in fact, no object in hurrying down stairs but to deliver a letter to a fellow aide-de-camp; his tarrying below to chat with the Marquis de

Irving added a few choice words about John C. Hamilton: that he was "oversensitive" and like a "caitiff" cur.[23] These epithets and indeed all references to discord of any kind between Irving and John C. Hamilton are absent, however, from the *Life and Letters*. As a matter of fact, Pierre went out of his way to be conciliatory. The sole reference to Alexander Hamilton in the fourth volume—ironically, an erroneous remark in a quoted letter from George Bancroft—includes a tribute to his "rare combination of talents."[24]

Another characteristic of Pierre's selections from his journals and other sources in the final chapters of the biography is their retrospectiveness. It is true, of course, that during the late 1850's Irving was to a degree abstracted from contemporary affairs and did enjoy recalling earlier scenes in his lifetime. By laying stress on his uncle's memories, Pierre not only brought the *Life and Letters* toward its close by presenting, as for recapitulation, incidents in Irving's life set forth in the preceding volumes,[25] but he also emphasized a real feature of Irving's character. At the same time as he gave prominence to recollections of the past, however, he was silently shielding from view the author's other ideas and activities in the present. Moreover, he reinforced this screening effect by including the correspondence he did; for while such quoted letters as the congratulations from famous persons on successive volumes of the *Washington* did pertain to a major interest of Irving's, the tributes were somewhat ceremonial exercises revealing

Lafayette, the general all this time remaining at the head of the stairs, had certainly an air of great disrespect, and we do not wonder that the commander-in-chief was deeply offended at being so treated by his youthful aide-de-camp" (*Washington*, IV, 211). In his letter to the *Intelligencer*—see footnote 20 above—Hamilton wrote of this passage: "What could have induced Mr. Irving, so happy in his use of language, to misapply so strangely the words 'tarrying' and 'chat'?" Finally, WI agreed to correct the passage, and on June 10, 1859, PMI recorded in his list of corrections for the work: "for 'chat' put 'talk'" (NYPL, Berg). See also above, p. 204, footnote 125.

[23] See above, p. 201.

[24] *LLWI*, IV, 282. As published in *LLWI*, Bancroft's remark was: "The sketch which Washington gives of Hamilton, on preferring him for the post next himself in the army, is the finest tribute ever paid to Hamilton's rare combination of talents." WI did not include any such sketch in the *Washington*, and neither Sparks' edition of Washington's writings nor any other which I have encountered includes one. In fact, when Colonel Scammell, Washington's Adjutant-General, resigned his post in 1780, Washington decided *against* nominating Hamilton to fill the vacancy; see Sparks, ed., *Writings of Washington*, VII, 315, 321. Washington had solicited the advice of the Marquis de Lafayette as to an appropriate person to designate as the new Adjutant-General, and in his reply (Paramus, New Jersey, November 28, 1780), Lafayette gave Hamilton a warm recommendation; see Jared Sparks, ed., *Correspondence Relating to the American Revolution* ... (Boston, 1853), III, 159-60. This is the only such recommendation extant.

The published letter from Bancroft in *LLWI*, with its testimony to the talents of Hamilton, may have included a misprint of "Washington" for "Lafayette." Or, of course, Bancroft himself may have been confused. In either case, the force of PMI's apparent compliment to Alexander Hamilton—and of his conciliatory gesture to the militant John C. Hamilton—was certainly reduced by his having published a reference to a commendatory passage which did not exist.

[25] See, for example, *LLWI*, IV, 301 (Burr), 284-85 (Humboldt), 273 (J. P. Kemble).

little in themselves except that the published writings had won the praise of respected judges.[26] They gave an impression of elucidating Irving's affairs, as in a limited sense they did; but at the same time they spared Pierre from intruding on the author's private life by drawing on other resources available to him.

A desire to relate his account of Irving's declining years to the pattern of the biography as a whole controlled Pierre's choice of material pervasively. Throughout his presentation of events in 1859, for example, he sought to evoke an atmosphere of melancholy and mortality.[27] How this aim conditioned his criteria for usable details is not difficult to imagine, and its result is typified in the use he made of his long journal entry for April 3, 1859, Irving's seventy-sixth birthday. Recounting the events of the day, he selected items of a predominantly lugubrious cast. The sun rose on a "dull, cheerless morning; overcast at dawn, and raining before seven." Later in the morning a "beautiful bouquet" of flowers arrived, a gift from a neighbour, but Irving received it with a wistful exclamation: "Beautiful flowers to a withered old man!" At dinner the table was "decked" with the flowers and other gifts, and the family "tried to be cheerful"; but when Irving was forced by "a spasm of coughing" to leave the room, those remaining "felt the uncertainty of another birthday with him . . . [and] all rose from the table in tears." The harrowing account of the day nears its conclusion with a glimpse of Irving unable to sleep, "terribly depressed and nervous, as the night before."[28] Certainly the insistent counterpoint of the flowers and the celebration against Irving's feebleness and depression achieved the effect Pierre intended! In order to make it do so, of course, he was obliged to suppress the portions of his journal entry which failed to contribute to the tone he desired.[29]

In his account of Irving's last day of life, November 28, 1859, Pierre sought even more obviously to set an appropriate tone of dignity and pathos by making judicious selections from and additions to his journal entry. He elected not to use the anecdotes Irving had told at the supper table that evening: two had dealt with wine-bibbing, one other was perhaps a bit heterodox, and they all conveyed an impression of joviality which would be discordant with the funerary atmosphere he wished to evoke. Rather, to do the day full justice he took the unusual step of elaborating upon his brief reference in the journal to "the brilliant sunset" that had been visible at suppertime, with "the

---

[26] See, for example, *LLWI*, IV, 194, 203-05, 206-09, 232-35, 281-82. Quoted reviews of *Washington* also filled much space.

[27] PMI signalled the onset of this melancholy tone at various points in his account of the year 1858 (*LLWI*, IV, 238-66). For example, he quoted WI's expressed recognition of his failing health in February of that year (IV, 239), and a few pages further on he referred to WI's fear of senility or severe physical debility (IV, 255).

[28] *LLWI*, IV, 278-79. PMI probably intended the 1859 birthday celebration to function in counterpoint to his portrayal of the happier one in 1858; see *LLWI*, IV, 244.

[29] See above, pp. 186-88.

brilliant bank of clouds lit up, &c."[30] In the *Life and Letters* he wrote that, while seated at the table, "the whole party were lost in admiration of one of the most gorgeous sunsets I have ever beheld. The whole western sky was hung with clouds of the richest crimson, while the scene had all the softness of our lingering Indian summer. Mr. Irving exclaimed again and again at the beauty of the prospect. How little did any of us dream it was to be his last sunset on earth!"[31] The autumn evening, a fitting symbol of a quiet and serene end, was more apposite to Pierre's aims than a final view of the aged author, hoarsely jocose at the supper table, shouting: " 'Sir, you may be a good judge of small beer, but by God! you're no judge of wine!' "

In his portrayal of Irving in 1859 Pierre made a constantly recurring motif of his uncle's nervousness, insomnia, and assorted other symptoms of debility. Here was one aspect of Irving's private life that he dealt with in tiresome detail. It seems odd in light of his concern to censor other information which one might consider private or privileged, that he should have adjudged these observations legitimate material for the biography. Perhaps he dwelt upon the medical minutiae because he regarded them as essentially clinical rather than personal in nature. Or, recalling the avidity of the public for this sort of thing during Irving's lifetime, he may have decided to include it on the assumption that it would still find favour. Another possible explanation of his emphasis on the medical history and suffering—Irving's exclamations of frustration and depression, his wishes to die[32]—is that they may have bulked large in his generalized memory of the final year. But if this was so, a careful re-reading of his journal would have shown him that his memory was in error. For by dwelling on matters of pathology throughout his account of the year, Pierre distorted the clear indication of his own contemporary record that Irving had regained much of his strength by June 1859 and had maintained it during the summer. Perhaps he assumed that by focusing on Irving's poor health he was evoking in a natural way an atmosphere of mortality,[33] but by overemphasizing his uncle's symptoms he only succeeded in misrepresenting the evidence and in rendering his closing pages a painful narrative to read. Too often his portrait of Irving in 1859 shows us no more than an aged bundle of nerves who bewails his fortune on bad days and reminisces amiably on good ones.

On the whole, it may be said that Pierre suppressed from the final chapters of the *Life and Letters* the varieties of information about

---

[30] See above, p. 238.

[31] *LLWI*, IV, 326.

[32] See *LLWI*, IV, 274, 289, 291, 306, *et passim*.

[33] This seems to have been his assumption. Summarizing WI's condition on January 15, 1859, for example, he abruptly switched his narrative from the past tense to the present and wrote this premonitory statement: "The faithful Doctor still encourages us and himself with the hope that this is only a morbid condition of the nervous system, which may pass off; but I have at times an ominous feeling as if we were watching his decline" (*LLWI*, IV, 268; see also IV, 312).

Irving's life and character which he was uniquely qualified to offer, and that he included in its place a quantity of the pre-packaged material which, during his own lifetime, Irving had granted to persons outside his household or near acquaintance.[34] By selecting the material he did and presenting it as he did, Pierre passed on through the *Life and Letters* essentially the same public image of his uncle which during the 1850's Irving had collaborated with the journalists and the public in fashioning. His characterization of the elderly author was of a superannuated dignitary, a "Patriarch of American Letters," recalling with mixed fondness and regret an earlier career which seems to have been almost wholly pleasant.

In his shrewd and largely favourable review of the completed work, Donald Grant Mitchell took note of the oversimplification in this "quiet and tranquil picture." Granting that "a conscientious man, in setting about the task of writing the life of a favorite author, would ask himself, over and over, how much should be yielded to the eager curiosity of the public, and how much a refined courtesy of feeling should keep in reserve," Mitchell affirmed that in the case of Washington Irving there was really nothing to hide. Pierre had portrayed him as "kindhearted to the last degree," and so he was:

> ... and yet, remembering as we do that sly look of humor which lurked always in the corner of his eye, we cannot believe but that in his freer moments he has pricked through many a bag of bombast, and made dashing onslaught upon noisy literary pretension. Of all this, however, we find nothing in the volumes before us,—nothing in his own books. Always, in his contact with the world, he is genial; the face of every friend is beautiful to him; every acquaintance is at least comely; in rollicking Tom Moore he sees (what all of us cannot see) a big heart,—in Espartero a bold, frank, honest soldier,—in every fair young girl a charmer,—and in almost every woman a fair young girl.[35]

Mitchell knew more than he wrote concerning Irving's vituperative and satirical moments,[36] but in his oblique manner he had pointed out the most serious shortcomings of the concluding chapters in the *Life and Letters*. While Pierre's solicitude to present a favourable image of his uncle and at the same time preserve his privacy ought perhaps to enlist our sympathy, the strictness of his guardianship over the information he withheld seems more severe than the material intrinsi-

---

[34] Although the almost uniform amiability and the constant bent for reminiscence in the portrayed WI bear out this statement in themselves, PMI's use of published accounts of visits to SS by William G. Dix, Theodore Tilton, and N. P. Willis (*LLWI*, IV, 315-25) gives a more striking confirmation of its accuracy. These quoted passages, with their formulaic material—Walter Scott, portraits of WI, WI in his study, WI's writing habits, Sleepy Hollow, Byron, and so on—took up eleven of the fifty-nine pages PMI devoted to recounting WI's life in 1859. See also *LLWI*, IV, 260-61.

[35] Mitchell, "WI," *Atlantic Monthly*, 13 (June 1864), 695.

[36] Mitchell recurred to the subject in his address to the WI Association at the commemoration of WI's centenary in 1883 (*WI. Commemoration*, p. 41). There, too, he reiterated his belief that PMI's guarded posture in relating the facts of WI's life and

326 / The Continuing Collaboration

cally merited. Perhaps the best we can say of his performance in these final pages is that, even though he would have better satisfied modern taste by a more open portrayal of the elderly Irving, he satisfied his contemporaries more thoroughly by adhering to the principles he at last decided upon. How would the *North American Review* have reacted in 1862 had he portrayed Irving as using the strong language he sometimes did? Or what of Irving's hilarity over his own gauche remarks about Negroes, or his dismissal of a contemporary worthy such as the Honorable Gulian C. Verplanck?[37] Such things had no place in a delegated biography.

George Putnam emphasized the permanent authoritativeness of the completed *Life and Letters* by referring to it grandiosely in his newspaper advertisements as a "delectable book for all time";[38] and in the decades that followed, the work did sustain unchallenged a high reputation. Between 1870 and 1900 a succession of shorter lives of Irving appeared, almost all of them wholly dependent upon Pierre for facts and dates, and most of these indicating an unquestioning acceptance of his portrayal.[39] In his *Memoir of Washington Irving* (1870), Charles Adams struck the keynote of absolute respect for the *Life and Letters* when he referred to it as "a model work of its kind."[40] This deferential regard for Pierre's monumental work was in important senses fully justified, for he had taken no significant liberties with chronology, and—except for two anecdotes wherein quotations attributed to Irving were somewhat expanded from notes in the 1859 journal[41]—there is no evidence that he had fabricated material. His portrait of the elderly Irving was rather stiff and two-dimensional, but it was faithfully executed in a medium—the delegated "life and letters"—wherein such an effect was desirable. His book was, as Putnam quaintly put it, "delectable" to nineteenth-century taste. With our present knowledge of what the fourth volume might have been, we cannot assent to Adams' judgment of it and the rest of the

character was unnecessary, since "we cannot honor him more than by recalling him in his full personality" (p. 44).

[37] See above, p. 234.

[38] New York *Tribune*, December 17, 1863, p. 6, col. 4.

[39] See William R. Langfeld and Philip C. Blackburn, *WI: A Bibliography* (Port Washington, New York, 1968—originally published 1931), pp. 89-90.

[40] (New York, Cincinnati, and San Francisco, 1870), p. 5.

[41] The passage in the journal, March 24, 1859—see p. 185 above—wherein WI spoke of his sister Ann, appeared in *LLWI* under the date March 24, and took this regularized form: "Mr. Irving broke forth into warm eulogy of her wit, sensibility, and humor—'delightful in every mood.' 'I was very meagre, when a child, and she used to call me a little rack of bones. How fond I was of having her sing to me, when an infant, that pathetic ballad of Lowe:

'The moon had climbed the highest hill
    That rises o'er the source of Dee.'

How it used to make me weep, and yet I was constantly begging her to sing it" (IV, 277). The other expanded passage from the journal was the entry of September 13 relating to Leigh Hunt; see above, p. 320.

Life and Letters as "a model work of its kind" unless we add that from a twentieth-century viewpoint the "kind" itself has serious limitations.

Pierre must have breathed a deep sigh of relief when, having corrected his last proofsheet, he stepped from his office in the Bible House[42] out into the wintry streets of New York, free at last. At some time in the indefinite future he intended to revise his work, uneven as it inescapably was, fitting it into the three-volume format he had first planned; but such a task was far from his mind just now. The city of New York was caught up in a mood of taut excitement aroused by the lengthening war with the Confederacy, and several of Pierre's colleagues had already set aside their ordinary occupations to devote their talents to the Union cause. Moses Grinnell was at work supervising hospitals for war casualties, and his huge shipping firm had become a vital link in the logistical chain of the Union armies.[43] James Watson Webb was serving as United States Minister to Brazil, where he was waging a tireless diplomatic battle against the aid being extended in South American seaports to Confederate privateers.[44] Early in 1863, George Putnam had been appointed Collector of Internal Revenue for the prosperous Eighth District of New York, and his duties of extracting from reluctant plutocrats the huge tax levies required to run the war had become so time-consuming that he had suspended active supervision of his business.[45] Pierre, having chafed while at work on the *Life and Letters* at being insulated by his gentle occupation from the affairs of the Union, may now himself have taken up some volunteer role, but if he did so no record of it has survived. He did invest heavily in United States bonds, and as his uncle's executor he allocated large sums from Irving's estate in the same manner.[46] Perhaps, too, he took comfort in the apparent truth of Putnam's assurance that the *Life and Letters* had aided his fellow-citizens by affording them a temporary respite from the routine of violence they were being forced, actually or at second-hand, to endure. In any case, while outwardly he and Helen seem to have kept up their old habits, renting rooms in New York and periodically visiting at Sunnyside, there was no avoiding the tensions and sacrifices of the war, even had they wished to. Late in 1864 they accepted a longstanding invitation from the Kennedys and spent a few days at their home near Baltimore. "Every hour had its enjoyment," Pierre wrote to R. C.

[42] PMI was listed in the *Trow New York City Directory* for 1860 through 1864 as keeping an office at 49 Bible House. He was unlisted in the *Directory* afterward except in the volume for 1869-70, where his home address was given as 281 Fourth Avenue—that is, the Clarendon Hotel.

[43] Grinnell was a member of the Union Defense Committee, a Commissioner of Charities and Corrections, and a tireless servant of the Lincoln administration during the Civil War. He also assisted generously in relief work (*DAB*, VIII, 5-6).

[44] *DAB*, XIX, 574-75.

[45] G. H. Putnam, *Putnam*, pp. 289-92, 334-52. G. P. Putnam turned over his stock to Hurd & Houghton, publishers, who sold and printed it on commission (DAB, XV, 280).

[46] Account Book, pp. 37, 39.

Winthrop a few years later, yet the "terrible war" overshadowed the visit. Kennedy was "full of interest on the subject and drove us about to all the points connected with the late Baltimore difficulties."[47] As it had done to thousands of families, the Civil War had divided them from their relatives in the South. Helen was cut off from her brother James Dodge, who still lived in North Carolina, but she and Pierre occasionally saw Dodge's son Richard, a Captain in the Union Army who was stationed at a training camp in Elmira, New York.[48]

The war lingered through the early months of 1865, culminating in tragic anticlimax with the surrender of General Robert E. Lee at Appomattox on April 9 and the assassination of President Lincoln at Washington five days later. Then, under the new leadership of Andrew Johnson, the nation turned ponderously away from military affairs while its leaders sought to institute a new civil order. The outsized tax levies were abated; civilians resigned from the wartime offices in which they had voluntarily served; brevetted officers, restored to their proper ranks, resigned from the Army; soldiers returned home, and a new era began. George Putnam continued at his post as Tax Collector until the spring of 1866, when, a victim of party politics in its vicious postwar resurgence, he was abruptly ousted from office, by Presidential order, on a trumped-up charge.[49] Putnam was not bitter, however. Recognizing that a reading public worthy of his attentions was re-establishing itself, he willingly gave over the duties he had accepted in the national interest and returned to his interrupted thirty-year's career in publishing. Resuming the full management of his business, he admitted his son George Haven Putnam into partnership and set his sights on achieving a cherished private aim of renewing publication of *Putnam's Monthly Magazine*, a first-class literary monthly which his financial misfortune of 1857 had forced him to discontinue at that time.[50] In order to attain the goal, of course, he must first amass capital; and thus he mounted his first postwar selling campaign by featuring anew his surest source of income in earlier years—the property which George Haven Putnam was later to call "the old standby"[51]—the revised works of Washington Irving. He produced various new editions of individual titles, such as "The Artist's Edition" of *The Sketch Book*, profusely illustrated and bound in Levant morocco, which sold for $20. He published a lavish new edition of the collected works, entitled the Knickerbocker Edition, and as he had done before the war he advertised "choice sets

[47] PMI to R. C. Winthrop, New York, October 17, 1870 (Exeter Academy).

[48] John P. Frothingham, Miscellaneous Papers (NYPL, MS). Richard Dodge continued his military career after the Civil War and saw service against the Indians of the Western territories. He was the author of *The Black Hills* (1876), *The Plains of the Great West* (1877), and *Our Wild Indians* (1882).

[49] Putnam, *Putnam*, pp. 352-55. His successor was a liquor dealer.

[50] Putnam, *Putnam*, p. 359.

[51] Putnam, *Putnam*, pp. 359-60. Putnam did succeed in reviving the magazine in January 1868, but the competition of such powerful magazines as *Lippincott's*, the

of the Writings of *Washington Irving*, in every variety of style and price."[52] Happily for himself, just as prior to 1861 Irving had been his largest moneymaker and claim to fame, the sales figures revealed that the late author still occupied that position.[53]

Putnam's canny advertising gambits in 1866 showed an important shift in emphasis away from his earlier ones, however—one which betokened his belief that Irving's relation to contemporary American life had fundamentally changed. Previously, he had portrayed Irving's works or Pierre's biography as offering something of immediate importance to the public at the moment they appeared. Now, in his pre-Christmas sales campaign for 1866, he adopted a new approach: "Every Intelligent Family Should Own the Writings of Washington Irving."[54] This slogan implied that Irving was no longer a contemporary writer, useful for specifically present needs despite his roots in the past, but that he had become an old favourite, a "classic." Putnam reinforced the suggestion of his headline by quoting beneath it the prophecy of William Cullen Bryant in 1860 that Irving would enjoy "eternal fame."[55]

The intuition that had led the publisher to abandon his claims of contemporaneity for Irving's works was sound, for clearly they were no longer so. To a post-Civil War audience, Washington Irving inevitably seemed remote. Henry Adams' remark in the *Education* concerning himself in 1865—that "he saw before him a world so changed as to be beyond connection with the past"[56]—must have been true in some degree for any one who had lived through the long trauma of the war. Irving's final work had been dedicated in part to forestalling the conflict which was to become an ineffaceable scar on the consciousness of Americans. As if to symbolize by its date his place in history, his funeral had preceded by only one day the execution of John Brown, the firebrand whom Melville referred to as a portentous "meteor of the war."[57] Irving belonged to an earlier era, and he was separated from the mentality of the Civil War's survivors by a gulf of emotion and

Century, the *Atlantic*, and *Harper's* was so strong as to make *Putnam's Monthly* a losing proposition. It ceased publication in December 1870, after six volumes in the new series.

[52] New York *Tribune*, December 12, 1866, p. 6, col. 1.

[53] In 1871 Putnam wrote that since he had begun publishing WI's revised works he had paid over $150,000 to WI or his representatives ("WI," p. 494).

[54] New York *Tribune*, December 13, 1866, p. 6, col. 4.

[55] In his *Discourse* Bryant had not actually used the phrase "eternal fame," but he had spoken of WI's "deathless renown" and "enduring fame" (pp. 45, 46), which came to much the same thing.

[56] *The Education of Henry Adams: An Autobiography* (Boston and New York, 1918), p. 209.

[57] "The Portent (1859)," in *Collected Poems of Herman Melville*, ed. Howard P. Vincent (Chicago, 1947), p. 3. On December 2 and 3, 1859, accounts of WI's funeral competed for space on the front pages of New York newspapers with reports of John Brown's last hours and execution.

loss. He might live on in reputation as an admired literary craftsman, or simply as an author whose works, for one reason or another, "Every Intelligent Family" should read. Enshrined in the *Life and Letters*, his engaging personality might still exert some of the charm he had possessed when living, but he was no longer in actual contact with the nation's affairs. No more an admired elderly contemporary, he was an old favourite.

Perhaps Pierre sensed this alteration of Irving's status in the public mind; but if so, he did not allow it to alter his plans as his uncle's literary executor. For several years he had intended to prepare for publication a collection of Irving's fugitive writings, and he still intended to do so. A few months before Irving's death, the author had expressed to him the wish that the nearly completed Spanish legends, the suite of narratives which had occupied him at intervals since 1826, should be edited and published at some future time.[58] Pierre made no public acknowledgment of his plan to comply with his uncle's request, but the reading audience had been apprised of the existence of the legends since 1850.[59] These, together with a miscellaneous mass of uncollected writings including Irving's youthful "Letters of Jonathan Oldstyle" (1802-1803), his biographies of naval worthies written for the *Analectic Magazine* in 1813 and 1814, scattered articles in the *Knickerbocker Magazine*, and contributions to still other journals, gift-books, cyclopedias, and even newspapers, comprised the corpus of material which had led a newspaper writer to speculate shortly after Irving's death that "several additional volumes will probably be added to his works."[60] Naturally, between 1859 and 1863 Pierre's work on the *Life and Letters* took precedence over the project of salvaging these minor pieces which Irving had not taken the trouble to assemble himself. In the second volume of the biography he did include a list of the almost-finished Spanish legends, recounting Irving's labours over them and observing that they were "still unpublished"—but he still gave no sign of his intention to edit them.[61] Possibly he had adopted this matter-of-fact tone as a lure to elicit some assurance of continuing public interest in the narratives. If so, he must have been gratified when within a few days of the volume's publication he received an inquiry from the Rev. Henry

[58] The only entry in the 1859 Journal suggesting a date on which this conversation may have taken place is that for April 3, when PMI recorded WI's showing him "his Spanish chronicles in manuscript—'Don Pelayo,' 'Fernando el Santo,' &c. Spoke of now being able to tell me anecdotes &c." The last sentence may suggest that WI was referring to his retirement from literary work. If so, then this would have been an appropriate time to show the manuscripts of PMI and suggest that he publish them eventually.

[59] See WI's "Preface" to *Mahomet and His Successors*, wherein he explained how his biography of the prophet had grown from a brief sketch first written to form part of a medley together with the still unfinished pieces (I, 7).

[60] "WI and His Books," an unidentified newspaper clipping in the Peters Scrapbook (NYPL, Berg).

[61] *LLWI*, II, 373-74.

Coppée, an old admirer of Irving, concerning his plans for these "valuable materials." On October 20, 1862, he replied to Coppée that "at some future and more auspicious period" he intended to publish "such of the intermediate chronicles as received from [Irving] something approaching to a final handling."[62] He did not write in so many words that he intended to wait until the return of peacetime, but that was certainly his meaning.

In April 1866, one year after the war had ended and more than three since his correspondence with Coppée, Pierre received a letter from one Edward Howell of New York which seemed to confirm the wisdom of his delay in bringing forth a collection of the miscellaneous writings. In a cordial reply to Howell, he wrote:

> I am gratified to have your opinion that the uncollected writings of Mr Irving in the "Analectic Magazine, Knickerbocker & elsewhere" would form an acceptable accompaniment to the revised edition of Putnam, inasmuch as I already engaged in preparing two additional volumes which will embrace the articles in the Analectic & Knickerbocker, together with other of his writings which have been long out of print and some unpublished manuscripts. I had hoped to have had these volumes out this Spring, but there has been some delay which will prevent their appearance before August or September next. A portion of the volumes is already in type.[63]

The nature of the "delay" is unknown; quite possibly it was associated in some way with the process of Putnam's re-assuming control over his firm. In any case, Pierre's prediction of the date when the work would be published was accurate, and *Spanish Papers and Other Miscellanies* was published on September 12, 1866.[64]

Spanish Papers merited the word "miscellanies" in its title, for it was a true salmagundi; yet it was not a receptacle for *all* Irving's previously uncollected writings, even all those of which Pierre was aware. For example, of the nine Jonathan Oldstyle letters which Irving had written for Peter Irving's *Morning Chronicle*, Pierre reprinted only the first five, omitting the four others with the explanation that he did so "in deference to the wishes of the author, who marked them as 'not to be reprinted,' when there was question of including the pamphlet of Oldstyle papers in a collective edition of his writings." Reading the letters thus proscribed by Irving and accordingly excluded by Pierre, one is at a loss to understand why the author should have thought them any more or less worthy than the others; they are all very slight, frothy performances. However, Pierre made no further attempt to explain his suppression of the four innocuous pieces. "Of the

---

[62] PMI to Rev. Henry Coppée, New York, October 20, 1862 (Historical Society of Pennsylvania).

[63] PMI to Edward J. H. Howell, New York, April 8, 1866 (Historical Society of Pennsylvania).

[64] New York *Tribune*, September 12, 1866, p. 5, col. 2.

literary merit or demerit of these productions," he wrote rather archly of the Oldstyle papers as a whole, "I do not propose to speak."[65] Yet even had he agonized in print over the question whether to transgress against Irving's desires in this small matter, it is unlikely that his decision would have made much difference to the great majority of the reading public. There is no record that his omission of the four letters was resented, or even noticed, by the contemporary readers of *Spanish Papers*. Who, except Pierre and a few score of Irving's intimates and most ardent admirers, really cared any longer whether he reprinted the letters or not? Gamely, Putnam declared in the newspapers that *Spanish Papers* was as "attractive in variety of topics, vigor of treatment, and grace of style, as the very best of Irving's works";[66] but sales were only moderate.[67] For the American audience of 1866, *Spanish Papers* could not be expected to command the interest elicited by another work which Putnam advertised along with it, F. B. Carpenter's *Six Months at the White House, with Abraham Lincoln.*[68] By deferring publication of *Spanish Papers* until what he had thought would be the "auspicious" period after the war, Pierre had issued the work to a public no longer caught up in uncritical affection for Irving. The period of idolization, during which the collection would probably have achieved popularity, had passed.

Sunnyside, which had excited such widespread interest and admiration during Irving's lifetime, remained something of a showplace in the years after the Civil War, even though the visitors came less frequently and probably left less well satisfied than before. Outwardly the property prospered in the absence of its master, for under the administration of Pierre it was maintained without stinting the heavy expenditures which had become usual during Irving's lifetime.[69] A show of hospitality was also made. A guest-book was kept in the library, and the families which had moved into the neighbourhood since Irving's death—the Goulds, the Harrimans, the Fargos, among others—were duly escorted about the grounds. Jay Gould, the industrialist and banker, was fond of entertaining his guests with tours of the neighbourhood, and he called quite often with parties of ladies

[65] *Spanish Papers*, II, [10].

[67] This is indicated by the brevity of the entry on *Spanish Papers* in Stanley T. Williams and Mary A. Edge, *A Bibliography of WI* (New York, 1936), pp. 141-43.

[68] New York *Tribune*, September 12, 1866, p. 5, col. 2. However, *Spanish Papers* was given top billing in the small advertisement.

[69] Annual expenses for the cottage as recorded by PMI in the Account Book, p. 149, were as follows:

November 28, 1859 to November 28, 1860:		$8,976.70
1860	1861	4,903.00
1861	1862	6,072.50
1862	1863	5,773.25
1863	1864	6,840.04

References in the Account Book to PMI's paying large sums to his cousin Edgar Irving, "for cottage expenses" (p. 29 *et passim*) suggest that Edgar took charge of day-to-day care of the property while PMI continued to act as comptroller and auditor.

and gentlemen.[70] The visitors to Sunnyside were most numerous, and apparently least unwelcome, on Decoration Day, May 30; but at other times, except on special occasions, Kate and Sarah preferred to keep themselves hidden inside the house or on the piazza behind the row of tuberoses which Robert still maintained for them.[71]

Irving's wish, often expressed during his lifetime and reiterated in his will, that Sunnyside should function after his death as an *"Irving homestead,"*[72] a gathering place for succeeding generations, was not to be fulfilled. Robert, Maria, and their brood still enlivened the place in the role of petted first family among the servants, but the only permanent residents were Ebenezer, now enfeebled and losing his sight, and Kate and Sarah. The Grinnells made their home, as before, on the adjoining estate.[73] In the summers Charlotte Grinnell, Ebenezer's youngest daughter, still journeyed from her home in western New York, and Julia Sanders, who had always loved Sunnyside and whose vivacity was unaffected by a cruelly increasing deformation of her spine, also visited at the cottage for a few weeks between her alternating sojourns in Boston and Washington.[74] Yet the tone of the place had become autumnal, and it was losing its character as a family center. In August 1868, at the age of eighty-six, Ebenezer died,[75] and in the following spring Kate and Sarah formally released Pierre from the duties as executor which he had performed with meticulous care and without remuneration for over eight years.[76] Long after Pierre had died, "the girls" continued to make their home at Sunnyside, although they fell into the custom of vacating it to take rooms in New York during the summers. On three such occasions they rented it for the season, but these experiments were failures,[77] and afterward they held their pride above a sometimes embarrassing want of funds.[78] For obscure reasons, enmity grew up between branches of the Irving family until some of its members were no longer welcome at the cottage.

In the few remaining years of his own lifetime Pierre never lost, nor sought to efface, the deep impression made on his character by his

[70] It is doubtful that this recurrent ritual represented a special dispensation in Gould's favour by Kate and Sarah alone. His welcome, such as it was, was more probably attributable to the $2 tip he left with at least one of the servants at the end of each visit (McLinden Interview—SHR).

[71] McLinden Interview (SHR).

[72] Appendix B, "Provisions of the Will," in *LLWI*, IV, 409.

[73] Scharf, *Westchester County*, I, 241.

[74] McLinden Interview (SHR).

[75] August 22 [?], 1868 (*Life*, II, opposite 255).

[76] Catharine A. Irving and Sarah Irving, to Pierre M. Irving, Executor. Release. New York, March 30, 1869 (Virginia).

[77] According to Catharine McLinden Richardson, they rented SS twice to Henry A. C. Taylor of Newport, R.I., and once to a "Mr. Swann" (McLinden Interview—SHR). The latter person may have been Otis D. Swan, who between 1857 and 1860 was co-Notary at the Bank of Commerce with Leslie Irving.

[78] See Putnam, *Putnam*, p. 231.

relations with his uncle. Over the decades Irving's circle of friends had gradually become the same as his own, and his own interests in literature and history had just as surely become almost indistinguishable from Irving's. Even though by 1866 he had completed his delegated work of writing the biography and editing *Spanish Papers*, in his subsequent activities Pierre continued to direct his interests and energies toward topics which had engaged him while Irving was alive. In 1869 he published his revised and condensed edition of the *Life and Letters*—omitting, interestingly, not only the Dawson-Fuller interpolations and most of his commentary thereon, but also the memorable quotations from Irving's autobiographical manuscript concerning his love for Matilda Hoffman.[79] Three years later he returned to his genealogical studies of the Irving family.[80] And throughout this period, of course, he was kept regularly employed in the role of ultimate authority on his uncle's life and character,[81] answering in his businesslike and at times acerbic style a succession of queries and requests from Irving devotees.[82]

In April 1873 he received an inquiry concerning Irving's love life from a gentleman with an ominous surname, Henry B. Dawson. Dawson, who was editor and publisher of *The Historical Magazine*, a miscellany which described itself as a "medium of intercommunication between Historical Societies, Authors and Students of History,"[83] has sought him out in the hope that he would write for the *Magazine* a new statement on this vexed topic. As Pierre's reply indicates, such hopes were vain:

[79] The "Revised and Condensed" edition was published on May 15, 1869 (New York *Tribune*, p. 8, col. 3).

[80] In 1872 he wrote out a new draft of "The Irving Genealogy, Compiled by Pierre M. Irving for the information of those of the name who desire to be certified / 'through whom / Their life blood tastes its parent lake,' and to secure and preserve the vestiges of an ancestry equally ancient and honorable" (Misc. Notebook).

[81] This was of course a role which PMI had become accustomed to playing even during WI's lifetime. For example, on January 6, 1858, WI had addressed a note to D. Appleton & Co., complimenting them on the newly published first volume of their *New American Cyclopedia of Biography*. In reply to their request for information about himself to be included in a subsequent volume, he had added: "My nephew Mr. Pierre M. Irving will furnish you with information for the article which you specify" (Virginia).

[82] See, for example, PMI to Clarence Moore, New York, May 10, 1864 (in Volume II, part II of the Memorial Edition of *LLWI* [NYPL, MS—Hellman Collection]); PMI to R. W. Lawrence, Irvington, October 18, 1865 (SHR); PMI to C. B. Tillinghast, New York, April 19, 1868 (Historical Society of Pennsylvania); PMI to Charles W. Stoddard, 281 Fourth Avenue, New York, November 2, 1869 (Virginia). Another letter indicating the kind of services PMI was called upon to perform was from Charles L. Elliott, dated October 31, 1864. Elliott explained that the sculptor Erastus Dow Palmer (1817-1904) had consented to execute a marble bust of WI, a commission for which work had been donated to the New-York Historical Society. The purpose of Elliott's letter was to solicit "any suggestions, assistance, or information you may be able to render" (Yale).

[83] Begun in 1857, the magazine was supported by private contributions. Dawson sent a copy of it to WI in 1859 and received a reply that it could "not fail to remain a most valuable and popular national work" (WI to Henry B. Dawson, SS, April 6, 1859—SHR).

Dear Sir:

Your letter of the 1st was delayed in reaching me from having been directed to Irvington on the Hudson which has long ceased to be my address. I discover no new matter in the article, Why Washington Irving was not married, copied into your magazine of November 1870 from the Albany Argus,[84] and to which you refer me for some sanction of its accuracy, or otherwise. After an ineffectual search of a few days I found this number of the Historical Magazine in the Astor Library, and upon reading the article I perceived that it was made up mainly from the Biography, and that I could not therefore well dissent from its accuracy. See Chaps. XIV Vol. I of the Life & Letters in four volumes, or Chap. XII, Vol. I of the later edition, "Revised and Condensed," in three vols. The supposed letter of Mr. Irving quoted by the writer of the article was not in reality a letter, as I had originally surmised, but extracts from some eight leaves of manuscript, written on both sides, and extending from page 3 to 18—part of a sketch of his early history which he had drawn up and left for perusal merely and not to be retained, with Mrs. Amelia Foster during their long and intimate sojourn at Dresden in 1823. It was submitted to the perusal of this lady to satisfy some curiosity expressed by her as to the incidents of his early life, (he was then 40) with a strict injunction that it should not be shewn, and should be given back to him, which was done. The first leaf was missing, and the closing page or pages, when I found it among his *private* papers, where it had no doubt remained since restored, but that part of the narrative which touched upon his relations with Miss Hoffman was complete. I repeat therefore that I find in the article to which you ask my attention nothing irreconcilable with the Biography. . . .

Yours very truly,

Pierre M. Irving

P.S. I write this merely for your own satisfaction, and *not for publication.*[85]

Like the majority of biographical commentary on Irving for two generations afterward, the anonymous article in the Albany *Argus* had been based on the *Life and Letters.* Even Pierre's letter to Dawson was filled with echoes of his own discussion of Irving's manuscript in volume four of the biography.[86] Concerning the Emily Foster affair he had nothing more—publicly at least[87]—to say.

[84] "Why WI Never Married" appeared in the *Historical Magazine*, 8, 2nd series (November 1870), 314-15. It began: "Much mystery has attached to the celibacy of Washington Irving. While, upon every point of peculiarity of the great writer's character and career, his familiar friends have taken pains to inform the wide circle of his admirers, an aggravating reticence has always met the questionings of those who were curious, as to why matrimony made no part of his experience" (p. 314).

[85] PMI to Henry B. Dawson, 140 Fifth Avenue, New York, April 11, 1873 (SHR).

[86] See *LLWI*, IV, 214.

[87] In his letter to Dawson, PMI reiterated Mrs. Flora Dawson's account of the autobiographical manuscript as having been given by WI to Mrs. Foster at Dresden. But

So far as Pierre sustained a wide reputation in the years after the *Life and Letters* was published, he was known as a dispenser of autographs and sheets of manuscript, an answerer of inquiries, and a corrector of misinformation; but as the life and works of Washington Irving moved from the center of public interest in the United States, the prominence which he had attained for a short time gradually diminished. During his last years of life, therefore, his long-cherished wish to live in independent comfort and privacy was realized, not merely through his own exertions but also because the public role he had been called upon to assume had lost its contemporary significance. Like the Irving whom he had portrayed for the new generation, Pierre became during his lifetime a relic of the past. He outlived many of his close friends—Charles A. Davis died in 1867, Kennedy in 1870—and most of his brothers and sisters—Oscar died in 1865, Ogden in 1869, and saddest of all, Julia Irving Grinnell in 1872.[88] Unlike his uncle, Pierre had no family gathered around him in his old age; and compared to Irving's his last years seem rather barren and anticlimactic. To the bustling society presided over by General Grant, he had nothing more to offer. His greatest comfort as he grew feeble was the understanding and wit of Helen, whose "heart of tendrils" he had praised so wisely forty years before.[89]

When he died in New York on February 25, 1876, Pierre was even more a relic of American history than his uncle had been in 1859. He had been a child in the house where some of the *Salmagundi* papers were written; he had grown up on Byron and "The Croakers"; and he had collaborated in writing *Astoria* at a time when the trans-Mississippi West was not even reliably mapped, let alone spanned by a transcontinental railroad. Like Irving, he had lived through an era of the nation which from a post-war vantage point seemed extremely remote, but unlike his uncle he was never admired simply because he seemed so agreeably out of place. Slightly over twelve years after he completed the *Life and Letters*, he died virtually forgotten. Perhaps, devotee of verbal economy that he was, he would have been pleased to see the spare death notice that appeared in the New York *Times* on February 27, 1876. One wonders, however, about his reaction to the garbled details summarizing his claims to remembrance:

> Pierre M. Irving died in this city on Friday in the 74th year of his age. He was the nephew of Washington Irving. He was chiefly known as the editor of his uncle's "Life and Letters," published in 1861-1867 in five volumes. He also collected and edited his "Spanish Papers and Other Miscellanies," published in three volumes in 1866.[90]

as he well knew, the manuscript itself contradicted that account; see above, p. 259, and Williams, *Life*, II, 262.

[88] "Children of William Irving and Julia Paulding," in Misc. Notebook. PMI noted here that Julia Irving Grinnell had died "at Genoa, Italy, February 23, 1872."

[89] See above, p. 55. Helen survived PMI, died on March 5, 1885, and was buried in the family plot at Sleepy Hollow Cemetery.

[90] New York *Times*, February 27, 1876, p. 2, col. 5.

The sole bit of obituary comment on the character of Pierre Munro Irving appeared in the New York *Tribune* on the following day. The *Tribune* repeated the notice in the *Times* and added one sentence: "He was a gentleman of unassuming, quiet manner and attractive social qualities."[91]

[91] New York *Tribune*, February 28, 1876, p. 4, col. 6. *Appleton's Annual Cyclopedia . . . for the Year 1876* (New York, 1888) included a short notice of PMI's death, also marred by errors (p. 619). PMI's funeral was held at the Church of All Saints, corner of Fourth Avenue and Twentieth Street, New York, at 9:00 A.M. Monday, March 2. He was buried in the family plot at Sleepy Hollow Cemetery.

Index